# Pageants, Parlors, and Pretty Women

BLAIN ROBERTS

# Pageants, Parlors, & Pretty Women

## Race and Beauty
### in the Twentieth-Century South

THE UNIVERSITY OF NORTH CAROLINA PRESS  *Chapel Hill*

*This book was published with the assistance of the*
*Z. Smith Reynolds Fund of the University of North Carolina Press.*

Designed by Sally Scruggs. Set in Miller and Meta by Tseng Information Systems, Inc.

The paper in this book meets the guidelines for permanence and durability
of the Committee on Production Guidelines for Book Longevity of the Council
on Library Resources. The University of North Carolina Press has been
a member of the Green Press Initiative since 2003.

Library of Congress Cataloging-in-Publication Data
Roberts, Blain.
Pageants, parlors, and pretty women : race and beauty in
the twentieth-century South / Blain Roberts.
pages cm
Includes bibliographical references and index.
ISBN 978-1-4696-1420-5 (cloth : alk. paper) — ISBN 978-1-4696-1421-2 (ebook)
ISBN 978-1-4696-2986-5 (pbk. : alk. paper)
1. Civil rights movements—Southern States—History—20th century.
2. Southern States—Race relations—History—20th century. 3. Race awareness—
Southern States—History—20th century. 4. African American women—Southern
States—Social conditions—20th century. 5. Black race—Color—Social aspects—
Southern States—History—20th century. 6. Human skin color—Psychological
aspects—Southern States—History—20th century. 7. Cosmetics—Social
aspects—Southern States—History—20th century. 8. Beauty, Personal—
Social aspects—Southern States—History—20th century. 9. Beauty
shops—Social aspects—Southern States—History—20th century.
10. Beauty contests—Social aspects—Southern States—
History—20th century. I. Title.
E185.615.R522 2014
323.1196′07300904—dc23
2013035602

# Contents

# Illustrations

# Acknowledgments

It is with great pleasure, and relief, that I am finally able to acknowledge the many people who have made this book possible. The seeds of this project were planted years ago, in an undergraduate senior thesis. Very little of that thesis remains in these pages, but Nell Painter, my adviser at Princeton, showed me what historians do. When she asked where my sources were, and when I responded that they were in faraway places like Atlanta and Charleston, she said, "Well, get yourself down there!" And I did, taking a road trip over fall break to comb through dusty boxes in southern archives. That experience helped me see history as a process of discovery. My first debt is to her.

On that adventure, as well as on subsequent research trips I took as a graduate student and faculty member, an army of knowledgeable archivists connected me with traces of the story I wanted to tell. I would like to thank archivists at the Robert W. Woodruff Library at the Atlanta University Center; the Auburn Avenue Research Library; the Dolph Briscoe Center for American History at the University of Texas at Austin; the Southern Historical Collection and the North Carolina Collection at the University of North Carolina at Chapel Hill; the Avery Research Center for African American History and Culture at the College of Charleston; the South Carolina Historical Society; the DeGolyer Library at Southern Methodist University; the Rare Books, Manuscripts, and Special Collections Library at Duke University; the Indiana Historical Society; the State Historical Society of Wisconsin; the Amistad Research Center at Tulane University; the Will W. Alexander Library at Dillard University; the Department of Archives and Special Collections at the University of Mississippi; the State Archives of North Carolina; the D. H. Hill Library at North Carolina State University; the W. S. Hoole Special Collections Library at the University of Alabama; and the William H. Sheppard Library at Stillman College.

I have benefited from the kindness of many institutions whose financial support helped me finish the manuscript. Two Mowry Research Grants from the University of North Carolina History Department, a Summer Research Grant from the Center for the Study of the American South, and a Newcomb College Travel Grant made possible early research trips. A University-Wide Dissertation Research Fellowship provided funding for a semester of research travel during which I drove from North Carolina to Texas and back again. A Royster Society of Fellows University-Wide Dissertation Completion Fellowship, awarded by the graduate school and the Center for the Study of the American South, gave me the freedom to write for an entire year, free of teaching responsibilities. The Citadel, where I took my first job, has an impressive research program for faculty members funded by the generosity of its alumni. In my two years there, The Citadel Foundation provided three grants that allowed me to work on the manuscript. At California State University, Fresno, Dean Luz Gonzalez and the College of Social Sciences have been especially supportive, awarding two course releases that gave me time to revise the manuscript. Two research grants from Provost William Covino, one given in conjunction with the College of Social Sciences, defrayed the costs associated with acquiring illustrations.

During my time on the road, family and friends provided room, board, and outstanding company. For their hospitality, I thank Geoffrey Kay, David Kay, Mitch Dean, Jo Ann Hengst, Laura, Joe, Will, and John DiCaro, Ray Hengst, Amy and Franklin Caputo, Chris Mogridge, Gail Quarles and the late John Quarles, Amy Burton Storey, Lisa Burton, Amy Moser Harrison, Kristin Hebert-Fisher and Lenzy Fisher, and John Zeigler. Outstanding company is one of the many fine things you will find in Chapel Hill, North Carolina. There may be better places to be in graduate school, but it sure would take a lot to convince me. For helping me become a better historian and quasi-respectable pool player, I thank Matthew Brown, Leah Potter, Joel Revill, Susan Pearson, Mike Kramer, Matt Andrews, Natalie Fousekis, Adam Tuchinsky, Jen Tuchinsky, Hans Muller, Jen Muller, David Sartorius, Josh Nadel, Eva Canoutas, Mariola Espinosa, Spencer Downing, Mike Ross, Stacy Braukman, Kerry Taylor, Bruce Baker, Marko Maunula, and Kevin Clark. Leah, Matt, and Mike, my writing group, read early versions of chapters and provided insightful criticism. There were many times in the years after we all went our separate ways that I wished we could gather to share a chapter and some beers.

At The Citadel, Bo Moore, the chairman of the history department, was a wonderful mentor during my first years as a faculty member. I also valued the friendship of Joelle Neulander, Kurt Boughan, Kathy Grenier, Keith Knapp, Jason Solinger, and Jack Porter, whose enthusiasm for happy hour I miss every Friday. In California, I am grateful for the support of my colleagues in the history department, including our two recent chairs, Michelle Denbeste and Bill Skuban, who accommodated this project's voracious appetite for photocopies despite our anemic budget. An entertaining and always distracting circle of friends has made living in the "other" part of California a pleasure. In particular, I would like to thank Brad Jones, Flo Cheung, Dan Cady, Lisa Bennett, Alex Espinoza, Kyle Behen, Lori Clune, Maria Lopes, Alice Daniel, Ben Boone, Nora Chapman, and Bill Skuban.

Anthony Stanonis, Vernon Creviston, Kyle Behen, and Jack Kytle took time out of their own busy schedules to read the manuscript in part or in its entirety, offering astute observations and drawing connections I had not. Two anonymous readers for the University of North Carolina Press provided criticisms that have improved the book substantially. Panelists and audiences at conferences have given valuable feedback over the years. Thanks especially to the participants at the Civil Rights and the Body in the American South Symposium in Chapel Hill; the Southern Historical Association Conferences in New Orleans and Richmond; the New England American Studies Association Conference in Portland, Maine; and the St. George Tucker Society Conference in Atlanta, Georgia. My editor at UNC Press, Chuck Grench, expressed interest in this book when I was still a grad student, which kept me motivated in the years thereafter. Chuck has been a steadfast supporter, sticking with me through the disruptions caused by two new jobs, and two new babies. I appreciate his patience. His assistants Sara Cohen, Alison Shay, and Lucas Church graciously shepherded me through the ins and outs of the publishing process.

Finishing a book about the South while living in California comes with some challenges. For visiting archives and libraries when I could not, I wish to acknowledge Anna Krome-Lukens in Chapel Hill, Laura Cunningham in Memphis, and Tyler Greene in Philadelphia. Here in Fresno, Cherith Fleming, Art Mendoza, and the rest of the Henry Madden Library interlibrary loan staff tracked down a variety of obscure sources. Steven Rendon proved a creative and enthusiastic digital archives researcher during a critical stage in the manuscript's final phase.

At the University of North Carolina, many professors supported my apprenticeship as a historian-in-training. Peter Coclanis was an early ally and champion of my work. He and Deborah also rescued me from the poverty of graduate student life more times than I can count by inviting me to dinner. John Kasson, Joy Kasson, Peter Filene, and Laura Edwards of Duke shaped this project in ways that I can still see. Jacquelyn Hall deserves much more than the thank you I can offer here. Jacquelyn is legendary, and rightfully so, for her commitment to her graduate students. She read everything I ever gave her, and returned it all, quickly, and with copious comments. During our conversations, she asked pointed questions that saved me from dead ends and redirected me down more fruitful paths. Indeed, I am especially grateful to her for encouraging me to return to southern beauty after a master's thesis on southern conservatism threatened to take me in a direction I didn't really want to go. She has continued to support me all these years later, providing revisions suggestions from afar. I value my friendship with her and Bob Korstad immensely.

I owe the most, of course, to my family. For years, my in-laws, Jack Kytle and Tari Prinster, have selflessly given of their time while pursuing their own intellectual projects. Josi Kytle is a fabulous friend and aunt whose visits we all cherish. Amazingly, my parents, Ron and Martha Lou Roberts, always told me that going to school for a long time was not a bad thing. In fact, they said it was good thing, and as it turned out, they meant it. How many children are so lucky? Even while they knew that a career in academia would likely take me far away from Louisiana, they cheered me on, believing that it was worth it. They were right. I am also fortunate to have embarked upon this career with my husband, Ethan Kytle, by my side. To have found two jobs not just in the same state, not just in the same city, but in the same department—how many academics are so lucky? The arrival of Eloise and Hazel has made our lives together all the more rich and, at least on most days, all the more enjoyable.

Pageants, Parlors, and Pretty Women

# Introduction

In her autobiographical novel, *The Bondwoman's Narrative*, fugitive slave Hannah Crafts provides a damning portrait of the planter class that kept her in bondage until her escape to the North in 1857. Although a few of the white women for whom Crafts worked displayed a paternalistic kindness that softened the cruelties of her life's station, most were consumed by the evils of slavery. Mrs. Wheeler, the last mistress Crafts served before escaping, was one of these. From the moment the two women met, Crafts felt uneasy. "Notwithstanding her sociality and freedom of conversation," Crafts writes, "there was something in her manner that I did not like." Crafts's suspicions were well-founded. Mrs. Wheeler was an impulsive, manipulative mistress, the embodiment of the excesses of power afforded by her class and race. After just a few days in her service, Crafts concluded that "[t]here seemed no end to her vanities, her whims, and caprices."

But Mrs. Wheeler got her comeuppance, one that nearly ruined her life. It came in a small box sold by a chemist to Crafts. And it was not, as we might expect, a poison, at least not in the traditional sense. The Wheelers had moved to Washington, D.C., from their plantation in North Carolina so that Mr. Wheeler might secure a position in the federal government. Having had no luck himself in the matter, the hapless Mr. Wheeler convinced his wife that she, as a beautiful woman, might succeed where he had not by persuading the gentleman in charge of patronage that her husband was deserving of an office. She agreed, but before undertaking the mission she asked that Crafts retrieve the box recently procured from the chemist. In it was a very fine and soft white face powder, which when applied, Mrs. Wheeler had been told, would produce a "most marvellous [*sic*] effect." "The skin, however sallow and unbeautiful," Crafts wrote of the product's promise, "would immediately acquire the softness and delicacy of childhood. Tan, or freckless [freckles], or wrinkles, or other unseemly blotches would simultaneously disappear." Wanting to look her best before going out into the world to attend to this most important task, Mrs. Wheeler applied the powder. According to Crafts, it seemed to work: "I had never seen her look better."

Two hours later, Mrs. Wheeler returned, frustrated by her inexplicable failure to acquire a position for her husband. For Mr. Wheeler, Crafts, and the rest of the household, the reason was obvious enough: Mrs. Wheeler's face had turned completely black. The transformation was shocking. "Heaven help me," Mr. Wheeler cried, "I fear that her beauty has gone forever." Oblivious to her altered appearance, Mrs. Wheeler had pleaded her husband's case as a black woman, unrecognized by her audience, mocked for her insolence. She returned with nothing to show for her effort, save her new black skin. Although the blackness gradually washed off with soap and water, the incident became the talk of Washington, D.C.—a "bit of scandal, so fresh and original," Crafts reported, "how the fashionable world loved it."

Explanations and interpretations abounded. Some speculated that Mrs. Wheeler had blackened herself on purpose, to win a wager. Others argued that she had done so in the playful spirit of "a little masquerade." A local minister gave the episode a serious spin, turning it into a morality tale. Crafts heard that he "held forth for two whole hours on the sin and wickedness of wantonly disguising the form or features and suggested it was a wonder of mercy that the presumptuous lady had not been turned irrecoverably black."

The gossip proved so malicious that the Wheelers left the city in disgrace, retreating to their North Carolina plantation. Mrs. Wheeler blamed Crafts for her misfortune, as well as for spreading rumors about the incident in North Carolina among the plantation slaves. She banished Crafts, a house slave her entire life, to labor in the fields. "With all your pretty airs and your white face, you are nothing but a slave after all," Mrs. Wheeler reminded her, "and no better than the blackest wench." Crafts was devastated at the prospect of her new fate. Her soul, she said, "actually revolted with horror unspeakable."

What do we make of this story? Although it is difficult, as Henry Louis Gates Jr. has noted, to determine which parts of Crafts's autobiographical novel are embellished, the story of Mrs. Wheeler and the face powder seems far-fetched, if intriguing.[1] Mrs. Wheeler was Crafts's mistress in Washington, D.C., and North Carolina, and she may have used face powder as a part of her toilet preparations, as grooming rituals were called during her day. But no powder would have changed the pigmentation of her skin so that she became black beyond recognition. The story is a momentary detour into allegory, and yet, as such, it presents its own truths, especially about one of its themes: female beauty. Indebted to centuries-old beliefs that prevailed on both sides of the Atlantic, most white south-erners in the antebellum era held that elite white southern women were inherently beautiful because of their class status and moral superiority. Their defining physical marker was their whiteness, a trait secured by their privileged position atop the social and racial hierarchy. Theologians, proslavery apologists, and artists alike praised southern ladies' beauty in the most extravagant terms. Antebellum plantation novels, for example, widely read in the South as well as the North, depicted the southern lady—and the belle, her younger, unmarried counterpart—as one of God's most beautiful creatures. Caroline Lee Hentz, a plantation novelist who was one of the three most popular writers in the United States as late as 1892, de-scribed the appearance of one of her heroines in typical fashion in 1852.[2] Of the young Eoline Glenmore, Hentz wrote that her complexion "had the fairness of the magnolia blended with the blush of the rose. Her hair, of a pale golden brown, reminded one of the ripples of a sunlit lake by its soft waves, giving beautiful alterations of light and shade. . . . Her eyes, blue, soft, and intense as the noonday sky in June, had a kind of beseech-ing loving expression—an expression that appealed for sympathy, protec-tion, love. . . . Such was Eoline in repose, a fair, delicate, and lovely young girl."[3] She was beautiful and fragile, worthy of admiration and yet in need of male protection, mindful, presumably, of the sexual subordination on which that protection was premised. Hentz's was the kind of description that slipped easily into prescription, an ideological construct that served the needs of patriarchy and white supremacy, gaining currency by force of repetition. It was also in large part a fantasy. Most white southern women were not of elite birth, and many of those who were would have been a far cry from the physical ideal.

If few women managed to embody the ideal of beauty, it was not for lack of trying. Mrs. Wheeler hoped the chemist's powder would even out a complexion made sallow by the passage of time and, Crafts suggests, by indiscretions in the sun. The tragedy that befell her was thus what some-one of her position might have seen as the ultimate physical punishment. The face powder completely took away her beauty, which Crafts reports had been considerable during her days as a belle. Mrs. Wheeler became black—"black as Tophet," or hell, according to her stunned husband—the opposite of beautiful. And when her beauty disappeared into blackness, so, too, did her standing and social status.

For blackness was actually much more than the opposite of whiteness. Since the beginning of European exploration in the fifteenth century, blackness had represented a negation of those qualities associated with civilization, morality, and beauty. European and American thinkers saw blackness as a degeneration not simply from "original color," as Winthrop Jordan has written, but also from the original state of man.[4] Just as a kind of circular logic governed whites' views of themselves, so, too, did it determine how whites viewed blacks. Dark skin and "African" features were a sign of supposed moral depravity and baseness; meanwhile, blacks' supposed moral depravity and baseness manifested itself in the aesthetically unattractive black body. In the slave South, the presumption of hypersexuality that was part and parcel of this black subhumanity was especially pronounced, serving to justify white men's rape of female slaves and, thus, the appreciation of their property.

Slaveholder Thomas Jefferson gave voice to these popular views of blackness in his *Notes on the State of Virginia*. "Is it not," he asked, "the foundation of a greater or less share of beauty in the two races?" And to skin color could be added "flowing hair, a more elegant symmetry of form, and [blacks'] own judgment in favour of the whites," which Jefferson argued was as certain "as is the preference of the Oran-ootan for the black women over those of his own species."[5] In this scheme, black women fared even worse than their male counterparts. Unattractive by virtue of their black skin, libidinal to the point of being animals (according to Jefferson, black women were prone to relations with apes), female slaves were the aesthetic and moral foils of their white mistresses.

And yet Crafts's story also shows that black women's homeliness fell along a continuum, something that Jefferson himself would likely have admitted. Black skin may have been repulsive to whites such as Mrs. Wheeler, but there were degrees of blackness. There were therefore degrees of unattractiveness as well. Crafts apparently boasted both "pretty airs" and light skin—Mrs. Wheeler went so far as to charge her with having a "white face"—both of which raised the ire of an already angry mistress. Crafts had white ancestry and had also enjoyed the material advantages that came with being a slave in the master's house. Mrs. Wheeler would probably have been in good company in seeing Crafts as more physically attractive than the "blackest wench." She did not, of course, say this directly. But her banishment of Crafts to the fields and her insistence that she was "no better" than the blackest female slave are suggestive, revealing an anxiety over a perceived threat to her own beauty and her status within the household.

Crafts's tale contains other intriguing glimpses into the meaning of beauty among antebellum women. Mrs. Wheeler felt she simply needed a bit of touching up before leaving home. Others, however, believed that her recourse to face powder represented an act of "sin and wickedness" and that her black complexion was divine retribution for attempting to be something that she was not—for attempting to construct a disguise of sorts. Or perhaps the real issue was that this disguise had emboldened her to enter the public sphere of politics, albeit briefly and informally, a place off-limits to ladies, desperate husbands aside. Another possibility was whispered. Some thought that Mrs. Wheeler might have deliberately pretended to be black, to have engaged, as they put it, in a "little masquerade." Crafts herself does not give much credence to this theory, but that some of the Wheelers' acquaintances could conceive of such a desire at all is fascinating. Why would a plantation mistress want to look like a black woman, given the widespread disparagement of black features?

Long before the emergence of modern department stores with their glittering cosmetic counters, of beauty pageants with their scantily clad young contestants, and of beauty parlors with their noisy hairdryers and chattering women, beauty occupied a conspicuous place in the actual and imaginative worlds of white and black southern women. Their pursuit of beauty, moreover, was far from a frivolous act undertaken merely to pass the hours. These facts did not change once the social order to which Crafts and Wheeler belonged died. Indeed, the dynamics that underpinned Crafts's story lived on, proving a complex inheritance for southern women of the Jim Crow South, women born into a society that was at once so different from, yet so similar to, the one that had bound together slave and mistress.

*Pageants, Parlors, and Pretty Women* examines the legacy of these ideas, uncovering how the female heirs of Hannah Crafts's and Mrs. Wheeler's Old South experienced beauty in their lives. I argue that beauty, at its core, was about power and, therefore, a hotbed of contention. As Crafts's story suggests, some conflicts arose from the South's racial politics. But there were also those that dealt less with race than with other forces that for so long made the region different: the entrenched class divisions in both the white and black communities that race leaders preferred to ignore; the agricultural rhythms that shaped southern life and that begrudgingly gave way to urbanization and modernization; and the conservative gender mores that determined what white and black women could and, more often, could not do. This book shows how, by pursuing beauty, southern women mediated the crises of modern southern history, a period bookended by the ascendancy of legalized segregation in the late nineteenth century and the crusade to destroy it in the 1950s and 1960s.

*Pageants, Parlors, and Pretty Women* thus offers a new interpretation of an old story. It tells us how Jim Crow and civil rights culture were expressed in southern women's bodies. Using female beauty as a lens, the book brings into focus an untold social and cultural history of southern women and of the South more generally.

STUDIES OF SOUTHERN WOMEN, black and white, have proliferated over the last forty years.[6] Indeed, no women of any other American region have received more scholarly attention than those living below the Mason-Dixon Line. Despite this extensive body of scholarship, no one has undertaken a historical examination of the pursuit of female beauty in the South. It is a striking omission. Bring up the topic in casual conversation, as I did dozens of times while writing this book, and people instinctively understand that southern women's relationship to beauty is somehow unique. "Right," they say, "southern women love the Miss America Pageant." Maybe, instead, they mention Scarlett O'Hara. These discussions tend to truck in stereotypes or involve some icon of popular culture, not quite firm ground from which to stake out a serious investigation of beauty. Plenty of what historians have uncovered about southern women, however, provides just such a jumping-off point and suggests that southern beauty might be a fruitful subject.

Historians such as Anne Firor Scott and Deborah Gray White long ago demonstrated how southern myths of femininity exerted a powerful influence in the lives of the region's women and shaped the contours of its culture.[7] To white southerners, these myths and ideals were tools for shoring up slavery and, later, segregation, providing justification for white supremacy, especially when it was under attack. Largely a function of white racism, ideas about black femininity and womanhood performed the same service, though black southerners often rejected these and embraced their own in an effort to subvert the logic of Jim Crow. In much of this scholarship, the degree to which the pursuit of beauty underpinned the images and norms to which women were held has been either left implicit or addressed only in passing. *Pageants, Parlors, and Pretty Women* puts beauty front and center.

A second contribution of this book follows naturally from the first. It adds a regional—and racially integrated—perspective to the history of female beauty in the United States. Studies of this subject, too, have multiplied in recent decades. But like the earliest forays in American women's history, many of the existing works on beauty in the United States suffer from a narrow view of the past. They have focused on beauty among elite and middle-class white women in the Northeast or on the silver screen, ignoring differences of race, class, and region.[8] More recently, several historians have successfully tackled these complexities. In her examination of the cosmetics industry in the United States, for example, Kathy Peiss takes into account the fault lines that separated black and white, wealthy and working-class, and urban and rural women.[9] Others, such as Tiffany M. Gill, Maxine Leeds Craig, and Susannah Walker, have redressed, specifically, the absence of black women from this beauty literature.[10] Given that the vast majority of African Americans in the United States resided in the South for much of the twentieth century, these studies do analyze black beauty in the region. Yet taken as a whole, this body of work either ignores regional differences in beauty practices or leaves black and white women's beauty experiences unconnected. A racially inclusive history of beauty in the South reveals southern women's distinctive relationship to beauty. Showing that white and black southern women were in conversation with each other in embodying their respective notions of beauty—both consciously and unconsciously—I argue that female beauty in the American South was, more so than in the rest of the country, deeply racialized. White beauty and black beauty were mutually constitutive in the decades after the Civil War, just as they were in the antebellum South. It is impossible to understand one without understanding the other. What it meant to be beautiful in the Jim Crow and civil rights South was determined largely by the presence of a racial other.

While race was the most salient factor in shaping southern beauty, it was not the only one. *Pageants, Parlors, and Pretty Women* also demonstrates how southern beauty practices resulted from the fraught relationship between a conservative, largely rural region and the rest of the nation. This book thus joins those studies that detail how economic modernization, consumer culture, and modernity informed southern identity.[11] At the same time, I stress the significance of gender and notions of femininity to these phenomena. Scholars of the "modern girl" have given us the most comprehensive analysis of this link, of the way in which the refashioning of the female body characterized the transition to modern life all over the world during the first half of the twentieth century.[12] Modern girls were defined by "their use of specific commodities and their explicit eroticism," which, combined, challenged traditional gender norms.[13] In the South, as

Susan K. Cahn has explained, adolescent girls from 1920 to 1960 bore witness to these developments. Though her primary interest is not the body or beauty per se, Cahn observes that changing sexual attitudes and behaviors threatened a breakdown in social order and stood in "for larger instabilities of the region."[14]

*Pageants, Parlors, and Pretty Women* builds on this work. I contend that as southern women experimented with new products and rituals at odds with the region's ideals of female behavior, their bodies came to represent the modern, in economic and especially cultural terms. Whether or not southerners celebrated this fact depended on who they were and what they wanted. Younger women rarely expressed reservations about beauty contests, for example. But their elders did, insisting the spectacles promoted an inappropriately sexualized femininity. Even then, qualms could be laid to rest if the financial stakes were high enough. White farmers needed beauty queens to drum up national and international interest in the South's commodity crops. As black southerners in particular understood, policing women's consumptive practices also represented an effective way to stave off the troubling consequences of consumer culture. Perhaps the most popular strategy in dealing with the bodies of modern southern women, however, was to racialize them, a tactic that reveals how inescapable race really was. By making women's bodies do important work on behalf of their race, both white and black southerners blunted their disconcerting modernity. Beautiful white women were transformed into symbols of white supremacy and, eventually, massive resistance. Beautiful black women, meanwhile, personified racial uplift and racial progress and, later, Black Pride.[15] More so than white southerners, though, black southerners worried that black women might embody their race in the wrong way. Sometimes critics condemned the aesthetic choices of black women as distasteful, by which they meant that their preferences were too black. Attempts to prescribe the appropriate parameters of self-presentation—to dictate what items of clothing to buy and how to wear them—thus suggest how consumption, itself, played into understandings of race.

By examining the interaction between the South and the nation and the function of beautiful bodies therein, this book challenges widely held assumptions about the continuity of southern women's experiences. Many southerners, and even some scholars, take for granted that the history of southern beauty from the antebellum era to the mid-twentieth century is seamless.[16] In some cases, it was. White southerners continued to herald white women for their beauty and, more often than not, mock black women for their African features long after slavery was gone. But significant conflicts also arose between earlier and later ideals of beauty. Young white women who used visible makeup in the early twentieth century may have believed they were carrying forward the tradition of the beautiful antebellum belle, but they were not. Attuned to the impact of cultural and economic modernization within the region, this book reveals the degree to which beauty practices in the postbellum South departed from those that had come before.

Finally, *Pageants, Parlors, and Pretty Women* posits a capacious conception of beauty, complicating our understanding of the significance of beauty in women's lives. I approach beauty as an expansive category that encompasses ideals, practices, rituals, labor, and even spaces. This book brings together a host of phenomena often studied in isolation—cosmetics, beauty and body contests, and hairdressing—to show that the pursuit of beauty encompassed a range of activities, large and small, intimate and public. In the same vein, I also emphasize the complexity inherent in the pursuit of beauty. On the one hand, this book incorporates the insights of feminist critics who emphasize the physical and psychological cost that beauty exacts.[17] An important product of second-wave feminism, this scholarship has exposed the negative consequences of a behemoth beauty industry in the United States, demonstrating how the emphasis on beauty serves, in Susan Bordo's words, as "an amazingly durable and flexible strategy of social control."[18] African American feminists have taken this critique further. They argue that black women have suffered from a system of pernicious images that normalizes racism, sexism, and black poverty.[19] In many ways, *Pageants, Parlors, and Pretty Women* finds common ground with this thinking. Throughout the twentieth century, white and black southern women submitted to beauty rituals in which they were objectified, often at the behest of individuals motivated by financial or ideological gain.

On the other hand, I am careful to balance the insights of feminism with the demands of my evidence. Failing to do so, I quickly realized, could result in an analysis too beholden to contemporary concerns. A properly historicized account of beauty in the South shows that white southern women might actually experience beauty in ways that, if not fully liberating, nevertheless bucked southern tradition. Many of the beauty practices that second-wave feminists would later condemn as tools of female subordination were perceived as dangerous instruments of female liberation to conservative southerners living in the interwar years. Makeup and beauty contests, for example, represented a threat to southern male power. While their meaning later changed, we should not lose sight of how they were initially received and interpreted. Even if they failed to upend southern sexual relations, these products and rituals created possibilities for a femininity that was deliberately crafted by women themselves.[20]

The pursuit of beauty might also entail welcome moments of sensory pleasure, a fact that the experiences of black women in beauty parlors highlight in vivid terms. Drawing on the field of sensory history, this book examines the tactile and olfactory dimensions of the beautifying process, especially, and argues that they formed the basis of a black female culture that had distinct benefits.[21] Nurtured in places overseen by black women, this free space might breed radical talk and even political activism. Black beauty parlors also show especially well how the beauty industry gave black women economic opportunities otherwise unavailable to them. My book therefore argues for a nuanced view of beauty, one that takes into account the fact that beauty might be one way for southern women to assert a degree of power in a society rooted in white male patriarchy.[22]

In the course of engaging these issues, *Pageants, Parlors, and Pretty Women* provides a fresh perspective on the anxieties that plagued southerners from the late nineteenth through the mid-twentieth centuries. Or, put another way, it reveals how the female body both informed and reflected the challenges of life during Jim Crow. This was the case in both the white and black South. Indeed, despite the significance of race to this story, and the very real disparities it created in southern women's lives, it was nevertheless true that the pursuit of beauty by white and black southern women stemmed from similar convictions and revealed common concerns.

Underscoring almost every conversation about beauty in the region were worries about morality and sexuality. Ideas about beauty always exposed a great deal about how southerners understood the moral character of women. To be sure, it was not uncommon for Americans everywhere to conflate a woman's outward appearances with her inner nature. In the South, however, guarding the moral character and sexuality of women was of utmost importance. White southerners did so to guarantee the female subservience so crucial to the maintenance of racial hierarchy. Black southerners did so to fight the assumptions on which that very hierarchy was based. Prescriptions about how or how not to achieve beauty thus often served as a way to control potentially wayward women, white and black.

The close correlation between the body and soul had other consequences as well. The subject of beauty had a way of provoking discussions
about what was natural or "authentic" in terms of bodily presentation
and, ultimately, in terms of one's identity. Efforts to change the outside, by
definition, suggested a desire to change the inside. A white woman who
beautified in the early twentieth century encountered charges that she was
being artificial, that she was covering up her true self to become someone
else. To their critics, black women who beautified were insufficiently black,
as they seemed to want whiter skin and straighter hair. In still other contexts, pursuing beauty became the way for white and black women to signify their commitment to their race, to literally embody it. The adoption of
the Afro during the Black is Beautiful movement of the late 1960s is a good
example. Black women who abandoned straightened hair signaled that
they were more "black" than women who did not. Regardless of whether
the beautifying actions of white and black women were welcomed or censured by their larger communities, the beautiful woman served as a proxy
for racial identity. Female bodies became the repositories of whiteness and
blackness. The focus on female beauty therefore had the effect of essential-
izing race, of locating what was a social construct in the biological body.

Black and white southerners also used female beauty as a veneer to
hide unseemly behaviors and circumstances that flowed from the region's
economy and racial politics. As they battled the legacies of slavery and the
deprivations of Jim Crow, African Americans harnessed female beauty to
demonstrate black capabilities and humanity. They deployed the beautiful black woman as part of the larger effort to dispute white beliefs that
African Americans were innately depraved and dirty, that their women,
especially, were sexually licentious. Often, in fact, attractiveness for a black
woman was less about achieving perfection of face and form than it was
about the daily effort to conduct herself in an appropriately feminine manner. Another result of this emphasis on the correctly adorned and con-
trolled black female body, however, was that poor women's style was disparaged. In their attempts to both mask the economic consequences of
segregation and confute white racism, middle-class blacks elevated their
own aesthetic above others. In rural areas, black home demonstration
agents, for example, spent much of their time convincing rural women
that their clothing—seen as loud, ostentatious, and unsophisticated—
betrayed the race.

White southerners also relied on female beauty to deflect attention away
from things they preferred to hide. Much more so than for black south-

erners, however, white southerners' intended audience was national. The white beauty queens that became so popular beginning in the 1930s with the onset of the Depression were dispatched to help resuscitate southern farming. But they also put a glamorous face on the cultural backwardness and racism that characterized the rural South. Similarly, during the civil rights movement, beautiful white women made a powerful statement to a concerned American public that the white South was not, all evidence to the contrary, a bastion of violence.

The constant invocation of female beauty placed a heavy burden on the bodies of white and black southern women. Still, southern women were not entirely passive recipients of ideas and ideals imposed by others. They employed beauty for their own ends as well. All told, the pursuit of beauty was complex, allowing southerners to achieve a variety of goals, from the personal to the political, from the progressive to the reactionary. Female beauty held the potential to both strengthen and undermine the racial, class, and gender assumptions that sustained Jim Crow.

A FEW POINTS OF clarification are in order before beginning. In terms of their age, the women that I examine fall somewhere between their teen years and middle age. Older women, and the issue of beauty and aging, lie beyond this study. Most beauty products, tools, and rituals of the Jim Crow era were designed to appeal to younger women on the cusp of adulthood. This was especially true of the body contests, such as health pageants and bathing beauty revues, that became popular in the first few decades of the twentieth century. Moreover, since beauty practices seemed to herald a new social order, one with which neither white nor black southerners were entirely comfortable, what younger women did at their dressing table and at the beauty salon mattered. These women represented the future of their race—and ultimately the future of how the South would be organized— and so provoked the most commentary. Middle-aged women, too, participated in the world of modern beauty by having their hair done, buying cosmetics, and modeling in dress revues and fashion shows, though even some of them, in the early years at least, objected to beautifying practices on the grounds that they challenged female propriety or racial authenticity.

The geographical boundaries of *Pageants, Parlors, and Pretty Women* are, in large part, the boundaries of the former Confederacy: Alabama, Arkansas, Florida, Georgia, Louisiana, Mississippi, North Carolina, South Carolina, Tennessee, Texas, and Virginia. Connected by their history as slave states that seceded from the Union, this South has provided the majority of the material analyzed in this book. At the same time, I have resisted a definition of the region that is too narrow. The significance of race in the developments I describe required a more expansive view. Those slave states that did not secede—Kentucky and Maryland, for example—shared much in common with those that did and were culturally oriented toward the Confederacy, as was a city like Washington, D.C., a bastion of southern racial mores well into the twentieth century. In many areas, this southern orientation proved tenacious, surviving the homogenizing effects of modern technological innovations and economic assimilation. Any place where de facto and de jure segregation still reigned in the 1950s and 1960s, as they did in parts of the border South, was more southern than not.

The centrality of segregation to these states, and thus to the history that I reconstruct, determined the book's organization. Although I considered weaving together my examination of beauty among black and white women in the pages that follow, I decided against it. It is true, as I have already indicated, that some motivations for, and consequences of, pursuing beauty transcended race. Nevertheless, the stories that emerged from the evidence were different enough to warrant a segregated approach. I want to honor these distinctive stories, to avoid diluting them, and so I discuss white women in the first chapter, black women in the second, and so on. Only in the final chapter, which looks at the move toward desegregation and the role that beauty played in that process, do I integrate my analysis of southern women and beauty. In organizing the book this way, my intention is not to portray black women as non-normative or to suggest that they were less important; rather, I hope to highlight the diverse experiences of black and white women within a framework that reflects the reality that governed their lives. Jim Crow shaped how black and white women understood and pursued beauty in very different ways. Part of conveying the power of Jim Crow in determining beauty practices and ideals, moreover, is acknowledging that even in the best of situations, black women's beauty choices were conditioned by the views and actions of white southerners. The structure I have chosen enables me to capture this fact.

*Pageants, Parlors, and Pretty Women* begins with the daily, and ostensibly private, beauty practices of southern women from the late nineteenth through the mid-twentieth centuries. Chapter 1 examines how white southerners responded to the new world of modern beauty accoutrements. The adoption of cosmetics and bobbed hair among white southern women was slow, hampered by the deprivations of rural life. Southerners in the countryside also saw cosmetics, especially, as dangerous tools of a new and threatening social order. To overcome this widespread opposition, manufacturers presented cosmetics as devices for the construction of white racial identity by manipulating ideas about the antebellum southern lady. This marketing tactic mitigated cosmetics' modernity and had the added benefit of bolstering Jim Crow by symbolically erasing class divisions among white women.

Chapter 2 analyzes how new beauty products and practices affected black women. Cosmetics presented problems for black southerners, too, but race compounded these complexities. Black women who used cosmetic products invited criticism for wanting to be white or for exuding disreputability in a society already inclined to see them as immoral. By focusing on the black beauty parlor, however, I also argue that the consumer products and services associated with beauty could be used for progressive purposes. As independent business women, African American beauticians plied a trade that allowed for economic security and the cultivation of personal beauty in the name of racial uplift. Beauticians helped black southern women endure Jim Crow by providing a means with which to appear attractive and by creating an atmosphere of intimacy that bred trust.

In Chapters 3 and 4, I turn to public rituals of beauty. Chapter 3 traces the history of beauty contests for white southern women. Initially controversial, beauty contests eventually earned approval because of developments in the rural South. Home demonstration agents and agricultural trade boards transformed a tradition of evaluating farm women's domestic products to achieve their goals. Demonstration agents hoped to bring farm families' tastes and living standards in line with national norms. Trade boards wanted to sell agricultural products in national and international markets. In the 1930s, these efforts coalesced to give rise to the agricultural beauty contest. This ritual provided rural women a new model of southern womanhood and a conspicuous role in the economic and cultural modernization of the South.

Chapter 4 explores the role of body and beauty rituals in black communities. I argue that contests that judged black women's beauty—or, in other cases, aesthetic or bodily performances—were important rituals for the cultivation of race pride and the projection of virtuous womanhood. Black colleges were especially significant sites in this effort. They provided institutional settings for the dissemination of an aesthetic of respectability among the women who would become race leaders. Because the middle class formulated this aesthetic, however, rural and working-class practices were stigmatized, on college campuses and beyond. Because the aesthetic of respectability relied on delineating appropriate consumer choices, it also underscores how consumption informed black women's racial identity.

Chapter 5 brings together white and black women, examining how they pursued beauty as segregation buckled under the weight of the civil rights movement. This revolution had a profound effect on how southern women experienced personal beauty. As the South's most wrenching confrontation with the nation since the Civil War and Reconstruction, the movement transformed white beauty contests into rituals of massive resistance. White southerners honored white queens as the embodiment of the southern "way of life." So, too, did the rest of the country: southern contestants did remarkably well in the Miss America Pageant in the 1950s and 1960s. Building on a practice that was fundamentally political, black beauticians, on the other hand, nurtured a form of political activism within their shops that proved crucial to the success of the civil rights movement. By the mid-1960s, however, younger southern black women reevaluated the aesthetic of respectability. They shunned older standards of beauty in favor of a style that supported the shift to Black Power. On college campuses, beauty contests celebrated this new ideal, making black women's bodies vessels of political and aesthetic blackness.

*Pageants, Parlors, and Pretty Women* ends, then, with the role that beauty played in the crisis that shook the foundations of southern society. It begins, however, in a seemingly quieter time – in the rural South of the early twentieth century.

CHAPTER ONE

# Making Up White Southern Womanhood

*The Democratization of the Southern Lady*

Like most politicians, Thomas Walter Bickett, the governor of North Carolina from 1917 to 1921, had a habit of delivering the same speech over and over again. One favorite topic was "civic righteousness," but he also tended to stray into more surprising territory. To all-female Tar Heel audiences, Governor Bickett often spoke on the subject of how to be beautiful: "Be beautiful. You must be. If you cannot be entirely beautiful, then wage an unwearying campaign to be as beautiful as you can be. No woman has a right to be ugly. An ugly woman is a mistake; a misfit; out of joint; out of tune; at war with the law and the purpose of her being. Whenever I see an ugly woman I know that somebody, somewhere, has either sinned or blundered, and the woman has been cheated of her birthright." Ugliness, he continued, was a "preventable disease. It belongs in the same category with smallpox, tuberculosis and typhoid fever." Concerned with outward beauty enough to make stump speeches about it, Governor Bickett nevertheless abhorred what he called the "bewildering labyrinth of hats and hairpins . . . flounces and frills, and whalebone and cosmetics." These were not, to his mind, the secrets to true beauty.

Governor Bickett insisted, instead, that women strive to be natural, a request that revealed his apprehensions about artificial beauty accoutrements, increasingly popular in some parts of the country. "Affectation spoils more faces than smallpox," Bickett declared. "You simply cannot develop grace and charm in a self-conscious personality. . . . Ours is an age of imitation, of sham. So many things are painted over, or powdered over, or plastered over, or veneered over. Notwithstanding the Pure Food and Drug Act, it is hard to find anything that is exactly what it purports to be."[1]

His reference to this piece of legislation is telling. Passed in 1906, the act made illegal the manufacture and sale of food and drugs that were "adulterated or misbranded."[2] Made-up women, in Bickett's mind, were both. Beauty sprang eternal from physical well-being and clean living, not from jars of creams and tubes of lipstick.

In opposing the "labyrinth" of modern beauty products and practices, Governor Bickett was in good company. Many of his contemporaries agreed that they posed a dire threat to virtuous, white southern womanhood and marred the natural beauty that was touted as its defining physical characteristic. For generations, beauty had been understood not so much as a physical entity that could be manipulated at will but as a reflection of female morality and obedience.[3] The modern beauty industry, which blossomed in the United States during the years that Bickett served as governor, seemed to challenge this traditional way of thinking. The growing recourse to cosmetics, especially, and to the beauty parlor, to a lesser extent, raised troubling questions about who white southern women were and what they wanted. If beauty was innate, a function of female virtue, what did it mean that a white southern woman might decide to make up her face or bob her hair? Who was she? The fact that a politician attempted to answer these conundrums is revealing. In the interwar South, for a woman to stake out a place in this new corner of consumer culture was not a small act. Habits that, at first glance, seem merely private, even frivolous, had consequences for the southern social order.

To be sure, it would be a mistake to assume that every white southern woman who indulged in new beauty practices did so to make some kind of statement about her place in southern society. At the same time, beauty products are potent cultural symbols, imbued with meanings by those who make, use, and see them. All consumer goods provide "marking services," a function that is particularly well served by beauty products, which literally mark the body with meaning.[4] Regardless of a woman's motivation, then, many observers of Bickett's generation interpreted the use of beauty products as a sign of an unforgivable artifice rooted in female rebellion. In the segregated South, moreover, any challenge to male supremacy was inherently a challenge to white supremacy. Modern beauty practices and products carried the potential to upset both. As they debated the meaning of a woman's desire to pursue beauty in novel ways, what southerners were really grappling with was the region's relationship to consumer culture and modernity and the sexual and racial changes that they threatened.

Not surprisingly, given pervasive opposition on ideological and moral grounds, cosmetics and beauty parlors were slow to take hold in the South. Further diminishing their appeal were difficulties created by availability, time, access, and purchasing power, issues that become even more stark when we remember that the vast majority of white southern women lived on farms in the late nineteenth and early twentieth centuries. Figuring out how to overcome these hurdles represented a considerable challenge to the manufacturers of beauty products that were springing up throughout the United States in the 1910s, 1920s, and 1930s.

By World War II, cosmetic manufacturers, in particular, had largely succeeded, settling on a strategy that involved a simple but savvy redefinition. Cosmetic companies and their advertising allies marketed cosmetics as key instruments in the construction and maintenance of elite white racial identity.[5] This tactic, which strengthened the culture of segregation, had the potential to alleviate concerns about the propriety of cosmetics use. By tying cosmetics to one of the most ubiquitous icons of the Old South, they reframed the new products as traditional, as the very antithesis of modernity. Ironically, this was an approach made possible by the new view of beauty as a physical entity rather than a moral quality.[6] Once beauty could be constructed on the body through the use of the right products, even the humblest, and most morally questionable, of southern women could be true southern ladies.

One of the most striking aspects of this story is the conspicuous role of younger southern women. More so than their mothers and grandmothers, high school and college-aged girls wanted to be a part of the exciting world of modern beauty improvements, to experiment with the tools that many feared. Some younger southern women also did not find the aesthetic of whiteness as captivating as cosmetic companies and their female elders might have liked, displaying, instead, a disconcerting attraction to the suntan. Through the pursuit of beauty, younger southern women did not simply exhibit the adventurous proclivities of youth but revealed, in a vivid manner, the disturbing effects of the new forms of self-presentation.

ALTHOUGH IT WOULD FLOURISH in the years following World War I, the beauty industry in the United States grew out of humble nineteenth-century origins. Eleven years before the outbreak of the Civil War, the value of toiletries produced in the United States was only $355,000.[7] Even then, most toiletries were not beauty products per se, but rather items such as soaps and patent medicines, the latter of which promised to cure everything from nervousness to irritability to kidney trouble. Some manufacturers did market cold creams, face powders, and even rouge and eye makeup, which during the Civil War enjoyed a brief period of popularity among the wealthy. But most elite and middle-class women shunned the use of color since the "painted woman" carried negative associations. Prostitutes had long announced their trade with the visible use of face paint, while actresses, another disreputable set of female professionals, used cosmetics on stage. Natural beauty was the ideal, prized as the manifestation of morality. Cosmetic artifice, by contrast, represented a breach of female propriety.[8]

In the South, racial slavery and male patriarchy bolstered these proscriptions against paint since ladyhood itself, crucial to antebellum social order, was intensified to the point of caricature.[9] As paragons of virtue and submission, southern ladies, precisely because of their innate goodness, were naturally and intrinsically beautiful. Although southern ladies were hardly as numerous as mythmakers would have us believe, the rules that governed their appearance were very real, determining how they—and other women who strayed from the ideal—were judged. A charitable observer of a painted woman in the antebellum South might have argued that she was defying the gender mores that dictated her obedience and her relegation to the private sphere. Commenting on the spirit of wartime rebellion that gripped some of Charleston's young elite women, for example, Emma Holmes censured two young belles for "rougeing" and blatantly ignoring their elders' authority.[10] Most observers would have remarked that such a woman was brazenly proclaiming her own sexuality, or, at the very least, of questionable character.

The emphasis on natural beauty as the outer sign of inner goodness resulted in an anemic cosmetics market in the nineteenth century, but it hurt aesthetic judgments as well. Some observers attributed beauty to a face when apparently there was none, as was the case with a young Mary Withers, in whom the candid Holmes admitted being "dreadfully disappointed" after having heard so much about her "far famed beauty." "Perhaps her beauty may grow upon me," Holmes confided to her diary, "but I expected to be dazzled by its exceeding loveliness."[11] The conflation of beauty with morality could easily lead southerners to ignore physical reality. The concurrent injunction against cosmetic artifice could also lead ladies to draw fine distinctions between which cosmetic practices were acceptable and which were not. New Orleans native Eliza Ripley recalled

Painting of Eliza Ripley by Theodore Sydney Moïse, ca. 1854. Ripley condemned most cosmetics, except for rice powder, which, she insisted, was not really a cosmetic. From Ripley's autobiography, *Social Life in Old New Orleans* (New York: D. Appleton, 1912).

that during her antebellum girlhood, no young woman of her elite social class used cosmetics, "except rice powder," which, she carefully added, was "not a cosmetic."[12]

Deeming rice powder acceptable because it helped women protect and even out their white skin, Ripley was unwilling to sanction the use of whitening enamels, which were often lead-based. More importantly, they were seen as a form of paint that artificially masked the face. She mocked a young bride, who hailed from "somewhere up the coast," for having her face enameled while on honeymoon in Paris. Not only was the practice inherently objectionable; it had a ridiculous result: "[the bride] had to be so careful about using the muscles of the face that she was absolutely devoid of expression. Once, in a moment of forgetfulness or carelessness, she cracked a smile, which cracked the enamel. She returned to Paris for repairs. I saw her on the eve of sailing, and do not know if she ever returned."[13] Ripley's humorous anecdote reveals the existence of antebellum beauty rules that had quite serious consequences for the women of her social class. In this case, the offending female was metaphorically cast out of society. Her presence, Ripley suggests, was never missed.

That the bride had felt compelled to apply a whitening enamel, how-ever, was the result of another quite grave injunction. As Ripley's own approval of rice powder indicates, ladies were to protect their white skin from the sun at all costs, a rule the wanton bride had perhaps violated. Rebecca Latimer Felton wrote that young women during her antebel-lum youth in Georgia "were emphatic on this line" and thus "sun bon-nets were always in evidence."[14] Lily-white skin distinguished ladies from the poorer sort who worked in the fields and whose tanned complexion was the marker of their inferior status. Describing a woman named Milly who was the recipient of her family's charity, Mary Boykin Chesnut stated matter-of-factly: "She was a perfect specimen of the Sandhill tackey race, sometimes called country crackers. Her skin was yellow and leathery; even the whites of her eyes were bilious in color."[15]

Most women of Ripley's and Chesnut's class who did seek out beauty help did not look to Paris for enamels and paints; they relied, instead, on ingredients that were readily available in their own homes and gar-dens to make beauty-enhancing concoctions that generally fell within the bounds of respectability.[16] Milk, lemon juice, sugar, and chalk could be used in homemade remedies designed to nourish, powder, or whiten the skin, while flowers and vegetables could be used, if a woman so desired, to lightly blush the cheeks. Simple ingredients for simple recipes. It did not take much for a lady to approximate the nineteenth-century ideal of white skin with a hint of healthy color, though the very use of these reme-dies shows that even the ideal of natural beauty required cosmetic tricks.

As the twentieth century dawned, the cosmetics industry took off in the urban centers of the Northeast, Midwest, and West Coast, where the pio-neers of the industry were located. Urban women of varying social classes moved beyond the relatively safe practices of cleansing and powdering, as a number of factors chipped away at the traditional association of paint with promiscuity.[17] Cities gave birth to vibrant consumer cultures, cement-ing women's identities as consumers and creating new spaces in which they could put themselves on display. In stores and on the streets, clothes, and increasingly cosmetics, became acceptable tools in the fashioning of one's public self. The saturation of popular culture with images of faces also facilitated the adoption of makeup in urban centers. For much of the nineteenth century, the face was less a fixed entity than a product of memory, idealized portrait paintings, and low-quality mirrors that only partly reflected reality. But the spread of photography, and the birth of a new technology, the film projector, conspired to surround urban men and women with pictures of real faces, particularly the made-up faces of stage and screen stars born of a new cult of celebrity. Some women followed in the footsteps of these stars, experimenting with lipstick, rouge, and eye makeup to correct perceived flaws, or to accentuate facial features.

Cosmetics both signaled and facilitated new female desires: a desire to participate in mass consumer society, to lay claim to a life beyond the home, to acquire that most necessary of twentieth-century possessions— a "personality," which, as Warren Susman has written, required that every American "become a performing self" in an ever-expanding, anonymous world.[18] Thus, while national cosmetic advertising redefined the meaning of the painted woman by equating cosmetics use with social mobility, romance, and perpetual youth, it also emphasized what might have seemed a paradoxical claim, according to Kathy Peiss. The industry argued that cosmetic artifice could help a woman present her "true self" in a society where seeing and being seen were more important than ever.[19] Cosmetics use, Peiss argues, was evolving into a "dramatic performance of the self in a culture increasingly oriented to display, spectatorship, and consumption."[20] Often adopted in a spirit of playful rebellion, the cosmetic look nevertheless pointed to serious changes in the lives of many American women. Sales figures provide the most eloquent testimony on the growing allure of cosmetics. In 1929 the value of cosmetic sales in the United States was $141 million, a tenfold increase from 1909. In the same time period, the number of manufacturers almost doubled.[21]

Hair care also became an industry in the early twentieth century. Previously, hairdressing had been an informal ritual, one undertaken by women and female relatives within the privacy of their own homes. For the most part, domestic hair care was more about cleansing than styling, though special occasions might warrant the use of old rags or chicken bones to transform straight hair into curly locks.[22] Wealthier women depended on the labor of servants to wash and then style their long hair into the elaborate updos that were the vogue for much of the nineteenth century. In the South, it was slaves, of course, who provided these hair-grooming services to the likes of Mary Boykin Chesnut and Emma Holmes. Over time, wealthy women in larger cities of the Northeast could patronize beauty shops that provided hair as well as skincare services and products. For those beyond urban borders, hairdressing products—tonics and washes that promised not only to cleanse but to prevent graying and drying of the hair as well—could be acquired through mail order. An 1873 mail-order ad for Lion's Kathairon for the Hair in a South Carolina newspaper reminded women why taking such steps was necessary: "Woman's glory," it proclaimed in the company motto, "is her hair."[23]

Referencing the biblical axiom that a woman's long hair was a sign of her obedience, this company gave voice to the most prevalent belief about women's hair in the years before World War I: long hair was divinely ordained. Indeed, this idea had such cultural currency that few women seem to have even thought about violating it. Women's diaries and other sources from this era are not replete with denunciations of shorn hair in the way that they are with condemnations of painted faces. Short-haired women were rarities in turn-of-the-century America, so odd as to invite diagnoses of sexual perversion. As one sexologist argued in 1886, lesbian proclivities "may nearly always be suspected in females wearing their hair short."[24]

Hairdressing changed drastically after World War I, however, when American women became enamored with the "bob." Increasingly the hairstyle of choice for screen stars in the late 1910s, the bob became emblematic of new, more liberalized attitudes toward female behavior and adornment; in fact, bobbing was to hair as cosmetics were to the face. As singer Mary Garden argued in a *Pictorial Review* article on the new style, bobbed hair "typifies growth, alertness, up-to-dateness, and is part of the expression of the *élan vital!*"[25] In the early years, women who wanted to chop off their locks had to either do it themselves or visit a barbershop, since beauty parlors that served women were few and far between. Only 5,000 existed in the United States in 1920. Ten years later, the number had grown to 40,000, an increase that suggests not only the popularity of the hairstyle but also the work that went into maintaining it.[26] Far from freeing women from the laborious hairdressing rituals that long hair demanded, the bob actually called for frequent care at the hands of a professional. "It was at first thought that bobbed hair would require but little attention," one observer noted in 1925, "but that is a fallacy that was quickly dispelled."[27] This was especially true once the permanent wave became popular. The increase in beauty parlors also reflected a democratization of modern hairdressing practices. Initially the provenance of the wealthy, now middle- and working-class women began to patronize beauty parlors. By the late 1920s, many American women made regular trips to the beauty parlor, where they could enjoy a variety of beauty services—shampoos, haircuts, permanent waves, facials, and manicures.

Southerners were not immune to these cultural changes, though the fact that nearly three in four still lived in a rural area as late as 1920 did diminish their effect.[28] Rural southerners had some access to the goods manufactured in the more industrialized North. Since the 1890s, when mail-order houses began marketing their wares in the region, southerners had sent off for patent medicines. By the 1910s, they were ordering items such as hair tonics, cold creams, face powders, and skin bleaching creams. The country stores that cropped up in the postbellum era also brought new products to rural southerners. Soap and patent medicines, in fact, were the first consumer goods widely available in southern country stores, which numbered 150,653, or about 144 per county, at the turn of the century.[29] Almost every country store had a shelf of patent medicines. "Country people," as one historian has dryly noted, "liked their pills and droughts."[30]

And why wouldn't they? Advertised in newspapers, almanacs, and even religious publications, bitters, tonics, and elixirs sometimes contained opium; almost all contained alcohol.[31] Lydia Pinkham's Vegetable Compound, a highly popular patent remedy for "female complaints," had about twice as much alcohol as the same amount of Schlitz beer.[32] Many patent medicines aimed at women, moreover, promised that curing the inner body could improve the outer body. A healthy woman could aspire to beauty, an Electric Bitters advertisement in a Georgia newspaper insisted, but one plagued by illness could not: "If she has constipation or kidney trouble, her impure blood will cause pimples, blotches, skin eruptions and wretched complexion. . . . Electric Bitters is the best medicine in the world to regulate the stomach, liver and kidneys and to purify the blood. . . . It will make a good-looking, charming woman of a run-down invalid."[33] A correlate to the link between morality and beauty, the connection between inner health and outer appearance was a common motif in the ads of these early patent medicine manufacturers.[34] That a woman might imbibe significant quantities of alcohol to become good-looking and charming did not seem to cause much public comment.

Still, a cornucopia of beauty products did not compete for shelf space with these high-octane patent remedies. General store ledgers from the years immediately following the Civil War show that women could buy items such as cologne, toothbrushes, combs, and hair oil.[35] Soap represented the most commonly stocked beauty-related product throughout the late nineteenth century, though more often than not ledger entries for soap represent the more traditional cleaning variety and not the "toilet" kind.[36] By the 1890s, nationally distributed goods such as Vaseline (originally a black jelly, used as medicine or as a cosmetic on the hair or eyelashes) were available in some areas. By the 1920s, rural white women could expect to find a limited selection of makeup in local stores. A 1929 ledger from a North Carolina general store, for example, indicates that women could purchase toilet soap and face powder. The powder was not a particularly lucrative item. The store sold only 10, while it sold over 180 bars of soap.[37] Within the region, moreover, patterns varied widely. One Alabama general store located in Wilcox County, today still one of the poorest and most sparsely populated counties in the state, stocked only talcum powder and Vaseline as late as 1939.[38] A researcher at the New York–based J. Walter Thompson Advertising Agency, which handled accounts for cosmetics manufacturer Cheesebrough Ponds among others, summed up his assessment of these distribution problems in rural areas quite simply: "Towns under 1,000," he wrote, "are hopeless."[39]

Even if stores did carry beauty products, there was no guarantee that white southern women would be able to buy them. The barriers were enormous. First were the difficulties particular to the rhythms of rural female life. The poorest tenant and sharecropping women were overburdened by domestic chores, childrearing, and field work. Beautifying took time and effort, neither of which they could spare. In her pioneering study of white tenant women in the 1930s, sociologist Margaret Hagood often mentioned the appearances of the women she interviewed. Very few of them impressed her, and those who did stood out because they managed to be simply neat or clean. More typical were women such as a Mrs. Perry, aged forty and mother of sixteen: "She has no time for primping, and stringy bits of colorless hair show beneath a 'stocking' cap on her head. She has no make-up on her face—only brownish stains at the corners of her mouth."[40] Hagood noted that even the basics of personal hygiene, such as hair brushing and face washing, were sometimes ignored.

A lack of free time undoubtedly contributed to such behavior, but so, too, did a lack of indoor plumbing. As late as 1940, only 16 percent of white tenant families in central Texas had running water in their homes.[41] For most rural southerners, taking a bath was no small chore since it involved collecting wood, starting a fire, hauling water in buckets, and then dumping heated water into a tub.[42] Letters to the editor of the *Progressive Famer*, a publication aimed largely at landowning farm families, reveal how onerous the process was even for those with more resources. One woman wrote longingly of her desire "not for one of those tiled and tinted bathrooms, but just for a faucet and one of those folding rubber bathtubs advertised in mail order catalogues."[43]

Having to use lye soap did not make the prospect of a bath any more

Sharecropping woman, Arkansas, ca. 1935. Most sharecropping women had neither the time nor the resources to use commercial beauty products, especially during the Depression. Courtesy of the Franklin D. Roosevelt Library and Museum, Hyde Park, New York.

attractive. One Texas farm woman remembered how much she preferred commercial shampoo to homemade lye soap since it made her hair "softer and smell better." But her family used lye more regularly because store-bought preparations "wouldn't clean any better."[44] They were, however, more expensive. Common pantry items also substituted for store-bought preparations. One Tennessee women recalled that her aunt, who never washed her hair with soap and water, used meal to clean her hair.[45]

Clearly, the rural economy presented hurdles. From the end of the Civil War through the Depression, cash was scarce in the agricultural South. Southern sharecroppers and tenant farmers relied on credit extended by country stores. Given that many of these southern families indebted themselves just to subsist, buying beauty products was not a priority. Even necessities might fall by the wayside, as they did with one tenant woman interviewed by Hagood. The woman and her husband hoped to buy land, and so for two years she had not purchased new shoes. To extend the longevity of her old pair, she had gone barefoot in the summers. The woman did make sure her hair was rolled up, Hagood remarked, "for she has not lost all thought of appearance" despite the fact that she had no money for "adornments."[46] Like their husbands, poorer farm women viewed consumer goods as luxuries that endangered their tenuous economic independence.[47] Country stores may have been, in the words of Grace Hale, "a temptation difficult to bear," but meager incomes prohibited spending sprees.[48] These southerners could not afford to see general stores as exciting sites of consumption. They viewed them, instead, as utilitarian clearinghouses that supplied the staples of living.

Frugality reigned in less cash-strapped homes as well. The beauty editor of the *Progressive Farmer* advised her middle-class female readers to set aside sufficient money for beauty aids by drawing up "beauty budgets" at the beginning of each new year. Recognizing that the best financial planning was no guarantee that a woman could buy what she needed, the beauty adviser continued to provide recipes for homemade face creams well into the 1930s even as the magazine carried ads for such products. These very real limitations on farm purchasing power preoccupied market researchers throughout the 1920s and 1930s, prompting concerns about whether to advertise at all in small-town and rural periodicals.[49]

For those rural women who did have the income to purchase consumer goods, the general store, itself, posed a problem. As elsewhere, the use of beauty products in the rural South was linked to women's access to public space. Women who did not feel welcome in the places where goods were sold had fewer opportunities to experiment with the new treats of mass consumption than women who did. Most southern women fell into the former category. Throughout the antebellum era and the late nineteenth century, stores in rural southern areas were gathering places for men.[50] Tied to the home by domestic duties, women rarely patronized them. The boisterous and bawdy conversations echoing from store front porches, moreover, likely offended female sensibilities. Although they might make annual or semiannual treks to stock up on household supplies, more often women sent their husbands on weekly trips with shopping lists. Alternatively, they made purchases in the private setting of their homes from the itinerant merchants who crisscrossed the region. One study of rural Mississippi in the late 1920s determined that women in some areas "did not get to town more often than once a month or even less often." Mothers of large families with little cash on hand, the report noted, "rarely ever left home" for any reason at all.[51] Margaret Hagood found that in white tenant families, "the wife doesn't 'tote the pocketbook' and neither she nor her husband thinks it right for a woman to do so." "A woman who is not at all a downtrodden wife," Hagood wrote of one interviewee, "says she just wouldn't feel right in a grocery store—it's no place for a woman."[52] For decades this pattern of consumption and sociability in the agricultural South persisted. Lu Ann Jones has noted that in Farm Security Administration photos taken of general stores in the 1930s and 1940s, women "were hardly to be found."[53]

Rural women's efforts to have their hair professionally groomed were hampered for similar reasons. Access was a big obstacle because beauty parlors, rigidly segregated along racial lines by the early twentieth century, were rare in sparsely populated areas of the South. In 1920, there were 167 white beauticians in Georgia, but 87 of those worked in Atlanta. In Alabama, there were 102 white beauticians, but 59 of those worked in Birmingham. In the entire state of Mississippi, white beauticians numbered only 22. The numbers of beauticians per capita were thus extraordinarily low—in Georgia, Alabama, and Mississippi there were 1:5,057, 1:7,093, and 1:19,408, respectively—for the most part lower than in nonsouthern states and the nation as a whole.[54] As we will see in Chapter 2, moreover, the minimal supply of white beauticians in 1920 contrasted sharply with an astonishingly high number of black beauticians throughout the region that same year.

The disparity between white and black beauticians highlights a range of issues, such as the slow advance of consumer culture among rural white women as well as their limited employment opportunities. The difference also suggests how black women responded to their own restricted job prospects. Early on, they saw in beauty work a viable alternative to the agricultural and domestic service jobs that confined them to the lowest rungs of the southern labor market. Given the scarcity of white beauticians during these years, most white women in the rural South continued to do their own hair or depended on female relatives for styling help. If a rural woman wanted to hop on the bobbing bandwagon and wanted the expertise of a professional to do so, a barber was her only option. Throughout the 1920s and 1950s, articles in the *Progressive Farmer* acknowledged the existence of beauticians in some villages and nearby cities but assumed that many rural women would have to rely on the services of a barber. One article that ran in 1930, for example, explored the wonders of "beauty parlor marcels and finger waves" while nevertheless instructing female readers on how to get quality bobs from barbers. "On your next visit to a city," the beauty columnist wrote, "go to the very best barber and have him explain to you just how he cuts your hair so you may, in turn, explain it to your home town barber."[55] Seven years later, the columnist still referred to the reader's hypothetical hairdresser as "him."[56]

Many rural women would have avoided barbershops altogether, however, since such spaces were, even more so than the general store, the epitome of male camaraderie and potentially hostile to female intrusions.[57] Indeed, the barbershop was historically linked to one of the most infamous of male habits—paying for sex—making a visit potentially problematic for all southern women, rural or urban. The difficulties presented by the barbershop, as well as the growth in demand for services more complicated than the bob (such as color and curling), encouraged more southern women to open their own shops for female customers. So, too, did the Depression, which drove white women into the labor force to help their families make ends meet. With relatively low barriers to entry, the hair-care industry represented an attractive option for women whose male relatives found themselves under- or unemployed.[58] By 1940, the number of white beauticians in the South had increased dramatically. That year, Georgia had 2,821, Alabama had 2,092, and Mississippi had 1,487.[59] The number of beauticians per capita rose commensurately in most southern states to more manageable levels; now, there was one beautician for several hundred, as opposed to several thousand, women.

In fact, in eight southern states, white beauticians, when compared to black, now constituted a disproportionate share of the state's overall beauticians.[60] Still, a beautician in Athens, Georgia, told a Federal Writers' Project interviewer in 1939 that many of her clients lived in towns that were too small to support a beauty parlor.[61] Many women, furthermore, would have found it difficult to make such a trip for a service not deemed a necessity. Even when there was a beauty parlor nearby, some women were not in a position to use it. In the late 1940s, town girls in one western North Carolina county frequented the local beauty shop, but rural girls still could not afford professional services. Instead, poorer young women in the countryside resorted to home methods, such as rolling hair in paper or stockings, to achieve their desired look.[62]

As this North Carolina example illustrates, the beauty industry made more headway in southern towns and cities. Mores that prohibited women from patronizing stores in rural areas were less restrictive in urban locales. Sites of consumption, moreover, multiplied in the early twentieth century. A midsize city such as Louisville, for example, was home to ten department stores and seventeen five-and-dimes by the end of the 1920s. A smaller town such as Durham, North Carolina, had welcomed four department stores and six five-and-dime stores in the same period.[63] The business-men who managed these stores recognized the potential profitability of serving the urban woman, especially those of means. Store owners made concerted efforts to lure them out of their homes by employing female clerks. Owners and manufacturers also placed ads for all manner of cosmetics and hair washes. Beauticians, too, marketed their services in urban periodicals, often touting the skills of a particular operator who had just been trained in the latest hair treatment system.

Younger urban women responded. Virginia Foster Durr, a member of the fashionable set in Montgomery, Alabama, in the late 1910s, recalled the elaborate beauty rituals she and her friends would undertake before going out on dates. "Everything would have to be just right," she recalled, "our slippers and stockings and underwear and our powder and paint and lipstick and rouge." Not yet bobbers, Durr and her friends took bubble baths and had their mothers curl their long, clean hair. "When we finally got it all done, we would look like beautiful flowers."[64] Even with the luxuries of indoor plumbing and shampoo and cosmetics, disappointment could result. After all that primping, Durr somewhat bitterly recalled, their dates always got drunk and ruined the carefully crafted aura of romance.

Elite young women in other cities were intimately involved in the new world of beauty products as well. Debutantes from Savannah, Birmingham, New Orleans, Atlanta, Nashville, and Richmond followed the ads in women's magazines for information about the industry's earliest and best-selling cleansing and moisturizing products—toilet soaps, cold creams, and vanishing creams—and bought them on a regular basis.[65] College women, too, were drawn to beauty products and services, taking advantage of their proximity to department and drug stores and to behavioral standards developed by a peer group prone to experimentation.[66] A quick perusal of any campus yearbook or newspaper shows that by the early 1920s, coeds clamored to wear makeup and chop off their locks. College and high school women represented the group most likely to use the tools of beauty to fashion themselves as flappers, the model of female liberation that became the icon of the 1920s and that was defined, in part, by her recourse to modern beauty products.[67]

Women with fewer resources also discovered new products and practices while wandering through urban stores. The agricultural crisis of the 1920s gradually pushed poorer farming families into towns, where wage labor jobs, such as those in the textile industry, waited.[68] Though they had to relinquish some of their earning to their parents, young working girls might still have cash to spend. Growing up in small-town Arkansas, writer Shirley Abbott was fascinated by her mother's beauty rituals, which the elder woman had learned while working as a maid in Hot Springs, Arkansas, after moving off the family farm. "[O]ne thing she had acquired in town was the ability to be glamorous, to divorce herself, by means of paints and polishes, from that other world. . . . I think the women in her family must have yearned for such things since the dawn of time," Abbott wrote.[69] Like buying their clothes rather than making them, using cosmetics and cutting their hair allowed young country girls to leave behind that "other world" of rural poverty, isolation, and backwardness. In their hands, beauty rituals became aspirational, signs of their independence, though even with these tools, country girls might fail to erase the signs of their lower-class status.[70] For a young girl newly arrived to town, homemade clothes could betray the sophisticated facade she had cultivated with makeup and a fashionable hairstyle.[71]

Regardless of their class status, urban women, too, risked crossing significant lines when they chose to beautify with modern beauty tools. Although beauty shops, unlike barbershops, were not historically linked to prostitution, they could bring together women of very different socioeconomic, even moral, universes. A Federal Writers' Project interviewer who visited Bonnie Baste's beauty salon in Raleigh, North Carolina, in the late 1930s witnessed an awkward moment for Baste and her patrons that illustrates this reality. As a young secretary and a member of the Junior League (with hands that "glistened with white diamonds and platinum") sat having their hair done, a woman with excessive and "clownish" makeup entered, raising eyebrows all around. Recognizing the sensitivity of the moment, Bonnie whisked the woman away to the back room where she could segregate her from respectable customers. And while Bonnie was willing to offer the painted woman her services, she did not relish the job. The beautician-client relationship necessitated close contact and touching. "[F]resh from the cribs," Bonnie said of the woman. "Hate to put my hands on her."[72]

The intimacy inherent in hairdressing was problematic for other reasons as well, especially in the early years of the bobbing craze when women might turn to a barber. In large southern cities, many barbers were black, transforming a white woman's visit to a barbershop into a sexually charged situation that violated the strictest taboo of the Jim Crow South. The city of Atlanta, for one, took action, passing an ordinance in 1926 that made it illegal for black barbers to cut white women's hair.[73] That Atlanta leaders felt such a measure necessary is curious. Census data from just six years earlier shows that white barbers outnumbered black barbers 394 to 241.[74] Perhaps the city envisioned its measure as purely preventative. Or perhaps some white women willingly patronized black practitioners despite the availability of barbers of their own race, an alternative that suggests adventurous white women may have been attracted to the titillation inherent in such a boundary-crossing experience.[75] Even when it was cut in a salon operated by a white proprietor, bobbed hair raised eyebrows. A mill worker in Spray, North Carolina, in the late 1910s and early 1920s, Nannie Pharis bobbed her hair to win a ten dollar bet. "When I come home," she recalled years later, "my son wouldn't even speak to me."[76]

Southerners struggled to reconcile these beauty practices with ideas about how women were supposed to present themselves, a tension that inevitably revolved around how women were supposed to behave. The prescriptive ideals of southern ladyhood had a profound effect on how southerners viewed southern women, even those, like Pharis, with no claim to elite heritage.[77] Perhaps the clearest window into how southerners interpreted modern beauty products in light of their views on women is the city, for it was there that enough women experimented to elicit reaction. In 1912, the *Baltimore Sun* sponsored a write-in contest for its readers, "Should Women Paint?," thus confronting the issue of cosmetics use head-on. The paper printed over four dozen responses to the question from women and men living in Baltimore, Washington, D.C., and Virginia. Opinions were mixed, but even those in favor of women turning to jars of paints and creams usually qualified their endorsement.

Women entering the business world, a female respondent argued, "will be more successful and demand more respect if they are attractive and well dressed." If painting and powdering makes a woman more beautiful, then, by all means she should do it, but only, the writer said, if she makes herself "natural looking." Opponents expanded upon this plea to strive for naturalness, betraying unease over the presence of made-up women in public spaces. Fears of female "deception" abound in responses. One reader wished made-up women could experience the perspective of the male gaze: "[I]f only the average 'painter' could see herself at work, shopping, or at the theatre," he wrote. "Surely she takes it for granted she is being admired when she is stared at quite often by inquisitive eyes."[78] In reality, men stared because they wondered how much money she wasted on her painted face and who, exactly, she was. Women who made up confounded an observer's ability to know them.

In a New South less and less rooted in place, cosmetics added to the confusion of a landscape in which anonymity and social mobility made it difficult to detect sincerity or, worse, "social counterfeits"—people, as Governor Bickett might have said, who were "not what they purported to be."[79] For white southerners, the most threatening social counterfeits, of course, were light-skinned blacks who attempted to pass, a trick cosmetics could facilitate. The consequences for gender relations bothered many. Rare were the readers who insisted, as one woman did, that painted women "be asphyxiated." But for most people, the implications of cosmetics use were serious, nonetheless. As one wrote, "No woman, in her natural desire to be beautiful, should seek outside aid when true beauty can be obtained through right living and right thinking, by observing the laws of nature and health, by living a useful, helpful life, and being content with that state of life into which it shall please God to call her.[80] Cosmetic artifice seemed to herald a new era in which the traditional route to beauty—whereby a woman remained content with her "state of life"— could be sidestepped for a different path.

Young women on college campuses came under fire for cosmetics use, too, sometimes by their own peers. One of the few universities in the region with a strong coeducational tradition, the University of Texas struggled with the significance of beauty products in the late 1910s. Grappling with the changes that World War I wrought in women's lives and expectations, the 1918 yearbook featured a campus beauties section with photos of made-up women dressed as soldiers, sailors, football players, and cowboys, coupling cosmetics with identities and roles that were explicitly male. The female students of UT were so offended by the looks the beauties had created that they assembled to pass a resolution denouncing the photos as "offensive and obnoxious" and unrepresentative of "student life, standards, and ideals."[81] Backed by the beauties themselves, who seem to have had second thoughts about the photo spread, the coeds also ensured that the beauties section was torn out of any undistributed yearbooks. High school girls fared no better. A poem in a publication at Dallas's Forest Avenue High School in 1923 warned young flappers that lipstick, rouge, bobbed hair, and revealing clothes made them nothing more than senseless painted dolls. A man might be attracted in the short run, but he would never commit: "Lonely you'll find your later life, When you'll be dropped; man wants a wife who's gentle, modest, pure, and sweet. He'll worship at her feet."[82]

The popularity of the flapper look, in fact, emerged as a leitmotif in

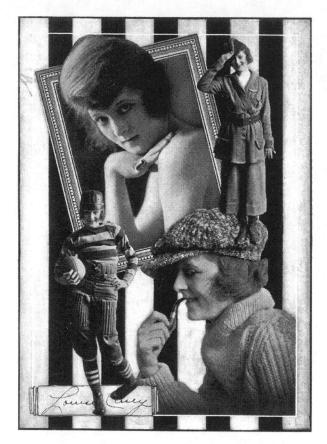

University of Texas campus beauty, in its 1918 yearbook. One of several campus beauties whose made-up face and male clothing sparked student outrage. Courtesy of the University of Texas Archives, Dolph Briscoe Center for American History, University of Texas at Austin.

publications on some campuses. The painted coed, with her eyes outlined by heavy pencil and her bee-stung lips dripping with crimson color, became a favorite subject of campus artists at the University of Alabama, for example, where the artists were no doubt male. Shorn of her locks, she was often captured in the act of making up, reveling in the public display of artifice, the sensuousness of her look, and the knowledge that she was being watched. The eagerness with which the Alabama humor magazine, in particular, featured caricatures of the artificially enhanced college woman suggests an interest tinged with a hint of admiration and a heavy dose of derision. Beneath one such illustration, an ode to "prom girl" captured the ambivalent appreciation of the coed's new style and what it represented: "Prom girl of today . . . You come—see—then conquer, More glory to you."[83] While in this drawing she displayed the conquering power of the New Woman, in other images and the accompanying text she was vain, stupid, unpredictable, or altogether inscrutable. These depictions stand

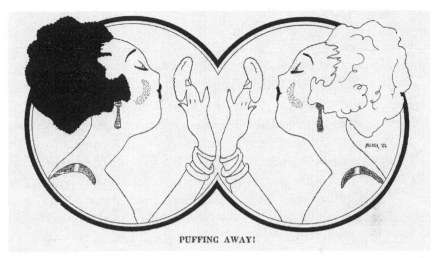

PUFFING AWAY!

*Rammer Jammer* drawing, 1925. In this drawing by a member of the class of 1926, which shows coeds reveling in the public display of artifice, the University of Alabama's humor magazine connected cosmetics to smoking. Courtesy of the W. S. Hoole Special Collections Library, University of Alabama, Tuscaloosa.

in stark contrast to those from the beginning of the century, which praise Alabama coeds for their modesty, purity, simplicity, and natural beauty.[84]

The timing of the novel look was significant in Tuscaloosa, as it must have been at other colleges. Although the University of Alabama was one of only six major public universities in the South that had been nominally coeducational since the turn of the century, the number of female students began to increase dramatically in the 1920s after the president made female enrollment a priority.[85] In poking fun at the made-up coed, male students may have been expressing resentment at the destruction of what had been essentially a boys' club. At the very least, the focus on her much-altered visage suggests that the practices symbolized, even to some of the region's young, a new kind of female self-presentation and power.

Unpainted faces and long hair stood as evidence of southern women's virtue, of their obedience—of their very identity as southern ladies. Southern women who beautified with modern tools seemed to reject all three. Checking this possibility was precisely the goal of John W. Porter, a Southern Baptist preacher from Louisville, Kentucky, and venomous campaigner against modern beauty practices. Writing in 1923, Porter lamented a loss of "womanly modesty" in "The Menace of Feminism," the first chapter of an entire book exploring this theme. Condemning feminists' efforts to destroy divinely ordained gender relations, he criticized the look that feminists adopted, one characterized by indecent, "peek-a-boo" clothing and visible makeup. In Porter's view, cosmetics seemed to help disobedient women achieve their feminist goals: "With her dear doggie, powdered face, painted cheeks, and penciled brows, the feminist goes forth to conquer, and it is to be feared, sometimes 'stoops to conquer.'" Porter argued that feminists' gains in the realm of sexual equality—and the look they cultivated as their badge—emasculated men and masculinized women. Feminists were masculine, in fact, to the point of being a third sex. He predicted that if the tide were not soon turned, "the grammarian will have to use three genders for the human race—he, she and it." To Porter, cosmetics, short hair, and revealing clothing were anathema to traditional femininity and an ally of a feminism that destroyed female virtue. He could console himself only by imagining that women knew not what they were doing: "Surely they must be ignorant of the fact, or careless of it, that such fashions originate among harlots and actresses and leaders in fast society."[86]

Defenders of beauty products and practices embraced precisely what Porter condemned. Perhaps no one better personified the new look than Montgomery native Zelda Fitzgerald, who in 1918 was voted the prettiest girl in her graduating class.[87] By the early 1920s, Zelda had become the most famous flapper in America and wrote several short essays that explained why young women had abandoned old-fashioned appearances and behaviors. Respectability, they had realized, was overrated. Boys actually did like girls who flirted and had sex. "Perceiving these things," Zelda wrote, "the Flapper awoke from her lethargy of sub-deb-ism, bobbed her hair, put on her choicest pair of earrings and a great deal of audacity and rouge, and went into the battle."[88] Zelda rejected arguments that beauty devices were bad for women. Not everyone was born a natural beauty, she observed, but with cosmetics, a woman could at least "be pleasant to the eye." Thus altered, she was empowered. Young women simply "wanted to choose their destinies—to be successful competitors in the great game of life."[89] The position that second-wave feminists would take in the 1960s—that the accoutrements of beauty were a source of women's subordination—would have perplexed both John W. Porter and Zelda Fitzgerald alike.

But for Porter and his ilk, the world of modern beauty practices represented an unwelcome challenge to traditional notions—not only of morality, but of order, stability, and certainty. Indeed, opposition to beauty products and services accompanied the much broader resistance to modernity within the South, a resistance most conspicuous in the battles between religious fundamentalists and liberal theologians in the 1920s.[90] In condemning makeup and bobbed hair, crusaders took on the gendered implications of these forces. New beauty practices fed the anxieties of modernity by upsetting the Victorian idea that a woman's appearance was a reflection of both her inner character and social role.[91] How could southerners distinguish between a southern lady who was respectable and one who was not when they both wore the same mask?

Modern beauty practices also seemed to motivate women to enter the public sphere of work, consumption, and politics and to proclaim their sexual liberation—all of which were cornerstones of the modernist impulse. In a fitting leap of logic, worried southerners of this era went so far as to transform the adolescent girl, in particular, into "a trope for the South's modernity," in Susan K. Cahn's words. When she danced, smoked, bobbed her hair, or made up, she did much more than threaten inherited ideas of how ladies should comport themselves. She threatened the entire southern social system, a Gordian knot of patriarchy and white supremacy that depended upon the sexual subordination—and sexual passionlessness—of white women. Any recognition of white women's sexuality, as Cahn observes, "might hasten the collapse of racialized distinctions between white virtue and black vice, not to mention the racial order that such ideas buttressed."[92] Seen in this light, the new methods of beautification were worrisome indeed.

ALTHOUGH ALTERING BOTH the face and hair came under fire in the early-twentieth-century South, criticism of cosmetics ultimately trumped concerns over hair bobbing and visits to the beauty parlor. Aimed at a conservative rural female readership, the *Progressive Farmer*, for example, contains no stern admonitions against bobbing in the 1920s or 1930s. The magazine did acknowledge that not every farm woman wanted a bob, offering readers advice on how to approximate the look without actually having to cut all their hair.[93] "Bobbing the hair is a matter of taste," it observed in 1924, adding, a few years later, that the style did have the advantage of making women look younger.[94] That the publication did not take special aim at the bob contrasts, as we will see, with its concern over the proper use of cosmetics during the same period. The *Progressive Farmer* was not alone. In public conversations about the new products and practices, it was face painting that proved the most disturbing to opponents, though there were exceptions. As late as 1941, one fundamentalist minister from Texas argued in a treatise on the subject that bobbing hair was a greater sin than using makeup. John R. Rice based his case on the fact that the Bible does not discuss makeup but does contain rules about women's hair.[95]

But to many who spoke out on these issues, the artifice inherent in cosmetics—and its suggestion of brazenness, disreputability, and deceit—seemed a more serious crime than cutting hair. The explanation for this belief is not terribly surprising: cosmetics use had a much longer, and much more problematic, history. The cosmetic habit was also easier to indulge. For most southern women, visiting a beauty parlor for a new hairstyle was not an easy thing to do given their relative scarcity, while maintaining the look afterward took more time, effort, and money than did applying a little lipstick and rouge. The structure of the two industries also contributed to the differences. Unlike many beauty parlors patronized by black southern women, those that catered to white southern women were more often independently owned and operated, which meant that haircare advertising was relatively small-scale and localized. Many cosmetic manufacturers, by contrast, tended to be regional or even national operations with larger, more coordinated marketing campaigns.[96] On the one hand, the ubiquity of such ads helped stoke the controversy that blunted the acceptance of cosmetics. On the other, it meant that cosmetic companies were in a position to quell southerners' fears, if they could find the right pitch—if, that is, they could redefine the meaning of cosmetics and make them safe for consumption, particularly among the majority of white women living in the rural South.

On this issue, the efforts of the Zona Toilet Company of Wichita, Kansas, in the years immediately following World War I are instructive. The Zona Toilet Company attempted to establish a presence in Charleston, South Carolina, after waiting out the economic disruptions caused by war. F. D. Aley, an agent for the company in Wichita, recruited James Allan to oversee the advertising and distribution operations in the port city. In January 1919, Aley was optimistic. "I feel that we have a big thing in Zona," he told Allan, "and you may be able to do us lots of good in the south."[97] They focused in the early months on selling the company's face powder. Allan began by setting up window displays in drugstores, placing boxes of the powder in beauty salons, and devising a series of ads for Charleston papers. The ads reveal a degree of apprehension about cosmetics use in the city: "To those old Fogies in Charleston who do not believe in Modern Improvements. Try Zona."[98] Another ad assured potential customers that "[t]he use of a good powder is not a question of morality but of good taste."[99] The ads worked, as the product initially sold well in the city, especially after Allan, recognizing that women trusted the expertise of female clerks, hired a salesgirl at the Paragon drugstore to sing the praise of Zona powder in return for 10 percent of the sales.

By the summer of 1919, Allan had noticed yet another reason the powder was popular. Young women were buying it to protect their skin while they were at the beach. "Perhaps," Allan suggested, "a good strong ad for Zona in the two Sunday papers stressing the advantage of Zona for the beach and in the surf would be good."[100] Noting that the same trend still applied two years later, Allan asked the company to send free samples to sixteen young ladies who would be vacationing at the seashore during the summer and provided their addresses, all of which were located in the tony neighborhoods of the city's peninsula.[101] For these upper-crust ladies, the powdering habit was prophylactic, adopted in an effort to prevent any change in appearance and to maintain their fair complexions—to protect their lily-white skin.

Allan's marketing was just the entering wedge that cosmetic companies needed. Although best known as products that black women used in their efforts to achieve the light skin that denoted elite social status, lightening products enjoyed popularity among white women all over the country in the early part of the century.[102] The allure of a genteel, Anglo-Saxon whiteness crossed racial lines. Yet outside the South, new trends, especially suntanning, began to shift cosmetic advertising campaigns into new territory. First appearing during World War I, the fad of suntanning caught on in the 1920s in resort circles in the West and Northeast, where bronze skin revealed an ability to pursue outdoor leisure activities and to avoid factory work.

Slower to industrialize and more attuned to the traditional class and race implications of tanned skin, most white southerners, by contrast, resisted suntanning. A suntan still indicated a life of outdoor field work, the exact opposite of aristocratic leisure, and it carried the taint of blackness. Shirley Abbott's mother and other older female relatives may have learned how to use paints and polishes to divorce themselves from their former lives as farm women. They were, as Abbott remembered, "gentled and domesticated by the time I came among them. But the marks were there," she observed. "Their skins were leathery from working outdoors."[103] Farm women's reminiscences unfailingly include memories of performing field labor dressed in sunbonnets and gloves to shield their skin from the sun and thus escape the telltale sign of poverty. One South Carolina woman recalled that during her childhood, some men even donned the long, woolen gloves worn by the females on her family's farm.[104]

Although the rules of decorum had relaxed sufficiently for young women of means to participate in outdoor sports in the 1910s and 1920s, they had not relaxed so much that they could tan themselves and expect to get away with it. Eliza Ripley noted with horror that her granddaughter's New Orleans cohort exposed their skin when golfing in the summer and acquired tans. More daring than the women of Charleston in that they did not protect their skin while they could, even these young ladies knew they could not keep their tans for long. "These athletic girls," Ripley lamented, "come back to city homes so sunburnt and with such coarse skin they have to repair to a skin specialist, and have the rough cuticle burnt off with horrid acids, and be polished up before the society season opens."[105]

The cosmetic businesses hoping to break into the southern market, then, turned the problem into a solution: they tapped into the allure of the southern lady's white complexion. Tying the lady's beauty to cosmetic artifice by emphasizing the white complexion that had always been her defining characteristic, they suggested that all southern women, regardless of their class background, could be beautiful southern ladies with the use of the right cosmetic products. Paralleling efforts in other arenas of southern culture, this strategy rested on the belief that white women of modest means could, as Glenda Gilmore puts it in her examination of early Jim Crow politics, "be boosted up to the pedestal."[106] Cosmetic companies, in short, democratized the lady's aristocratic whiteness by making it available through bleaching creams and face powders. Whiteness was the lynchpin, the link between the beautiful southern lady and makeup. White southern women were encouraged to construct a racialized beauty, one that afforded all the benefits of white racial identity and class privilege but that carried none of cosmetics' threatening gender or sexual implications. Artifice was no longer a questionable game of deceit or an act of impropriety—indeed, it was not artifice at all—when the intended result was the uncovering or restoring of one's true white skin.

In the cities and larger towns where women of Ripley's class resided, newspapers carried ads for protective skin powders and whitening agents. These ads absolutely monopolized the women's sections of southern rural periodicals, playing on an undercurrent of perceived insecurity among rural women. Typical was the approach by Othine bleaching cream, which admonished women to remove the "ugly mask" of freckles and tan and reveal the "milk white" complexion that lay underneath.[107] Invoking insider knowledge, a common tactic in these appeals, promotions for Wilson's Freckle Cream, manufactured in Charleston, South Carolina, touted the product as "The Secret of Southern Beauty" in southern and nonsouthern newspapers alike. Ads promised "to *positively* remove freckles, tan, sunburn and clear the skin."[108] Many of these spots featured dramatic before-and-after drawings in which a dark grey complexion magically disappeared with the use of the advertised product. In the dichromatic newspapers and magazines of the early twentieth century, these transformations were always rendered as a change from black, or some shade of it, to white.

Among the most ubiquitous ads for face powders and bleaching creams were those of the National Toilet Company, headquartered in Paris, Tennessee. Founded in 1899, the company marketed its powders and creams in urban and small-town newspapers and farming periodicals. During the height of its media campaign in the 1920s, the National Toilet Company engaged the services of Dorothy Dignam, a pioneering female copywriter at the McJunkin Advertising Agency in Chicago. She gave the company a national name as well by developing ads for mass circulation women's magazines and newspapers across the country. Equally significant, however, were her efforts in expanding the company's market share within the South.

Dignam helped the National Toilet Company sell its products to white southern women, who were not, in fact, the original consumers of its whitening products. Black women were. The company hoped Dignam could help broaden its appeal, though at the time she apparently did not know this. To the top of one National Toilet Company advertisement she designed for Atlanta-area newspapers, Dignam later attached a note that read, "An odd one! This line made in the South was largely sold to the Negro market. The advertising was a planned attempt to capture the white market also. (I was never told!)"[109] This planned attempt revolved exclusively around using the imagery of the antebellum South and the antebellum southern lady. Clearly, the Tennessee-based operation played a significant role in determining the content of company ads. Yet Dignam executed the company's plan, translating its ideas onto paper. Her involvement highlights the fact that northern perceptions of white southern women's desires informed the marketing strategies of cosmetic companies in the South, even when those cosmetics were manufactured in the region. The racialized beauty sold to southern women was thus partly a manifestation of northerners' interest in—and invention of—southern identity in the late nineteenth and early twentieth centuries.[110]

The National Toilet Company invited white women to think of themselves as contemporary incarnations of nineteenth-century aristocratic southern ladies and belles. Ads for Nadine Face Powder, one of the company's leading products, targeted southern women directly and promised a powder made specifically for them. "Southern Women!" one declared. "This is your own—your individual face powder! Nadine was created for Southern women. It has been used for years by Southern beauties." The lengthy copy for these ads focused on the skin that made the lady so exquisite and predicted that every southern woman would soon be able to call it her own. "Every Southern Girl a 'Southern Beauty,'" another announced, noting that for generations southern girls had been "the fairest of women." Yet it continued, "This homage and admiration belongs to *every* Southern girl—not to a favored few. Every Southern girl *can* be a 'Southern Beauty!'" Achieving this look may have been difficult in the past, but Nadine face powder had finally made it possible for "thousands of women to look their loveliest." Blended to match a southern woman's "natural coloring," Nadine powder would protect skin from the ravages of wind and sun.[111]

Just as her great-grandmother, real or mythic, had guarded her pure aristocratic beauty through purity of thought and deed, a modern southern woman could ensure that her fair, white skin would remain unspoiled. For the modern southern lady, the task was easily accomplished. All she had to do was powder her nose, an act that gave her a claim to social, racial, and moral superiority and a connection with the region's antebellum aristocracy. Spots for Southern Flowers Face Powder, another product in the company's line, literally drew this connection for female readers in the ads themselves. Next to a sketch of a box of Southern Flowers powder stood an iconic image of an antebellum plantation with a stream of belles in hoop skirts emerging from under its columned porch.

Advertisements for Nadinola Bleaching Cream, one of the company's best sellers, promised a more dramatic service than did those for its face powders. The very existence of the cream not only called into question the efficacy of its powders but also undermined the company's signature claim that all southern women were born ladies who avoided outdoor labor. Promising to make outdoor complexions "clear and fair again," one ad portrayed the bleaching cream as a regionwide trick in the collective female beauty arsenal. "Here in the Southland, where the 'sunburn season'

## It's here—
# Southern Flowers

—the unusual
new face powder
of the Southland

PREPARED with the special purpose in mind of producing a perfect powder for Southern skins and Southern temperatures, Southern Flowers has achieved even more than its sponsors dared expect.

Never have you known such a powder. It agrees with skins that no powder suited heretofore. Its tissue cream ingredient nourishes the skin while protecting it, and it adheres no matter how sultry the weather.

All this combined with a new alluring fragrance—the most enchanting odor developed in years.

Why accept less in a powder than Southern Flowers can give you? Don't postpone trying it. You'll be glad you used it.

*You will find Southern Flowers Face Powder at the leading toilet counters. Look for the lovely flower garden box or send us $1.00 and state your choice of tints — flesh, pink, brunette or white.*

THE FULL PRICE WILL BE REFUNDED IF YOU ARE NOT ENTIRELY PLEASED.

## Southern Flowers, *Perfumers*, Paris, Tennessee

*SOLD IN ATLANTA BY*

M. Rich & Bros. Co.; Davison--Paxon--Stokes Co.; Keely Co.
and other leading toilet counters

Southern Flowers Face Powder advertisement, 1924. The National Toilet Company, headquartered in Paris, Tennessee, made whitening products for black women but began marketing them to white women in the 1920s. Courtesy of the Wisconsin Historical Society.

is so long, thousands of women regularly renew the creamy whiteness of their skin with Nadinola Bleaching Cream. It's an old Southern Beauty secret." Another ad revealed "How Southern Girls Keep Their Wondrous Complexions." "Everyone knows the Southern sun's intensity," the text observed, "yet the peach-bloom skin of Southern belles is the envy of women the world over. For years and years Nadinola Bleaching Cream has been the beauty secret of Southern women. It whitens discolored skin to milky purity. It banishes deep freckles and tan. . . . One cream that both whitens the skin and clears it . . . Nadinola never fails."[112]

Like the makers of Wilson's Freckle Cream, the National Toilet Company played on the idea that southern women possessed a secret unknown to women living elsewhere. The antebellum southern woman assumes the role of twentieth-century beauty expert in these Nadinola Bleaching Cream ads. Five modern women cast their gaze at a portrait of an antebellum lady who insists on white skin and sanctions the use of cosmetic artifice to achieve it. Yet by focusing on Nadinola's restorative effects, the National Toilet Company neutralized any suggestion that such artifice was untruthful. Whether the result of her need to do outdoor labor or of her decision to participate in outdoor leisure activities, a southern woman with tanned skin had "discolored skin." The use of cosmetics, at least the kind that protected and whitened, was not problematic if the purpose was to reclaim a natural beauty that circumstance had taken away. The democratization of white skin thus rested uneasily on a central tension: southern women who powdered and bleached constructed a whiteness—in effect, they put on "white face"—that they had possessed all along. And in becoming a southern lady marked by beauty, a southern woman overcame the problem of identity that cosmetic practices precipitated—she became scrutable. Regaining her white skin, she was now a lady, a respectable social type that every southerner knew well.

Lipstick and rouge had to be broached with more caution. The National Toilet Company did not overtly tie the southern lady to the use of these more contentious products, but many of its advertisements from this period did so subtly. At the bottom of the ad for the bleaching cream, adjacent to a small portrait of the lady, appeared a list of other "Nadine beauty requisites." Among these were "lip rouge" and, for the face, a "compact rouge," both of which were sold at stores alongside the company's whitening products. Once a woman had purchased products that lightened her skin, perhaps she would grow comfortable enough with the idea of artifice to take the next step and experiment with cosmetic color.

# How Southern Girls Keep Their
# Wondrous Complexions

Everyone knows the Southern sun's intensity—yet the peach-bloom skin of Southern beauties is the envy of women the world over.

For years and years Nadinola Bleaching Cream has been the beauty secret of Southern women. It whitens discolored skin to milky purity. It banishes deep freckles and tan. It fades the redness of windburn, softens and refines the skin coarsened by exposure.

Nadinola clears the skin of every blemish and imperfection. One cream that both whitens the skin and clears it—gives you a soft, fresh, satin-smooth complexion. Nadinola never fails. We guarantee that, or your money refunded. Begin tonight to use Nadinola. Watch the daily improvement. Full directions in each package. At toilet counters, two sizes, 50c and $1.

*Send today for our interesting booklet, "Beauty Secrets of the South," telling all about Nadinola and the other Nadine preparations. National Toilet Co., Paris, Tenn.*

### Nadine Beauty Requisites

| | | | |
|---|---|---|---|
| Nadine Flesh Soap | 25c | Nadine Rouge Compact | 25 & 50c |
| Nadine Vanishing Cream | 50c | Nadine Lip Rouge | 25c |
| Nadine Cleansing Cream | 50c | Nadine Face Powder | 50c |
| Nadine Almond Lotion | 50c | Nadine Face Powder | |
| Egyptian Cream | 50c | Compact | $1 |

# Nadinola Bleaching Cream
## The Lure of Southern Loveliness

Nadinola Bleaching Cream advertisement, 1924. This National Toilet Company advertisement features the antebellum lady, ready to bequeath her trademark white skin to early-twentieth-century women whose own skin was too dark. Courtesy of the Wisconsin Historical Society.

This marketing tactic made sense. By associating these cosmetic products, lightening or otherwise, with the antebellum southern lady, the National Toilet Company tempered the sexual modernism that they represented. As Karen L. Cox has shown, the images of the antebellum South that circulated so widely in early-twentieth-century popular culture served a particular function. Created by northerners for northerners, these images assuaged the anxieties of life in the industrialized North. Modernity, which sprang from the twin forces of industrialization and urbanization, was frightening, even to those best poised to reap its benefits. So, the Old South—in songs, in films, in advertisements—became a balm for those northerners who "longed for a return to America's pastoral and romantic past."[113]

As the case of the National Toilet Company demonstrates, mythmakers assumed that southerners, too, might find the icons of an arcadian Old South an appealing antidote to the uncertainties of the emerging economic and cultural order, uncertainties from which southerners were hardly immune, despite their rural provenance. In this case, southerners might come around to cosmetics if they could learn to see them the right way. To connect cosmetic products to the southern lady, in other words, was to suggest that there was nothing new or modern or troubling about them at all. The recourse to the southern lady in cosmetic ads is striking because the most pervasive image in cosmetics marketing at the time was the Modern Girl. Ubiquitous in national and international advertising for the first several decades of the twentieth century, the Modern Girl epitomized the possibilities afforded by consumer culture: female liberation and sexual desire—even, to some observers, interracial sexual desire.[114] She was hardly old-fashioned. The southern lady was her foil, serving to reposition cosmetics within a context of traditional values.

Determining how white southern women viewed early cosmetic products is difficult. Beauty regimens only rarely elicited comment in diaries and memoirs. Beauty advice, however, can begin to fill the void. Beauty columnists served as mediators between cosmetic companies and female consumers, rescuing the latter group's voice from obscurity and the din of marketing rhetoric and offering important clues about how cosmetics were consumed. For over thirty years, the predominantly rural female population of the South had just such an expert to whom it could turn for help in negotiating the changing world of female beauty. Beginning in 1930, Sally Carter, the beauty adviser for the *Progressive Farmer*, wrote a regular column that addressed everything from clothes to hair to cosmetics. The most popular periodical in the region, farming or otherwise, the *Progressive Farmer* likely represented the main source of information about the cosmetics market for many white rural southern women during these decades. It boasted close to a million subscriptions in the 1930s and claimed almost four and a half million readers in the 1950s, most of whom were from middle-class, home-owning families.[115] Some farm women of lesser means managed to take the *Progressive Farmer* as well, including one, interviewed by Margaret Hagood, who recalled her disappointment at having to cancel the family's subscription during the lean years of the Depression.[116] According to the *Progressive Farmer*'s own research, nearly a quarter of all white rural females over the age of ten read the magazine by the postwar period.[117]

Sally Carter and the cosmetic ads that appeared in the women's section thus came to be regular features in the daily lives of many white women learning about the world of consumer goods that lay beyond the home. To be sure, the beauty advice dispensed in the pages of the *Progressive Farmer* was not formulated in an environment free of marketing influence. Carter had a vested interest in the success of the companies that advertised in the publication. She responded by pushing products that appeared in the ads on her page. Despite this mix of business with beauty advice—or, in part, because of it—Carter's column is illuminating. It shows how rural southern women gradually changed their view of cosmetics, as well as the nature of their own beauty.

First published in 1886 in Raleigh, North Carolina, the *Progressive Farmer* ran neither a beauty column nor advertisements for beauty products for three decades, devoting most of its space to articles about advances in farming and housekeeping methods. The cover of a 1923 issue, however, did play on the assumption that southern women were inherently beautiful, a theme that would later inform many of Sally Carter's columns. Beneath a large photo of a farm woman kneeling between two calves, a caption announced that "[t]he South is blessed with good looking women but is in dire need of more purebred calves of the dairy breeds," drawing a comparison between women and farm animals that, as Chapter 3 will demonstrate, was important and influential in its own right.[118] Starting in the 1920s, as its circulation began to reach into the Deep South, the farming periodical included grooming articles on the women's page. But it carried few ads for cosmetic products that might help with the grooming process, advertising, instead, pills and tonics that cured indigestion, colds, and constipation. As late as 1928—by which point references to hair bobbing had become a recurring and unexceptionable event on the women's page—an article about cosmetics discussed the virtues of antiperspirants, toothpastes, and depilatories, not face powder and lipstick.

By 1930, when the magazine had become staple reading in southern farm homes, the advertisements had begun to change, and Sally Carter had assumed control of the grooming column, now called "Out of Miss Dixie's Bandbox." Face powders, cleansing creams, cold creams, and bleaching creams, including those made by the National Toilet Company, captured adjacent ad space. Taken together, these ads and Carter's advice suggest that attaining soft, white skin represented the most important goal of a beauty regimen for farm women, who would have had a difficult time protecting themselves from the sun. Bleaching cream ads, for example, assured readers that true beauty was waiting to be rescued— "Under your freckles, you are beautiful—remove the ugly mask"—while spring and summer inevitably inspired columns by Carter about the necessity of keeping the complexion white.[119] Year after year, she returned to the topic, by far her favorite, even as discussions of other trends began competing for space in her columns.

Carter's refrain was simple. She admonished her readers to avoid the sun at all costs and to bleach away any signs of not having done so. Acknowledging that suntanning had become popular in places such as California, she had a difficult time understanding the motivations behind the practice. Recalling in 1930 a recent vacation to the West Coast, Carter wrote that she had been "horrified" to see girls deliberately tanning their skin. "I kept wondering why anybody would want to look like that," she mused, "and how they'd ever get that tan off." She warned that sun exposure could "permanently coarsen and darken the skin, or at best make it very hard to recover its natural tint."[120] Carter insisted that her readers keep their skin "smooth and white as though you never ventured out of doors," directing them to the skin whiteners advertised in the pages of the magazine if they needed effective remedies for skin that had endured the sun.[121]

Carter did not concern herself with the need for more purebred dairy calves, but the South's good fortune of having so many beautiful women became her rallying cry. Like national and regional cosmetic companies, she called on the myth of the beautiful southern lady to convince modern southern women that white skin, and thus beauty, lay within their reach. Citing the "homage . . . paid to the loveliness of Southern women," she reminded her readers that it "was up to us to live up to the tradition."[122]

Betraying her sense that modern southern women might be reluctant to try even whitening cosmetics, Sally Carter let her readers in on a secret. The antebellum lady did occasionally use beauty aids. "[M]y!" Carter whispered. "How secretly she used them!" The lady's beauty, her whiteness, was not completely natural after all. It depended on an external source— homemade beauty concoctions that had been made by her black mammy. "Mammy," Carter wrote, "was actually one of the first beauty specialists in our country, and a most successful one, judging by results." Mammy devised secret recipes for face powders and hair tonics, and even allowed her mistress to use beet juice on her lips and cheeks.

The loyal slave focused most of her attention, though, on protecting her lady's complexion. Mammy spent hours in the garden and kitchen "turning out jars of snowy creams and bottles of perfumed liquids that gave her 'baby' a skin of such magnolia petal fairness."[123] If, for some reason, the skin of her mistress "became the slightest bit tanned or freckled . . . Mammy lost no time." Gladly ignoring her other responsibilities, she went to work immediately. Despite Mammy's best efforts, of course, not every antebellum woman could benefit from her wisdom and labor, and those unfortunate women certainly could not buy mass-produced cosmetics. There was, in short, no "organized attack against ugliness as there is nowadays."[124] Modern cosmetics had changed everything. "More of you are 'beauties' than ever before," Carter observed, able to go to the store or send away for "beauty aids that don't require so much effort."[125] Agreeing with Governor Bickett, who had argued that ugliness was a "preventable disease," Carter prescribed a cure that might have made him uneasy.

Intended as an amusing tale of the Old South, Carter's story cuts to the core of the racialized beauty that was marketed so creatively to white southern women in the early decades of the twentieth century. It captures how the racial and sexual politics of the South allowed white women to wrest their famed beauty from the hands and bodies of black women. More astute than she perhaps intended, Carter's metaphorical reading of southern history points to the labor dynamic that enabled southern ladies to revel in their beauty. Female slaves provided not simply the "jars of snowy creams" that made a lady's skin white and beautiful, but the prerequisite that made it possible: they freed the lady from field work. Safe in the knowledge that antebellum ladies had turned to slave-made remedies, farm women could now enjoy the gift that black women had bestowed— white skin—themselves, even though they might not be able to enjoy the leisure that had been the lady's birthright. By associating cosmetics with the familiar imagery of the premodern Old South, Sally Carter, like the National Toilet Company, assured farm women that the recourse to cosmetics was not the handmaiden of a dangerous modern womanhood.

Although the antebellum lady may have used the juice of vegetables to add a hint of color to her cheeks and lips, throughout most of the interwar years the *Progressive Farmer* did not carry advertisements for rouge, lipstick, or eye makeup. Manufacturers opted not to advertise them in the farming periodical, at least directly. A 1931 ad for Plough's Peroxide Cream, a skin bleach, trumpeted its whitening power while also observing that it could hold powder and rouge on for hours, but went no further.[126] Jane Simpson McKimmon, the first agent of North Carolina's home demonstration program, would have understood why. She remembered when the agents under her supervision, who were generally more urban and better educated than the rural women they visited, began to use rouge. "It was quite . . . disturbing," she recalled. "We . . . had to consider our conservative group whose opinion we valued highly." Gradually, she and her staffers concluded that "color could be used with restraint" and that the effect was beneficial if it was not detectable. "The agents began to use rouge in a faint blush," she later wrote, "which slowly increased but rarely passed nature's blush line."[127]

McKimmon's observations indicate how controversial cosmetic products made their way into farm women's beauty regimens. Once they had grown accustomed to the idea that they were bona fide southern ladies who were born with beautiful white skin but sometimes needed help uncovering it, they could more readily accept the idea that the use of visible color was just another way to highlight their natural beauty. Sally Carter pursued this line of reasoning in her columns throughout the 1930s, slowly cracking the wall of opposition to face "paint." As early as 1931, she wrote a piece titled "Making Friends with Make-Up" in which she tried to help her readers negotiate the intimidating world of cosmetic color. Again assuring readers that they were the heirs of their "Dixie belle" grandmother's inherent southern beauty, Carter argued that all cosmetic products could be used "to enhance your loveliness" if one simple rule were followed: "Apply only enough to look perfectly natural."

Carter predicted that many southerners could conceive of a woman using powder but would oppose the use of rouge—and absolutely revolt at the sight of lipstick. She even admitted that she, herself, had not yet come to terms with eye shadow and mascara. The problem, she insisted, was that those individuals with reservations had observed "the wrong kind of make-up, or the right kind wrongly used." Makeup could "be a bitter enemy, bent on making you look silly or grotesque or even ill-bred," but it could also be a friend, if used to imitate nature.[128] Carter advocated this policy as the surest way for women to overcome the objections of men, who still needed convincing in the late 1930s. She acknowledged that a husband might not like the idea of his wife using makeup but argued that he inevitably liked the effect when well done. "In other words," she concluded, "he wants make-up to be so artfully used that neither he nor anyone else thinks of it as make-up."[129]

Obscuring the artifice inherent in applying color was the key to making it acceptable. Acknowledging this element of subterfuge, Carter regularly listed "Tricks in the Art of Make-Up" as one of the mail-order pamphlets that were available to interested readers. Carter was especially concerned about proper cosmetics use among high school girls, who more eagerly welcomed visible color than did older women. In her advice on how to apply rouge and lipstick before school, Carter wrote that blending these products well was essential if a young girl hoped to become attractive and, just as importantly, if she hoped to avoid the criticism of mothers and classmates. Being a "smoothie"—a girl who looked "vital" and "well-groomed"—was every girl's dream. But no one wanted a face that announced to the world, "Here goes Painted Polly."[130] In the same vein, Carter criticized the obvious artificiality of colored hair. If the *Progressive Farmer* is any indication, gray hair was an unwelcome sign of age to many farm women. Yet "[m]ost dyed hair looks dyed," Carter stated matter-of-factly, continuing, "you will fool nobody."[131] Indeed, even before Carter took over the reins of the beauty column, hair coloring—not bobbing—was the cardinal hair sin in the pages of the periodical.[132]

Carter did not let go of her opposition to hair dye, which may say as much about the technology of early- to mid-century hair coloring and its lack of subtly—its obvious artificiality—as it does about any deep-seated opposition to the practice. By the late 1930s and early 1940s, however, the sense that there was any fundamental difference between antebellum and modern cosmetic practices had disappeared from the pages of her column. Making up had apparently been the wellspring of natural, aristocratic beauty all along. Carter, meanwhile, invoked the plantation lady time and again as the justification for modern farm women's beautification efforts. Actually, she turned to the trope more and more during these years, suggesting its staying power in the lives of rural southern women. Then there was *Gone With the Wind*. The release of the movie in 1939 elevated the myth of the plantation lady to new heights of popularity. In her Christmas column that year, Carter conceded that the days of Christmas balls on plantations "when the Scarlett O'Haras and the Melanies of the Old South beguiled the hearts of men" were over. The New South's yuletide festivities would be just as merry and glamorous, however, with "you, today's Dixie belles, no less anxious to be your loveliest."[133] Images of Scarlett and Melanie, as well as other real southern belles renowned for their beauty, continued to pepper the pages of the *Progressive Farmer* into the 1940s.

At the same time, pitches for formerly controversial cosmetic products began to appear in the magazine with more frequency. Carter herself had facilitated this development, but it was also was the result of events far removed from her offices at the *Progressive Farmer*: the United States' entry into World War II in 1941. Once America was at war, the pursuit of beauty emerged as a national concern. The government and corporations told women that it was their patriotic duty to embody femininity, creating advertisements and propaganda that framed the cosmetic mask as a central component of the feminine ideal. The overt message was twofold. First, women had to make up to prove they were worth fighting for. Second, they had to maintain the nation's morale, as well as their own, during this time of crisis. Underneath, however, was a hope that the gender challenge posed by women's entry into male work spaces could be mitigated through made-up faces.[134] Women, in other words, would remain women, even though they were doing men's jobs. Significantly, this wartime emphasis on cosmetics included not just face powders and cold creams but also products that in the rural South, at least, had been off-limits for decades. Melissa McEuen has argued, in fact, that no single item was as important in accomplishing these ideological ends or was as symbolic of American femininity during the war years as lipstick.[135] American women answered the call of duty. Between 1940 and 1945, annual sales of cosmetics, perfumes, and toiletries—which were not subject to the severe rationing that restricted consumption of other items—jumped from $400 million to $660 million.[136]

Many of those who contributed to this dramatic sales increase were cosmetics novices, women whose new employment opportunities afforded both the exposure and money to make up. Rural women were among these. "Farm women going into war plants," *Business Week* observed after the war, "learned the morale-building qualities of lipstick." A "whole new segment of the population," it concluded, "has been introduced to the perfumes, toilet waters, lotions, deodorants, and other articles that make up the cosmetic and toiletry line."[137] In the South, some of the rural women who took up war work migrated to towns and cities for good; others remained behind on the farm and commuted. Even those who did not engage in wage labor were not immune from the rhetoric connecting makeup to patriotism or from the relative accessibility of cosmetic products. Indeed, at a time when there was more money in the rural South than ever before but a shortage of most consumer goods, cosmetics may not have seemed a lavish or frivolous purchase.[138]

By late 1945, Sally Carter's columns indicated the issue was settled. She was advising her readers to think of coordinating their lipstick and rouge in the same way they would their hats, gloves, and handbags.[139] Cosmetics were as pedestrian—and as essential—as clothing. Still, despite the boost provided by the war, southern women lagged behind women elsewhere in their annual cosmetic purchases. In 1948, women in all of the former states of the Confederacy, as well as Kentucky and Maryland, spent less than the national average of $8.59 on makeup. Mississippi women, ranking dead last, spent only $2.88.[140] The research of several social scientists who studied southern communities in the wake of the war also showed that cosmetics had not been incorporated into every southern woman's routine. After attending a meeting of the Women's Business and Professional Club in Camden, Alabama, a tiny town in Wilcox County, one observed that the attendees were all dressed up as they might be for Sunday but that only some wore cosmetics.[141] Another who visited a small mill town in South Carolina interviewed the wife of relatively high-ranking mill worker. He wrote in his field notes that she "uses lipstick," a detail he included because it seems to have stood out as an unusual habit.[142]

Sally Carter, for her part, continued to argue that visible cosmetic color could still call a southern woman's virtue into question, but only if used incorrectly. The implication was that most modern Scarletts knew, by now, what they were doing. Perhaps this was so. But the transformation that occurred in the pages of the *Progressive Farmer* beauty column, and presumably among some of its readers, also rested on a new way of seeing.[143] To the newly trained eye, cosmetic artifice came to seem natural, while the absence of artifice was unnatural, if not downright ugly, a deliberate choice to shun one's birthright of beauty, to make oneself unpresentable. To venture into public with an unpainted face was now the transgression. The gradual rise in popularity of the term "makeup" itself perhaps best reveals the paradox of the transition in how southerners viewed cosmetics.

Invoked with no sense of irony by Carter and others, "makeup" described cosmetic products that made southern women look more like their true selves. Another irony, of course, was that the new cosmetic artifice granted southern women of modest backgrounds an artificial, even false identity as southern ladies. The deceit inherent in this ruse, though, smoothed over class differences in the service of Jim Crow.

If Sally Carter led many readers, particularly older ones, to embrace visible cosmetic color, her columns indicate that some led her to embrace another aesthetic trend—the suntan. This was the one beauty innovation she was loathe to welcome, and beneath her injunctions against sun exposure runs a continual current of apprehension. Younger readers, it seems, were less convinced than she might have hoped by the valorization of white skin both in her column and in the advertisements of cosmetic companies adjacent to it. Just as they were with makeup, young women living on farms and in rural communities were more accepting of tanned skin than were their elders, and by the middle of the 1930s, Carter was almost forced to take notice. Still condemning sun exposure and praising the virtues of whitening and bleaching, she nevertheless acknowledged that some rural women were increasingly interested in acquiring a suntan. But, she wrote in 1935, these women were achieving the look from "a bottle sold them by the druggist and not from Old Man Sol."[144] A year later, she reiterated her claim: "no matter how much a girl wants the golden brown sun tan that is now the mode, they no longer flirt with Old Sol to get it . . . they *protect their faces* from the sun, and get their tanned complexion by the camouflage of sun tan powder!"[145]

For Carter, the concern was not simply that girls should avoid the sun's damaging rays but that they should be able to instantaneously get that "tan off," as she had once put it. Her reluctance to sanction even the "camouflage" of the temporary tan is captured in the column's title. "Summer Make-Up," it read, "Bows to Fashion." This was not an aesthetic transition she accepted with ease. But within the next few years, the beauty editor began to rethink her position. This change of heart must have been hastened, at least in part, by the allure of advertising dollars. Products to facilitate suntanning or give the illusion of a tanned skin, the druggists bottles and suntan powders, were inching out skin whiteners. By 1941, Carter was advertising "Suntan vs. Sunburn" as one of her mail-order pamphlets, while a few years later she addressed this distinction in depth, won over by the beauty of bronzed skin. She assumed, in fact, that many of her readers were already sun worshipers. "Most Southern Belles hardly need to be told how to acquire a suntan! . . . If, however, your tan is not deep enough to please Dame Fashion and yourself," she assured readers, "you can deepen it by using a suntan preparation that sifts out the infra-red (burning) rays."[146] A deep tan, of course, was precisely the kind of semipermanent change in skin tone Carter had resisted for so long, though no evidence of her earlier opposition appeared in these later columns. Any disjuncture between the past and present disappeared, just as it did with respect to cosmetic color.

An unsullied whiteness had proven attractive to a generation of rural southern women indebted to the aesthetic prescriptions of the nineteenth century. Its appeal was bound to wane, however, as their daughters and granddaughters came of age. Indeed, the job of serving as the magazine's beauty sage had likely been passed down to a new "Sally Carter," a younger southern woman less beholden to older beauty ideas and practices than her predecessor(s) had been. Even as the beauty sage was dispensing her advice during the interwar years, industrialization and urbanization were altering the landscape of southern social relations and leisure patterns, just as they had earlier in the North. By 1945, only one-third of southerners lived on farms.[147] Areas like the Carolina Piedmont, where factory work had been plentiful for decades, had gradually transformed the meaning of tanned skin. Upstate "country crackers," as Mary Boykin Chesnut had called them, were once "yellow and leathery." But one researcher observed that the cotton mill workers in South Carolina were now "as a rule, pale and sallow" without the "healthy transparency seen among the townspeople."[148] In this new context, young women who could afford to spend time outside tanning their skin showed with their bodies that they did not have to work indoors. A boom of swimming pool construction across the region, which began in the 1920s and accelerated during the Depression with the availability of New Deal funds, facilitated this pastime.[149]

The emergence of the bathing beauty in the South, long the epitome of youthful leisure elsewhere, was perhaps the most salient symbol of this shift to suntanning. That her roots within the region were largely rural, as we will see in Chapter 3, demonstrated just how much traditional proscriptions against tanned skin lost their relevancy in the years around World War II. Gone was the suggestion, moreover, that a young woman might forfeit her status as a southern lady by tanning her skin. Her identity had been secured by decades of marketing and prescriptive rhetoric.

She was still a "Dixie Belle," a "New South Scarlett," a modern reincarnation of her aristocratic, if mythic, grandmother, albeit with tanned and painted skin.

As white women transformed themselves into made-up southern ladies, black women, meanwhile, did not stand by or concede the possibilities of pursuing beauty. On the contrary, they countered the version of racialized beauty white women had come to embody by cultivating their own beauty practices and standards and, in the process, forged a unique weapon in the battle against Jim Crow.

## CHAPTER TWO

# Shop Talk

*Ritual and Space in the*
*Southern Black Beauty Parlor*

During the Depression, black workers at the American Tobacco Company and Liggett and Myers Tobacco Company frequented a barbershop/ beauty salon in the black business district of Durham, North Carolina. Years later, Julia Lucas, who ran the beauty salon part of the operation, recalled why the establishment was so popular. The grooming services were important, of course, but that was not all. "We didn't have that many private places, other than churches, that we could discuss . . . anything that concerned black people's advancement," Lucas observed. Factory workers spoke their minds in the shop, she said, because "they felt secure."[1] They discussed unionization and criticized the city's black leadership, which tended to oppose decisive action on controversial projects. After NAACP headquarters decided to fight for a salary raise for black teachers in North Carolina, for example, Durham NAACP officials proceeded slowly.[2] Most of Lucas's customers, however, wanted action: "They'd come in . . . and say 'Yeah, let's do it. Let's do it.'" Lucas understood well the function the beauty salon and the barbershop played in the lives of Durham's working-class blacks. "A place," she concluded, "does make a difference in how you express and when you feel free to express something that you know is controversial."[3]

Lucas captures the civic significance of the work that went on inside beauty shops, which beauticians and patrons alike termed "beauty culture," or the grooming of hair. Rooted in assumptions and structural realities unique to black communities, this work, and the spaces where it occurred, occupied a conspicuous place in southern black neighborhoods and economies. As did white southern women's encounter with beauty products, black women's participation in the modern world of beauty afforded tools for constructing visions of self and community. For the first half of the twentieth century, white women turned to cosmetics to fashion an exclusionary, racialized femininity. Sometimes, black women found their own consumer choices conditioned by this same ideal. The conviction that "whiter" features were more attractive than "black" ones gave rise, for example, to commercially prepared hair straighteners and skin bleaches. The availability of these controversial products, as well as of cosmetics that elicited anxieties about female morality, meant that the pursuit of beauty was fraught with contention in the black community. The historical record reveals these tensions, exposing the emotional and especially physical cost black women bore as they pursued beauty with the aid of modern beauty products.

But as Lucas's memory indicates, black women also found themselves heirs to a beauty tradition with different ideological underpinnings and, at times, quite different uses. Black beauticians who plied their trade in the early- to mid-twentieth-century South helped their clients construct a femininity that blunted the harsher edges of Jim Crow. What was at stake for many black women was the respectability that well-groomed hair conferred, a status that was particularly significant for poorer black women, whose financial and occupational position made fighting negative stereotypes difficult. Through the expanding market of consumer goods and services, southern black women wrested a small degree of power from an antagonistic audience by presenting themselves in ways intended to demand respect. The beautifying process itself was also significant, providing overworked black women opportunities for relaxation and pampering.

In addition to the efficacy of their products and services, black beauticians also emphasized that their line of work was a valuable vehicle for the economic uplift of the race. Black women with little capital could enter the profession without going into debt, a fact that allowed scores of working-class black women to set themselves up as beauticians and thus free themselves from economic dependence on both black husbands and white employers. Perhaps most importantly, since they operated beyond the watchful gaze of white employers, black beauticians presided over important free spaces in black communities. Nurtured by this freedom—and, significantly, the content of beauty rituals themselves—a culture of beauty shop talk emerged in many African American beauty parlors. The practices and physical spaces of black beauty parlors, in short, reveal the political potential inherent in certain types of consumer behaviors.[4]

On the whole, black southern women forged a more intimate—and more active—relationship with the burgeoning world of beauty than did white southern women. By comparison, most white southern women experienced a distant connection to the new marketplace of beauty, at least in the early years. They seemed to be relatively passive consumers of products and services that, while full of potent cultural meaning, nevertheless carried little of the same import. In one sense, this distinction was the result of a racially divided economy wherein black women, by necessity, had to work and were therefore more likely to be proprietors who offered beauty services. In another sense, this difference was a function of black women's ongoing struggle to be recognized as attractive and the significance of such services to this effort. In still another sense, black women were more likely to find the beautifying process itself a salve for the psychological and physical wounds inflicted by Jim Crow, wounds white women did not endure.

Despite the possibilities inherent in black beauty culture, problems remained. Financial stability was not a guarantee, especially during the Depression. Purveyors of beauty products and services also had difficulty answering the challenges their work presented. To critics, a black woman who had her hair groomed, or pressed, in the lingo of the day, seemed to indicate a desire to be whiter, and the beautician who helped her was guilty of promoting discriminatory beauty ideals. Finally, by framing well-groomed women as the embodiment of racial progress and respectability, beauty culturists placed a heavy burden on black women. Because of black women's sex as well as their race, in other words, the complexities of beauty were compounded. Ultimately, black beauty culture reveals especially well the ways in which the pursuit of beauty in the Jim Crow South could be at once restrictive and liberating.

BLACK WOMEN WHO chose to groom hair in the twentieth-century South were indebted to traditions that stretched back several hundred years before the importation of slaves to America.[5] Diverse though they were, African societies valued hair as a medium of communication. Within African cultures, for example, differences in hairstyles might correspond to differences in status or point to one's surname, as clans often adopted signature looks. Although slavery drastically curtailed the attention that men and women of African descent could devote to hairstyling rituals, they did adapt their practices to the harsh realities of the plantation. In fact, the styling of hair, as Shane White and Graham White argue in their examination of slave runaway advertisements, "was one of the few areas of which it could be said that whites allowed blacks a relatively unhindered scope for cultural expression."[6] Slave owners' descriptions of runaways in the eighteenth century show that slaves created a variety of looks with plaits, curls, and knots. Their aesthetic often struck their owners as curious if not downright baffling. Distinctive hair arrangements seem to have been less in vogue in the nineteenth century, suggesting a new preference for shorter hair or perhaps new circumstances less conducive to intricate hairstyling.[7]

Photographs, Works Progress Administration interviews, and memoirs reveal the tension that must have underscored all efforts to clean and style hair—the desire to make the best of an oppressive situation. Slave women wore colorful, patterned bandanas that allowed for individual expression and became emblematic of a rural black style. Still, the practice was born of necessity. Head coverings protected from sunstroke and preserved the fruits of grooming labor, which slaves could perform only once a week, on their day off. Combing and separating their hair with "cards" on Sundays, slave women wrapped sections of hair with cotton or strips of material, a technique that kept hair manageable for the rest of the week and that also created loose curls that could be let down on special occasions. Ever present in the minds of slave women, especially those with white ancestry and straighter hair, was the knowledge that their work could be undone at the whim of an angry master or vengeful mistress. Responding to a specific offense, or upset by such a visual reminder of miscegenation, white southerners—women, most often—might cut a slave woman's hair as punishment, an increasingly popular choice of retribution toward the end of the antebellum era.[8]

A few black women in the nineteenth century were able to parlay their skills into full-time jobs, though most of them were free and lived in the North, working primarily for an upper-class white clientele. Eliza Potter, a free black hairdresser, spent much of her time serving the women of Cincinnati but lived in New Orleans in the 1850s. There, she not only styled wealthy white women's hair but also traveled to nearby plantations to teach enslaved women what she knew.[9] Sometimes, slave women were given the opportunity to show off their talents as the personal hairdressers to their mistresses. According to Elizabeth Fox-Genovese, they labored to make their mistress look attractive and "outshine the other ladies."[10]

In the decades after emancipation, newly available commercial beauty preparations presented a challenge to a tradition of hairstyling that had afforded a sense of pride. Beginning in the late nineteenth century, white-

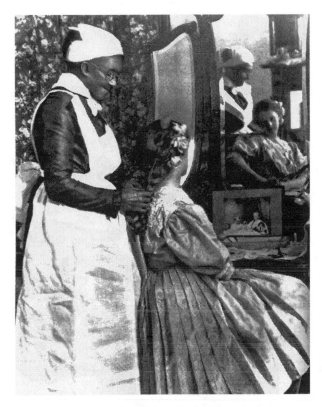

Jane Bond, a Kentucky-born slave, braids her white mistress's hair, n.d. From Gladys-Marie Fry, *Stitched from the Soul: Slave Quilts from the Antebellum South* (Chapel Hill: University of North Carolina Press, 2002).

owned companies in the North and South marketed an array of po mades that promised to straighten black hair. In a typical appeal, Nelson's Straightine, made in Richmond, assured black women that it could turn "knotty, kinky and curly hair straight."[11] Ozonized Ox Marrow, manufactured in Chicago, made the same claim, promising hair that was "soft, pliable and glossy."[12] Ads for hair straighteners that appeared in African American newspapers often featured before-and-after sketches that would seem laughable to twenty-first-century eyes if they were not so appalling. Not only did these products demean black features, but they were also harmful. Hair straighteners contained alcohol and other damaging ingredients that could break hair and burn the scalp. Although black manufacturers made these products, too, critics were quick to point out that the companies most likely to manufacture and market dangerous concoctions were white-owned. Members of Booker T. Washington's National Negro Business League pleaded with the already sympathetic organization to condemn publicly these white companies. Mrs. J. H. P. Coleman, a black pharmacist who spoke at the league's annual meeting in 1912, saw both the products and advertisements of such manufacturers as "positive insults to our self-respecting ladies." She wondered why, during demonstrations, white salesmen used rubber gloves to apply their company's hair preparations to black women.[13]

Other African Americans focused on the vexing questions that beauty products like these raised about female sincerity and morality. This line of thinking paralleled white southerners' assessment of modern beauty practices: women who rejected natural beauty forfeited their feminine virtues. As Chapter 4 will demonstrate more fully, administrators at black southern colleges and normal schools, for example, expected female students to exhibit good taste and modesty. "Neatness, cleanliness, industry, and economy," declared the 1892–93 Spelman Seminary catalog, "are with us indispensable virtues."[14] But coeds were to avoid excess finery and disabuse observers of any impression that they might waste money on fashionable clothes, spend too much time primping, or seek to cultivate an artificial beauty. The cardinal sin, as nearby Atlanta University put it, was to appear "showy."[15] Mary Armstrong, wife of Hampton Institute's principal Samuel Chapman Armstrong, wrote her advice book, *On Habits and Manners*, in part, so that Hampton students might see the "folly" of such a desire. A woman should "take every care of her teeth, her hair, and her skin," she advised, but should shun beauty aids.[16] Armstrong's condemnation stemmed from class-based notions of propriety and morality but was echoed in poorer, less cosmopolitan circles well into the twentieth century. Mamie Garvin Fields, a teacher, clubwoman, and beautician from Charleston, South Carolina, saw this firsthand in the 1920s on a sea island outside the city. She tried to help her female students groom their damaged hair. One girl's mother was not pleased. "'You let ee he-yuh stay like I hahv' 'em,'" Fields remembered the enraged mother shouting. "I can still see that lady now, standing in the road with her hands akimbo, mad," Fields continued. "A conservative lady, that mother, and she wore her hair wrapped in the traditional way, with multicolor thread and a bandana on top."[17] Thereafter, Fields asked permission before styling her students' hair.

The issues that black women confronted in beautifying their hair went beyond concerns over morality and modernity. There were practical considerations as well. Working primarily as domestics and field laborers, most southern black women suffered from the same hardships that made grooming difficult for poorer white women. Bathing was arduous and often relegated to a once-a-week affair since water had to be brought in from a well and heated. As Mary Mebane, who grew up in rural North

Carolina, drolly explained, "a bath was an undertaking of considerable proportions" for rural people.[18] Yet differences in degree, if not in kind, resulted in a problem that made even the simplest beauty regimen irrelevant: hair loss. A low-protein diet, excessive sun exposure, and a belief that washing hair once a month was sufficient to ward off diseases such as eczema and psoriasis combined with the naturally dry nature of African American hair to make black women vulnerable to hair loss.[19] And as Fields's recollection reveals, so, too, did the major styling method among rural black women in the late nineteenth and early twentieth centuries — hair wrapping. She believed the practice was the main reason her students' hair was falling out. "Back then," she wrote in her memoir, "every little neighborhood had an official hair wrapper, and those ladies would pull the hair so tight until it receded from the temple and around the forehead."[20] Many hair tonics and straighteners advertised as remedies for hair loss only made the problem worse, stripping hair of its natural oils and further drying out the scalp.

It was the combination of natural hair loss and the deleterious effects of products manufactured by dishonest companies that motivated black beauty culturists to stake out a place in the consumer market of goods and services aimed at black women. Carrying forward the expertise that had provided moments of pleasure during slavery, black female beauty entrepreneurs offered their knowledge to women struggling to claim beauty in a hostile environment, using traditional folk remedies to nurture damaged hair. In the first two decades of the twentieth century, dozens of black women throughout the country went into business for themselves, selling hair pomades and hair growers door-to-door and through mail order. This upsurge in black female entrepreneurship, as Noliwe Rooks has argued, shifted the content of advertising copy away from appeals to explicitly racist beauty norms.[21] To be sure, not all black women who sold hair products in the turn-of-the-century South divorced themselves from a beauty aesthetic that posited black features as ugly and inferior. Nor did those companies that did push such an aesthetic suddenly retreat from the market. For decades, hair straighteners continued to fill the shelves of southern stores, declining in popularity only with the rise of the Black is Beautiful movement in the late 1960s. But many entrepreneurs who were black and female drew on different life experiences and had different motivations than those who played on insecurities over kinky hair.

The most famous of these beauty culturists were the two pioneers of the industry, Annie Turnbo Malone and Madam C. J. Walker, who shared

Pressing comb, ca. early 1920s. Metal combs, used with hot oil, were essential to the pressing process. This all-brass comb cost about $1.75. From the author's collection. Photograph by Jackson Kytle.

their hair-care systems with thousands of southern black women in the early twentieth century. Both women suffered from diseased scalps and brittle hair (Walker, in fact, developed bald spots), and both took advantage of the fact that the barriers to entering the hair-care-product market were low. Experimenting in their homes, Malone and Walker created "hair growers," or shampoos, based on traditional folk remedies. In 1902 Malone set up her business in St. Louis, hiring Walker the next year as an agent to sell "Poro Wonderful Hair Grower," a concoction that contained sage, sulfur, and eggs. By 1905 Walker had left Malone's Poro Company to strike out on her own, establishing the headquarters of the Madam C. J. Walker Company in Indianapolis in 1910. Claiming divine inspiration for her recipe, Walker, too, used well-known healing agents such as coconut oil and sulfur in her "Wonderful Hair Grower." Malone and Walker developed entire "systems," or hair-care regimens, that included regular shampooing, scalp massage, and hair "pressing"—or "straightening," as it was also commonly called. Using hot oil and a heated, wide-tooth metal comb, a beautician pressed hair and then manipulated it into any number of styles that varied according to the latest trend.

Despite the labels assigned to their work by the public, then and now, Malone and Walker omitted references to "hair straightening" in their advertisements and public speeches. They focused, instead, on the many benefits of their products and of working at their companies. First, of course, was the claim that their remedies cured scalp disease and encouraged hair to grow. Walker, for her part, demanded that newspaper writers not characterize her work as hair straightening but as hair cultivation. In an interview conducted by an uncooperative reporter in 1918, Walker interrupted his questioning to prevent any misunderstanding: "Right here let me correct the erroneous impression held by some that I claim to straighten the hair. I grow hair. I want the great masses of my people to take a greater pride in their personal appearance and to give their hair proper attention. I deplore such an impression because I have always held myself out as a hair culturist."[22] Walker emphasized the maintenance of a healthy, well-groomed body as key to the cultivation of personal and race pride, and as an antidote to the negative images of black women that were pervasive during her day. Some customers seem to have taken Walker at her word, like one woman who wrote a desperate plea for help in 1918. In a brief letter, Marie Cane asked Walker for advice in growing her hair no fewer than six times.[23] With no hair to speak of, Cane failed to meet even the most minimum standards of respectable self-presentation. Suggestive, too, is the fact that Walker's Wonderful Hair Grower, and not the company's glossine—the oil used during the pressing process—represented the company's best-selling product until the late 1920s.[24]

In underscoring the connection between personal appearance and race progress, black beauty culturists such as Walker and Malone echoed the sentiments of other early-twentieth-century African American leaders. Booker T. Washington, Hampton graduate and founder of Tuskegee and the National Negro Business League, displayed, as Peter Coclanis has put it, an almost fetishistic "fixation upon matters hygenic."[25] By paying attention to physical appearance and health, poor southern blacks, in Washington's view, not only challenged stereotypes; they also internalized the moral and social virtues necessary for climbing the socioeconomic ladder. Black church and club women, too, targeted the body as central to what they termed "racial uplift," or the elevation of the entire race through the social service efforts of middle-class and elite blacks.[26] The Woman's Convention of the National Baptist Convention, for example, preached a "politics of respectability" to the primarily working-class constituency of the black Baptist Church, distributing tracts such as "Take a Bath First" and "How to Dress." The goal was to bring readers' habits in line with those of middle-class America and thereby undermine racist ideas that served as justification for their subordination.[27]

Initially, though, Washington and a handful of prominent church and club women rejected the claim made by African American beauty culturists that their work could help black women construct more positive images of themselves. As a former Hampton student under the influence of Mary Armstrong, Washington probably opposed all modern beauty aids on moral grounds, failing to appreciate their growing importance in the lives of white and black women negotiating the public sphere.[28] Washington may have also struggled with the gender implications of female-owned manufacturing companies. Similarly, church and club women may have felt their class-based positions of authority challenged by working-class beauty culturists advancing an economic form of racial uplift from below.[29]

Most importantly, critics could not see what hair regimens that called for the use of straightening or pressing irons had to do with respectable self-presentation. More than the safety or morality of the process, straightening offended because it seemed to indicate a desire to be white. Washington did not distinguish between black hair culturists who argued they wanted to cultivate black women's beauty and those who made harmful products designed to make them look whiter. He went so far as to lump hair straightening together with fortune-telling, writing to the editor of the *New York Age* in 1911 that they subjected blacks "to the ridicule of even our best white friends." He declared that the advertisements for both practices that appeared in the paper detracted from the "prestige" of the historic publication.[30] Nannie Helen Burroughs, member of the Woman's Convention and the National Association of Colored Women, the umbrella organization for black women's clubs, stated similar opinions in the *Voice of the Negro* in 1904: "What every woman who bleaches and straightens out needs, is not her appearance changed, but her mind changed." She concluded that "[i]f Negro women would use half the time they spend on trying to get white, to get better, the race would move forward apace."[31] Burroughs's National Training School for Women and Girls in Washington, D.C., in fact, used pictures of dark-skinned women in advertising posters, revealing her hope that women with a range of physical features would feel comfortable at the institution.[32] The school motto—"Bible, Bath, and Broom"—succinctly captured her view of efforts to improve the body. Cleanliness was a worthy, even godly, goal. Beautifying to look like white people was not. The same year that Burroughs admonished black women for attempting to look whiter, Cornelia Bowen, a Tuskegee graduate and founder of the Mt. Meigs School in Alabama, told a group of club women gathered in St. Louis that "[i]t is foolish to try [to] make hair straight when God saw fit to make it kinky."[33] She bragged of the Mt. Meigs Anti-Hair-Wrapping Clubs, which female students had established at the institution to put an end to hair straightening.

Washington and Burroughs, for their part, would later change their

Nannie Helen Burroughs, ca. 1900–1920. Burroughs argued in the early 1900s that black women who pressed their hair were trying to be white. She later changed her mind. Courtesy of the Prints and Photographs Division, Library of Congress, Washington, D.C.

minds. And both their vehemence—and prominence—may suggest that reservations about beauty practices ran deeper in the black community than they actually did. Still, the intellectual paths these early opponents traveled, from opposition to acceptance, are significant nevertheless. They reveal much about the ambivalence that underlay black beauty culture in the early twentieth century and the thin line that beauty culturists walked in denying charges that they straightened hair to help black women look white.[34] Indeed, these examples point to the ambivalence at the heart of the politics of respectability, which leaders were loath to confront, at least publicly. As scholars of uplift ideology and middle-class reform have noted, notions of what qualified as respectable were not shaped in a racial vacuum. Exhortations to look and act in certain ways, whether made by a club woman or a working-class beautician, were influenced by whites' normative judgments.[35]

In early debates about hair straightening, what was at issue was the question of what it meant to be black, or how to define racial authenticity through physical appearance.[36] Critics of beauty products and services framed the possession—and embrace—of darker skin and naturally curly hair as "a more authentic form of black embodiment," in the words of Maxine Leeds Craig.[37] As Burroughs had framed the problem, black women who used beauty products were guilty of trying to "get white," of rejecting their race. Elite opponents of modern beauty practices were not alone in giving voice to this line of reasoning. One lower-middle-class black woman interviewed by Hortense Powdermaker in her study of Indianola, Mississippi, in the early 1930s—whom Powdermaker called "very black and Negroid in features"—remarked that darker individuals were "more pure in blood." Another woman who preferred "very Negroid" individuals like herself stated hair pressing was not "right."[38] The equation of race with biology, of course, served as the lynchpin of segregation, informing the "one-drop rule" that made someone with the smallest trace of African ancestry black. In the black community, those who condemned hair pressing for stripping away a woman's blackness inadvertently condoned the same essentialization of race. Such criticism had the effect of locating race in the body, of naturalizing it and making it physical. That the charge might be leveled by someone like Booker T. Washington, who had a lighter complexion himself, must have seemed rich to black women with "Negroid" features who viewed their grooming efforts as a way to look more respectable and improve their status.

Despite the pitfalls of their critique, opponents raised a crucial question. Did the desire to look respectable mean, by definition, the desire to look white? Walker, as we have seen, insisted that it did not, further arguing that her system produced "a beautiful head of hair in *natural* condition."[39] Black women who followed her hair regimen were not striving for whiteness; they were striving for a natural beauty hidden by factors beyond their control. Walker denied the charge of "straightening" because a clean, healthy, well-styled head of hair—straightened with a heated comb and then curled in the way deemed fashionable—should not be seen, to her way of thinking, as white. Walker's and Malone's projects, then, were a calculated challenge to white women's exclusive purchase on natural beauty, respectability, and fashion. Featuring their own life stories and images, their marketing campaigns drove home the point that working-class black women could be attractive just like their wealthier counterparts, some of whom took notice.[40] According to Mamie Garvin Fields, a member of Charleston's black middle class, "When [Madam C. J. Walker]

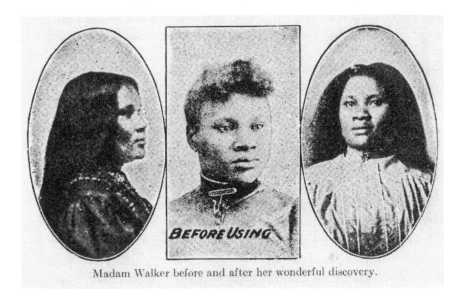

BEFORE USING

Madam Walker before and after her wonderful discovery.

Madam C. J. Walker advertisement, ca. 1906. Walker featured "before and after" photographs in her advertisements to illustrate the efficacy of her products. Courtesy of the A'Lelia Bundles/Walker Family Collection, Washington, D.C.

stood up to talk, a go-ahead, up-to-date black woman was talking, and the women listened to what she had to say."[41]

Other beauty culturists acknowledged that their work stood on complicated ideological ground. After retiring, Catherine Cardozo Lewis, who helped run a Washington, D.C., beauty salon with two of her sisters, reflected on how, in the interwar years, they had understood their jobs as beauticians. Like Walker and Malone, she stressed their desire to boost clients' self-esteem. Unlike these beauty culture icons, Lewis suggested that the criteria for attractiveness may not have been determined by blacks alone: "We just thought that one of the things that we were doing actually was contributing to the self-respect of Negro women at that time [who] felt that they should be well groomed." "And one of their ways of being well groomed," she continued, "was to have their hair fixed as close as possible to the way the white people felt."[42] Mamie Garvin Fields stated without reservation that before Walker came along, "Negro women didn't straighten their hair" but that she had "made it possible for black women to straighten their hair and then style it whatever way they wanted to."[43] Fields had no qualms about labeling her work "straightening."

Catherine Cardozo Lewis's assessment of the influence of white standards may have been a product of the Black is Beautiful movement (in the interview she alludes to the late-1960s campaign). But her view also suggests that we take seriously the range of possibilities available to black women living during the early decades of Jim Crow. It is essential to contextualize pressing, to locate the bodies of black women in the particular spaces and in the particular time in which they moved. If the politics of respectability championed by prominent black women was, by necessity, a reflection of the values of white America, these women also knew that adherence to its tenets might be the most realistic way to subvert the logic of racism.[44] Once it became clear that the regimens of Walker, Malone, and other beauty culturists worked—that they did not cause irreparable physical damage in the pursuit of a caricatured whiteness—the subversive potential of their products and services quashed the most strenuous opposition for the same reason. By 1928, for example, Nannie Helen Burroughs had agreed to speak at the annual Walker Company convention in Indianapolis, though illness kept her away.[45] In 1936, she gave the commencement address at the Apex Beauty School in New York City, offering a spirited defense of beauty culture. In addition to stressing the field's financial rewards, Burroughs insisted that black women "should not be apologetic or feel ashamed of the desire to make ourselves more presentable and beautiful."[46] As uplift reformers well knew, the radical implication of embodying respectability was to suggest that it was not the property of whites alone, to denaturalize its long association with whiteness. In time, Burroughs saw beauticians' work as compatible with this larger goal.

Burroughs also understood beauty culture's pecuniary potential. This second benefit of beauty work constituted the major focus of Walker's and Malone's appeals to potential customer-agents. They argued that working-class black women could take charge not just of fashioning their own self-representations but of their own economic well-being. While uplift reformers focused on nurturing black motherhood and black homes, then, beauty culturists offered a different understanding of racial uplift, insisting that black women's domestic contributions could be financial.[47] By becoming official agents for their companies and reaping the profits from door-to-door sales, from their own company-affiliated beauty shops, and from women they themselves recruited as agents, black women could support their families. They might even achieve financial independence from whites. Indeed, black beauty culturists envisioned their line of work as a way to promote a separate black economy.[48] It was, in the end, this emphasis on financial autonomy, as much as the racism of white beauticians reluctant to serve black women, that promoted the racial segregation of the hair-care industry and, as a result, provided a degree of protection from white competition. (And it was the desire to defend beauty culture from the threat of white encroachment that prompted Burroughs to remind Apex graduates that beauty work "is ours, and we should keep it ours.")[49]

Malone's Poro Company addressed the economic possibilities of beauty culture by focusing on what must have been a burning issue for most southern black women. "How can I," a typical ad in the *Dallas Express* posed, "a woman without training and experience, earn the money so necessary to the welfare and happiness of myself and those I love? Our Answer: Become a Representative of Poro. . . . You can have a profitable occupation right in your own home and build for yourself a permanent income by serving your neighbors, friends, and acquaintances and others with Poro Hair and Scalp Treatments."[50] Orphaned at a young age, Malone must have known the difficulties that black women faced. Walker certainly did, and she chose to weave her hardscrabble biography throughout the fabric of her entrepreneurial sell, using her life story as an example of what beauty culture could do for poor black women with few options for earning a living. At the Thirteenth Annual Convention of the National Negro Business League in 1912, Walker told the audience of her spectacular financial success—offering her annual revenues for the previous seven years as evidence—and of how beauty culture had provided her a way out of the low-paying, menial jobs most black women were forced to take. Born to former slaves in the Louisiana Delta in 1867, Walker had used beauty culture to rise above her fate: "I am a woman that came from the cotton fields of the South; I was promoted from there to the wash-tub; then I was promoted to the cook kitchen, and from there I promoted myself into the business of manufacturing hair goods and preparations. Everybody told me I was making a mistake by going into this business, but I know how to grow hair as I know how to grow cotton."[51] Espousing the same self-help philosophy that formed the backbone of Booker T. Washington's organization, Walker was well-received by the members of the National Negro Business League.

Still, Walker had a harder time convincing Washington that her line of work was a worthwhile calling. She had already sought Washington's approval before the convention, asking him to invest in her company, an invitation he refused. Walker's address to the National Negro Business League Convention, in fact, came only after Washington had ignored a request from the floor that she be allowed to speak. Rising in defiance of Washington, who was moderating the proceedings, Walker pleaded, "Surely you are not going to shut the door in my face."[52] He did not. He granted her the floor and, in 1914, passed a resolution, for which she had repeatedly asked, that praised her success and endorsed her line of work. Finally Washington had been persuaded by Walker's argument that her aims differed from those of manufacturers who hawked straighteners that demeaned black features.

Despite this public seal of approval, Washington was reluctant to accept the claim that beauty culture could provide his own Tuskegee students with a useful occupation. "Would it be asking too much of you," Walker wrote to Washington in the spring of 1914, "to take [beauty culture] as a part of your school work and teach it as you would any other industry, as this work is an industry where by [students] can make more money than they could by sewing, or cooking or any other of those industries."[53] Several times he declined her offer, arguing that the "time was not ripe," but by 1917 he had been convinced.[54] Other schools more eagerly accepted her proposal. Mary McLeod Bethune's Daytona Educational and Industrial Training School for Negro Girls in Florida, Wiley University in Texas, the Utica Normal and Industrial Institute in Mississippi, and the Arkansas Baptist College all welcomed the $100 Walker provided for the furnishing of a training room to be run by a faculty member who attended the Walker Beauty School in New York City.

Washington likely experienced a sincere change of heart in accepting Walker's professed goal of encouraging self-respect in black women. But he would have also had a hard time ignoring her generosity. In 1911, she donated $1,000—one month's income—to the Indianapolis YMCA. In 1914, she provided scholarships to five students at Tuskegee. Walking testimonials, albeit exceptional ones, to the possible economic rewards of beauty culture, both Walker and Malone began to emphasize a third benefit to their profession as their own fortunes grew.

They argued that beauty culturists, as independent businesswomen unhindered by white employers, possessed a unique ability—and, therefore, a responsibility—to undertake social welfare projects. Walker organized the first Madam C. J. Walker Benevolent Association in 1916, and one year later convened the first national meeting of Walker agents to learn new hair-care techniques and discuss community concerns. She awarded prizes to members for excellence in sales and in charitable giving. She also made the first of a series of overtly political gestures at the conclusion of the convention, when she and the assembled delegates sent a telegram to President Woodrow Wilson asking him to pass a federal anti-lynching law. Malone similarly envisioned her Poro College in St. Louis as a kind of combination beauty school and settlement house. She offered courses in beauty culture as well as music and theater and urged her agents everywhere to "be an active force for good" by organizing Poro clubs with business and charitable objectives.[55] This expansion to include social engagement was important. Walker and Malone turned what was already a potentially political set of practices in a markedly political direction. Of course, not every black woman who got her hair done did so in order to assert her self-worth or to make a political statement about the respectability of black women, but some did. Others would go further, embodying Malone's and Walker's charge to take seriously their responsibility to secure racial justice. The legacy of this early focus on community activism should not be underestimated. By the end of 1920, the Walker Company alone claimed to have trained 40,000 agents throughout the country.[56]

Walker and Malone spread their messages of healthful beauty, financial gain, and racial uplift directly to potential customers and agents. Both women marketed heavily in the South, placing advertisements in southern newspapers.[57] As early as 1907, Walker had determined that the best markets for her products were in this region, where 90 percent of the nation's black population still lived.[58] That year, she embarked upon a seven-state tour to sell her hair grower and recruit agents, continuing these trips for the next decade. Agents, too, went on promotional tours. F. B. Ransom, the company's lawyer and general manager, implored one traveling agent in 1918 to "thoroly [sic] canvass Virginia, North and South Carolina." "There are more Negroes and more money there," he argued, "than in all other states combined."[59] Ransom promised that Walker herself would make an effort to help with this important drive and would attend at least one meeting.

During typical sales gatherings, Walker demonstrated her system at a local African Methodist Episcopal or Baptist church, fraternal organization, or boardinghouse, an arrangement that would anticipate and nurture the emerging public significance of black beauty culture. Walker sold interested women starter kits for $25. As licensed agents, these women then went into business for themselves doing hair and training new agents if they so chose, which allowed them to earn even more money. Walker was a forerunner, in other words, in developing what would become known as direct selling, a business model later made famous by companies like Tupperware and Avon.[60] So, too, was Malone—and innumerable other early black beauty culturists, for that matter, many of whom employed the same approach. Charlestonian Mamie Garvin Fields, for example, learned the Poro system from a friend. She fondly remembered how her new line of work benefited her customers and her own family. Doing hair outside so passersby could admire the results, she soon had so many customers that she had set up a shop in her home. Already relatively comfortable, Fields was able to use the money she made as a Poro representative "to put lots of little extras" in her house.[61]

BY THE EARLY 1920S, both Walker and Malone had added skincare cosmetics, including face powders, to their lines of hair-care products. The move was significant. Hairdressing, at least, had deep roots in black culture. Making up did not.[62] Since the mid to late nineteenth century, black critics, like white, had denounced cosmetics for encouraging artifice and vanity. Mary Armstrong insisted in her advice manual that "no lady should use cosmetics in any form." Paint and powder may have names like "'Liquid Bloom,' or 'Lily Enamel,'" she continued, "but remain always unclean, false, unwholesome, a disgrace to those who use them."[63] The association of these products with sexuality was of particular concern for black women. White women who used cosmetics raised unsettling questions about their innocence. Black women who did so ran the risk of reinforcing deep-seated beliefs about black female licentiousness. Marjorie Stewart Joyner, who trained as a beautician in the 1910s and later worked for the Walker Company, remembered that in the early days black preachers linked cosmetics to prostitution in their sermons. "You must be interested in a red light district," they would declare, "or you wouldn't be putting that rouge and lipstick on you."[64]

But in some quarters, at least, cosmetics signaled other things. In 1921, Alice Dunbar-Nelson, the famous Creole poet from New Orleans, described how she looked on a Pennsylvania outing in a way that positioned cosmetics as tools for constructing an imposing public image: "I a made-up face, tall, broad-shouldered Juno," she wrote in her diary.[65] Others connected paint and powder to the necessity of fashioning a public appearance that, if not imposing, nevertheless announced a modern womanhood. A columnist in *Half-Century* magazine, a publication underwritten by black cosmetics entrepreneur Anthony Overton, argued in the same year that "[i]f rouge and face powder help to keep women youthful and progressive, let them pile it on thick."[66] In the *Apex News*, the trade publication for the Apex News and Hair Company, one woman gave thanks in 1938 that society's moral judgment against cosmetics had finally dissipated. Even though men considered the products "a nugacity," or a trifle, women knew cosmetics created an "irresistible charm."[67]

Black women also insisted that cosmetics gave them an edge in "the game of life," as one Georgia woman wrote in a beauty column sponsored by the Larieuse Beauty Foundation, a St. Louis–based cosmetics company.[68] Beauty-aid convert Nannie Helen Burroughs divided this game into two parts: work and romance. She told Apex graduates that women had to "take up where nature left off and strive to make of themselves a thing of beauty." Then, she predicted, they would hear of "fewer divorces and fewer jobs being lost."[69] A Baltimore woman informed readers of the Larieuse beauty column that working girls had to do everything in their power to appear charming. An employer is "only human," she observed, and will choose the applicant who looks the best. Makeup could help job hopefuls stand out from the crowd, though caution was in order. Powders needed to match the skin's natural tone, and items like rouge had to be "subdued to a faint hint of color."[70] The Georgia writer agreed, warning, "Avoid the 'painted look.'"[71] Charlotte Hawkins Brown, head of the Palmer Memorial Institute in Sedalia, North Carolina, advised her female students of the same rule: "Lipstick and rouge should give one a natural, life-like appearance, and be used so that they can scarcely be detected."[72]

The embrace of cosmetics by women like Dunbar-Nelson, Burroughs, and Brown indicated changing opinions during the interwar years. Manufacturers' marketing efforts played no small role in this transformation. As some of the evidence above illustrates, in fact, it is difficult to distinguish between the views of actual women and company-sponsored content. By tying cosmetics to career success, heterosexual romance, and natural beauty, companies used these forums and advertising more generally to distance their products from age-old associations with sexuality and immorality. Cosmetics were said to promote racial advancement, too. Walker Company ads from the 1920s, for example, emphasized that "[n]o greater force is working to glorify the womanhood of our Race" than Walker hair and skin preparations.[73]

Although such efforts won over some skeptics, the conviction that cosmetics were at odds with respectability persisted. Looking back at how blacks in Memphis attempted to appease whites in the 1930s, one African American man emphasized the significance of appearances. "No black went into high school in my day without a tie on and shoes . . . shined," he recalled. "Girls did not wear lipstick and they had to wear stockings. Take pride in yourselves."[74] In his memory, cosmetics contradicted racial pride

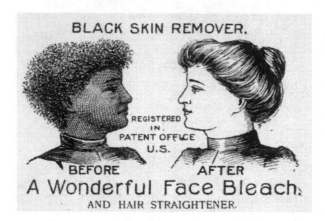

Black Skin Remover advertisement, 1900. Black Skin Remover promised to bleach black skin in forty-eight hours. The box also included a hair straightener. *Richmond Planet*, 24 November 1900.

and played into white perceptions that African Americans were disreputable. For this reason, some of his female peers, at least, did not use them. During her childhood in North Carolina in the 1940s and 1950s, Mary Mebane's mother never wore makeup or jewelry. Her father was vocal about his preference for "plain, unadorned women." Her mother apparently did not object. Not only did she avoid modern beauty accoutrements herself; she also waged a protracted campaign to limit the influence of an aunt who, with her "strange, big-city ways," Mebane later wrote, "smoked cigarettes on the sly, used rouge . . . and put unsuitable notions in my head."[75]

The cosmetics market for black women included another category of products that caused consternation: lightening and bleaching agents. Significantly, Annie Turnbo Malone and Madam C. J. Walker did not follow the lead of other companies, black and white, in manufacturing these items. Skin bleaches and lightening powders were pervasive nonetheless and, according to the incredible claims made in ads, capable of dramatic results. Black Skin Remover, said Richmond-based manufacturer Thomas Beard Crane, turned the complexion "of a dark-brown person half-white, mulatto to perfectly white."[76] The refusal of Walker and Malone to sell these products highlights the distinction they made between hair pressing and face bleaching. The former helped a black woman achieve her desire to look respectable; the latter helped a black woman achieve her desire to look white.

Made with ingredients such as mercury, which gradually poisoned skin, bleaches and lightening powders could also be dangerous. A woman from Paris, Tennessee, wrote *Half-Century* to alert readers of the unscrupulous practices of a company in her town. One of its powders had made her skin sore. "[I]f I live a hundred years I will never put any powder on my face that is made by white people," she declared. "I feel confident that no colored person would knowingly make a preparation that would injure our women's skin."[77] A Georgia woman said in the same publication that a friend had used a bleach, made by a white company in Memphis, that caused her skin to peel off.[78] Mary Mebane recalled that she could never account for the odd look of a woman she knew, until she figured out that the woman "at some point in her life used a cream that had leached all the color out of her skin, taking with it the skin's natural elasticity and vibrancy."[79]

Madam C. J. Walker, at least, could not preserve her wishes from the grave. Despite the physical problems they caused and the censure they invited, bleaching products were in demand. After her death in 1919, the Walker Company introduced a product tellingly called "Tan-Off." Lauding it as the "most effective bleach on the market today," the company promised that it could eradicate "dark spots" or a "blotchy, cloudy complexion."[80] By 1930, the company reported that Tan-Off was its "best seller in some sections" of the country and observed that agent-operators would be asked by customers to bleach their skin.[81] The popularity of the bleach actually coincided with a drop in demand for Wonderful Hair Grower, likely the result of greater competition from white-owned companies.[82] Though Walker Company records do not indicate how individual products sold by geography during this period, given the strong business of the company in the South overall, southern black women must have responded enthusiastically to Tan-Off.[83] In 1928, for example, two of the three agents with the highest sales of Walker products hailed from Atlanta and New Orleans.[84]

High-Brown Face Powder, manufactured by the Overton Hygenic Company of Chicago, did do well in the region. Anthony Overton founded his company in 1898 and quickly rose to the top of the national black cosmetics market, largely by convincing some of the biggest jobbers to sell High-Brown to retailers.[85] Overton's company did most of its wholesale and door-to-door business in a few states in the Midwest and the majority of them in the South. By the early 1910s, Overton reported that jobbers in Texas, Arkansas, Alabama, and Mississippi had made some of the biggest purchases from his company. Overton did not market his High-Brown powder as a lightening product, a choice that fit with his business philosophy. Like Walker and Malone, he classified his company as a "Negro enterprise" that fused moneymaking with race pride. He also left a blank space on High-Brown Face Powder boxes for a picture of the most beautiful black woman in the world—once she had been found, he jokingly remarked—allowing his consumers to envision themselves as that woman, regardless of their skin tone.[86] Yet High-Brown advertisements featured light-skinned women. The names of the five shades offered by the 1930s— brunette, high-brown, pink, flesh-pink, and white—suggested, moreover, that some women may have used the powder for lightening.[87] The Beckwith Manufacturing Company of Cleveland, Ohio, was typical of a smaller black-owned firm that sold beauty products, including skin bleach and lightening powders, to black women in the South.[88] In the summer of 1921, Madam Beckwith spent six weeks in Columbia, South Carolina, training agents in her system. By the end of the course, thirteen women—whose home addresses were conveniently provided in the local black newspaper—had learned about the advantages of her hair grower, as well as her face powders (in brown, flesh, pink, and white) and "Bleachine, for those desiring a lighter complexion."[89]

White-owned companies did not cede the traffic in bleaching products to black companies.[90] In fact, white companies increasingly impinged upon the black cosmetic market in the first three decades of the twentieth century, taking advantage of larger advertising budgets and distribution channels through national chains and drugstores. The Plough Chemical Company of Memphis set up shop on Beale Street, the heart of the city's black business district, in 1914 and marketed a skin bleach as part of its Black and White line. Dr. Fred Palmer's of Atlanta contended that its skin whitener would not only lighten dark skin but, in a mysterious process left unexplained, also result in "a luxuriant growth of straight, soft, long-hair."[91] As we saw in Chapter 1, the National Toilet Company began as a manufacturer of lightening products for black women and represented a major player in the market by the 1920s. Recognizing that the appeal of the Old South among black women may have been limited, the company tended to eschew plantation and southern imagery in Nadinola bleaching cream advertisements that ran in black newspapers, favoring, instead, more generic pictures of women with no obvious regional or historic markers. The National Toilet Company sometimes emphasized Nadinola's effectiveness—it "never fails to bleach the skin," one ad claimed.[92] In others, the company connected light skin with social status, contending that Nadinola had lightened a socialite's skin "three shades" and finally given her the "fashionable light skin of other girls."[93]

Company claims and promises aside, what did black women want when they purchased bleaching and lightening products? As Kathy Peiss has pointed out, answering this question is challenging in the absence of market research or company correspondence about these goods that in any way rivals the material relating to hair products.[94] Black women were also reticent about bleaching agents in memoirs, letters, and interviews. Their reticence contrasts sharply with the ample record they left behind on hair-care practices, which will be examined later in this chapter, and may be indicative of the fact that bleaching remained controversial, and thus a topic to be avoided, while pressing did not. Regardless, it seems reasonable to assume that some light-skinned women relied on bleaching creams and lightening powders to pass.

The diary of Alice Dunbar-Nelson, who often passed by virtue of her light skin, provides hints that she used lightening cosmetics for this purpose. Dunbar-Nelson, in fact, did not consider herself a Negro, the accepted term for an African American during her time, but instead a person of color or a mulatto. Mulattos were a "class apart," as she once argued, "separated from and superior to the Negroes."[95] In the same 1921 entry in which she described going out as a "Juno" with her "made-up face," for example, she bragged about being "prosperous and white-looking," raising the possibility that she had brushed on a lightening powder to achieve an even whiter complexion. Living in Wilmington, Delaware, in the early 1930s, Dunbar-Nelson endorsed Plough's Black and White skin bleach, lending her photo to the company for its ads in national black newspapers. She did not say in her diary whether she liked Black and White herself, but she did admit to bleaching, and injuring herself in the process. Her face, she noted in 1931, resembled a "sieve" because of the peroxide and almond meal masks she used to bleach her skin. She went to a local beauty parlor for a reparative facial, as well as a manicure, shampoo, and wave, which cost her $6.25. "The price of beauty!" she lamented. In pursuit of beauty the following year, Dunbar-Nelson made an appointment at a white beauty salon, not knowing if she would "get by," in her words. She successfully passed, adding triumphantly, "Beauty problem solved."[96]

The act of passing was rare, but color prejudice within the black community was not, a reality that manufacturers of bleaching agents exploited. From the late nineteenth century and throughout much of the twentieth, common wisdom held that lighter-skinned blacks belonged to a more affluent, more refined, and more educated class than did those with darker complexions.[97] Such beliefs were a function of the fact that the majority of upper-class blacks—the "aristocrats of color," as Willard B. Gatewood has labeled them—did have fair or light skin because of their mixed ancestry.[98] Mamie Fields, the Charleston beautician, demonstrates that biology could be more complicated: children with the same parents could have very different physical features. She was, in fact, darker than her sister. As a child, Fields did not attend the Avery Normal Institute, the local school for the children of Charleston's black elite and middle class, because "the colored people there discriminated against dark-skinned children. It was easy for sister Hattie to go, because she had light skin. . . . I heard right along that if you were black, you couldn't get school honors, no matter how well you studied." Her family decided that she should attend nearby Claflin, which was more tolerant on this issue than Avery. Fields's brother Herbert, who was also dark, was accepted at Avery and enjoyed an active social life. "Herbert got invited to all the parties and had many girlfriends," she recalled. "But if you were a little black girl from the same very nice family, that was something else. It kept you from being invited to parties."[99]

Fields's recollections confirm the observations of other southerners who believed that black women felt the effects of color prejudice more severely than did men. Julia Lucas, the Durham beautician, recalled that the fair-skinned women of her 1920s youth had the "best choice of marrying men."[100] Those with darker skin, meanwhile, selected from a less desirable pool of suitors. Some of the most detailed reports on views of skin color come from the social scientists who, eager to capture the contours of southern culture, descended upon the region beginning in the 1930s to conduct interviews.[101] The studies of these regionalists show that negative assessments of dark skin affected women's romantic fortunes into the 1930s and 1940s. According to one local black man, many African Americans living in the Natchez, Mississippi, area were "color-struck," and one family, the Yanceys, was especially so. "One boy married a dark-brown girl," the man stated, "and the Yancey family like tuh died."[102] One Indianola, Mississippi, man, himself light complexioned, told sociologist John Dollard that he had been taught by his mother to favor "brighter" Negro girls. Dollard speculated that he viewed a light-skinned woman as a status symbol but reported that certain factors, such as a particular skill or profession, might mitigate against the defect of a woman's darker complexion.[103] A dark-skinned woman was also less likely than a dark-skinned man to escape the class into which she was born—it was "the most difficult step in upward mobility" within the black community.[104]

Even if the greater discrimination against darker females was not universal, black skin was equated with ugliness more so than other, lighter skin tones. In his survey of black youths in the rural South, African American sociologist Charles S. Johnson asked his male and female interviewees to describe "the ugliest girl you know." Fifty-five percent of the boys answered that she was either "black" or "dark brown"; 46 percent of the girls said she was "black" or "dark brown."[105] A darker complexion, moreover, was not just a mark of lower-class status or ugliness. It carried a host of negative associations. Researchers noted that southern blacks viewed dark skin as indicative of primitivism, animalism, ignorance, and overall disagreeability. "My grandmother wuz uh little black woman," one man declared, "an' she wuz one of the evilest black women God evah made! . . . Dey really evil!"[106] During her time in Indianola, Mississippi, Hortense Powdermaker observed that many black women bleached their skin, proving, she stated, that beauty standards in the black community were white. A few women even altered photographs of themselves, making them "invariably lighter than the original" and more "Nordic."[107] Johnson noted, too, that his interviewees, male and female, consistently stated that their own skin was lighter than it actually was.[108] Dollard went so far as to state unequivocally that since whiteness represented the ability to participate fully and equally in American society, blacks "prefer to be as light as possible."[109]

Dollard overstated his case, as an array of evidence—even another of his studies—highlights a more complex attitude toward skin color. Light skin may still have represented status, but by the interwar period, aesthetic preferences were more varied. Some black southerners did not view a light complexion positively. The lyrics of blues songs from the 1920s, for example, point to the acceptance of a broader color spectrum. Though some songs praised "yellow" women and condemned other hues as signs of evil, lighter skin was sometimes equated with untrustworthiness. "You never can tell," according to the lyrics of one tune, "When de yaller gal's lyin.'"[110] And dark black skin, too, was not disparaged altogether. References to black "crows" appear regularly in blues songs. "You want some good loving," Frankie "Half-Pint" Jaxon proclaimed, "get yourself an Old Crow Jane."[111] Some male singers were taken with the beauty of the contrast between very dark skin and pearly whites, a look that women might accentuate by placing diamonds in between their teeth or having them covered in gold.[112]

Black women and girls also testified to the fact that being as light as possible was not necessarily a blessing. A young Creole girl in New Orleans complained to Allison Davis and Dollard himself of her "dilemma."[113] She could play neither with white children nor with black children who were darker than she. Since the nineteenth century, novelists had explored this sense of limbo—of being caught between the white and black worlds— and concluded that the light-skinned progeny of mixed-race relationships were doomed to suffer as outcasts. In most stories, the "tragic mulatta" met an unfortunate fate.[114] In real life, southern blacks might indeed view lighter skin as an unwelcome sign of interracial sex that, far from bestowing status, had compromised racial purity. As a child in Georgia, singer Lena Horne was taunted by her darker peers, who called her "a little yellow bastard." She found that having a light complexion was a liability, evidence, she said, "that your lineage has been corrupted by the white people."[115] Darker skin was a matter of racial pride among her cohort, though the popularity of skin lighteners confused the young Horne and indicates that there was not a clear consensus on the issue. One light-skinned woman told Powdermaker that if she had a choice, she would become darker since "race mixture is bad." "A race ought to be a full race," she stated.[116] Charles S. Johnson heard similar claims: "Yellow is the worst color because it shows mixture with whites," and "Yellow don't have no race, they can't be white and they ain't black either."[117]

E. Franklin Frazier and Charles H. Parrish, two other prominent black sociologists who, like Johnson, focused on the views of black southern youth in the late 1930s and early 1940s, reported still other reasons light skin was criticized. Frazier, querying adolescents in Louisville and Washington, D.C., heard one young girl announce that "'Mrs.——— is one of them ole yellah hussies. I hate her . . . she thinks she's cute because . . . she got a little money.'"[118] Parrish found similar class-based associations among his subjects in Louisville, who contended that blacks with light skin and Caucasian features had a "superiority complex which makes them conceited" and want to "act like white people."[119]

The most desirable skin tone, in fact, seems to have been in the middle of the color spectrum. As Lawrence Levine has noted, blues songs typically rejected both very light and very dark skin in favor of a medium-brown tone, celebrating brown women as more dependable mates: "If I get drunk, who's goin' ter carry me home? Brown-skin woman, she's chocolate to the bone."[120] Sippie Wallace, a blues singer from Houston, bragged about her brown complexion in "I'm So Glad I'm Brownskin," recorded in the early 1920s. She saw her color not as a deficiency but as an asset. "I've got what it takes," she proclaimed, to keep a "tailor made" man.[121] Levine speculates that the desire to achieve a brown tone, rather than a light one, may explain why some black southerners turned to skin lighteners.[122]

With a few exceptions, researchers who elicited opinions about skin color in the interwar South confirmed this preference for brown skin. Of the rural youth in Charles S. Johnson's study, 44 percent chose "light-brown" and 15 percent picked "brown" to describe "the most beautiful girl you know."[123] Charles H. Parrish reported that that shades ranging from light to dark brown were most linked to beauty among young black men and women in Louisville.[124] E. Franklin Frazier turned up like-minded assessments among his subjects, with most men and women stating they hoped their future mate had a brown complexion.[125] Frazier concluded: "It appears from the answers of these youth that the Negroes are gradually developing a conception of themselves as brown people rather than black people."[126]

Laila S. Haidarali has observed that the research of these three African American sociologists indeed underscores the emergence of a new brown-skin ideal during this period, which, given their interest in promoting black welfare, they posited as a possible solution to intraracial color discrimination.[127] Their studies, Haidarali argues, also highlight a dynamic that they themselves failed to fully articulate. The emerging consensus was a "gendered hierarchy of color," meaning the brownskin ideal was more important for black women than men, and when females did not measure up, judgments were harsher.[128] Several other African American researchers noted the growing acceptance of brown, too. Their observations, however, indicate that this change was, in some places, dependent upon a narrowing range of skin tones within the community.[129] Even Johnson, in positioning brownskin as the "victor in the colour battle," in Haidarali's words, observed that rural black southerners had less exposure to mixed-race individuals.[130] This was the case, he reasoned, because mixed-race blacks tended to migrate to cities.[131] These findings indicate a qualified triumph for the brownskin ideal, as it may have been less influential in larger urban areas with more light-skinned blacks.

Taken as a whole, though, this body of research suggests that while some southern black women may have wanted to be as white as possible and used lightening products to that end, others did not. They may have turned to lightening agents, as Levine conjectured, to alter their complexion in a more subtle fashion, to become a version of "brown." Other evidence supports this conclusion. The Georgia woman who wrote to *Half-Century* magazine to criticize the white-manufactured bleaching cream, for example, stated that a friend had started using it since her skin "was a bit darker than she wanted it to be."[132] The woman who told readers about the damaging face powder made in Paris, Tennessee, said that she initially refused the salesman's plea to try it. "I told him I liked _____ Powder because it matched by complexion perfectly and always looked smooth," she wrote, despite eventually relenting.[133] Given Overton's interest in boosting his own company's bottom line, taking these complaints too seriously is ill-advised. Still, the way the two women describe the purpose of these cosmetic products seems revealing. In one case, the goal was to lighten the skin a shade; in the second, it was simply to smooth out her complexion with a powder that matched her skin. Other women may have purchased bleaching agents because of assurances that they could rid the skin of bumps and blemishes.[134]

The efficacy of bleaching products was, of course, another matter. Some bleaches may have diminished blemishes. Some may have removed old skin, making complexions appear brighter. But none actually produced drastic transformations in the color of the skin, lightening it, in the words of the National Toilet Company, by "three shades" (an arguably immeasurable feat). By contrast, the process of pressing hair could result in a dramatic change. One young woman interviewed by Charles S. Johnson noted this reality. "[Y]ou can fix hair and make it look pretty," she stated, "'but you can't change color.'"[135] A few of Johnson's interviewees also commented that darker women, compared to those with lighter skin, "can't use makeup," an observation that suggests some black women may have questioned the utility of cosmetics in their beauty regimens.[136]

Perhaps, then, the abundant evidence black women left about hair straightening speaks to several issues. Beauticians provided a service that worked—they transformed the texture of hair, at least until water or humidity made it curly again. Just as importantly, these women reframed the ritual and the end result as catalysts for promoting respectable womanhood and for uplifting the race. There was another possibility, too. Black sociologist Hylan Lewis asked the black residents of York, South Carolina, in the late 1940s to make a choice. If they could be born again, which would they prefer, "good hair or light skin"? The majority said good hair. He continued: "The evidence is that hair texture is probably a more important criterion than skin color for beauty. Usually when the beauty, or lack of beauty, of a woman is remarked upon the quality of the hair will be mentioned before her color." He further reported that the concern with hair was "particularly pronounced" among schoolgirls and that several said they hoped to become beauticians themselves. "I want other people hair to look good," one remarked.[137] Lewis conducted his interviews after World War II, but this preference for "good hair" is intriguing and may be another reason for the proliferation of black beauty culturists in the early twentieth century.

And proliferate they did. "Madams" were ubiquitous in the advertising sections of early-twentieth-century black newspapers. "If you are bothered with falling hair, dandruff, or any hair trouble," a Birmingham beauty culturist announced in the same year that Walker died, "try a box of Frances Willard Howell's Mor-Life Hair Grower. It makes the hair soft and silky. Agents wanted. Liberal terms."[138] In language almost identical to that of the luminaries of the business, Madam Luella McDaniel of Greenville, Texas, advertised herself as a "scalp specialist and beauty culturist," while the maker of Star Hair Grower guaranteed "good money" and announced that it wanted 1,000 agents so that one could be found "in every city and village."[139] It is unclear if the company reached its goal, but it is probably not a stretch to conclude that a black beautician could be found in even the tiniest of southern towns by 1920. That year, black beauticians outnumbered white beauticians in every southern state except for Maryland, despite the fact that the white populations were larger—significantly so, in most cases.[140] There were, for example, 898 black beauticians in Georgia (compared to 167 white); 665 black beauticians in Alabama (compared to 102 white); and 535 black beauticians in Mississippi (compared to 22 white). Black beauticians thus also constituted a vastly disproportionate share of beauticians in terms of the overall population in every southern state, even in Maryland. Though Arkansas was 73 percent white, to take just one example, 85 percent of its beauticians were black.

These numbers tell us several things. For one, the early stigma associated with hair pressing declined rapidly. It is hard to imagine that so many women could have worked as beauticians—even if they did so part-time—otherwise. For another, black southern women were far more likely to find a woman to care for their hair than their white counterparts. Indeed, these statistics, along with similar findings in nonsouthern states, support Julie A. Willett's supposition that the black hairdressing industry matured earlier than the white.[141] At the same time, a comparison of data from southern and nonsouthern states shows that customer access and entrepreneurial opportunity were not as good for black southern women. Black beauticians, in other words, were even more overrepresented among the ranks of beauticians in places such as Illinois, New York, and Pennsylvania, the per capita ratios of beautician to female residents even lower.[142] Although thousands of black southern women participated in beauty culture as proprietors and clients, living outside of the region—where business conditions were better, and legalized segregation not nearly as severe—provided black women a far more favorable environment to do both. Geography mattered.

PROMISING IMPROVEMENTS IN personal appearance and economic security just as Madam C. J. Walker and Annie Turnbo Malone did, many women ran shoestring operations out of their kitchens, conducting business in relative obscurity. Very few would have achieved the dazzling success of Walker, for example, who was worth about $600,000 at her death in 1919.[143] If we dismissed these women as mere imitators, however, we would miss the point. Walker and Malone were the most visible practitioners of a line of work that met the needs of many black women with restricted employment and educational possibilities. Becoming an agent for one of the more well-established beauty companies or striking out as an independent beautician represented attractive alternatives to the drudgeries of factory, field, and domestic labor. Going into beauty culture, moreover, did not call for access to large amounts of capital. Beauty culture was also one of the few lines of work that afforded women professional status but did not require that aspirants hold a high school or college degree, no small matter for young black women who lived in an area that offered blacks no secondary education or who, by choice or necessity, dropped out of high school.[144]

For some black women, beauty school took the place of high school or college. Several young girls in rural Tennessee told Charles S. Johnson in the 1930s that they had settled on beauty culture because they predicted they could make a good living without having to graduate from college.[145] Beauty schools themselves became more central to the profession throughout the 1920s and 1930s as the beauty industry began to offer increasingly structured, supervised training. Responding to an increase in consumer demand, to new state regulations that created licensing requirements, and to a desire to improve beauty culture's professional status, successful African American beauticians around the country transformed their beauty shops into full-fledged beauty schools. The Madam C. J. Walker Company, for example, boasted six large schools by 1940, including one in Dallas and one in Washington, D.C.[146] Hundreds of colleges were also owned by independent beauticians of much lesser means. Like those affiliated

Fort Worth Cosmetology School, 1946. Beauty schools like this one flourished throughout the South as beauty culture became increasingly professionalized. Courtesy of the De-Golyer Library, Southern Methodist University, Dallas, Texas, Collection of African American Photographs, Ag2002.1415.

with national companies, independent beauty schools offered courses that might last from six weeks to six months, cost from $75 to $250, and reward their successful students with elaborate graduation exercises, often held at local churches.[147] Larger towns and cities benefited the most from this growth in beauty culture education. By 1944, Atlanta had four black beauty schools, two of which were not affiliated with the big national companies, while Louisville was home to two schools, an independent and a Walker affiliate. Durham, North Carolina, boasted one independent, Madam DeShazor's Beauty College.[148]

Professional organizations for beauticians also increased in number and influence in the interwar years. Established in 1919, the National Beauty Culturists' League (NBCL) emerged as the umbrella organization for local and state leagues around the country.[149] The NBCL and its affiliates worked to disseminate information about hair care techniques, improve the public image of beauty culture, secure better regulation of the industry, and advance the welfare of black communities. Founded by Ella Martin in the early 1930s, for example, the NBCL-affiliated Atlanta Beauty Culturists' League was intended to help the city's black beauticians, as the bylaws' capacious language stated, "solve our mutual problems."[150] An employee in the mail-order department of Annie Turnbo Malone's Poro Company in St. Louis in the 1920s, Ella Martin had been struck by the volume of orders the company received from Atlanta and moved to the New South city in 1930. She opened a Poro salon and beauty school in the Auburn Avenue business district. Motivated by her mentor's mantra— "to be helpful and useful in our communities in all areas"—Martin organized the Atlanta Beauty Culturists' League to achieve both professional and social justice goals.[151] Through the local and later the state league, which she also started, Martin not only taught unlicensed beauticians the science of the trade so that they could meet new state cosmetology regulations and remain in business. She also enlisted beauticians to volunteer their shops for voter registration drives and for voter education projects. By the end of World War II, a southern black beautician could expect to join a highly organized network of businesswomen—the regional Southern Beauty Congress, for example, held its first convention in 1945—that afforded her with continuing educational and professional support.

Who, then, were the women who became beauticians, and what did they say about their professional choice and experiences? Blanche Scott, a Durham, North Carolina, native, was one of thousands of black women living in the South for whom beauty culture made sense. Born into a family of tobacco factory workers, she found in beauty culture an escape from the grind of stemming, bundling, and hanging tobacco. Her parents worked for the American Tobacco Company throughout the 1910s and 1920s, while her maternal grandmother was an employee of Liggett and Myers. Her grandmother's daily routine, and the meager financial reward, made an especially vivid impression on her as a child: "I looked at my grandmother. [She] would get up in the morning. There used to be a whistle blow at 6:30. She got up one morning, and the 6:30 whistle was blowing, and she was late. She got up in a hurry, nervous and everything. . . . She went running. I looked at her running, going to work. I thought about that. I wanted to be so when I growed up that maybe I wouldn't have to go out like that. . . . I looked at my grandmother and I wanted to do better than that as I grew up. I wanted to have something because my people, they didn't own their homes. They didn't own anything, just poor people, but I wanted something before I died."[152] Because her family needed the money, however, Scott found work as a part-time stemmer in a tobacco factory in 1918 at the age of twelve. She dropped out of school four years later and became a full-time employee at Liggett and Myers, working nine-and-a-half-hour days for the next twenty-eight years.

But Scott held onto her childhood dream to one day "have something." In 1946, when her health began to fail from the long-term effects of handling tobacco, she and other disgruntled coworkers enrolled at the new Madam Rogers's All Queens Beauty College in Durham. Scott and her friends attended classes during their off hours, finishing nine months later. Graduating with her peers at Mt. Vernon Church, Scott finally had the satisfaction of finishing school—she had earned the highest marks and thus the honor of delivering the graduation welcome address—and of having a job that allowed her to enjoy a more comfortable life than had her grandmother and parents. A beautician for nearly thirty years, Scott earned enough to buy a house. "I'm not rich now," she said after her retirement from the beauty business, "but I got more than we had then."[153]

Paying for beauty school, however, might represent a significant expense for young women from families with modest incomes. Ada McWilliams of Enfield, North Carolina, grew up wanting to attend nursing school, but her family's financial circumstances did not allow it. A landowner near Enfield, Ada's father had managed to send her two older sisters to beauty school. Seeing the fruits of their training every time they returned home, Ada decided that beauty culture was a good second choice. Along with a friend and her twin sister, Hazel, she made the ninety-mile journey to Durham in 1943 to attend Madam DeShazor's Beauty College. Located in the Hayti, the black business district, Madam DeShazor's Beauty College offered a six-month program in hairdressing, hygiene, and anatomy, which must have appealed to someone like Ada McWilliams with dreams of going into medicine. As did other beauty schools that attracted students from the surrounding countryside, DeShazor's provided dormitories for its students, but Ada and Hazel could not afford to live in them. Boarding with a generous Durham family, the McWilliams sisters received some money from their father to spend on food and other necessities but still struggled to make ends meet. McWilliams vividly remembered the week that they ran short on money and resorted to eating raw sweet potatoes until their father could bring more food from Enfield.

Ada McWilliams pursued a career in beauty culture because she could not be a nurse, but the field provided alternatives to black women in a number of ways. One mother, concerned that her daughter was running with the wrong crowd—"girls of the ultra mode," as she called them—was sure that she would choose better friends if she became a beautician. "I feel that training in beauty culture may improve her taste," she told Nannie Helen Burroughs in the early 1930s.[154] By far the most common destiny black women hoped to avoid was domestic work. Mary Elizabeth Roberts of New Bern, North Carolina, became a domestic in the late 1910s because, as she recalled, it was "the only kind of work" open to black women.[155] She really wanted to become a beautician since, as she recognized at the time, "There's good money in that stuff if you know it good." After beauty school, Roberts set up a shop in her mother's home in nearby James City, where she worked at night and on Saturdays to supplement her earnings as a laundress. Helen Dunson, also of New Bern, asserted that as proprietor of a local beauty school, her sister hoped to keep black women "out of being a domestic." She wanted to "give them a trade," she remembered, so that they could "do something for themselves."[156]

The benefits of independence from white households were not purely financial. Becoming a hairdresser rather than a domestic spared black women from the danger of sexual exploitation. Bernice Robinson, director of the first Citizenship School sponsored by Highlander Folk School, attributed her decision to attend beauty school, in part, to her mother's cautionary tales. Growing up in segregated Charleston, Robinson remembered that family discussions of the region's racial caste system were rare. The one exception was her mother's unwavering assertion that no daughter of hers would ever work in a white house. Robinson understood as she grew older that "what was in her [mother's] mind was that if you do domestic work and the white man comes home and he wants to have sex with you, you can't do anything about it. You have to give in. . . . She wasn't going to have that with her girls." Leaving Charleston in 1936 for New York City because she could not find anything to do except to work as a domestic "making a dollar a day," Robinson later returned to the port city and set up a beauty shop in her home.[157]

Toiling in white kitchens for low pay and low status under the constant supervision of white women presented other problems: a lack of leisure time and control over work hours. Even domestics who enjoyed a relatively good relationship with their white employers often worked well into the night and on weekends. "The hours was long," according to Alice Adams, who spent her entire adult life as a domestic for an Atlanta family she liked very much, "just long hours. I worked from seven to seven. . . . I couldn't go to church because I had to work. I wanted to go to church and I wanted to visit friends and take care of my house. And you didn't have time, you just had to work."[158] Although most black beauticians also had to work long days to make a living, some could determine their own hours and schedule appointments around church, social, and civic activities, especially if they had other sources of income. Ruby Parks Blackburn, an Atlanta hairdresser and leader in the city's African American civic organizations, adjusted her appointment book in the 1950s according to the demands of her volunteer work and her financial need. Sometimes taking just one or two customers a day, Blackburn earned as much as $57.00 and as little as $11.00 a week at her shop on Simpson Street in the black business district of Atlanta.[159] Ada McWilliams made a good living styling hair at her Lafayette Beauty Shop in Enfield, North Carolina, but found she could earn more money working at a local peanut mill. For two years, McWilliams worked in the mill during the week and supplemented her wages by moonlighting at the shop on Saturdays. Accumulating a small savings, she returned to beauty culture, which she preferred, full-time.

In addition to the kind of commercial shop Ada McWilliams ran with her sister, neighborhood or kitchen salons also thrived. They gave women not only the flexibility to set their own work schedules but also the option to operate their businesses at home. Kitchen beauticians could hold several jobs and also combine work with family responsibilities. Mamie Garvin Fields set up her Poro salon in a bedroom in her home and was able to keep an eye on her young children while she took care of customers. Elizabeth Cardozo Barker, who established the Cardozo salon with her sister in 1928 in Washington, D.C., worked out of her apartment until 1937 when new regulations forced them into commercial space. The initial arrangement was one of the main benefits of beauty culture, as she was assured that her children were "growing up nicely because I was able to be at home with them." "It had worked," she said, "the idea of being at home with my children and making a living at the same time."[160] A Poro agent in Athens, Georgia, told a Federal Writers' Project interviewer that she had moved her shop to her house so that she could more easily take care of her domestic chores but that the switch had an unexpected benefit. Now able to stay open as late as she wanted, her business had increased as well.[161] Kitchen salons might also be more informal, familial affairs. Mothers pressed their daughters' hair at home to extend the longevity of a professional hairstyling or to substitute for one if money was tight. Until they were old enough to graduate into the adult world of hair pressing, younger girls also had their hair washed and braided at home, often on Saturday nights, in anticipation of church the next day.

Despite the ease with which some beauty culturists could combine their work with other forms of employment and their own domestic concerns, not all women who opted for beauty culture fared well. Rosa Grantham's main goal as a child was to become a beautician, and she opened a shop after World War II. But she soon tired of the work because "you had to do so much for a little bit of money." For around $2.00 a head, "you washed their hair, you comb pressed it, then you had to hard press it if the person wanted it, then you curled it." After nine years she closed her shop to take a job in a school cafeteria. "Beauty culture," according to Grantham, "was not paying enough money."[162] Beauticians also endured long days, sometimes starting early in the morning so that clients could have their hair done before going to work, staying late so that others could come afterward. The schedule was demanding, the physical toll—being on their feet all day—grueling.

For some black southern women, beauty culture's financial promise failed to deliver not during the post–World War II years but during the Depression. It is true, as Tiffany M. Gill has noted, that the number of black beauticians in the United States increased from 1920 to 1940, a period that coincided with the blossoming of beauty culture in the South as elsewhere and with the waning years of the Depression. In 1920, black beauticians numbered 12,660 nationally. By 1940, that number had risen to 14,782.[163] Such an increase demonstrates that the black beauty industry in the 1930s, in Gill's words, "not only survived but thrived" and proves the disadvantage theory of economics, or the idea that the higher the level of unemployment or underemployment in the labor market, the higher the level of entrepreneurship among minority groups.[164] More black women chose to become beauticians during the Depression, in other words, because their employment prospects in other sectors of the economy were diminished.

On close inspection, however, a much more complex picture emerges. Census data shows that black beauticians in the South were more vulnerable during this economic downturn than those living elsewhere.[165] The number of beauticians did increase in many nonsouthern states, but beauty culture in the South was not, as one black beauty salon chain claimed at the time, "Depression-proof" after all.[166] By 1940, the number of black beauticians had decreased from 1920 levels in every southern state for which comparative data is available with the exceptions of Texas, Virginia, and Maryland. In six southern states—Alabama, Arkansas, Florida, Louisiana, Mississippi, and Tennessee—there were fewer black beauticians in 1940 than there had been in 1920 despite an increase in the number of black female residents over the previous twenty years. By

1940, then, black beauticians were disproportionately underrepresented among the ranks of beauticians throughout the South.[167] In reality, it was white women, as we saw in Chapter 1, who flooded into the profession in the years before World War II.

How do we explain the decline in southern black beauticians?[168] Most obvious, of course, is that demand for their services and products plunged, given the economic straits into which so many of their clients fell. A study by the Women's Bureau published in 1935 confirmed that a lack of purchasing power affected black beauticians across the country. According to the report, which examined the industry in Columbus, St. Louis, Philadelphia, and New Orleans, black beauticians had dropped their prices from around $1.50–$2.00 to about $1 or less for a shampoo and press by the winter of 1933–34. In New Orleans, however, the discounts were drastic. New Orleans beauticians charged twenty-five cents per visit, a practice that seems to have resulted not just from a lack of purchasing power but from the existence of a large group of unlicensed hair pressers who worked in their own homes, or who traveled to their clients' homes. This latter type of "itinerant" presser, in particular, represented the "bane" of regular, licensed shop owners, who regaled investigators with "many disparaging tales" of how these women bartered their services "for food, clothing, or anything else of use."[169] Similarly, Hortense Powdermaker found that black beauticians in Indianola, Mississippi, were still making ends meet in the early 1930s, but observed that clients might offer items such as chickens as payment.[170]

These examples attest to how attached black women had become to hair pressing. But they also attest to how this economy required a degree of flexibility that may have, over time, precluded a living wage for beauticians in the cash-poor South. Some women probably visited their beauty shop less frequently, and stretched their tins of pressing oil, often acquired at the salon, to make them last longer. Yet another challenge to black beauticians was launched from within their own ranks. Building on earlier efforts to professionalize their trade, beauticians with commercial shops campaigned for greater regulation of the industry during the Depression to end the cutthroat competition the Women's Bureau documented in New Orleans.[171] Black beauticians did not encourage federal regulation, believing that the "Code of Fair Competition for the Beauty Parlor Concessionaires" proposed by the National Recovery Administration in 1933 failed to sufficiently account for the fact that their work was different.[172] Though the code never went into effect, its maximum hours stipulation would have hurt black beauticians more than white, given the large number of domestics black practitioners served.

At the state and local level, however, beauticians did organize to push for licensing requirements. By 1940, every state in the Union had passed legislation that governed the training of beauticians and the sanitation of their shops. The 1935 Texas law, for example, stipulated that beauticians finish one thousand hours of instruction at a licensed beauty school and pass written and practical exams. State provisions also required that licensed beauticians stock their shops with certain items, such as dressers with mirrors, permanent wave machines, and sterilizing equipment. As Julia Blackwelder has argued, these furnishing requirements alone might easily cost the operators of even the smallest salon about $100, an amount that "exceeded the resources of the average person of color."[173] Women could ignore the new provisions, but licensed beauticians might take note—as they did in New Orleans—and action, as they did in Dallas, Texas. In 1939, black beauticians in the Texas city approached a local merchants association for help in dealing with the "unfair competition" resulting from "persons dressing hair who are not licensed."[174] New regulations also inspired the formation of statewide black beauticians associations that, in addition to promoting community welfare, policed the profession. Associations affiliated with the National Beauty Culturists' League were founded in South Carolina (1936), Kentucky (1937), North Carolina (1939), Florida (1939), and Arkansas (1940).[175]

On the whole, these Depression-era developments may have affected black beauticians in the South more than those working elsewhere. The evidence collected in New Orleans by the Women's Bureau suggests that southern black beauticians were less likely to be licensed in the first place. The costs of attending beauty school and setting up a shop may have driven many women from the profession. Alternatively, some women may have simply been driven underground, reluctant to advertise their work to licensed competitors and prying Census Bureau employees. Finally, some southern beauticians may have left the region for the promise of a better life, setting up shop in a northern or western state, thereby contributing to the growing ranks of beauticians elsewhere.

Still, the newly regulated environment would prove beneficial for commercial beauty salons as the economy emerged from the depths of the Depression. In towns and cities across the South, beauty parlors consistently ranked among the most numerous black-owned and -operated businesses

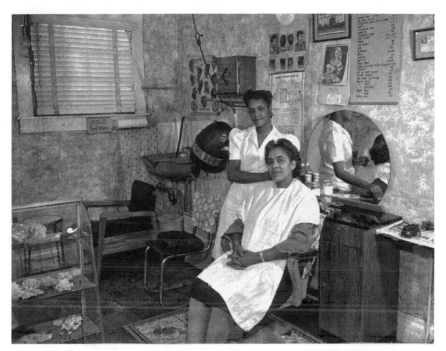

Black beauty shop, Memphis, ca. 1940s. After the Depression, commercial beauty shops thrived, too. Courtesy of the Rev. L. O. Taylor Collection, Center for Southern Folklore, Memphis.

after World War II. A survey of city directories conducted by the National Urban League from 1944 to 1946 illustrates this fact. According to the study, Atlanta had 225 black-owned restaurants, 89 beauty shops, 72 barbershops, and 63 grocery stores. Durham, North Carolina, was home to 20 restaurants, 16 beauty shops, 13 barbershops, and 37 grocery stores. Memphis had 112 restaurants, 70 beauty shops, 65 barbershops, and 34 grocery stores. New Orleans, finally, claimed 29 restaurants, 41 barbershops, and 36 beauty shops.[176]

By the 1940s, beauty shops and the services they offered had become so important to black women that earlier objections to hair pressing were rarely if ever raised.[177] Beauticians had succeeded at portraying their work as catalysts of personal respectability and racial progress. World War II likely helped erode lingering reservations over pressing as well. A well-coiffed head of hair had become a part of the patriotic femininity for which all American women, white and black, were to strive. With the influx of women into the labor force, and a concurrent shortage of consumer goods, beauty shops also became logical spots to spend money.[178] Black beauty culture in the South continued to recover in the 1950s as postwar prosperity afforded black women disposable income. Given increased demand, many states also revised their regulations to allow for the proliferation of in-home beauty shops, a change that professional associations now welcomed, seeing it as good for business.[179] By 1960, black beauticians were more readily available throughout the region than they had been in 1920.[180]

INSIDE BLACK BEAUTY SHOPS, rituals of beautification converged with rituals of socialization. African American beauty salons offered the same services, more or less, regardless of location. Beauty operators would shampoo, press, and then sometimes put curls or waves back into the hair by finger waving, crignoling, or marceling. Before the Depression and again during the postwar years, shop owners charged $1.50–$2.00 for the entire process, while kitchen beauticians, with little overhead, could charge less.[181] Better-equipped beauticians in bigger towns and cities also offered other services, but elsewhere it did not pay to do so. The Poro agent in Athens, Georgia, stated bluntly that "[t]here aren't more than four Negro women in this town who could afford facials and manicures at a price that would enable an operator to clear the expense of the treatment, to say nothing of overhead for taxes, water, lights, heat and things like that."[182]

In terms of their size and setup, shops varied dramatically. Kitchen shops were intimate places that might use household furniture and facilities to accommodate clients. Salons in business districts might have several booths, each with a shampoo bowl and chair, some of which were rented to beauticians who lacked the resources to establish their own shops. Ada and Hazel McWilliams's Lafayette Beauty Shop in Enfield had six booths and employed four full-time operators, while the Cardozo sisters of Washington, D.C., eventually constructed a ten-booth parlor, complete with a reception area, a shampoo area, and a dining area for the operators. Despite the sex segregation of the hairdressing industry, a few shops catered to both men and women. Memphis, Atlanta, and Durham had a handful of such establishments in the mid-1940s.[183] Often the beauticians and their clients were sequestered in separate rooms, but they might fix hair in close proximity to the male barbers, as was the case at the barbershop/beauty salon run by Julia Lucas and her husband in Durham where a "lady barber" took care of female customers.[184]

Of course, many women were unable to escape domestic, factory, or field labor for a job that offered financial independence, opportunities to pursue civic or leisure activities, or time to attend to their own domestic concerns. For patrons, regular hair-pressing sessions at the beauty salon or with a female relative provided welcome moments of pampering, self-indulgence, and sociability. Embedded in the practice of beauty culture were moments of physical pleasure and emotional connection. The women who sat in the chairs, in other words, found in beauty culture small ways to cope with life in the segregated South. Recognizing the value of these moments, Madam C. J. Walker believed that helping clients relax during their appointments was just as important as helping them look better. A former sharecropper and laundress herself, Walker understood that the ritual of shampooing and styling might represent the only occasion a working woman had to unwind. She instructed her agents to "secure absolute rest for the patron if she is to get the most beneficial results."[185] The instruction manual for her agents envisioned beauty shops as refuges from "the cold hard facts of the world," arguing that beauticians had a responsibility to surround a patron "with an atmosphere of peace, beauty, purity and restfulness which will compensate for her seeking your shop after a hard or nerve-racking day."[186]

Beauticians' recollections about the unusual hours they worked provide eloquent testimony of the importance of the weekly or monthly visit to the salon to women who spent their days at arduous, often dirty tasks. Ada and Hazel McWilliams served an enthusiastic clientele at their salon during the 1940s and 1950s. Before heading off to the factories and fields of Enfield, McWilliams remembered, the "working ladies" who patronized their shop in the black business district would come to have their hair done.[187] Some customers arrived before the sisters did and, during the winter, made a fire in the street to keep warm until they could go inside. Hortense Powdermaker found that the beauty business thrived in the black community of Indianola, Mississippi, during the depths of the Depression. "Even women who are very poor go to a hair-dresser regularly, to have their hair greased and 'pressed,'" she observed.[188]

Beauticians themselves found pleasure in fixing hair. After learning the Poro system, Mamie Garvin Fields and other Poro agents reveled in the intricacies of their new work. "Oh, my, didn't we have fun working on each other's heads. We tried out the Sayman soap mixture, the sage rinses, the egg rinses, the pressing oil, the hair-growing pomade, and the special finger movements to make thin hair grow," she later remembered, adding almost parenthetically, "they worked, too."[189] Looking back on a life characterized more by strife than joy, one North Carolina woman singled out the ritual of doing hair as a bright spot. She was not a professional beautician but a mother with eight daughters. "[Back] then we were into straightening hair," she recalled, "and we'd get out there in the back yard and we'd just have the best time. I'd be doing heads while we'd be playing."[190] In a letter to headquarters, an early Walker agent succinctly summed up the pleasure beauticians took in practicing their trade. "We's here to help one another," she wrote, "and feel's each other'[s] care."[191]

Henry Louis Gates Jr. has talked about how his mother occasionally set up shop in their kitchen to do hair when he was a child in West Virginia. She did so, he argues, "because she enjoyed it, rather than for the few dollars it brought in." Describing the hot comb and iron curlers heating up on the kitchen stove, Gates remembers how the ritual affected his mother, her friends, and even himself, the observing child poised just outside the contented circle of women: "I liked what that smell meant for the shape of my day. There was an intimate warmth in the women's tones as they talked with my mama while she did their hair."[192] Singer Lena Horne, who spent part of her early childhood in Georgia, remembered the weekly washing and pressing session at the girls' dormitory at Fort Valley Junior Industrial Institute, where her uncle was dean. Like Gates, Horne observed the ritual as an outsider, for she was too young to participate. She also had straight hair, a condition that rendered the use of a straightening iron unnecessary. "I wanted so much to join in," she said; ". . . it seemed a denial of my right to share in a group activity with my associates."[193] The act of doing hair conferred a sense of belonging and camaraderie, one that many young women desired.

Not everyone recalled these moments so fondly, however, as not every stylist knew how to use the hot instruments well. Even those, like Mary Mebane, who had no quibble with the pressing ritual itself, recalled the injuries that could result. "Sometimes burns on the top of the ear were so severe," Mebane explained, "that they blistered and peeled."[194] For this reason, skilled stylists were never short on clients. Trudier Harris, who grew up in Tuscaloosa, Alabama, found hair pressing "an uncomfortable and at times dangerous process to endure" and hated having it done. Harris observes that she was one of many black southern girls who had to be dragged "kicking and screaming" to sit at the feet of someone wielding a hot iron. Disliking the process was of little importance. "If you were born black and female in the South in the mid-twentieth century," she has written in her memoir, "you did not have an option: you got your hair straightened."[195] No doubt there were legions of black women who, like Harris, would have preferred to avoid hair straightening altogether. Memories like hers provide a useful reminder that the pursuit of beauty could exact a high price. Paying for beauty with pain—even burned skin—was not insignificant. The line between beauty and pain was also easily violated. The "heavy metal tools had the power to make me feel pretty," as one woman stated, "or, when they accidentally touched my skin, to inflict pain."[196]

What is most striking about personal reminiscences of pressing is how just as often they resemble the ones penned by Gates and Horn. Striking, too, is the fact that similarly nostalgic descriptions of the sensory dimensions of beautifying are not as prevalent in white southern women's memoirs. In fact, the olfactory pleasures of pressing—and the way such pleasures were tied to physical comfort and closeness—are a recurring theme in black women's writings.[197] Suffering from a fever and aching head, Alice Dunbar-Nelson stopped off at a beauty shop in 1929 "for warmth—even the smell of fried hair, being warm, is attractive," she confided to her diary; "I sleep."[198] Fellow poet bell hooks, who grew up in Kentucky in the 1950s and 1960s, similarly recalled how the aromas of pressed hair and domestic life made for an intoxicating blend. As she and her five sisters sat in the kitchen while their mother did their hair, they enjoyed "[s]mells of burning grease and hair, mingled with the scent of our freshly washed bodies, with collard greens on the stove, with fried fish." In hooks's memory, fixing hair is associated with acts of nurturing, like cooking food. This "ritual of black women's culture—of intimacy," in her words, was also one that marked one's initiation into womanhood. She and her sisters were all eager to leave behind childhood braids and enter the grown-up world of pressing. The former had been a comforting routine, but the latter afforded a "deeper intimacy." "It [was] not a sign of our longing to be white," she insists. "There [were] no white people in our intimate world. It [was] a sign of our desire to be women." In fact, hooks resented that she, unlike her sisters, had been born with "good hair" that did not require the manipulation of the pressing iron. In her adolescent mind, good hair represented a barrier to intimacy, and she was thrilled when her mother finally let her join the Saturday ritual even though she did not need to.

Although hooks would later criticize hair pressing as a concession to white beauty standards, she still believed that the ritual of hair pressing had afforded a moment of change, both physical and emotional, to black women. The beauty parlor, in particular, she asserted, was "a place where one could be comforted and one's spirit renewed," especially since there were no children or husbands around. For all of these reasons, hooks has insisted that we acknowledge beauty culture's complexity: "These positive empowering implications of the ritual of pressing mediate but do not change negative implications. They exist alongside all that is negative."[199]

Some black women describe the hot combs and nimble fingers of the stylist as almost electrical conduits of nurturing. After finding her childhood straightening iron in a box of memorabilia, historian and southerner Willi Coleman recalled Saturday nights at her house, which were reserved, as her mother had always put it, for storytelling and "taking care of them girls' hair." "Political correctness be damned," Coleman wrote in 1987, "we loved the ritual as well as the end results. Both were powerful lines of love held in the hands of women and shaping the lives of girls." Coleman and her sister would relay the quotidian pains of childhood while their mother, a domestic who worked six days a week, would tell of her triumphs over "folks that were lower than dirt" and white men who saw her as sexually available: "She combed, patted, twisted and talked, saying things which would have embarrassed or shamed her at other times. There were days when I was sure that she had ceased to be the mother we all knew. The smell of warm oils, clean hair and a Black working woman's anger had transformed her into somebody else. She talked with ease and listened with undivided attention. Sometimes the magic lasted for hours." The magic manifested itself in Coleman's changed appearance, which her mother always suggested "bordered on the truly wonderful," and in the "life sustaining messages," she wrote, "which had seeped into my pores as I sat on the floor."[200] Like hooks, Coleman later conceded the complicated meaning of a hair regimen that culminated in the use of a straightening iron. Yet she insisted that beauty culture had provided a defense against the hazards of being a black child in the South.

For both generations, the talk and practice of beauty culture combined to produce a physical barrier—in the form of clean, stylish hair—as well as an emotional barrier against the ruthless world that lay beyond the protective confines of the kitchen. These recollections about the pleasures and comfort of beauty culture seem all the more significant given their source. Henry Louis Gates Jr., bell hooks, and Willi Coleman are academics; Lena Horne became a civil rights activist. None of them, in other words, lacks the kind of racial consciousness that invites critical examination of such cultural practices. Despite the misgivings they acknowledge, the benefits of beauty culture, in their estimation, remain.

The informality and domestic familiarity of kitchen floors and shops would seem to have been especially conducive to conversation and camaraderie between beauticians, customers, and family members. Many main street beauty shops, however, brimmed with conversation as well. Customers expected to find out what was happening in their neighborhoods and communities while they had their hair shampooed and styled. Harriet Vail Wade's childhood recollections make this point clearly. Growing up in the 1940s, Wade spent many hours in her grandfather's James City, North Carolina, barbershop and in the beauty salon her aunt later opened in the rear. Both acted as "more of a meeting place" for the men and women who frequented them: "The beauty salon and the barbershop . . . were gathering places for information, like the newspaper is now or like television is. People spoke of their accomplishments, bragged on their children, talked about how hard times were."[201]

Other people's lives entered the conversation, too. A Charlotte beautician, who opened her shop near the end of World War II, remembered that soldiers and their dating status were a hot topic of conversation among her customers, as were women—likely young, unmarried girls—rumored to be pregnant. Julia Lucas, who ran her Durham barbershop/beauty salon with her husband, also claimed people would "talk about it all," including "who's good church people, who is the nothings."[202] Ada and Hazel McWilliams's salon in Enfield was so alive with "beauty shop talk" or "gossip," according to Ada, that women would stop in to chat even when they were not having their hair done.[203] In her New Bern beauty parlor, Helen Dunson recalled that she often felt "sort-of like a bartender," dispensing wisdom and sympathetic words to women who were just as concerned with talking about their family and relationship problems as they were with having their hair fixed.[204] Outsiders also noted the close relationships that developed between beauticians and clients and the importance of conversation in their interactions. Hylan Lewis, for example, concluded that the "function" of the five black beauticians in York, South Carolina, was to "play a confidant-listener role" in the lives of their customers.[205]

At some beauty shops, talk, or certain kinds, was not welcome. The McWilliams sisters' primarily working-class clientele expected to participate in conversations, but the relaxed atmosphere of a shop could lead women to go too far. Though her aunt's salon had long acted as a gathering place for information, Harriet Vail Wade tried to stem what she considered to be the vicious flow of gossip at the shop when she became an operator there. "You walk out," she stated, summing up the pattern, "they talk about you."[206] Other beauticians worked hard to ensure that talk did not interfere with the sensual pleasures of having one's hair done and suggested that their clients' middle-class status was the motivating factor. The Cardozo sisters of Washington, D.C., also appealed to women who worked throughout the 1930s and 1940s, but their customers tended to be wealthier and viewed the Cardozo salon, with its regular appointment system and elaborate facilities, as a refuge from worldly matters. The physical intimacy of shampooing and grooming was one thing. Social intimacy and interaction—between customers themselves as well as between operators and customers—was quite another. "Because they'd come in tired and worn out," Elizabeth Cardozo Barker argued, "and they would want to relax, come in and get their hair treated, and not be hearing about anybody's problems or not be hearing any gossip, they'd just want a relaxed, quiet atmosphere. Some people say we were 'hinkty'! They didn't like to go to a beauty shop with all that quiet. 'Think you're going to church.'"[207]

Class status affected the perception of beauty work. The dictates of professionalism did not sanction the kind of gossipy talk that characterized the decidedly unprofessional domestic sphere. The goal in silencing talk, then, was not just to make customers feel more comfortable, according to Barker, but to encourage operators "to be professional, to be businesslike ladies."[208] This pattern of beauty parlor socialization continued in some southern areas for decades. Studying black beauty parlors in Newport News, Virginia, in the 1970s, one scholar found that operators working at shops that served upper-class black women "rarely engage in conversation with [customers] or with each other." Working-class women, on the other hand, "make extensive use of the beauty parlor as a setting for communication," while middle-class women fell somewhere in between.[209]

Clearly, then, not all black beauty shops, main street or otherwise, were cauldrons of conversation. Yet those that were shared certain qualities with other institutions in the black community that nurtured debate and activism. The church was among the most prominent of these. Because their access to civic and social institutions was restricted, southern blacks transformed churches, as Evelyn Brooks Higginbotham has argued, into "discursive, critical arenas" where they could discuss their lives with friends and neighbors.[210] Like fraternal lodges, schools, and mutual aid societies, churches resided below the radar screen of the southern white community, serving as safe spaces where such talk could transpire. Black churches were vital public spaces in black communities, filling the void created by legal disfranchisement and segregation. According to Higginbotham, in fact, the church represented a kind of counterpublic, a place that fostered activities and speech directed against the very public that sanctioned racial discrimination.[211] Through their local religious institutions, southern blacks, especially women, battled inequality and worked for the welfare of their families and their neighbors.

Whether they were situated within homes or located on main streets, beauty parlors enjoyed a somewhat similar position, located beyond the gaze of southern whites but squarely within the daily routines and commercial districts of ordinary black southerners. Combined with the fact that black beauticians were independent of white employers, answering only to themselves or to their black boss, beauty shops provided a comparable freedom to their owners and patrons, too. They could engage in debate and activism that, in other contexts, might have proven impossible, even dangerous. But beauty parlors were different in important ways as well. Rather than seeing them as purely public spaces like churches, we might more accurately characterize them as having a hybrid nature, as institutions that mediated between the public and the private.[212] Discussing beautician Vera Mae Pigee and her civil rights work in Clarksdale, Mississippi, Francoise N. Hamlin invokes the analogy of "mothering" to describe the role of the beautician and, as a result, the distinctive quality that beauty shops acquired. As Hamlin puts it, the beauty shop is "a kind of public household where the mothering of the domestic sphere is renegotiated in a public, yet special place."[213] This dual quality applied quite literally, of course, to those shops that were run out of kitchens or other rooms in beauticians' homes, but even main street beauty shops boasted within their walls an ambiance of comfort. Beauticians provided patrons a physical attractiveness that directly challenged views of black women as degraded and subhuman. Leaving a beauty shop with the knowledge that one's appearance would strike observers as stylish or pretty was a potentially uplifting and empowering experience.

The content of beauty parlor practices mattered, too. The rituals of shampooing, pressing, and curling themselves created, as we have seen, an environment in which African American women enjoyed moments of physical and psychological release, moments when their senses were indulged. Such moments fostered intimacy between the women who had their hair done and those who did the grooming. Even shops in commercial districts were linked with the safety and nurturing of home since most black women first had their hair groomed as children by mothers and sisters as they sat on the kitchen floor. Beauty shops were thus enveloped in a veil of trust and comfort, one that was conducive not only to the gossip we might expect in same-sex social institutions but also to talk with political implications.[214] The act of gossiping, in other words, did not always just fill the hours or satisfy personal curiosity.[215] It could serve community needs, as Julia Lucas's recollections about her Durham, North Carolina, beauty shop reveal well. Once the campaign for black civil rights assumed the proportions of a mass movement in the 1950s, the full implications of this fact would become clear.

The work of southern black beauticians in the early to mid-twentieth century demonstrates that the pursuit of beauty is more complicated than we might initially think. This observation holds true for white southern women as well, though in different ways, and for different reasons. To be sure, white southern women did not have to struggle as most black women did to have their racialized beauty recognized. Yet white women were not able to effortlessly adopt every practice and ritual associated with the modern pursuit of beauty, a fact that informed the history of cosmetics in the region and that also impinged upon the history of beauty contests, as the next chapter will show. Even the spaces that nurtured beauty among white women present their own surprises. Glamour, it turns out, could be cultivated in the most unglamorous of places.

## CHAPTER THREE

# Homegrown Royalty

*White Beauty Contests in the Rural South*

Taking a break from his usual subjects, sports commentator Frank Deford spent the better part of 1970 pondering the Miss America Pageant, the nation's premier battleground of competitive femininity.[1] In the book that resulted, he noted that southerners were especially likely to win the coveted tiara. He was right. During the previous fifteen years, five women from the South had been crowned Miss America. And at the end of Deford's journey through the Miss America Pageant system—which began at preliminary competition in Wilson, North Carolina, and ended at the big event, in Atlantic City—it was a southerner that again rose to the top. Texas's Phyllis George took home the crown, becoming Miss America 1971. (Titleholders serve the year after they are crowned.)[2] Needless to say, all six of these southern winners were white, since black women were excluded from the state preliminary system in the South (as they were, for that matter, throughout much of the country). One of Deford's interviewees, herself a former Miss America from the region, offered a theory about southern women's attraction to and success in the contest. "We don't have many metropolitan areas," she explained. "We have all those little towns . . . and Jaycees that don't have anything better to do than run beauty pageants." Really, she said, "it's the country girls. The chances of a girl winning from Atlanta or New Orleans are just about as good from Boston or Chicago."[3] While the former Miss America attributed southern small-town and rural interest in beauty contests to the abundant leisure time of the Jaycees— or the Junior Chambers of Commerce, who sponsored the preliminaries for the Miss America Pageant—Deford preferred another explanation. He thought that rural girls believed beauty contests would smooth away their rough edges.[4]

By insisting on the importance of the rural South in breeding a spe-

cial interest in beauty contests within the region, Deford and his interviewee were on to something. To be sure, urban locales had hosted beauty
contests throughout the twentieth century. Preliminaries for the Miss
America Pageant, in fact, were often held in cities or in seaside resort
towns where the bathing beauty revue had first emerged in the early decades of the twentieth century. But the history of the beauty pageant in
the South is one with deep rural roots, a fact that Deford observed but
declined to explain.[5] To understand the popularity—and just as significantly, the function of beauty contests in the South—we must look to the
pre–World War II countryside, to the farming communities where the cultivation of tobacco and cotton and other crops provided the basis of local
economies and structured the rhythm of life. To a large extent, developments in the rural South cleared the way for the beauty contest, making it
one of the most enduring symbols of white southern culture.

Conditions in southern communities, urban and rural, initially mitigated against the bathing beauty contest, just as they slowed the adoption
of cosmetics. Few farm women could afford the time and energy required
to achieve the comeliness that characterized the bathing beauty, a symbol, among other things, of leisure. More importantly, in both cities and
sparsely populated areas, moral objections to the public display of female
flesh ran deep, echoing concerns about women embracing cosmetic artifice. The made-up woman advertised with her face a cultural modernity
that made many white southerners uneasy. The bathing beauty did so with
her entire, seminude body, often in front of a crowd. In the years after
World War I, however, efforts to modernize rural life and to penetrate
markets with southern agricultural products gave birth to a bumper crop
of bathing beauties. Two groups were primarily responsible for sponsoring the programs that gave rise to this phenomenon: home demonstration
agents, the region's ambassadors of cosmopolitan living and sensibility,
and agricultural trade boards, which devised new promotional techniques
as the market economy transformed the South into a region of profit-
oriented, commercial farming.

Together, these two groups altered indigenous rural practices into
forums for the evaluation of women's bodies. Farm women had long participated in contests that judged their productive capabilities, receiving
prizes at agricultural fairs for their household labor. As home demonstration agents and agricultural trade boards discovered, the step from evaluating women's domestic contributions—their soaps, their hand-sewn
dresses, even their babies—to evaluating their face and form was not a

difficult one to make. It was facilitated by attempting a balancing act, by linking bathing beauties to the land and to the crops that it nourished. Rather than presenting women's bodies as commodities, beauty contest sponsors offered women's bodies as commodity crops, which tempered the troubling implications of the bathing beauty ritual.[6] The economic and cultural modernization of the South, we might say, thus ruralized women's bodies, even as it refashioned them in new ways. In the process, it also racialized women's bodies, celebrating a bevy of beautiful southern ladies who deflected attention away from the racial system on which southern agriculture rested.

The translation of the bathing beauty contest into a visual and rhetorical language that rural southerners understood worked. Denunciations of the bathing beauty contest in the South subsided. Qualms about beauty pageants, however, have never dissipated entirely. The most potent critique has been forged by feminists, who tend to characterize beauty contests as arenas for the objectification and oppression of women. They also argue that beauty competitions elevate a standardized, white ideal of beauty that does a disservice to women of color in particular.[7] Rural beauty contests did advance a white ideal of beauty, one that would become the face of the South to southerners and nonsoutherners alike. Yet what it meant for white southern women to participate in beauty competitions is a more complicated matter.[8] By contextualizing the rural beauty contest, we can see that it propagated a more complex vision of beauty, one that was potentially destabilizing, if only for a short time. The sexual, cigarette-smoking, farm girl tobacco queen of the 1930s, to take the most striking example, was not the comely maiden of traditional southern womanhood. If rural beauty contests ultimately failed to provide a route to southern women's liberation—and I think it is fair to say that they did— these rituals allowed some rural women to construct new forms of rural female identity and to integrate previously male commercial spaces. At the very least, the contests afforded a break from the tedium of country life.[9]

Relying on women's bodies to achieve economic and cultural integration with the rest of the nation was bound to have complicated consequences. By the postwar period, in fact, the rural bathing beauty exuded a glamour less agrarian than contest proponents might have anticipated or liked, no small irony for their project. Making the South more modern required pushing rural southern women into the consumer market. As this happened, the rural southern beauty came to embody the sexualized femininity that was its trademark.

THE MODERN BEAUTY CONTEST stems from varied sources and antecedents. It is an eclectic amalgam, as Lois Banner has noted, of high- and
lowbrow entertainments.[10] Many of its precursors were eighteenth- and
nineteenth-century adaptations of Old World chivalry and fertility rituals. They thus resonated in a region where the antebellum elite boasted
aristocratic pretensions and where military defeat heightened devotion
to a romanticized past in the decades following the Civil War. Other fore-
runners dovetailed with the region's idealization of white womanhood and
its penchant for turning to women to embody community values. As we
might expect, these rituals raised women to the status of queen without
challenging ideas about proper female conduct. Respectability—rooted
in deference to traditional gender mores—characterized women's participation.

May Day celebrations, held at antebellum girls' schools in the North
and South to welcome the arrival of spring, culminated in the selection of
a queen. In elaborately staged tableaux with dozens of costumed participants, May Day rituals kept alive the ancient association of women with
beauty and fertility before the Civil War and continued to be held in some
schools long after. The ring tournament, a re-creation of a medieval eques-
trian competition that tested the skills of male riders, also concluded with
the crowning of a queen. Wealthy white southerners sponsored ring tournaments at private parties and agricultural fairs in the 1840s and 1850s
and at Lost Cause celebrations in the early twentieth century. The winner,
whichever rider was the fastest at removing three small rings suspended
from a bar, might win a horse, money, silverware, or medals. He invariably had the honor of crowning his very own Queen of Love and Beauty,
usually his sweetheart or wife, clad in a white dress. A third event that
turned southern women into royalty was the civic or community festival.
The most famous of these was New Orleans's Mardi Gras, which origi-
nated in 1699 and crowned its first queen in 1871.[11] San Antonio, similarly,
chose its first queen in 1896 as a part of its Fiesta celebration, an event
inspired not by the religious calendar but by the more common desire
in late-nineteenth- and early-twentieth-century America to memorialize
local historical events in grand historical pageants.[12] Fiesta honored the
naming of San Antonio and the Battle of San Jacinto, in which Texas won
its independence from Mexico.[13] Invoking history as proof of past successes, the festival queen symbolized a city's progressive spirit. She announced that the community possessed the enthusiasm and resources
necessary to attract settlers and new businesses.

The southern town envisioned its community spirit, and the women chosen to embody it, in regional terms. From the end of the Civil War to the end of World War I, many civic celebrations in the South were manifestations of the Lost Cause, the regionwide commemoration of Confederate valor.[14] Lost Cause organizers devoted much of their energy to honoring the bravery of Confederate soldiers at Memorial Day festivities and veterans' reunions.[15] Women occupied a prominent position in these celebrations, especially after the founding of the United Daughters of the Confederacy (UDC) in 1894 and the organization's increasing stewardship of Lost Cause activities throughout the next three decades.[16] Not only did UDC members spearhead the incorporation of Confederate women's wartime sacrifices into the official narrative of the Lost Cause, they also placed female bodies at the center of Lost Cause rituals. The Daughters, comprised of elite and middle-class women whose number reached nearly 100,000 by the end of World War I, exercised an enormous influence in fixing the symbolic value of the beautiful southern woman during the first few decades of the twentieth century.

At veterans' reunions, young UDC members acted as "sponsors," or representative southern women, who were called onstage to praise the aging veterans and to provide visual reminders of the genteel womanhood that soldiers had battled to defend. Dressed in virginal white gowns, sponsors embodied the values of a white community wistful for the culture of the Old South, shoring up white southern manhood in the wake of humiliating defeat. Elizabeth Lumpkin, one of the most popular sponsors on the reunion circuit, highlighted her symbolic function in a typical greeting to Georgia veterans in 1904: "I love you," she proclaimed, "you grand old men who guarded with your lives the virgin whiteness of our South."[17] Veterans responded enthusiastically to Lumpkin and other sponsors, clamoring to embrace them and kiss their hands after they had delivered their odes to male bravery. The UDC also featured young girls at ceremonies that celebrated the unveiling of new Confederate monuments. White dresses were the uniform of choice at these festivities as well, as were the kinds of sashes that would later adorn participants in beauty contests. When a new monument was dedicated by the UDC in Huntsville, Alabama, in 1905, for example, the *Confederate Veteran* reported that "thirteen beautiful girls, representing the Confederate States by appropriate banners" gathered decoratively around the pedestal during the ceremony.[18]

Like festival organizers everywhere, UDC members drew a connection between civic spirit and beautiful young women, underscoring this re-

United Daughters of the Confederacy monument dedication in Marietta, Georgia, 1908. At monument dedication ceremonies, young girls often wore sashes imprinted with the names of the Confederate states, anticipating the look of beauty contestants in later decades. Courtesy of the Vanishing Georgia Collection, image no. cob718, Georgia Archives, Morrow, Ga.

lationship with appeals to the past. UDC members parted ways, however, with local boosters who crowned festival queens. They did not invoke local history and present beautiful young women to pave the way for civic and economic progress, much less to announce a general willingness to embrace the future. The United Daughters of the Confederacy was not interested in creating a New South. As Karen Cox has argued in her study of the UDC, they found the very term abhorrent—an "expletive," in fact—since it suggested that the Old South was somehow deficient or in the wrong.[19] The UDC's recourse to female bodies in the performance of Lost Cause rituals was designed to support arguments for traditional gender and race relations. Reunion circuit sponsors and Confederate monument beauties testified to their innocence, to their respectability, and to their need for male protection.

Because they conformed to an Old South model of femininity, beauties of May Days, ring tournaments, civic festivals, and Lost Cause rituals gave little offense—none, quite likely—to the audiences they encountered in the decades leading up to World War I. These women reflected the values of white southerners taken with notions of romance and chivalry. Perhaps most importantly, the young women honored at these rituals were never valued for their attractiveness alone; or, to be more precise, organizers never pointed to the bodies and faces of the participants as the primary visual focus. The symbolic value of beauty royalty remained paramount.

Even as white southerners were enjoying these rituals and their emphasis on the allegorical meaning of female beauty, change was under way. By the mid-nineteenth century, the physicality of women's bodies began to receive more attention. Slowly the female form emerged as an object of public evaluation, a development that can be traced, in part, to a novel kind of competition that featured the bodies of much younger contestants: the baby show.[20] Baby shows rewarded babies deemed "finest" by a panel of judges that completed their evaluation process in front of an audience. The shows were first held at agricultural fairs in the 1850s, where organizers framed participating babies as manifestations of women's home production (like bread or butter), thus attempting to integrate this new ritual into a familiar rural context. Within the next few decades, baby shows were sponsored to raise money for community organizations, as entertainment at local festivals, or by entrepreneurs hoping to earn a profit. Fittingly, P. T. Barnum was among the first of these, staging baby shows at his American Museum in New York City beginning in 1855.

Baby shows helped give rise to the modern beauty contest in a number of ways. First, they began to alter the meaning of the public exhibition of the body. For much of the nineteenth century, forums that featured the human body had emphasized difference. The dime museum and circus, for example, trafficked in human freakery, and so the act of being shown was, to critics at least, a degrading form of public spectacle. The baby show erased these traditional associations, placing bodily display within the realm of normalcy and teaching Americans to view the exhibition of the body in a positive light. Second, in most baby shows, mothers accompanied their babies onstage, which meant that audiences became accustomed to seeing not just any bodies, but the bodies of respectable women, as sources of amusement. For some male viewers, in fact, the babies were not even the main attraction. A Savannah, Georgia, newspaper noted in 1867 that young men had recently attended a local baby show not to gaze at the infants but "to see the young ladies, of course."[21] By the 1870s, baby show from California to New York had taken this development to its logical culmination, adding prizes for the best-looking mothers. The baby show was, as Susan J. Pearson's argues, "a gateway to the overtly spectacular female beauty contest."[22]

The opening of this gateway was gradual, however, as opposition to the public display of the female body had a long history. Since the eighteenth century, white women who had entered popular public leisure spaces met with suspicion. Women attending the theater faced the censorious stares of male theatergoers who, often quite rightly, assumed them to be prostitutes. Well into the nineteenth century, audience members believed actresses to be prostitutes, too.[23] Middle-class women of virtue avoided sites that sanctioned the flaunting of such overt sexuality. Although the theater gained a veneer of respectability as the nineteenth century progressed, the immediate postbellum period saw the rise of burlesque in the theater, an entertainment form showcasing explicit female sexuality.[24] In short, public women, especially those onstage, violated a host of mores that dictated how middle-class women were to behave. The format of the baby show challenged these gender proscriptions. It drew attention to the materiality of bodies on display, blurring the line between private domesticity—the appropriate domain of children and women—and the public.

A ritual like the baby show helped erode reservations over the spectacle of the public woman onstage, but early beauty contests reveal just how contentious the proposition could be. Indeed, opposition to the display of the female form sank the initial scheme of P. T. Barnum to sponsor what has been called the first modern beauty contest at his museum in 1854.[25] The wrong kind of women applied to participate—Barnum could "count only that female population that the French . . . call *lorettes*," or kept women, one observer wrote—forcing an alteration of the contest.[26] Barnum scratched the requirement that contestants appear in person and asked that interested women simply submit daguerreotypes. Despite the fact that the contest was never held (the images failed to arrive before he sold the museum), the idea provided a model of marketing, as well as a new kind of popular amusement, that took hold in various venues across the country. In New York and Chicago, dime museums that catered to a working-class male clientele, sites where standards of decorum were more relaxed, managed to sponsor the kind of beauty contest originally envisioned by Barnum throughout the 1880s and 1890s. P. T. Barnum's less objectionable alternative to the beauty parade, the daguerreotype contest, also bred devotees, as newspapermen adopted the idea in an effort to boost circulation.

Carnivals and midways provided fitting settings for early beauty contests, too.[27] The Midway Plaisance at Chicago's Columbian Exposition in 1893 featured within its mix of international exhibits a World Congress of Beauties, a collection of forty women from around the globe.[28] Two years later, organizers of the Cotton States and International Exposition in Atlanta adopted a similar ploy to attract crowds to their midway. A writer for *Metropolitan Magazine* judged the show a success, observing that its managers "realized its profitableness as a drawer of the crowd and its dollars . . . for a bevy of fair women on parade can wheedle where cotton-ginning machinery and what-not possess no charm."[29] The participants, at least in the photos published after the fact, exuded an aura of exotic, sensuous beauty, suggesting that the beauty parade was a function of the midway's emphasis on spectacle. Yet in a departure from midway tradition, bodily difference was not the reason these beauties were on view in either Chicago or Atlanta. The women may have been stand-ins for a variety of ethnic "others," but being shown, in this context, was an act intended to inspire admiration. Just as the inclusion of the midway itself in fairs indicated a change in middle-class taste in popular amusements, these beauties reveal especially well how the public evaluation of the female body was evolving into an acceptable act of pleasure.

It was the beach, though, that provided the quintessential setting for beauty contests by the early twentieth century. At the seaside resorts that began cropping up along the Atlantic, Pacific, and Gulf Coasts in the 1890s, Barnum's vision for beauty competitions between women in the flesh could be realized. Indeed, the new leisure spots were ideal. Beach resorts were designed for a kind of frolic—swimming—that demanded not just the public exhibition of the female body, but the exhibition of the female body in abbreviated attire. Reflecting new cultural trends that accompanied late-nineteenth-century industrialization, seaside resorts were increasingly accessible and desirable, both for members of the working class and for wealthier men and women who had more than enough leisure time to spare. The beach afforded opportunities for play and flirtation and stamped vacationers with the physical mark of leisure—the suntan—which announced, often in contradiction to a person's actual employment status, that he or she did not work in a factory.

The first beach resort to realize the financial potential of the beauty contest was Rehoboth Beach, Delaware, which, in 1880, sponsored the "Miss

United States" competition as a publicity gimmick to attract more tourism.[30] This early contest did not require that participants don a bathing suit. Scruples still dictated that women wear voluminous costumes while they swam. But the physical pleasures of beach culture, combined with the fact that bulky swimsuits were dangerous for those women who actually wanted to swim, meant that bathing clothes were bound to lose yardage and the corset—long seen as a necessary check on female sexuality—and thus incite the interest of admirers and critics alike.[31] By 1908, the revolution in bathing attire had occurred. That year, Annette Kellerman, a competitive Australian swimmer eager for freer movement, popularized the one-piece bathing suit, with stockings but without a skirt, when she was arrested for indecent exposure wearing the suit at Boston's Revere Beach.

Kellerman's arrest ushered in a new era—the era of the modern swimsuit, of the bathing beauty contest, and of intense efforts to police both. As soon as the smaller swimsuit appeared, beach censors took to the sands to punish women for baring too much skin and the bathing beauty revue emerged to reward the very same phenomenon. Neither knew regional boundaries, as both bathing beauty revues and decency regulations appeared all along the East and West Coasts and in hinterland cities with lake and river resorts.[32] A Kentucky legislator, for example, addressed the new bathing suit phenomenon in the statehouse in 1922, proposing a bill that would prohibit women from wearing swimsuits in the streets of resort towns such as White Mills, located on the Nolin River. Apparently, some young women wore their suits on the way to and from the river, in full view of townspeople. In support of the measure, a colleague insisted that lawmakers had a duty "to protect the eyes of the old men and the morals of the young men." "Incidentally," he added, "we are planning to legislate modesty into the bathers themselves." The issue was serious. The bill's sponsor announced that he would resign his post as representative, lobby for

Second International Pageant of Pulchritude, Galveston, Texas, 1927. Like most bathing beauty revue contestants of the era, those at this Galveston contest had to abide by rules governing their behavior. Courtesy of the Prints and Photograph Division, Library of Congress, Washington, D.C.

an appointment as deputy sheriff in White Mills, and ensure that "no fair violators escaped punishment."[33] In nearby Louisville, Baptist preacher John W. Porter, the antifeminist, anticosmetics crusader, chimed in on the issue of women's swimsuits as well, writing that they were "too indecent to describe, without appearing vulgar." "Mermaids, to be sure," he quipped, "are not supposed to wear clothes, and many maids seem disposed to follow their example."[34]

In this context, any competition between women dressed in bathing suits was sure to be surrounded by an aura of scandal, and thus as a marketing ploy, the bathing beauty contest was irresistible. Elevating the bathing beauty as the paragon of leisure, youth, and modernity, resort promoters quickly altered the precedent set at Rehoboth Beach to incorporate contestants wearing swimming attire. One of the earliest bathing beauty revues was sponsored in the South when businessmen in Galveston, Texas, banded together in 1920 to promote the amenities of their coastal city. For the next several years, young women traveled from all over the United States to participate in the contest, attracting publicity for the resort in their local newspapers, which carried photos of the beauties. A few years later, foreign women were invited to enter the contest, rechristened the International Pageant of Pulchritude. Organizers struck a careful balance between titillation and propriety in putting on such a show. They had to ensure that the beauties' reputations remained above reproach if they wanted the contest to attract the right crowd to the beach. While it is unclear whether contestants, or female beachgoers in Galveston, had to conform to regulations governing the length of their swimsuits, crown hopefuls did have to follow rules restricting their behavior. Contestants could not go into town without a chaperone, nor could they smoke. Having a cigarette, as a French contestant put it, "didn't go over much better in Galveston than eating an apple had in Paradise."[35]

For some observers, the organizers' efforts to give the contest a patina of respectability fell flat. R. H. Wynn, a Methodist minister from nearby Lake Charles, Louisiana, condemned his city's plan to host a bathing beauty revue modeled on the one held in Galveston. Sounding much like his contemporaries who criticized cosmetics, he lambasted the bathing beauty revue as a faulty gauge of true, inner beauty. "Girls who are beautiful in character, no matter what may be their charms of person," he asserted, "cannot afford to participate in such a parade. It is not a beauty contest in any high sense." Wynn urged his fellow citizens to free themselves from the clutches of greed: "The money argument for a thing of this kind should never outweigh a valid moral objection. Galveston's craze should not cause Lake Charles to lose its head."[36]

Contest sponsors might approach the problems posed by the bathing beauty revue by securing the services of the right judges. One option was to place an artist on the judges' panel, since his presence implied that the revue had more in common with the highbrow world of painting and sculpture than with the lowbrow world of commercial entertainment.[37] Businessmen in Wrightsville Beach, North Carolina, pursued this course in 1925. They asked John J. Blair, the first president of the North Carolina State Art Society, if he might be able to persuade sculptor Gutzon Borglum (who was working on Stone Mountain and would later carve Mt. Rushmore) to serve as judge of their upcoming beauty revue. Any artist, in the end, would do. "If the above artist is not available," the organizer wrote to Blair, "please advise as to whether you would suggest anyone else, and if not whether you could come yourself. I believe that you have great discernment in connection with the lines of beauty, grace, skill, etc."[38] Wrightsville businessmen may have believed that their contest judged women as works of art, but surely they knew that framing the evaluation process this way was smart public relations.

Promoters in Atlantic City had adopted the same strategy when they introduced the first Miss America Contest in 1921 as a way to extend the tourist season beyond Labor Day weekend, selecting Howard Chandler Christy to serve as the sole judge. The Men's Business League hoped to stave off criticism, as the beaches of Atlantic City were among those subject to dress codes.[39] When Margaret Gorman walked away with the first Miss America title, she managed to do so with her knees uncovered. But the local newspaper did think her appearance, as well as her competitors', worth noting: "The Bather's Revue was remarkable for the uncensored costumes. Nude limbs were in evidence everywhere—and not a guardian of the law molested the fair sea nymphs who pranced about the sands."[40] The businessmen in charge of the revue somehow managed to keep the guardians of the law at bay.

For the first seven years, Atlantic City organizers were adept at striking the right balance between respectability and sensuality. Taking care to paint their contest as a showcase of wholesome beauty, members of the Men's Business League drew up promotional material in the early 1920s noting that the majority of contestants did not bob their hair—Gorman, herself, had had long hair—and did not wear cosmetics. Contestants, in short, were not "fast" like flappers who brazenly flaunted their sexuality. Despite the fact that they stood around in swimsuits waiting to be sized up by a crowd of spectators, they were more traditional, more Victorian, than many of their female contemporaries. Sponsors of the bathing beauty revue in Savannah, Georgia, in 1926 hoped to cast their contestants in the same virtuous light, as the press took pains to point out that one winner "used cosmetics in a limited quantity" while another "used practically none."[41] Such efforts did nothing to allay the concerns of some opponents of the Atlantic City contest, at least, including a bishop from Raleigh, North Carolina, who in 1927 condemned the contest as "an exploitation of feminine charm by money-mad men."[42] Women, including members of the YWCA, expressed outrage, too. Responding to this barrage of criticism, contest officials toyed with the idea of dropping the swimsuit component of the contest. In the end, they abandoned the Miss America competition altogether, having decided that the publicity being garnered for the city was a net liability.

On the whole, then, the bathing beauty contest of the 1920s was a highly charged marketing tool that, in the South, made an occasional appearance at seaside and resort towns. White southerners appreciated the symbolic power of beautiful women, to be sure, but harnessing that power in the bathing beauty revue format required behavior that was unbecoming of a white southern woman. Like cosmetics, bobbed hair, and short skirts, the bathing beauty contest became a lightning rod for larger debates about proper decorum, women's roles, and modernity. Moreover, so long as whiteness was the beauty ideal for which southern women should strive, the popularity of the bathing beauty contest was certain to remain low. A beauty ritual that asked participants to compete in bathing suits forced them to risk a suntan, the dreaded marker of class and racial inferiority within the region.

To understand how beauty contests became so popular in the South, we must turn to the countryside—or, more accurately, to the relationship between the rural South and the rest of the nation and the world. The rhythms and rituals of rural southern communities, especially when deployed in the service of achieving greater cultural and economic integration with the rest of the nation, opened the region to the modern beauty contest.

SINCE THE EARLY nineteenth century, American farmers and their wives had gathered at local agricultural fairs for social and educational purposes. Although southern fairs struggled to stay afloat in the antebellum years—few white plantation owners were enticed by the promises of agricultural modernization that constituted the fair's raison d'être—they enjoyed popularity in a postbellum South more open to scientific innovation and crop diversification.[43] Agricultural societies in most southern states had revived defunct state fairs by the end of the 1870s and saw steady growth in smaller county fairs for the next fifty years. Farm men and women made the annual trek to the fair to learn the latest methods for improving their work and to display the fruits of their labor. Based on the principle that competition bred improvement, fair organizers offered cash prizes—or "premiums," as they were called—for the best entry in a range of sex-segregated categories. Reflecting the division of labor on the farm, the contests rewarded men for superlative cows, bulls, corn, and grains, while women won for the best homemade jams, pies, textiles, and soap. The establishment of the federal Cooperative Extension Service in 1914 further strengthened the viability of fairs as well as the tradition of education and competition among southern families. Under the auspices of the extension service, male extension agents and female home demonstration agents trained by state land-grant colleges fanned out across the United States. Their goal was to help rural families achieve more productive farming lives. This work was especially important in the rural South, where poverty and isolation compounded the already considerable challenges of a rural existence.

The extension service pursued a common agenda in most southern states, often working through the farm bureau, a public/private organization that provided the institutional base for activities at the county level.[44] Male agents taught farmers scientific methods for raising superior crops and animals. Female agents taught their wives and daughters how to create comfortable and efficient homes. Annual fairs played a central role in this program of agricultural modernization. Agents regularly spearheaded the organization of fair contests to promote interest in their educational classes and reward men and women who excelled in them. Motivated by the money and prestige that accompanied a blue-ribbon entry and encouraged by the extension agents who came to work in their communities, hundreds of thousands of white rural southerners had become accustomed to the rituals of judging that were the focus of agricultural fairs by the eve of World War I. Segregated along racial lines, the extension service did reach out to black southerners as well. African American agents brought many of the same programs and contests to black farming families, though, as we shall see in Chapter 4, funding disparities and cultural distinctions set a different tone for the black agenda.

The centrality of evaluation at the agricultural fair was crucial in laying the groundwork for the rise of the beauty contest in the South. Fairs not only sanctioned competition and judging but also served as sites for the evaluation of farm women's domestic contributions. The nature of their contributions, moreover, changed during the early twentieth century. Throughout the 1910s, 1920s, and 1930s, farm women spent more of their productive energies directly on the improvement of human bodies, including their own. As the emphasis shifted from growing better tomatoes to growing better bodies, so, too, did the kinds of competitions women entered. The transformation was gradual, and rural women certainly never altogether abandoned their traditional labors in the garden, kitchen, or chicken coop. Yet the push toward the modernization of the southern countryside led, in many instances, directly to contests that judged farm women's beauty.

The roots of this transformation extend back to the mid-nineteenth century, when rural mothers began bringing their babies to agricultural fairs and entering them into baby shows. Winners were those babies deemed "finest," as one North Carolina fair announced in 1876, an evaluation that usually meant cutest or prettiest.[45] Although they were still popular at the beginning of the twentieth century, baby shows were quickly supplanted by better baby contests, a new kind of competition first held at the Louisiana State Fair in 1908.[46] Like the move to bring cooperative extension service agents into the communities of rural America, the evolution of baby shows into better baby contests was forwarded by the Progressive Era desire to reform and modernize farm life through science and education. Indeed, better baby contest organizers looked at baby shows and saw a lack of objective criteria. Baby shows, they believed, valued sentimentality over science, rosy cheeks and dimples over signs of health and normal

First Better Baby Contest, Louisiana State Fair, 1908. Better baby contests, which judged babies like farm women's other domestic products, were important precursors to the beauty contest in the rural South. Courtesy of the Mrs. Frank de Garmo Collection, MS 1879, University of Tennessee, Knoxville–Libraries.

physiological development. The home demonstration agents and middle-class club women who sponsored better baby contests deemed it their responsibility to bring the knowledge afforded by their education and exposure to their less fortunate rural sisters. They hoped to keep babies safe from the perils of growing up in the early twentieth century—infant mortality, disease, malnutrition, and poor hygiene.[47]

Demonstration agents and club women organized better baby contests in some cities and mill villages, but the contests were most prevalent at the fair. Sponsors, as well as the doctors who served as judges, argued that if farm products could be raised and evaluated according to the principles of science, then so could babies. Contest promoters in Salisbury, North Carolina, put the issue this way in 1914: "The babies are entered like any other exhibit at an agriculture fair, but with this difference, they are not on exhibition all the time. They are examined by judges, just as livestock, grain or apples are examined." Salisbury sponsors reminded mothers of potential contestants how effective competitions for these other farm products had proven over the years: "The farmers who thought they were raising pretty good live stock and mighty fine grain, entered them in competition with what other farmers were raising. Sometimes they learned that they were raising prize winning products; again they found that their farm products were far below the standard set by the judges. And what did they do— these men who took second, third, and last prizes? They went back to their farms, took better care of their live stock, raised better grain the next year, and they have been doing that ever since."[48] Successful farm communities depended on well-bred babies just as they depended on well-bred crops. If livestock and grain could be improved by the application of tested rules and rigorous judging, children could be, too.

Better baby contests, then, drew heavily on eugenics; in fact, eugenics itself owed much to the belief that it was possible to create a "better stock" of animals by developing better animal breeding practices. Helping to sort the good from the bad, the logic went, better baby contests could do the same among humans, thus advancing the larger eugenic project. The contests would produce stronger, sturdier babies who would mature into stronger, sturdier adults who would, in turn, pass on their superior genes to their offspring. Eugenics, of course, had adherents throughout the country, particularly among nativist thinkers who feared "race sui- cide" among whites. It bears keeping in mind, however, that such anxi- eties took on a special import in a society whose cornerstone was white supremacy.[49] The vitality of white babies was essential to white southern- ers. Drawing analogies between babies and cows and corn, these contests placed healthy white bodies at the center of the rural South's modernizing agenda. And though they downplayed the importance of a baby's attrac- tiveness, the distinction was specious. Given the eugenic undercurrents of the contests, cute and attractive babies had a way of seeming to be the healthiest as well. Better baby contests continued to appear sporadically at agricultural fairs in the 1920s and 1930s, but by World War I, the craze had run its course.[50] Explanations for the contests' demise vary, though scholars tend to agree that the increased authority of the medical profes- sion, facilitated, in part, by the contest itself, made this amateurish event less attractive to the women who acted as sponsors.[51]

Yet by widening the lens of analysis, we see that the project of cul- tivating bodily health through rituals of competition did not disappear from efforts to reform the countryside; nor, for that matter, did women's stewardship of these contests wane. In the years following the war, home demonstration agents continued to include lessons in health and hygiene along with those on cooking, canning, and cultivating kitchen gardens as a part of their extension agenda. They also continued the steady conver- sion of the body into a product that—like southern cotton and tobacco sold in national and international markets—could be commodified. Their efforts resulted in a new ritual, a descendent of the better baby contest, that legitimized the evaluation of women's bodies in public settings: the health pageant.

Health pageants were the purview of young women and men in 4-H clubs, the organizations that formed the youth branch of extension work. Extension agents used 4-H clubs, which prioritized health as one their four main objectives, to inculcate in rural youth the habits that bred healthy bodies.[52] Agents provided medical information and access to health care providers to young women and men who might otherwise have gone without. Rather than teaching parents only, as better baby contest sponsors had done, demonstration agents focused on older youth, capable of internalizing health lessons themselves. Club leaders taught female 4-H'ers how to care for their hair and nails. They also identified ill and underweight members in need of medical attention, not insignificant in a region still suffering from malnutrition and pellagra in the 1930s. The health pageant represented the annual climax of this effort, and all over the South agents sponsored such pageants for youth on the county, district, and state levels.

Agents conceived of health pageants in much the same way as earlier agents had viewed better baby contests, envisioning youthful bodies as capable of improvement through the ritual of competition. Health pageants drew attention to the bodies of participants and to any deficiencies of nature or habit, only in this case the bodies were much more developed and the forum was much more public. Health pageant contestants appeared onstage before an audience, where doctors scrutinized their bodies and filled out elaborate scorecards. "Eyes clear, bright, without dark circles or puffiness; mucous membranes of eyelids bright pink," were a few sample criteria in a South Carolina contest. The doctors then chose as winners the young man and woman who scored closest to 100 points.[53] A newspaper reporter declared the 1930 North Carolina state king and queen to be "perfect specimens of physical manhood and womanhood." Dr. Campbell, the judge, was said to have remarked that "he seldom had the pleasure of seeing young folks in such splendid condition."[54] A North Carolina state health king from another year, according to newspaper coverage, had won first prize in a better baby contest at the state fair when he was three.[55] Some winners had, apparently, been in splendid condition all of their lives. Like earlier baby contests, the health pageant walked a fine line between health and comeliness. Jane McKimmon, the head of

**FOOD HELPED MAKE THE DIFFERENCE**

WINNERS IN 1923 HEALTH CONTEST — BOYS AND GIRLS CLUB WORK

**LEARN TO BUILD STRONG, SHAPELY BODIES**

4-H health pageant winners in North Carolina, 1923. Health pageants, which sometimes featured their older participants in bathing suits, followed on the heels of better baby contests and also laid the groundwork for the rural beauty contest. "Food Helped Make the Difference," #0000987, courtesy of the Special Collections Research Center, North Carolina State University Libraries, Raleigh.

demonstration work in North Carolina, described the health queen of one local county as the "lovely, rosy" Janice Fairless.[56] And though many contests seem to have judged contestants fully clothed, not all did. Photos of some health pageants show male and female winners in swimsuits, which allowed for a more thorough investigation of the contestants' physical development.[57]

Health contests were not the only body ritual sponsored by the cooperative extension service in the interwar years. Agents schooled farmers' wives and daughters in how to improve personal appearance, too, placing special emphasis on their clothing. Although lessons that focused on clothing were designed to help the entire family, the demonstration clothing program targeted women since they were the producers of homemade wardrobes. At demonstration club meetings, weeklong "short courses" held at land-grant colleges, and 4-H club meetings, agents emphasized the importance of planning and budgeting. They held workshops, for example, on refurbishing outdated dresses, men's suits, and hats to fit new fashions. The skills that demonstration club women and 4-H girls mastered at these meetings conferred economic and psychological benefits. As one extension clothing specialist wrote in 1938, the clothing program "contemplates a wardrobe for the farm family so planned and selected that it will improve appearance, give confidence, and poise, protect health and keep within the bounds of the family's purse."[58]

Even when the farm woman's circumstances prohibited purchasing new fabric for dresses, agents focused on how she could be stylish with the meager materials at her disposal. Nowhere was this more evident than in the agents' lessons in transforming cotton bags into clothing. Throughout the South during the 1920s and 1930s, agents taught women and girls how to sew dresses from feed, fertilizer, flour, and sugar sacks, which were made of cotton. Georgia farm women, according to one report, had as a result learned how to "admire real beauty and cleanliness and to make the most of simple and inexpensive materials."[59]

Underlying these sentiments was the assumption that rural families compared their wardrobes to those of town and city dwellers and found their own wanting. Growing up outside of Mayfield, Kentucky, on a dairy farm, writer Bobbie Ann Mason recalled that as a young child she was "acutely conscious of being country." "I felt inferior to people in town," she later wrote, "because we grew our food and made our clothes, while they bought whatever they needed. . . . We weren't poor, but we were country."[60] Assisted by extension agents, generally college-educated and armed with an urban sensibility, farm families could take pride in their appearance, assured that their clothing did not betray their geographic origins.

Home demonstration agents thus concerned themselves with inculcating habits not simply of economy but also of taste, which emanated from places such as Raleigh, Atlanta, and New York City. "Good taste," according to one agent who taught clothing classes, dictated that rural women choose color palettes appropriate both for their complexion and for the occasion and ensure that colors, as a general rule, "fit together pleasingly" and "harmonize."[61] Good taste also involved deportment, or the ways in which the bodies inside fashionable clothes moved. In this realm, too, differences existed between urban southerners and those from rural backgrounds. As late as the 1940s, mill workers in York, South Carolina, suspected that their daughters never placed in the town high school beauty contest because of "the way they walked."[62] Responding to this kind of perception, demonstration agents saw the clothing program as a means to achieve poise and grace, going so far as to argue that the right clothing would inspire a sophisticated demeanor. By the agents' accounts, these lessons succeeded. Jane McKimmon praised a group of farm women in

Johnston County, North Carolina, for making evening gowns that were as beautiful as any fashioned in New York. At the social gathering during which they modeled their handiwork, McKimmon continued, they had also proved "that they had gone far toward learning 'How to wear clothes when we mix with people and how to act when we wear them.'"[63] Similarly, a Mississippi demonstration worker wrote in a 1932 annual report that "one frequently hears the observation that country girls now go as well dressed as town and city girls."[64]

The highlight of the demonstration program in clothing was the dress revue, a cousin of the better baby contest and the health pageant that mimicked the fashion show. As dress revue participants walked across a stage in view of an audience and panel of judges, they announced their names and the cost of their homemade ensemble. Revues varied in size, but the 1933 competition held at North Carolina State University, which featured county winners from across the state, was typical of a larger affair. Forty-eight women modeled outfits in six different categories: house dresses, general wear, "remodeled," sack garments, afternoon, and evening. Willie Hunter, the state's extension specialist in clothing, reported that "the auditorium was full, mostly women," but a few men attended, too.[65] Hunter also recorded some of the highlights, which included a dress made of twenty-year-old lace curtains (sewn at no cost), a woman's suit made of a discarded man's suit, and a woman's suit made from a fertilizer sack. Agents saw the events as testaments to rural women's good taste and good sense. A casual observer, McKimmon remarked of one revue, might "lose sight of the fact that one was attending an amateur style show staged by farm women."[66] And while the participants' clothing was ostensibly the most important part of these competitions, judges actually paid a good deal of attention to overall grooming. A 1933 contest in Virginia, for example, graded entrants on "General Appearance," a category that included posture as well as neatness of hair, teeth, skin, and nails.[67]

Some county agents took pains to make sure the women in their programs mastered their lessons and did well in dress revues, ushering them through every level of competition. Ruth Jamison, demonstration agent in Augusta County, Virginia, accompanied fifteen-year-old Edna Hulvey Garber to the department store to buy materials for the dress she was to make for the 1931 county revue. Garber won, so Jamison again took her to town to procure the accessories she would need (shoes, hat, underwear) for the state contest. At the state competition in Blacksburg, Jamison managed to talk her way into a stranger's home so that the pair could use a sewing machine to place a last-minute button hole on Garber's dress. Victorious again, Garber was slated to compete in the national competition in Chicago, but not before Jamison convinced the young woman to get her hair thinned at the beauty shop—without her mother's permission—so that her beret would sit better. Foreshadowing the way chaperones and coaches would attempt to mold beauty contestants in later decades, Jamison left little to chance.

Garber, for her part, did not mind Jamison's efforts to get her ready. Her parents were too busy on the farm to even take her to town. "I would never have gotten my special trip to Chicago," she recalled, "if I hadn't had special help through her."[68] Echoing Garber, young women who entered dress revues at the district and state levels often recalled how exciting the experience was. Revues might occasion their first trip to a city. In 1924, the Iredell County, North Carolina, extension agent noted that only one of the five girls she took to the state dress revue had ever made the three-hour trip to Raleigh before.[69] The other four were daughters of tenant farmers who rarely left home. At the same time, these trips provided an opportunity to compare their clothes and deportment with those of urban dwellers. Champion dressmaker Eunice Whitley of Wilson County, North Carolina, wrote that on such trips she "noticed the hair, clothes, coloring and posture of the people [and] found that often the people who had signs of being wealthy were often dressed carelessly and had bad posture." She concluded, "Educated people often miss this point, too, I observe."[70]

Young girls and older women alike often framed their initial experiences with extension clothing lessons as revelations, as exposures to the exciting world of fashion and beauty that lay beyond the isolating confines of their own farms. Women who had participated in dress lessons and revues in the 1910s and early 1920s fondly recalled, as the *Raleigh News and Observer* wrote in 1923, that demonstration work had represented "an awakening to beauty and to the subtle touches of simple tasteful dress that have made of them better looking women through the suggestion of the Home Demonstration agent." According to the article, men had noticed that change, too: "One woman got an appropriation for the Home Demonstration work in her county from the skeptical, uninterested board of county commissioners when she went before them and told how the Home Demonstration agent had showed her how to keep from looking so fat and dumpy . . . to tone down the redness of her face by a softening touch of color in the neck of her dress. Every woman wants to look attractive, the best she can and the men like it so the woman won her case and got the appropriation."[71] Husbands had required some convincing as well. A historical pageant on early extension work in North Carolina featured a male character who, in an apology to his wife, admitted his initial reservations: "I'm sorry I ever said anything against your coming to these sewin' meetin's. I'm downright ashamed of myself, Millie—when I see how much better you look in that pretty new dress!" Apparently some men worried that their wives' efforts at beautification would increase their own work. And perhaps they did, but, at least to this fictional character, it was worth it: "I'd druther have a pretty happy wife to help me some of the time than a sad worn out one to help me *all* the time."[72]

For all of the emphasis that agents placed on attractiveness in dress revues and sewing classes, they were not, nor did they want their pupils to be, overly concerned with appearances. A preoccupation with beauty was unbecoming for farm women who had other, more pressing tasks to perform. They deplored vanity and habits that suggested one was "fast." After speaking before a statewide convocation of demonstration club members in North Carolina in 1923, one agent noted approvingly that there was "not an ear-bob [earring] nor a plucked eyebrow among 'em." "Guess they get their plucking exercises with the broilers," she concluded, referring to their work in the chicken coop.[73] Another demonstration agent, lecturing a group of 4-H girls at summer camp in 1927, announced that they were there to ensure the "cultivation of womanly qualities within ourselves," and suggested that the wisest among them would throw away their rouge. For this agent, attractiveness was rooted in superior health, which girls achieved through work, swimming, and playing games. Cosmetics had no place in her vision of the ideal farm girl. She also added one caveat to her endorsement of swimming: "A bathing suit is beautiful when its wearer is swimming but not," she warned, "when lolling on the shore."[74] Good taste and good health were worthy goals for young rural women; lolling about in a swimsuit was not. Bathing suits were utilitarian garments intended to facilitate bodily exercise, not bodily display. In the same vein, while demonstration agents encouraged young 4-H women to make "underclothes" rather than buy them because doing so was cheaper, equally important was another motivation. They hoped to control the style of these items of clothing, a particularly pressing concern since corsets—and their suggestion of a female sexuality firmly under control—had declined in popularity.[75]

Regardless of their intentions, by furthering the agricultural tradition of judging women's household contributions in the name of rural uplift,

demonstration agents also hastened the judging of women's bodily performances—whether that meant the production of better babies, healthier
bodies, or better-dressed bodies. They sought to cultivate a rural femininity notable for its robust health, thrift, and productivity. Unwittingly,
they ushered in the sensuous femininity that was the hallmark of the bathing beauties on the coasts and of modern consumer culture more generally. Health and dress revues may have positioned the evaluation of
women's bodies as a tool of edification, but it was a slippery slope toward
the world of pure spectacle and even objectification. This change in the
way rural women's bodily productions were judged received a catalyzing
jolt in the 1930s with the onset of the Depression. Requiring new tactics
to shore up agrarian commerce, the economic crisis revealed how fruitful
the groundwork laid by extension agents could be.

AT THE FEDERAL LEVEL, the New Deal provided a host of innovative, experimental measures designed to alleviate the hardships of farmers. South
of the Mason-Dixon Line, agricultural interests devised their own solutions, some of which were unique, indeed. Tapping into the precedent of
evaluating rural women's agricultural contributions and linking their contributions to the body, they turned the previously suspect bathing beauty
contest into the highlight of the agricultural festival. They commodified
women's bodies in the service of commodity crop farming, making rural
beauty queens the embodiment of everything from tobacco to cotton to
strawberries. The need to penetrate national and international markets
with high-quality crops in a time of overproduction and underconsumption, in short, produced a bumper crop of high-quality beauties. The extent
to which home demonstration agents directly sponsored this new breed of
female competition in the 1930s is unclear, though evidence does reveal
that in some areas the county's experimental station farm, run by the extension service, provided the venue for contests.[76] Visual records of some
competitions suggest agents' involvement as well. Crop beauty competitions differed in an important way, however, from earlier contests of rural
women's prowess, bodily or otherwise. Although they had always been
segregated along racial lines, fair and demonstration club contests that
judged the best tomatoes, babies, dresses, and bodies were held for white
as well as black women. As a marketing tool of the region's major agricultural interests, by contrast, the overwhelming majority of crop beauty
contests were closed to black women. Within the region and as far away as
Europe and Latin America, then, southern agriculture had a white face.

The Brightleaf Tobacco Belt, stretching from the Virginia and North Carolina Piedmont down through parts of South Carolina and Georgia, provides a particularly good window through which to view the rise and function of agricultural beauty queens in the 1930s. As the decade dawned, the rhythms of tobacco culture remained largely as they had been since the nineteenth century.[77] Landowning and tenant farmers, white and black, brought their cured tobacco to a market town at the end of the growing season. Once there, they chose a warehouse in which to sell it to a buyer from a domestic or foreign cigarette manufacturer. By the turn of the twentieth century, most market towns had organized trade boards or tobacco associations to facilitate the auction process, institutions that attempted to attract farmers to their member-warehouses and buyers to their towns. From the beginning, these trade boards employed an array of techniques to cultivate customer loyalty, such as offering credit and rebates to farmers deemed dependable and providing bunks for overnight stays. As markets for southern brightleaf opened up with the disruption of European production in the 1910s and then as tobacco prices fell in the 1920s and 1930s, newer selling strategies were in demand, even after the introduction of New Deal crop subsidies and acreage reductions.[78] Building on this tradition of savvy marketing, many trade boards decided to add an aura of excitement and glamour to the auction experience. Trade boards began to sponsor elaborate tobacco festivals for farmers and their families. These events were somewhat different from state and county fairs since they celebrated the cultivation of a single crop, but they celebrated the same principle: evaluation. And to the tobacco festivals, market town trade organizations added tobacco queen contests.

This idea had antecedents within the industry itself. North Carolina's own James "Buck" Duke had pioneered the use of beautiful women to sell cigarettes at the turn of the century when his American Tobacco Company began including trade cards with images of attractive women inside cigarette packs. The photographs skirted the edges of respectability—critics, including his father, deemed them "lascivious"—which of course ensured their success as a marketing scheme.[79] Like Duke, and the seaside resort owners who sponsored bathing beauty revues, tobacco queen contest sponsors hoped to use beautiful women dressed in abbreviated attire to stimulate business. The idea was to catch the eye of everyone from the company buyer to the average smoker to the lowliest tenant farmer. Yet rather than importing the bathing beauty revue whole cloth from coasts and resort towns, tobacco entrepreneurs altered the event to fit the familiar context of agricultural evaluation. Especially adept at turning young women into rural royalty, they did so in visually striking ways.

Danville, Virginia, was at the forefront of the new trend, hosting one of the first tobacco queen contests in 1934. In Danville and elsewhere, participants were not dressed in regular swimsuits but in swimsuit-like costumes made out of the crop itself. The event centered around the presentation of women as agricultural products and avoided the explicit presentation of women as seminude, sexualized spectacles: woman-as-commodity became woman-as-commodity crop.[80] Contestants in competitions from Danville down to Douglas, Georgia, appeared during at least part of the beauty contest wearing outfits made of dried tobacco leaves. Marjorie Poole, a contestant in the 1938 Mullins, South Carolina, Tobacco Festival queen contest, was photographed in a typical costume by the Columbia newspaper. "All decked out in tobacco leaves," the caption read, "she might be aptly termed 'Miss Venus.'"[81]

She looked like a contestant in a bathing beauty pageant, but her existence owed much more to the culture of the agricultural fair and agricultural education than it did to the leisure spaces of urban and coastal areas. For decades, rural southerners had justified the evaluation of babies by equating them with farm products. In tobacco queen contests, the evaluation of women for commercial purposes could be justified—visually—in the same way. Contest sponsors suggested that these young women were akin to corn and apples just as they had been as babies. The equation of product and person, however, was now made manifest on the body itself. Young rural women became tobacco incarnate. Contestants in some competitions were even photographed in ways that made them look like a part of the tobacco plant, their heads seeming to sprout from the top like the flower that farmers routinely cut off to spur growth of the leaves. Photographs from contests in many tobacco towns also show the influence of home demonstration agents. The tobacco outfits, as well as the shorts-and-shirt sets worn during contest activities that required more mobility, were identical, made from a common pattern. If agents did not design the costumes and distribute the patterns themselves, mothers and daughters almost certainly cooperated through the familiar channel of the demonstration club to decide on the final design.

This strategy of presentation hardly desexualized contestants altogether. Doing so, after all, would have made bad business sense. The idea seems to have been, instead, to strike a balance, to draw on familiar agrarian practices and age-old associations while embracing sensuality.

The sell was rooted in a complicated dialectic between the invocation of agrarian innocence and of a modern sensibility of sexuality. Some contests preferred to locate themselves on the more conservative end of the spectrum. The photograph of Poole from the Mullins competition, for example, while showing a fair bit of leg, conveyed a wholesome femininity. She was the good farm girl next door.

The Wilson Tobacco Board of Trade, sponsor of the annual festival in Wilson, North Carolina, embraced both innocence and sexuality by selecting two queens. In one contest that represented the culmination of the tobacco festival, beauties dressed in flowing evening gowns appeared onstage in the tobacco warehouse where they vied for the title of Queen of the Smoke Flower and Golden Weed. This event was reminiscent of the scores of dress revues in which local farm women had participated for the last twenty years or so, yet in this case, it was appearance alone—not ingenuity or thriftiness—that mattered. In anticipation of the competition in 1938, the *Raleigh News and Observer* reported that each of the forty-eight beauties from across the state would appear onstage and "will simply carry a number and will not be known by name." Knowing a young woman's name or hometown, presumably, might have compromised the purely aesthetic judgment the contest demanded. The second contest at the annual Wilson festival was a bathing beauty revue, held one night before the Queen of the Smoke Flower and Golden Weed was crowned. Face and form mattered in the bathing beauty revue, too, of course, though in this contest the participants were much more exposed. In the final round of the 1938 competition, the winner "was selected upon first inspection," according to the newspaper account, hinting at the close scrutiny to which the bodies were subjected.[82]

The Wilson festival pushed the envelope with its bathing beauty revue, leaving little to the imagination in its presentation of woman-as-commodity crop. In the days leading up to the bathing beauty contest, competitors, dressed in tobacco leaf outfits, traveled to a local tobacco farm. There they participated in a variety of suggestive field events for an audience of farmers, contest sponsors, photographers, and young men who were the contestants' official escorts. Participants did their fair share of frolicking, serving as visual reminders of the arcadian pleasures of rural life, but they also demonstrated that their farm girl innocence was tinged with a significant dose of sexual knowledge. Some photographs, for example, show contestants wearing two-piece tobacco leaf bathing suits and sitting on tobacco bundles. From the edge of the frame extends a male

Wilson Tobacco Festival Bathing Beauty Revue contestants, n.d. The Wilson Tobacco Festival bathing beauty contest put participants up for evaluation and auction. Courtesy of the State Archives of North Carolina, Raleigh.

arm—the arm of a "buyer," who, simulating the process by which tobacco was judged during an auction, was evaluating the beauties to determine which should receive the highest bids.[83]

Several field events featured contestants smoking, playing up the sensuality of what had traditionally been an illicit female activity. Indeed, the Wilson field events were suffused with sexual innuendo and phallic images. Some photographs, for example, feature contestants competing to finish foot-long cigarettes.[84] Removing their fragile tobacco costumes for their more durable shirt-and-shorts sets, contestants also participated in relays in which they ran while clutching corncob pipes in their teeth.[85] Other pictures capture men looking on with rapt interest as women smoked the pipes.[86] Precisely what these male observers are pondering is left for the viewer to determine. It is unclear exactly why organizers in Wil-

Wilson Tobacco Festival Queen contestant, North Carolina, ca. 1940. Organizers of the Wilson Tobacco Festival bathing beauty contest also used phallic imagery to link female smoking with sexuality. Courtesy of the State Archives of North Carolina, Raleigh.

son sponsored two separate beauty contests, but if these photographs are any indication, some young women may have preferred the relative conservatism of the Smoke Flower and Golden Weed competition.

The Wilson Festival photographs reveal especially well the target audience for tobacco queen contestants and winners—men. Tobacco farmers had long been able to take their tobacco to any number of market towns in their immediate vicinity. Building on the tradition of employing publicity gimmicks to lure farmers to their doors, warehouse owners in market towns incorporated the tobacco beauty into their arsenal of tricks. Advertising their competitions as farmers were finishing up the curing process, sponsors plastered photos of contestants in area newspapers to trumpet the higher prices and better warehouses that distinguished their market town. The implicit message was that the town boasted pretty women, too.

This message would not have been lost on those farmers who looked forward to the fraternizing of the male-oriented market culture, which, as one farmer later recalled, always included heavy drinking and the enthusiastic circulation of "girlie pictures."[87] Maidens of tobacco generated business on the local level in a second way. Some contestants might hail from a market town itself, but most were out-of-towners, young women invited to represent a nearby locale. Tobacco queen contestants thus linked outlying communities to a particular commercial center, giving farmers yet another reason to choose Wilson, North Carolina, over Whiteville, or Lumberton over Fairmont: they had a local girl to cheer on to victory.

Trade boards advertised the advantages of their respective markets in area black newspapers, too. Whiteville, for example, placed ads in Durham's *Carolina Times* for the 1937 selling season, welcoming black farmers to its warehouses. It is difficult to know whether white queens would have been an attraction to African American tobacco farmers, but a photo of the Whiteville queen did appear that year on the front page of the paper. Wearing not a bathing suit but a full-length evening gown, the queen sat atop a pile of golden weed that "sold above $30," according to the caption.[88] The spot thus emphasized the prices commanded in Whiteville, rather than the sexuality of the young woman who reigned as queen. Given the racial etiquette that would have prevailed in warehouses, moreover, tobacco queens likely had little physical interaction with black farmers. Still, the fact that a market town might use the image of a white woman to stimulate black interest is significant, suggesting how high the financial stakes were. Whatever the thinking of Whiteville boosters, in all market towns, the presence of these beauties lent a genteel mask to the annual proceedings in the warehouse, the physical and institutional center of a tobacco system that trapped many black tenant farmers in a continual cycle of indebtedness and poverty.[89]

Buyers who worked for cigarette companies, the men who traveled the region in search of the best and cheapest brightleaf, also had to be lured to markets. So the largest centers for marketing tobacco held enormous queen competitions with dozens of contestants from all over the Southeast. Festival organizers in South Boston, Virginia, invited seventy-five "princesses" to their competition in 1936, using the event not just to promote their own market but also to let dozens of other communities advertise their own. Many princesses would have been sent, in essence, to keep their hometown and home state on the radar screen of company buyers. Redoubling their efforts to maintain access to foreign markets during the

A tobacco queen with the Union Jack, North Carolina, 1941. Brightleaf Belt tobacco queens appealed to buyers in both domestic and foreign markets. Courtesy of the State Archives of North Carolina, Raleigh.

Depression, festival organizers from large market centers also used queen contests to cultivate international ties. The South Boston, Virginia, festival even dispensed with competition altogether in 1936, inviting the daughter of an English knight to reign as queen of the event, a move that rendered the other "princesses" mere delegates from their communities back home. And since experts, including the *Progressive Farmer*, predicted that expanding tobacco sales in Latin America represented "the best potentiality for recovering export trade," queens from south of the border were in demand, too. South Boston organizers chose as queen the daughter of Cuba's ambassador to Great Britain in 1937 and the daughter of the Mexican ambassador to the United States in 1938.[90] Tobacco festivals that stuck with homegrown beauties targeted international markets as well. In response to an embargo on American brightleaf imposed by Great Britain with the outbreak of World War II, a measure designed to save foreign exchange, one North Carolina festival dressed its 1941 queen in a tobacco leaf dress, placed her on a wagon-throne, and photographed her with a Union Jack.[91]

The state of North Carolina, for its part, did not leave promotion to individual festival organizers. The North Carolina Department of Conservation and Development received funding from the legislature in the 1930s to advertise the state's resources in the United States and abroad. The department regularly sent a photographer to the annual event at Wilson to capture the young beauties and their publicity stunts on film. It also dispatched photographers to beauty contests that celebrated other crops, some of which employed a similar, if less visually arresting, fusion of woman and crop. Department photographers traveled to Gastonia, North Carolina, for example, to photograph the Gastonia Cotton Festival and parade, where they snapped images of the pageant winner wearing a cloak made out of bolls of unprocessed cotton.[92] A contestant in the Wallace Strawberry Festival beauty contest was captured in her swimsuit as she reclined on wooden strawberry crates, provocatively poised to enjoy the sensuous pleasures of the fruit.[93] The Edenton Peanut Festival did not require that contestants wear dresses made out of peanut shells (though they could not have been much less comfortable than those made out of tobacco leaves), but the beauty contest did apparently serve the same function as nearby tobacco beauty pageants. Contestants from over a dozen towns made the trip to Edenton, riding on a float in the parade where they flanked the winner.[94] Like those from tobacco contests, the photographs documenting the festivities surrounding these agricultural beauty contests were a part of a system of agricultural marketing that operated on several levels. Farmers, civic boosters, state officials, and extension agents all used these images—and the real, live beauties themselves—to trumpet the superiority of their homegrown produce to local, state, regional, national, and international audiences.

Growers and sellers of the region's other major commodity crop were also skilled at using the agricultural beauty contest to stimulate business during the Depression. In 1931, boosters in Memphis founded Cotton Carnival to promote the Mississippi Delta's cotton crop.[95] The annual Carnival celebration elevated two young women to royal status. The queen, secretly selected from among the city's elite families, reigned as the symbolic head of the festivities but was not a beauty queen per se. That honor fell to the Maid of Cotton, who was chosen at a beauty contest and assumed the responsibility of advertising cotton with her body. In 1938, the newly formed National Cotton Council (NCC) took over the Maid of Cotton contest. The NCC's activities reflect the different trajectories of tobacco and cotton farming. Cotton cultivation was already moving down the road of mechanization, farm consolidation, and tenant displacement. The NCC was thus less concerned with building ties with individual farmers than local tobacco boards were. It focused, instead, on solving the problem of underconsumption, spending most of its energy expanding national and international consumer interest.[96] Demand for cotton had declined because of the Depression, but on the horizon was a new, more troubling threat—synthetics. The NCC envisioned the Maid of Cotton as a solution to both problems.

Welcoming young women from cotton states to Memphis, where they competed for the title, the Maid of Cotton competition hewed a more conservative line than some other agricultural beauty contests. It shied away from erotic games with phallic symbols in cotton fields—the contest was held in a city, after all—and did not require that contestants participate in a swimsuit competition (though they might wear them later, during fashion shows). The young women selected as winners did serve the same symbolic purpose as tobacco and other crop queens. Their bodies showcased the crop itself, in this instance processed and spun into a sophisticated all-cotton wardrobe that they modeled in advertising campaigns, in fashion shows, and in personal appearances on a promotional tour.

The National Cotton Council teamed up with Lever Brothers, manufacturer of Lux Flakes, a popular laundry detergent, to get more exposure for their commodity crop. The arrangement was born of necessity, as the council lacked the resources to fund a marketing campaign, but it was one that paid off.[97] The 1941 Maid of Cotton, for example, appeared in a four-page pictorial layout in the *New York Herald Tribune*, touting the superiority of clothing made from southern cotton and proclaiming the ease with which it could be cared for with Lux. Having beaten more than 138 other contestants from the cotton-growing South, Alice Beasley of LaGrange, Tennessee—a "titian blonde with milk-white complexion" and one of the "newest to be singled out in the South's long tradition of beauties"—had already logged 14,000 miles before arriving in New York. The copy also suggested that Beasley was of aristocratic origin. One photo showed her standing in a cotton riding outfit in front of a columned mansion. Another showed her in a cotton hoopskirted dress, "like those her grandmothers wore amid the same scenes," the copy noted.[98]

The promotional campaign thus not only appealed to fantasies of wealth and privilege but also lent respectability to Beasley's identity as a beauty queen. She was the modern embodiment of the antebellum plantation lady. Just as the National Toilet Company did in its advertisements for face powder and face bleach, cotton promoters used the plantation lady to justify women's participation in a consumer culture that centered on new forms of female display. In the case of brightleaf tobacco queens and Delta cotton queens, it was ultimately white southern women's particular connection to the land—as the South's crop par excellence, the most important fruit of all that agricultural labor—that lent them not just their credibility, but visual power, too.

The NCC's packaging of Beasley as a beautiful, exquisitely dressed southern belle with an Old South pedigree reveals another important audience for this marketing system—women. The fact that it was the female form, and occasionally overt sexuality, that characterized these contests did not preclude female interest. The iconography of the brightleaf marketing campaigns, in fact, was intended to help young rural women chip away at objections to female smoking. Tobacco festival organizers invited women to think of themselves as cigarette smokers by coupling the act of smoking with sexuality. Theirs was a bold scheme, given that Americans had frowned on female smoking throughout the nineteenth and early twentieth centuries. Among women, only prostitutes and bohemians had dared to smoke cigarettes, reinforcing the association between cigarette smoking and immorality. In recent decades, younger and more urban women, particularly college coeds, had begun to smoke publicly, but even the cigarette industry, fearful of a possible backlash, was reluctant to advertise to them directly until the late 1920s.[99] Respectable southern women, especially rural ones, did not pick up the cigarette habit as quickly. One young woman who moved from the North Carolina countryside to a mill town recalled that many of her contemporaries used snuff, but cigarettes were off-limits. "You never saw a woman smoking cigarettes back then," she said. "The awfullest looking sight I ever saw was a woman smoking a cigarette."[100] Taboos against female smoking remained strong in agricultural areas well into the 1930s. A survey taken in 1935 revealed that only 8 percent of rural women smoked, compared to about 40 percent of urban women.[101]

In this context, participation in a tobacco queen contest was significant, indeed. Young women who wore tobacco costumes—and thus made the link between women and tobacco visible on their own bodies—announced that they no longer had to abide by the old rules. So, too, did contestants who joined in field day events like those held in Wilson. The contestants photographed with their phallic cigarettes and pipes testified to the sensuous pleasures of smoking. In these images, the symbolic woman-as-commodity met her social counterpart, woman-as-consumer, who deliberately flirted with indecency.[102] Young women who helped establish the new visual landscape—and those who subsequently picked up the habit, contestant or otherwise—were redefining what it meant to be a southern woman from a small town or farm. Just a few years before the tobacco queen was offered as a respectable if sensual symbol of femininity, in fact, cigarette smoking had played a very public role in defining female disreputability in North Carolina. In 1931, sixteen teenaged girls at Samarcand Manor, the state's facility for white female juvenile delinquents, had allegedly set fire to two dorms. Press accounts of the arson trial that subsequently riveted the state revealed that the incarcerated girls begged visitors for cigarettes and matches. In the narrative of the ordeal that developed among concerned North Carolinians, smoking pointed to the girls' sexuality and, thus, their guilt.[103]

Once tobacco queens did become conspicuous in the region, the image of a young beauty pushing tobacco use might prove too much for some individuals. Sarah Blanding, the dean of women at the University of Kentucky, asked that the Kentucky Association of Deans of Women study the phenomenon of college beauties serving as commodity crop royalty. The association issued a report that condemned, in particular, tobacco queens as distasteful. Thereafter, the University of Kentucky forbade campus queens to compete at the Kentucky Tobacco Carnival. The university still allowed coeds to compete in other civic and commodity crop contests, a fact that the Lexington newspaper mocked, arguing that tobacco mattered more to the local economy than mountain laurel and rhododendron.[104]

Challenging the rules of propriety was not the only reason a rural woman might be attracted to crop beauty contests. Maids of Cotton traveled the country during their yearlong reign as queen, a significant experience even for the daughters of wealthy and middle-class farmers. Some years, the itinerary included trips to Europe and Latin America as well. In addition to her travels, Alice Beasley also won a crash course in modeling from the Powers Agency in New York. All told, according to the *Herald Tribune*, she had "literally stepped through the looking glass . . . and found herself something of a national figure overnight."[105] Her star seems to have faded when she surrendered her crown the following year, but some winners may have gone on to enjoy a career in modeling or in the entertainment industry. Nineteen fifty-seven Maid of Cotton Helen Landon appeared on the *Ed Sullivan Show*, cotton bolls in hand.[106] If most agricultural beauty contests drew from a less wealthy demographic than did the Maid of Cotton competition, this reality only underscores the role these contests played in the lives of young farm women. Beauty contests offered what must have seemed exhilarating chances to escape the family farm by traveling to a nearby town or state. For a few women, winning a beauty competition may have provided a ticket off the farm completely.

Contests associated with market days, such as tobacco queen contests, offered an enriching social function for all rural women, contestant or not. Seeing dollars on both sides of the gender line, tobacco festival organizers knew that contestants would bring with them an entourage of mothers, sisters, and other farm women for whom social opportunities were few and far between. As we have already seen, most commercial spaces in the early-twentieth-century South, including the general store, were reserved for men. The market culture surrounding the annual sale of tobacco was no exception, and so queen contestants and the women who came to cheer them on to victory integrated what had for decades been an almost exclusively male domain. In some cases, as in Wilson's Smoke Flower and Golden Weed Queen Contest, the queen was even crowned in the very center of agricultural exchange: in the tobacco warehouse.[107] With a new stake in what went on at market—their teenage daughters were up for evaluation, after all—farm women may also have enjoyed more power in determining where their family should take its tobacco.

Women living outside the South did not experience these contests in the same direct fashion, of course. They did, however, constitute part of the audience for the competitions and their attendant promotional campaigns. Depending on their background, nonsouthern women who saw images of tobacco queen contestants and who were inspired to smoke may or may not have been pushing at the boundaries of acceptable behavior. What is certain is that nonsouthern women, and men, were being asked to buy into a southern consumer culture that derived its power from romantic notions of an arcadian southern past. In the National Cotton Council campaigns, that past was even more idealized. Alice Beasley probably hailed from a wealthy planter family, as the biggest beauty contests associated with the celebration of southern agriculture (the Maid of Cotton competition was certainly first among them) drew the daughters of the well-heeled.

Whether or not the Maids were, in fact, wealthy southern belles was beside the point. The images of southern womanhood disseminated by the NCC were constructed to evoke this impression, as were the narratives explaining women's selection and travels. After crowning Beasley, the Maid of Cotton judges, the *Herald Tribune* noted, had been "pleased . . . upon discovering that the family of their choice had been engaged in the cultivation of cotton for the past 100 years."[108] Nowhere in this national advertising campaign would readers have seen evidence of the tenant farmers, white and black, who were so integral to the production of the region's cotton. Nor would they have seen their daughters, whose wardrobes were perhaps fashionable but almost certainly more humble than Beasley's. Obscured by the council's glossy advertising campaign was the fact that many poor southerners likely interpreted the symbolic meaning of cotton quite differently.

Hardly evocative of wealth and privilege, cotton represented hardship, oppression, and poverty.[109] Indeed, mill workers who labored in textile factories to transform raw cotton into ready-made clothing were disparaged as "lintheads" because of the cotton fiber that clung to their hair as they worked. The NCC actually had a separate marketing campaign for the region's rural poor and middling classes, one that made the pages of publications like *Agricultural Review*, rather than the *Herald Tribune*. To increase demand for the cotton sacks used to package staples such as flour and feed (paper was making inroads), the council launched the "Sewing with Cotton Bags" promotion in 1940. Ads featured women wearing attractive but modest dresses made from cotton sacks, proving that even housewives of humble means could enjoy the benefits of cotton.[110]

In the end, what we can see is that southern agricultural boosters exported far more than crops to the rest of the nation and the world. They exported an iconography of southern agriculture that feminized the land—their livelihood—during a time of economic uncertainty and anxiety. Notable, too, was the way in which this new visual landscape of homegrown beauty royalty underpinned the whiteness of the consumer culture arising out of southern farming. Cigarettes manufactured with Piedmont tobacco, dresses made out of Mississippi Delta cotton, packages of Georgia peanuts that made those Coca-Colas taste so good—these and a host of other consumer products circulated within the South and beyond. As they did so, they carried with them hints of the racialized femininity that had supported the region's system of agricultural production since well before the Civil War. Individuals who bought these goods were consuming more than products that simply relaxed, clothed, or fed the body. They were consuming—and in the process, affirming—visual representations of the southern social and economic order that hid as much as they revealed.

This whitewashing of southern agriculture stood in stark contrast to the gritty portrait that emerged from New Deal photography during the

A National Cotton Council pamphlet, 1940. In its "Sewing with Cotton Bags" campaign, aimed at southern women of modest means, the National Cotton Council insisted that thrift did not demand a sacrifice of style. Courtesy of the National Museum of American History, Smithsonian Institution.

same years. The most ambitious of these was undertaken by the Farm Security Administration (FSA). From 1935 to 1942, twenty FSA photographers took more than 13,000 photographs of the South, exposing the dark underbelly of southern agriculture to shore up support for progressive New Deal policies.[111] In fact, Dorothea Lange and her contemporaries so successfully captured the intense suffering of the region's poor tenant farmers and sharecroppers that, by the late 1930s, their boss was lamenting that in FSA photos "everyone is too old to work and too malnourished to care."[112] He wanted, as he put it, "[m]ore contented-looking" people.[113]

Crop queens offered just such an alternative picture of the South. Whether agricultural trade boards deliberately attempted to counter unflattering images of the Depression-era South is unclear, but some southerners were concerned about how the region was portrayed to the rest of the nation. In 1940, FSA photographer Marion Post Wolcott told the head of the agency that the South's most downtrodden residents submitted themselves to the camera with no objections. "But these more prosperous farmers, and middle 'classes,'" she observed, "they will have none of it, unless they look right, well dressed, powdered,—and unless they know who you are and what it's for."[114] Wealthier rural southerners wanted, in short, to make a good impression. As a form of iconographic dissemblance, agricultural beauty queens served this purpose well.

THAT RURAL BEAUTY QUEENS could serve this function signaled a shift in the meaning of beauty contests in the South. By 1941, when Alice Beasley was heralded as the face of southern cotton, the beauty queen was not as much of a threat as she had been in the 1920s. She made the region look good since, as the National Cotton Council asserted, she was a beautiful southern belle who would have made even her grandmother proud. Earlier opposition to the bathing beauty revue had diminished as the contests gradually became regular, annual rituals, situated within a familiar context of agricultural celebration. The sight of a young woman wearing a bathing suit, or a two-piece tobacco costume, was no longer as novel or as shocking as it may have once been.

The rural world of agricultural evaluation and marketing was crucial in sustaining this transformation, but there were other developments in the interwar period that played a role, too. The most important of these was the explosion of municipal swimming pool construction in the 1920s and 1930s. Before 1920, a few southern cities had public pools. Both Atlanta and New Orleans, for example, had four pools for their white residents.[115] Elsewhere, pools were few and far between, a situation that changed with the economic prosperity of the 1920s. Larger cities such as Dallas, Fort Worth, and Nashville all added pools in the 1920s, most of which were for whites.

Most significantly, even small towns could finally afford pools. Florence, South Carolina—a market town located in the heart of the Brightleaf Belt and home to a tobacco queen contest—had a pool by the end of the decade. Although municipal pool construction slowed with the onset of the Depression, it spiked again once the New Deal began pumping millions of dollars into art and infrastructure projects across the country. Between 1933 and 1938 alone, the Civil Works Administration (CWA) and then the Works Progress Administration (WPA) built 750 pools nationwide. (Federal agencies also built 1,681 "wading pools" during the same period.) To avoid favoring certain areas or regions over others, the government made a point of spreading money for pools around, which meant that the South came out well. In 1936 alone, 7 WPA pools were built in Alabama, 5 in

Louisiana, and 27 in Texas, numbers that compare favorably with non-southern states like Connecticut (10 pools), Indiana (9), and Iowa (12).

This wave of municipal pool construction in the 1920s and 1930s transferred the pleasures of the beach, including scantily clad bodies, to locales away from the shore. And whereas pools in the late nineteenth and early twentieth centuries tended to be segregated by sex, pools of this era were not, since public officials were increasingly inclined to see these social spaces as tools for fostering family and community stability.[116] Some southerners, however, viewed this development with concern. Carbon Hill, Alabama, population 2,500, was the beneficiary of a WPA pool that, according to William C. Pryor, chief of the Photographic Section of the WPA, was the only one between Birmingham and Tupelo, Mississippi. It was, therefore, very popular. Yet when the city commissioners announced that it would be open to males and females at the same time, a group of local ministers protested. As Pryor noted, until this point, Carbon Hill girls and boys were rarely allowed to socialize together, not even on the school playground. A progressive leader on the city commission prevailed—the foresighted man, in fact, who had spearheaded the effort to obtain New Deal funds—and Carbon Hill's pool was sexually integrated. "It is now taken as a matter of course," Pryor wrote in 1938, "and thus the New Deal has been instrumental in modernizing some of Carbon Hill's thought as well as some of its physical attributes."[117]

The design of interwar pools played a role in liberalizing attitudes toward pool use as well. Many offered new amenities that evoked the leisure of the seashore rather than promoting swimming as exercise. With sandy beaches, grassy lawns, and concrete decks, pools of the interwar period transformed what people did when they went to the local pool. They lounged, sunbathed, and gazed at each other, making pools the perfect sites for self-display and voyeurism in a mixed-sex setting. According to Jeff Wiltse, this shift in the way people utilized pools altered their sense of decorum. Not only was the public objectification of the body increasingly acceptable, but "public decency came to mean exhibiting an attractive appearance rather than protecting one's modesty."[118] The addition of bathing beauty contests at municipal pools reflected this evolution in the meaning of public decency. A competition that judged female bathers on how well they looked in their swimming attire was a natural outgrowth of the pool's altered purpose.

In the South, the sponsorship of bathing beauty contests at municipal pools revealed the degree to which crop queen contests helped further this transformation as well. Even at the new pools that were built in the 1920s and 1930s, the rural influence was evident. In 1934, New Deal funds paid for the construction of a new bathhouse and pool at Pullen Park, in Raleigh, North Carolina, replacing a turn-of-the-century structure that had segregated male and female swimmers. By 1938, Pullen Park had become the venue for two concurrent beauty contests with a connection to nearby tobacco queen contests. In the first beauty contest, one woman was chosen to represent the city in the tobacco queen contest in Mullins, South Carolina, while a second winner was chosen as the delegate to the Wilson Queen of the Smoke Flower and Golden Weed Contest. In the second competition, a bathing beauty revue held on the same day at the new swimming pool, the judges selected a young woman for Wilson's bathing beauty contest. (Wilson, it will be remembered, had both a bathing and nonbathing beauty revue at its annual festival.) The *Raleigh News and Observer* reported that a crowd of 10,000 had gathered for the events and, interestingly, that several who had applied to enter the competitions "failed to appear."[119] One wonders if something simply came up, or if the no-shows were concerned about reactions to their participation. Regardless, at the municipal pool, city girls — one was even a former Miss Raleigh — vied for a chance to compete in rural beauty contests, to become a part of the system of agricultural marketing that used pretty faces and shapely bodies to sell crops. They may have been crowned in the state capital, but the next stop on their path to beauty glory was the tobacco warehouse, maybe even the tobacco field.

The connection between town and country in these Raleigh beauty contests is also important for what it suggests about rural women's lives as the Depression gave way to post–World War II prosperity. Farm women were not as isolated, not as cut off from their urban counterparts as they once had been. Since the early twentieth century, home demonstration agents had championed an agenda of modernization in the South, an agenda premised on the adoption of new habits and tastes among rural women. They had encouraged rural women to acquire a more urban, middle-class understanding of gender roles, respectability, and domesticity.[120] Propelled by rising standards of living and the move toward commercial farming, the vision that home extension agents had advanced for decades was realized among the wives and daughters of the region's most prosperous farmers by midcentury. Not every farm woman had to work in the same ways, or to the same extent, as she had throughout the 1920s and 1930s to contribute to her family's livelihood. Farm women's contributions to the sustenance of the household became less significant. Capable farm women did not have to possess productive skills that were as highly honed as they once were, nor did they necessarily want to. In 1941, agents in Augusta County, Virginia, noted that many rural homemakers preferred the convenience of store-bought goods.[121] As Melissa Walker has argued, "conspicuous consumption and leisure activities symbolic of wealth and affluence" became more important—more possible—to some southern farm women.[122] It was, thus, their consumptive skills that increasingly mattered.

In this new climate, lessons in making clothes on a budget lacked their earlier urgency. Likewise, home demonstration programs focused less on rituals that showcased healthy bodies and female thrift. It was the beauty queen that fit more and more comfortably within the changing nature of farm women's lives and labors. Demonstration agents joined trade organizations and became heavily involved in the sponsorship of beauty contests at county fairs and agricultural festivals during these years, most often working through local 4-H clubs and the county farm bureau to recruit contestants. Nearly every southern county farm bureau crowned a new queen each year, dispatching her to surrounding areas to advertise homegrown products. Home demonstration agents helped push to its logical conclusion the decades-long evolution in how farm women's contributions were judged. They supported contests that cultivated beautiful, even decorative bodies, bodies that were more involved in consumption than they were in production. The ubiquitous agricultural queens of the postwar years were marketed as alluring consumers of cotton, peaches, and rice. They were charged with the task of encouraging more women in the South and beyond to be consumers, too, to buy the commodities they represented with their bodies. The region's increasing participation in the market economy meant, in essence, that more women found their bodies commodified in the service of the agricultural economy.

Even those beauties that did not represent a specific crop testified to the changed context of rural southern women's lives. In 1940, Sally Carter of the *Progressive Farmer* penned a beauty column entitled "Rearing Prize-Winning Daughters—A Quizzical Quiz on How to Make Daughters Beautiful."[123] Such an article would have seemed out of place, even inappropriate, just fifteen years earlier. By the end of the 1940s, young 4-H women in North Carolina were making swimsuits out of feed sacks and were featured in area newspapers as the new face of rural female life. More a publicity gimmick than anything else, the photos nevertheless revealed

Lumberton Tobacco Festival Queen, North Carolina, 1947. By the postwar period, tobacco queens brazenly announced their sexuality. From the *Raleigh News and Observer*, 7 August 1947, courtesy of the State Archives of North Carolina, Raleigh. © 1947 McClatchy.

how these women saw themselves—they were no longer captives of back-breaking labor or of moral qualms about showing their skin. The change was captured succinctly in the caption underneath one such photo: "Feed Bags Now Holding Bathing Girls."[124] The queen of the 1947 Lumberton Tobacco Festival similarly indicated a new view of beauty and sexuality, teasing the camera with her barely-there tobacco leaf.[125] Indeed, the leaf was not even attached to her body. With one movement, it is obvious that she could be topless. Hardly an innocent farm girl, the Lumberton queen was a classic pinup, reminiscent of the scores of sexualized beauties that had become icons during the war just a few years before. A more modern and materially prosperous agricultural South did not have to spend all of its energy and resources staging contests designed to raise awareness about poor health conditions or to help struggling women scrabble together a modern wardrobe. It could afford to appreciate and reward a new kind of feminine beauty, albeit one with a quaint rural touch. Nearly nude beauty queens were hardly problematic. They announced that the region had, in certain respects, arrived. They also revealed how this transformation in the region's fortunes rested on a complicated redefinition of rural femininity. The 1947 Lumberton winner, like many of her queenly contemporaries, exuded an ambiguous fusion of sexual power and sexual objectification.

After decades of nurturing rural beauties, the South was poised in the postwar period to arrive in Atlantic City, too. Southern contestants would soon find that the region's system of rural pageantry had positioned them well for the newly popular Miss America Pageant, which had been revived in 1935 after a seven-year hiatus. Once the pageant director finally succeeded in removing all hints of impropriety from the event, and once the white South found itself mired in a violent struggle to preserve its "way of life," southern beauty queens would take the stage in Atlantic City by storm. Until then, white women would continue to sell cotton, peaches, and tobacco with their bodies.

Black women, meanwhile, used their bodies to sell something that, on its surface at least, might have seemed an easier pitch to make—the idea that they were attractive. As it turns out, it was hardly a simple proposition, and not just because of white racism. Conflicting ideas about beauty divided black southerners along a number of fault lines.

## CHAPTER FOUR

# Thrones of Their Own

*Body and Beauty Contests among*
*Southern Black Women*

In August 1971, *Ebony* magazine ran a photo spread titled "Belles of the South." The layout did not, as white southerners might have assumed, include the pictures of white beauties, but rather included the images of sixteen black women. The editors hoped to counter "the impression that the only beautiful Southern women are white and all of [the region's] black women are either frazzled maids, overweight mid-wives or unkempt domestics." "In reality," the article insisted, "the South has always been a haven for beautiful black women." Most of the featured women were students at, or recent graduates of, historically black colleges; several had been chosen beauty queens on their campuses. All were "irresistibly attractive."[1] Making a case for comeliness of black southern women, *Ebony* was engaging in what, by this point, had become a long-standing tradition—celebrating black female beauty. The beauty of black women was a constant subject of conversation and labor throughout the first half of the twentieth century. While black beauty culturists were honing their craft, various organizations in the African American community were experimenting with body rules and rituals for black southern women. As the *Ebony* story suggested, in the most basic sense, the function of a ritual like the beauty contest was to prove that white southern women did not enjoy a monopoly on physical beauty in the region. It is hardly surprising that the magazine would feel the need to make this statement, given that images of white southern beauties had been a part of the nation's visual landscape for decades.

But beauty contests for black southern women during those same years were more than a demand for recognition. From the perspective of the black middle class, poorer African Americans in both cities and the countryside failed to exhibit habits that would ensure the survival of the race and shore up its public image. To achieve these ends, reformers, religious and civic leaders, and educators tackled issues like domesticity and childrearing, but their efforts focused on appearances, too. The beauty rituals and other body-related initiatives they sponsored can best be understood as the corporeal component of this larger project, as an effort to help black southern women embody the politics of respectability.[2] They were an attempt to change women's aesthetic practices and ideals, to help the "frazzled maids," the "overweight mid-wives," the "unkempt domestics"—as well as another infamous type, the hypersexualized jezebels—adopt a representational style that did the race proud.

Their mission proved difficult. Some black women struggled to attain an acceptable appearance because they lacked resources. But black women with access to consumer goods such as clothes, jewelry, and cosmetics posed their own problem. They made extravagant purchases, bought the wrong items, or disobeyed rules about how to put them together or act while wearing them. Individuals concerned by these perceived indiscretions envisioned their rituals and regulations as tools to channel women's consumption, to prescribe appropriate consumptive choices and thereby refashion the black female body. Correctly disciplined and presented, black women's bodies could dispute white perceptions that all black women were depraved and sexually promiscuous, poised to take African Americans down the road of racial degeneracy.[3] Even when physical beauty per se was not at issue, then, its constitutive elements—femininity, deportment, and modesty—were.

Body contests and regulations thus abounded in the rural South, where home demonstrations agents sponsored health pageants and sewing classes, and in the urban South, where middle-class matrons embraced the fashion show. They were particularly numerous in a setting that brought the dynamics of both of these locations together—the black college. *Ebony* was right to search out beautiful black women at the region's historically black colleges and universities. Since the late nineteenth century, these institutions had insisted that the shaping of young female bodies was as essential as the shaping of young female minds. And it was on the black college campus that the tensions of class, geography, and—just as significantly—generation played out in the starkest terms. Administrators believed that young women bore a special responsibility to advance racial uplift. As vessels of race progress, their bodies showcased black potential, but only, of course, when they were styled in a suitable manner. Over time, the challenges of this body project intensified, since coeds increasingly turned to modern consumer culture to satisfy their sartorial desires. Colleges used dress codes and, later, beauty contests to rein in the young women who were their charges.

The many contests and rules to which black women were expected to submit—on college campuses, but also on city streets and in rural hamlets—bring to the fore familiar themes: the ways in which consumer goods challenged traditional morality and accentuated a new, modern sexuality. They are especially revealing, however, of the role of consumption in defining women's bodies in racial terms. Black and white critics of the way black women adorned themselves both argued, in essence, that their aesthetic was too black. At the same time, southern whites sometimes contended that middle-class black women were attempting to be white through the use of consumer goods. Consumption was not a race-neutral practice, in other words, but figured into how southerners understood black women's racial identity. Body rules and rituals for black women also show how race leaders self-consciously utilized black women's bodies to prove not just their individual capabilities but the capabilities of the race itself.

Like the politics of respectability more generally, body regulations and body contests for southern black women betrayed an uneasy awareness of an ever-watchful audience, one poised to point out failings without hesitation. Black beauticians, as we have seen, also invoked the politics of respectability, pitting dirt, disease, and unkemptness against cleanliness, health, and attractiveness in promoting their work. More so than grooming hair, these contests and regulations put a stamp of approval on a black body aesthetic that bore the traces of a distinct class interest. Instilling respectability in the black female body meant erasing a style that was an expression of working-class and rural black culture. Beauty rituals that did not necessarily justify their purpose in terms of a class-based notion of respectability, such as newspaper photo contests, still left something to be desired. More often than not, they rewarded an ideal of black female beauty indebted to white standards.

The effort to help black women embody a respectable femininity made good sense, given the lack of respect many southern black women endured on a daily basis. Body and beauty rituals also supported the economic uplift of the race just as black beauty culture did. Using contests to raise money, southern blacks combined two political activities in a mutually supporting relationship—disseminating flattering images of the race while strengthening the financial stability of local organizations in the black community. But it was also true that the strategy of using black body contests to validate black women's beauty became more and more problematic over time. By the postwar decades, it was unclear whether it was sufficient for black women to be "belles of the South," as *Ebony* called them, or whether they needed to be something else altogether.

IN CONTRAST TO WHITE crop queens, black crop queens were not a conspicuous presence in the regional or national media in the early to mid-twentieth century. When images of African Americans were used at all in promoting products, in and out of the South, the preferred genre was racial caricature, which trucked in the denigration of black features.[4] One of the most popular advertising icons of the century was, after all, Aunt Jemima, the mammy figure extraordinaire, hardly famous for her beauty.[5] Other obstacles had an impact, too. In addition to white domination of the region's trade organizations and marketing boards, the smaller investment in black home demonstration work prevented the growth of rural beauty contests that in any way rivaled those for white southern women.

The number of black beauty contests at black agricultural fairs paled in comparison to the number of white competitions. Black rituals were also latecomers to a rural beauty scene already saturated with white queens who, not surprisingly, received much more press attention. One of the few rural beauty contests for black women in the state of North Carolina, for example, began in 1954 at the fifth annual Chatham County Colored Agricultural Fair, nearly twenty years after rural white women in the state had begun entering beauty contests.[6] Sponsored by the local black home demonstration agent, the contest continued for the next several decades. But it was one among a handful of such contests for black women. One major exception existed to this regional pattern. In Memphis, white women were not the only cotton royalty. Beginning in 1936, black women also did important body work on behalf of the Delta's most important commodity crop. Similar to their white counterparts in some respects, in still others the black cotton queens from Memphis demonstrate the difficulty of using black women to sell southern agriculture.

The origin of the Cotton Makers Jubilee—black Memphis's answer to the white Cotton Carnival—can be traced to concern over the public image of black men and women in the city. In 1935, dentist R. Q. Venson and his wife Ethyl took their nephew to a parade sponsored by the Cotton Carnival. At the end of the parade, the young boy wondered aloud why all the black men had been pulling mules and all the black women had been placed on cotton bales.[7] Concerned with the message the carnival was sending to the city's black population, especially its youth, the Vensons founded the Cotton Makers Fiesta (later renamed the Cotton Makers Jubilee) as a protest.[8] But it was more than that. It was also a demand for recognition. "The objective—the principal one—of the Memphis Cotton-Makers Jubilee celebration," an early event program announced, "is to symbolize the great and important part which the colored people of this area have played in the history of cotton." While Cotton Carnival failed to acknowledge the role of Delta blacks in the cotton economy, Jubilee promised to make it front and center. As Venson and his fellow boosters saw it, there was no way to leave blacks out, since growing, processing, and selling cotton "touches all phases of life in this section, and makes no distinction among classes or colors in its influence."[9] On one point Jubilee organizers and Carnival sponsors agreed. Selling cotton was a matter of utmost importance, and so Jubilee, too, was to be a promotional celebration, alerting consumers to cotton's advantages. The two festivals occurred during the same week, though Jubilee organizers had to ensure that their events did not conflict with Carnival attractions that drew big crowds.

The Vensons envisioned royalty as a central component of their project. In 1936, the first year of the event, Mrs. Venson simply declared herself queen and reigned with a local funeral director who acted as king. For the next several years, Jubilee queens and kings won their titles by raising the most money for the annual festivities. Thereafter, the contestants who garnered the most votes in a popularity contest emerged victorious. No matter how it claimed the throne, the royal couple embodied the dignity the Vensons wanted to highlight through their celebration. That a black queen in particular existed, and that she served as the star attraction in a parade through the streets of the city, even if the route was restricted to the black business district, were remarkable, indeed. "[N]obody had seen a black queen or anything like that," Mrs. Venson stated years later, "[and] the streets were just lined with people. They were white and black people . . . there were as many white people as black people." Non-Memphians were struck by the novelty as well. In 1937, *Life* magazine sent several photographers to Memphis to do a story on Carnival and Jubilee. According to Mrs. Venson, the photographers left Carnival after hearing that Jubilee had a black queen because they wanted to take her picture. When Carnival organizers got wind of what had happened, they were so upset that they "came down and yanked those fellahs away!"[10]

Within the next few years, Jubilee's royal pantheon expanded. As with white crop contests of the same era, festival sponsors invited princesses from various Delta towns to a Jubilee beauty contest. In 1940, the winner earned the title of the "Sepia Venus of the Mid-South." From 1948 to 1956, Jubilee added the Spirit of Cotton Pageant, a black analogue to the white Maid of Cotton Contest. Competitors were students at historically black colleges and universities throughout the cotton-growing South, and the winner, like the Maid of Cotton, was to tout the wonders of cotton to consumers on promotional tours. In the early years, Mrs. Venson played a big role in the contest. Some young hopefuls, it seems, were not attractive enough to represent the cotton industry should they be selected as the winner. "I hold if you let them in," she stated, "they have the right to win."[11] In such cases, intensive training and makeovers compensated for perceived deficiencies.

With Mrs. Venson as chaperone, Spirit of Cotton queens embarked upon publicity trips that took them to cities across the country and even to Cuba and Haiti. Typical were events held in New Orleans and in Washington, D.C., in the early 1950s. In the Crescent City, the 1950 Spirit of Cotton winner, the "traveling emissary of Cotton Fashions and good will," modeled thirty "stunning" cotton dresses at a fashion show.[12] In D.C., the 1953 queen met with the assistant secretary of agriculture to explain her promotional campaign and then modeled part of her thirty-five-piece cotton wardrobe at a luncheon. The department did its part by issuing a press release detailing the visit. The trip had the desired effect. A department official later wrote Mrs. Venson that several luncheon attendees were interested in acquiring patterns to copy the queen's clothes or in learning where they might purchase them ready-made.[13] For a few years, Jubilee volunteers donated the time and material necessary to create the queen's cotton wardrobe, not an inconsequential sacrifice for a program whose economic benefits to the Delta's black community were minimal. For five years, the National Cotton Council stepped in and contributed the material to the Spirit of Cotton winner, but not the services of a seamstress.

Jubilee and its royalty clearly played second fiddle to Carnival and its royal entourage, but for black critics of the event—and they did exist—this was not the issue. Rather, from the beginning, some black Memphians rejected the Vensons' contention that blacks needed a venue in which to celebrate cotton and their role in its production. Black teachers were among these. When the Vensons approached black teachers about providing the money to finance the first annual festivities and about encouraging children to participate, they declined. Their argument, Mrs. Venson said, was that "cotton had not done anything for us; . . . we were on the bottom of the hierarchy."[14] Initial support, instead, came from members of Dr. Venson's American Legion post, who had just received bonuses for their service in World War I. That same year, John Handcox, Southern Tenant Farmers' Union organizer and poet laureate, penned a poem that echoed the concerns of Memphis's black teachers. His target was not Jubilee, but Carnival and its white boosters. "Why do they celebrate Cotton?" he asked. "Because they cheat, beat and take it away from labor every year. . . . The money spent for decorations and flags, Would sure have helped poor sharecroppers who are hungry and in rags. . . . When cotton is King of any nation, It means wealth to the planter—to the laborer starvation."[15] To many blacks in Memphis and the surrounding countryside, cotton was hardly cause for revelry.

The glorification of King Cotton continued to bother Jubilee's detractors for years. By 1947, critics had become so vociferous that Dr. Venson included a pointed defense of the festival in the annual Jubilee program. In language reminiscent of Booker T. Washington, he lambasted those "who regard it beneath their dignity to cling to the earth from which all of our blessings flow."[16] Where Handcox and others saw deprivation, Venson saw blessings, at least in public pronouncements like this one. Therein lay the irony of the Vensons' event and its beautiful queens. In providing a more dignified role to local blacks in the city's celebration of cotton, Jubilee buried the unseemly sides of southern farming beneath a patina of boosterism, merriment, and feminine charm. The event had much in common, in short, with agricultural festivals and beauty contests in southern white communities. The difference was that some Memphis blacks, in contrast to southern whites, exposed the practice for what it was.

White Memphians were more likely to take issue with Jubilee and its royalty for other reasons. After *Time* magazine ran a story in 1946 about the local Democratic Party boss in Memphis—a feature that included a photo of the Jubilee king and queen with a caption that misidentified the couple as the Carnival rulers—a man wrote to complain. "Why . . . did [you picture] the Negro king and queen of the Cotton Carnival?" he demanded. "Anyone in Memphis five minutes would know the whole carnival centers around the duly elected [white] king and queen. You have done Memphis and the Cotton Carnival an injustice. . . . You delight, it seems, in trying to hold the South up in ridicule."[17] To this white southerner, black crop royalty represented an insult, an inversion of the way things should be. The appeal of black crop queens beyond the black community was, in sum, limited.

Despite the challenges posed by Jubilee as well as a dearth of crop contests like it, other kinds of black body contests connected to southern agriculture did exist. On this score, black women had more in common with white women than we might initially think. As daughters and wives of farmers and sharecroppers, black women, too, found their lives marked by the rhythms of the agricultural calendar and by agricultural contests that evaluated healthy and well-dressed bodies.

The rise of Jim Crow in the late nineteenth century spelled the end of the racially integrated crowds that had attended southern agricultural fairs in the immediate postbellum period. But rural black families continued to participate in fairground activities similar to those of whites. The North Carolina State Fair created a "colored day" in 1891, which featured an "Exhibit made by the Colored People from each of the Southern States, separate and distinct from the Exhibit of the White People, in separate buildings," while some southern states and counties had black-run fairs.[18] South Carolina, for example, became home to a "Colored State Fair" beginning in 1890. In 1898 Booker T. Washington started a fair in conjunction with his famous Farmers' Institutes at Tuskegee, providing local farmers and their wives an annual opportunity to show off the skills they had learned at monthly Institute classes. The success of the fairs at Tuskegee inspired the organization of black fairs across Alabama and eventually throughout the entire South.

Tuskegee also led the way in training African American extension and home demonstration agents in the South, partnering with the federal government to create a black extension service that had helped over 400,000 African American families by midcentury.[19] In contrast to their white colleagues, black agents were perennially underfunded and overextended, especially during the Depression. North Carolina, for example, did not hire its first permanent black home demonstration agent until the early 1920s, and the entire state had only half a dozen black agents through the mid-1930s.[20] In Florida, the total expenditure for white home demonstration work in 1930 was $131,009 but was only $25,526 for both black agricultural and home demonstration work.[21] In some southern states, white administrators of the extension program appointed only one black male extension agent per county, who was to work with both men and women.[22] Despite disparities in support, a small coterie of African American demonstration and extension agents existed in most southern states by the end of the 1920s, creating the same kinds of programs that were sponsored for white farm families and using the fair to evaluate black progress.

Bodies figured prominently in these programs. Health and hygiene, as we have already seen, were key items on the extension agenda in the rural South, but the health crisis among the black population and among black children in particular was dire. The infant mortality rate for blacks in some states was twice that for whites.[23] Along with middle-class club women, black home demonstration agents sponsored better baby competitions as a part of the educational activities associated with National Negro Health Week, first held at Tuskegee in 1915 and observed in roughly 2,500 communities by 1930.[24] Better baby contests at black fairs, like their white counterparts, often conflated cuteness with health. Health revues for older African American girls and boys in 4-H clubs served the same purpose, providing blacks in the rural South access to information about hygiene and disease, transforming those who best internalized the experts' advice into royalty. In all of these contests, black agents and participants drew on the eugenic tradition to undermine the belief that African Americans were of inferior stock and on the verge of "race suicide," often rewarding, in the process, the most attractive specimens of racial vitality among the entrants.[25]

Black home demonstration agents were also concerned with appearances and, in this arena, too, pursued an agenda that had much in common with the one embraced by white agents. Black agents sponsored sewing classes and dress revues, helping their pupils economize and learn the basic principles of style. They noted with pride how the farm women in their classes were shedding their rural ways, dressing more like middle-class urbanites. The African American agent who worked in the Raleigh area, for example, bragged to her superiors in 1937 that it was now impossible to "pick out country women on account of their ill fitting clothes and unbecoming colors." "The women," she continued, "have developed poise, self-respect and independence."[26]

But this achievement did not necessarily carry with it the same meaning as it did in the white community. Body rituals and regulations promoted by the cooperative extension service among rural black women spoke to a belief among the black middle class that black rural style was, in the larger quest for racial progress, an embarrassing obstacle. The charge that black women living in the rural South wore "ill fitting clothes" in "unbecoming colors" had been leveled at African Americans since at least the eighteenth century, when a unique black aesthetic emerged. Slave dress was characterized by varied materials and patterns and bright, contrasting colors.[27] This style was a reflection of the innovative uses to which slaves put hand-me-down clothing from their masters and mistresses. Although standard-issue slave clothing was of uniform cut and color and sewn of coarse, drab materials, slaves received a motley assortment of old waistcoats, dresses, stockings, hats, and petticoats from their owners, part of the rewards and punishments system on plantations. Incorporating hand-me-downs into their wardrobes and changing any details that they did not like, slave men and women showed little concern, as Shane White and Graham White have observed, that "such an item should coordinate in style, color, or anything else with the rest of their garb."[28] Shunning their masters' aesthetic for one of their own making, slaves fashioned an eclectic look that struck white observers as odd and even laughable. Unable to appreciate the different rules that governed how slaves adorned themselves, whites may also have missed the subversive mocking of white preening and privilege that underscored some slaves' dressing habits.[29]

Other factors contributed to the distinct fashion sensibility of slaves as well, especially West African traditions of textile-making that slave women had inherited and altered in the New World. African textiles were characterized by a purposeful mixing and matching of colors and patterns, a look enslaved women incorporated into the cloth they made, particularly after they took over the production of clothing for slave communities during the nineteenth century. Using berries, roots, and barks to dye thread of "de prettiest kind of colors," as one South Carolina slave remembered, slave women made vibrant homespun cloth.[30] Slave women also used this aesthetic tradition in mending worn-out clothes with scraps of material, repairing pants and dresses in irregular patterns that might eventually resemble a patchwork quilt. Finally, by the mid-nineteenth century many slave women had adopted the head wrap or bandana, worn to protect clean and untangled hair as well as to block out the sun's rays.

Compared to southern whites living in the mid to late nineteenth century, southern blacks looked different indeed. Traveling through Charleston at the end of the Civil War, northern newspaperman Whitelaw Reid summed up the overall visual effect in a description of newly freed slaves gathered to hear a speech in a black church. On one side of the church was "a motley, but brilliant army of bright-colored turbans, wound around wooly heads, and tawdry bandanas, and hats of all the shapes that have prevailed within the memory of this generation, and bonnets of last year's styles, with absolutely a few of the coquettish little triangular bits of lace and flowers which the New York milliners have this year decreed. Some of them wore kid gloves, all were gaudily dressed." For Reid, the audience gathered that day was, in short, "a study."[31] A writer for *DeBow's Review* described black dress among the freedmen of Virginia's cities the same way. Sundays brought out women adorned in "slop work cloth and sham jewelry and gaudy dresses and brilliant bonnets." "As in dress, so in manners," he concluded, "they are a showy, fantastical people . . . without very frequent evidences of taste in the one, and grace in the other."[32] Shocked by what they deemed the tawdriness before them, both men nevertheless seem to have been taken with the appearance of the freedmen and -women. The care with which they described their clothing reveals an ambivalent blend of ridicule and curiosity.

The aesthetic that these writers captured in their travelogues persisted, informing African American style in a New South that did not eradicate economic scarcity but did open up the possibilities of consumption. Similar assessments come from the social scientists who embedded themselves in southern communities in the 1930s and 1940s.[33] Their observations bear the imprint of their outsider status, as well as the judgments of the local whites and upper-class blacks who were among their interviewees. As sensitive to different mores as they may have been for their time, many academics—white and black—concluded that southern blacks could not quite get it right. Describing the Sunday dress of African Americans in the mill town of York, South Carolina, a University of North Carolina researcher who provided Hylan Lewis with information for his study reported that their style was "ostentatious in the extreme . . . the color combinations are as loud and striking as possible."[34] Using this and other, corroborating observations, Lewis ultimately concluded: "What often occurs in the case of dress and grooming can be attributed to a 'distortion' of the conventional . . . to the not wholly successful absorption or practicing of available or model customs in the larger community."[35] Despite their best efforts, and their limited but nevertheless real ability to buy clothing through mail order or in local stores, blacks in town exhibited "[g]aucheries in dress and adornment," wore "irregular combinations," adopted "cheap or exaggerated imitations of current styles," and relished "cast-off, second-hand, or handed-down clothing."[36] Researchers reported that head clothes on women and gold teeth or fillings were also prominent features of this ostentatious southern black style.

It was the rare outsider who voiced appreciation for the rural black aesthetic, but a few did. Lura Beam, a white northerner who taught at black southern schools in the early twentieth century, wrote admiringly in her memoir that "Negroes put red and pink and orange together before Matisse did."[37] Observers did note that not all blacks shared this aesthetic. In York, head wrapping was primarily a practice of poor, rural women who came to town to do their shopping on Saturdays or who had moved there from a nearby plantation. "As a general rule," one University of North Carolina researcher stated, "the educated, the more sophisticated, the urbanized, the ME church attenders do not wear them."[38] Hortense Powdermaker noticed a similar class division among the blacks of Indianola, Mississippi. Middle- and upper-class black women "deliberately avoid bright colors," according to her 1939 study, "and are offended if clerks in the stores assume that they want something 'loud.'"[39] Not surprisingly, wealthier southern blacks "frowned upon" goldwork in the mouth as well.[40]

Black rural women who wore loud clothing, adorned themselves in a garish manner, and exaggerated current styles seemed, in the eyes of disapproving blacks and whites alike, to lack the aesthetic and bodily restraint that was the hallmark of femininity. The problem went far beyond not quite getting it right; it indicated an indifference to the boundaries and rules that constituted the very core of femininity, a concept rooted in self-control and moderation.[41] The appearance of most rural black women suggested, in short, that they were unwilling to obey the rules that required their sexual subordination and purity in exchange for social respect. The critique of rural black women on this score reflected the class- and race-bound definitions of femininity that prevailed throughout much of the twentieth century.

Like the academics who published their observations, black home demonstration agents who roamed the southern countryside teaching black women how to look attractive furthered this version of femininity nonetheless. Middle class themselves—by 1930, for example, all black agents in South Carolina were required to have a college degree and were expected to own a car—they understood their efforts as part of a larger battle to improve the image of black womanhood.[42] Thus, while agents' dress and clothing lessons were informed by many of the same concerns that motivated white agents, a different dynamic ultimately defined their work. In helping black women learn to refurbish old clothing or master the finer points of color coordination, black home demonstration agents were not simply concerned with helping rural women become stylish or sophisticated. Instead, these terms were often code for one overriding concern: that their pupils

Home demonstration club meeting, North Carolina, ca. 1930s. In dressmaking classes, home demonstration agents taught black farm women how to economize, as well as how to achieve a more urban, middle-class fashion aesthetic. "Instruction in Foundation or Dress Patterns," Image #0000512, courtesy of the Special Collections Research Center, North Carolina State University Libraries, Raleigh.

shun a provincial—and fundamentally racialized—aesthetic. Rural women needed to understand that the clothing they typically made and bought helped to construct a femininity characterized by its blackness and, thus, a femininity that compromised their claim to respectability.

The agent in Guilford County, North Carolina, for example, stressed the economic hurdles that her rural students faced in trying to put together wardrobes, but equally important was their inability to appreciate what was attractive. While she was pleased with the progress her students had made in the clothing program, she also believed that more classes were necessary for, as she said teasingly, "we like the brightest colors."[43] Millinery classes, another staple of the demonstration program, gave black women the skills to make more fashionable alternatives to the bandana, or head wrap, seen by some black women, who "frown upon its use," as a "symbol of servant status and coarseness."[44] The sponsorship of a state-wide program, the Head to Foot Club in South Carolina in 1924, took aim at the whole body. Head to Foot students learned the basics of hygiene, how to care for their hair and teeth, and how to dress properly. Members responded enthusiastically to sewing lessons, making over 2,600 dresses and coats and 2,978 pairs of underwear that year.[45] African American demonstration agents in Mississippi who several years later organized a parade of black women wearing fertilizer- and feed-sack garments to march down Jackson's Capitol Avenue surely hoped, as one white agent later wrote, to highlight their pupils' "industry, skill, and economy."[46] But black agents and club members may have seen the march as an aesthetic performance, an opportunity to offer visual evidence—in the heart of the state's biggest city—that rural black women were quite capable of rejecting rural habits of dressing for those that were more urban and refined. In Texas, agents used such images for more pointed purposes. They took pictures of activities like sewing classes to prove the success of their programs and to secure more funding from the whites who allocated scarce demonstration resources. The black women and men who posed for these photographs, many of which were taken by professional studios, dressed in their finest, showing off polished shoes and hats. Though well-intentioned, this public relations campaign also deflected attention away from the very real obstacles black agents, and rural women more generally, faced in segregated Texas.[47]

Also at work was the desire to change white beliefs that blacks, especially those who were poor and rural, were dirty. Regionalists invariably heard whites complain of body odor and bad hygiene among the black population. As Mark M. Smith has noted in his study of the sensory dimensions of race, it was probably true that some southern blacks gave off an unpleasant odor by virtue of their living and working conditions.[48] The home demonstration program allowed black women not only to overcome these hurdles to respectable self-presentation but also to avoid situations where white perceptions of black filth were most likely to cause humiliation. Buying clothes was one of these, for as Allison Davis and his team of researchers found during their stay in Natchez, Mississippi, "The idea of uncleanliness is also extended to any clothing worn by Negros."[49] In small towns without a black business district, black women shopped in white-owned stores. Some stores prohibited blacks from trying on clothes altogether; some allowed the practice but insisted that black patrons do so over the clothing they already had on.[50] Establishments that had liberal rules still created awkward moments for black patrons. "Shopping downtown was so unpleasant," recalled a woman who grew up in Albany,

Georgia, "that my mother often traced the outlines of my feet on paper and shopped for my shoes without me."[51]

Slights and insults abounded. A clerk who gave a black woman a pair of shoes to try on, but offered no help, revealed a visceral reaction to her supposed dirtiness and an unwillingness to bow at her feet when racial etiquette demanded the reverse.[52] One white clerk in Natchez was appalled that her manager allowed a black woman to return a coat she had bought earlier. "'Who wants a nigger coat?'" she demanded. "'Some little white girl will probably come in and buy it and not know it is a nigger coat.'" Davis observed that she "hung it up very gingerly and didn't touch it any more than necessary."[53] It is doubtful that the patron was present for this exchange, but black women undoubtedly found themselves in embarrassing circumstances like these more than they would have preferred. Teaching black women how to make fashionable clothing at home imbued principles of thrift and, perhaps just as importantly, spared them from these assaults on their dignity.

Implicit in the extension program, too, was the fear that middle-class efforts at respectable self-presentation were called into question by the style of poorer rural blacks. But the dress of middle-class and elite black women did not escape censure, suggesting the fine line these black women walked in the Jim Crow South. The desire to achieve a respectable femininity could backfire. Southern whites might mock black style for its gaudiness and for its "distortion" of accepted ideals, but underscoring this criticism was also the worry that blacks with access to consumer goods might be too successful in their desire to embody fashion and beauty. Even in the antebellum South, whites had betrayed a sense of unease over blacks' access to smart clothing. As slavery and the old social hierarchy crumbled, those fears became more pronounced. One week before the surrender of the Confederacy, Charlestonian Emma Holmes commented in her diary on the appearance of Rachel, a Virginia "mammy" with whom she was acquainted. Holmes praised Rachel for wearing a "handkerchief turban," which she deemed "respectable and becoming" for a black women of her position. Other local blacks, however, dressed in ways that were inappropriate to their station, particularly for special occasions, such as going to church. "The other negroes at church were all in the most ludicrous and disgustingly tawdry mixture of old finery," she complained, "aping their betters most nauseatingly—round hats, gloves and even lace veils—the men alone looking respectable."[54]

Voicing the familiar criticism that black style was tawdry, Holmes reveals a deeper anxiety over the meanings of dress and adornment in a society soon to be formally free. Would African Americans think themselves the equals of whites if they could dress like them? Holmes implied that they might, though she never could bring herself to voice this concern outright. She couched most of her observations in aesthetic terms, insisting "how much better in every way a plain, neat dress for the working classes, as in other countries, and indeed among our country negroes formerly."[55] Like black women who took pains to groom their hair, those who dressed well in the postbellum South challenged whites' exclusive claim to respectability and beauty. Judging by the frequency with which the issue appeared in studies about, and memoirs of, the South, the act of dressing well seems to have been a worse transgression than the act of cultivating healthy, stylish hair. Yet the oft-stated white preference for head wrapping reveals how closely connected the two concerns really were.

Certainly black women of means recognized the consequences of dressing well in the New South. Mamie Garvin Fields, the Poro agent from Charleston, worked as a seamstress in high school. She once made herself a beautiful dress just like several she had made for a young white bride. Her employer was furious. "How dare you?" she shouted. "The white people would take their work away from me if they found colored people wearing those dresses." In this case, Fields did wear her dress, without incident, yet her immunity from white censure might disappear beyond the borders of Charleston. As a child visiting relatives in the South Carolina countryside in the 1890s, Fields learned that sometimes "it wouldn't do," in her words, "to ride around and let the white people see you with your fine things." Traveling to the local general store to buy a crochet needle with her reluctant country cousins, more savvy about the mores of the area than she, Fields endured the incredulous berating of Ruth, the woman behind the counter. "Oh, Lord," Fields recalled. "Here I was, the no-manners Charleston cousin trying to tell this Ruth—*Miss* Ruth, you know—about a crochet needle, standing there in my citified dress. . . . The crackers didn't like it, and Ruth was one."[56] As a black girl, Fields should not have looked the way she did, nor should she have known how to crochet. It is also possible that part of Ruth's consternation resulted from what she perceived to be a confusing incongruity. Fields's clothing and demeanor seemed to suggest she was trying to be "white," but her complexion was not white, or even light. Ruth may have felt the affront of dressing too well was all the more egregious because the black girl standing before her had dark skin: a poor, low-class black should have known better.

Mamie Garvin Fields, 1913. Well-dressed black women like Fields sometimes irked white southerners, who believed them to be "uppity." Courtesy of the Avery Research Center for African American History and Culture, College of Charleston, Charleston, S.C.

Proscriptions against blacks attempting to dress too nicely survived well into the twentieth century in the rural backways and mill towns of the state. Describing York, South Carolina, in the 1940s, Hylan Lewis noted that there were "certain pressures that operate from the white community with respect to dress and manner."[57] A black woman in Mississippi reported that she often felt "criticized by white eyes" when she went out "in a tastefully designed dress." Whites, she said, "resent seeing a colored person dressed up and looking nice."[58] While blacks might choose to ignore such pressures and dress well or carry themselves confidently, those who did so were considered uppity or "smart niggers."[59] An African American woman who abandoned the trappings of the countryside—or who, like Fields, had never known them intimately in the first place—ran the risk of trying to seem too white.

THE POLITICS OF DRESS informed the lives of southern blacks living in urban areas as well, shaping intraracial struggles over what constituted the ideal black woman in city spaces. Concerns about urban black women's bodies show up with more frequency in the historical record, in fact, largely because of the sheer concentration of African Americans in cities and the anonymity of urban life. In cities, appearances offered clues about strangers. Cities were also home to black newspapers and magazines, publications that gave these issues a public platform. Urban areas, moreover, represented the settings in which female appearances became most entangled with the freedoms—and dangers—of consumerism, leisure, and sexuality.

Working-class blacks in southern cities, often just a few years removed from the plantation or sharecropper's cabin, viewed dress and fashion as central to their enjoyment of leisure time and urban amusements.[60] Forced to wear factory, maid, and cook uniforms during the week, urban black men and women set aside these work clothes on Saturday nights for outfits of their own choosing. Wearing whatever they wanted, rather than uniforms that signaled servility, was both a declaration of personal dignity and a way to draw a bright line between work and play.[61] Alice Adams, a domestic for an Atlanta family, put the issue succinctly. "[W]hen I went out," she said, "I wanted to look different."[62] Some observers noted the pride working men and women exuded as they strolled the streets of black commercial districts thronged with like-minded pleasure seekers. George W. Lee, an African American civic leader in Memphis, wrote in his celebratory portrait of Beale Street that weekend revelers came out to enjoy the satisfactions of conspicuous display: "The working folks are on parade; going nowhere in particular, just out strolling, just glad of a chance to dress up and expose themselves on the avenue after working hard all the week."[63] Their ostentatious style rivaled that of the entertainers they flocked to see. The female blues singers who toured the region under the auspices of the Theater Owner's Booking Association showed up to the theaters and clubs of black commercial districts dressed to the nines. In advertisements for her performances, Ma Rainey often donned lamé headbands, beaded dresses, and necklaces and earrings made out of gold eagle dollars.[64] During a stint in Norfolk, Virginia, in 1921, Mamie Smith told a local newspaper that she had no choice but to wear extravagant costumes. "I believe my audiences want to see me becomingly gowned," Smith insisted, "and I have spared no expense or pains . . . for I feel that the best is none to [sic] good for the public that pays to hear a singer."[65]

For centuries enslaved men and women had been subject to a system intent on denying their ability to move or dress in ways that revealed their individuality and subjectivity. In the late nineteenth and early twentieth centuries, blacks faced similar, if less violent and institutionalized, physical confinement as domestics in white homes or as workers on the factory floor. Removed from settings rooted in the disciplining of black bodies, black women asserted their bodily freedom by insisting on their right to wear whatever they wanted. And as Mamie Smith suggests, they held performers to a high standard, as models of what was possible when money was not an issue. Like leisure activities themselves, the clothes that black women wore while pursuing them provided an avenue for the "symbolic and physical restoration of their subjugated bodies."[66]

Despite their own poverty, urban working-class women could generally satisfy their fashion desires. In rural areas and smaller towns, blacks' ability to patronize general stores was circumscribed by rural isolation, a cycle of indebtedness, and Jim Crow prohibitions against trying on clothes. Enjoying a small but significant discretionary income, poor urban blacks generally had an easier time purchasing items in the new sites of consumer culture—the variety and department stores—that were built in the early twentieth century. In his study of the purchasing patterns of blacks in Nashville, Birmingham, Atlanta, and Richmond in 1929–30, for example, Paul Edwards concluded that the apparel of the black family in the urban South was "as a whole, of better quality than the occupations of the majority would suggest." This observation was true for professional and working-class blacks. Both groups paid the same amount for clothing as did their white socioeconomic peers. Store account lists in these cities also revealed that more professional blacks and working-class blacks patronized "the better types of stores" than did whites.[67] In addition to enjoying the ability to buy clothing in stores, even if they had to pay by installment, urban working-class women were also targeted by stores themselves as a part of the broader effort to cultivate female consumers, regardless of race or class. Store advertisements on billboards and in local newspapers bombarded black women in cities.

Some urban domestics fulfilled their sartorial desires by taking advantage of the generosity of wealthy female employers. Willie Mae Cartwright worked for a well-to-do white woman in Atlanta who allowed her to buy and borrow used items. Yet even in an urban environment with segregated leisure spaces, the act of wearing a white woman's clothing out in public was fraught with potential conflict. One night, Cartwright—dressed in "a gray georgette dress and gray slippers, and gray dropstitch stockings . . . and a load of Mrs. Duke's jewelry"—went out for some fun on Decatur Street, the thoroughfare frequented by the city's working-class blacks. A white policeman noticed her finery, took her to the police station, and released her only after a phone call to the Dukes confirmed that the items were not stolen.[68]

Black criticism, too, came to bear on women like Cartwright. Although individuals such as Memphis's George W. Lee may have been sympathetic toward working-class women and their freedom to consume, other black observers were less able to appreciate, much less condone, the fashion desires of black women in search of urban amusements. Since the late nineteenth century, black Baptist reformers had taken aim at the venues young women patronized—dance halls, juke joints, saloons—as well as the clothes they wore while there. In the 1880s, former Memphis schoolteacher and Baptist leader Virginia Broughton had railed against the "gaudy colors and conspicuous trimmings" of young black women in cities.[69] *Ringwood's Journal*, a nationally read fashion magazine for female migrants to urban locales, shared these concerns. Shaped by the elite status of its editors and writers, many of whom were members of the National Association of Colored Women, the Cleveland-based journal declared that young women who shunned "garish and gaudy dress may demand more consideration and respect" than those who did not. But the issue was more pressing for some black women than others. "The fact must be especially impressed upon our young women of the South," one article insisted, "who are constantly exposed to the depravity and lechery of the fair-skinned destroyers whose hearts are blacker than Erebus."[70] To exude virtue and escape white predators, black women in southern cities were advised to avoid the color red and clothing with fringe. Just as in the countryside, "loud" and "gaudy" were often coded terms in cities, pointing, in this context, to a working-class sexuality perceived to be out of control. That white men might interpret this aesthetic as a sign of sexual availability, even licentiousness, made its eradication all the more urgent.

The critique of this look became intertwined with concerns over the movement of the bodies contained within the much-maligned clothing, which was somewhat abbreviated among women seeking the attention of the opposite sex. One church man lamented that the woman going to a dance hall, in fact, "will scarcely allow wrapping to touch her body."[71] Gaudy and skimpy clothing seemed to feed the immoral behavior that transpired there, and vice versa. Working-class women who were dressed for play risked compromising black female virtue, especially since dancing was the primary activity in many commercial establishments. Early-twentieth-century black vernacular dancing offended middle-class sen-

Juke joint, Memphis, Tennessee, 1939. Both the dress and dancing of Juke joint patrons, like these in Memphis, offended black middle-class sensibilities. Courtesy of the Prints and Photographs Division, Library of Congress, Washington, D.C.

sibilities, shunning boundaries and discipline and encouraging physical intimacy.[72] As Arkansas educator E. M. Woods argued in his etiquette manual, many modern dances "excited[d] animal passions which tend to lead the participants astray."[73] This possibility hardly dissuaded working-class blacks in Atlanta. While wealthier blacks did the waltz and polka, the workers who frequented Decatur Street embraced new dances that reflected the sensuous rhythms of the blues. In the 1910s, for example, the "slow drag" became popular in southern night spots. According to a cor-netist, couples doing the slow drag would "just grind back and forth in one spot all night." The daughter of a honky-tonk owner remembered women doing the "funky butt," a dance in which they "pulled up their dresses to show their pretty petticoats." One woman had a reputation for "pulling up her skirts and grinding her rear end like an alligator crawling up a bank."[74] Touching, caressing, and bumping—all characterized the dances that took place in working-class establishments and that spilled over into the street itself.

The bodies of the black working class, dressed in flashy clothing and moving to their own rhythm, threatened middle-class control over the public representation of blackness. As Tera W. Hunter has noted in her study of black working-class Atlanta, however, critics may have over-reacted, at least when it came to clothing. Hunter observes that early-twentieth-century photographs of dance halls feature women who largely appropriated middle-class styles and then added "their own twist," like skirts that hugged the hips and thus showed off the buttocks.[75] For some critics, the issue may have been that nighttime revelers did not, in fact, take the time to dress up before going out. Woods complained of women dancing "in soiled aprons and unironed dresses," suggesting they beat a hasty path from work to play.[76]

Still, middle-class critics felt the need to take action. One of the most important body rituals of the urban black South—the fashion show—was born, in part, of this disdain for working-class black style. A ritual that first appeared in black communities in the 1920s, the fashion show helped middle- and upper-middle-class black women establish themselves as the arbiters of good taste.[77] As such, these events were much more than a re-sponse to blacks' exclusion from the fashion shows sponsored by major departments stores. Like their extension service counterparts, shows re-flected the unique experience of black women, though the element of up-lift was somewhat muted by organizers' class interests. Home demonstra-tion agents hoped to help farm women learn new ways of dressing. While fashion show organizers may have hoped to teach working-class women the elements of style, they were just as concerned with refining the skills of those already in the middle class and with burnishing their image among whites: organizers seem to have never invited working-class women to be models.

Cities all over the country—New York, Chicago, Kansas City—hosted fashion shows in the early to mid-1920s. In the South, New Orleans boasted one of the biggest and, purportedly, most successful. The first Crescent City Style Show was held in 1926 and served as a fund-raiser for a charitable cause in the local African American community, an ar-rangement that tied the showcasing of black female bodies to racial up-lift. In this case, the proceeds went to Straight College, one of the institu-tions that later merged to form Dillard University. An informal association of the city's middle-class matrons promoted the event in the local black newspaper, the *Louisiana Weekly*. Early publicity predicted that the event would be "the greatest and most elaborate show of its kind staged in the South" but would still be "similar in all respects to those shows of the

East and North," an assertion that suggests the centrality of the major metropolitan centers of the Northeast as fashion and cultural capitals in the minds of black southerners.[78] The success of the fashion show relied on proving that black New Orleanians were not hostages of a distinct or "backward" southern style. The local black community, moreover, was not the show's only audience. Organizers and participants hoped to capture the attention of white New Orleanians as well. They were noted to have taken an "unusual interest" in the event and were being given a few seats at the affair.[79]

The fashion show did draw a big turnout on 16 April 1926. Capacity crowds overtaxed the theater where 300 young girls and women from the city modeled the season's latest trends. The second annual fashion gala in 1927 moved to a larger theater to accommodate increased interest. The goal this second year was the same, though organizers strengthened their aesthetic authority by incorporating the city's most elite young black women, the year's crop of debutantes, as models. The event was even more successful than the first. The women's social page editor thanked the organizers for helping local ladies pick out appropriate spring and summer wardrobes. "[T]hey are better able to discriminate in their respective choices," she wrote, "and they owe much of this valuable information to the excellent work of the Style Show."[80] This project of teaching women how to be discriminating in their clothing choices found enthusiastic proponents in nearby Baton Rouge, where local women also sponsored their first fashion show in 1926, as well as in most southern cities with a sizeable black middle class. The ritual proved eminently adaptable. In New Orleans, alone, style shows quickly became regular events on the annual calendars of schools, churches, and civic organizations. Revolving around the commercial exploitation of the female form, fashion shows came down on the side of propriety. They established the parameters of good taste and raised money for a good cause. Fashion shows also highlighted the existence of hundreds of dignified, well-dressed urban black women.

Sometimes, the fashion show appears to have served a different, subversive function. Such was the case in small-town Indianola, Mississippi, where one black church sponsored a fashion show with the theme "A Night in Paris." The female models, members of the town's black upper and middle classes, staged an elaborate performance in which they paraded in front of the audience before being seated at a table and served tea by a young girl dressed as a maid. Then the models enjoyed various musical acts, such as one by a young woman who played a Brahms waltz that, she proudly announced, she had learned in Germany. "Loud laughter greets her sally," fashion show attendee Hortense Powdermaker remarked, "as everyone knows she has never been out of Mississippi." Contestants, for their part, engaged in conversations intended for the amusement of the audience. Powdermaker reported that they talked "in affected tones about the banking situation, and throw in a remark *en passant* about Roland Hayes," a famous African American tenor.[81] At the end of the event, one woman at each table won a prize, an honor bestowed not because of the superiority of her clothes but because of the superiority of her performance. For the black women of Indianola, the show may have advertised their fashion sense, but it also provided a forum for the mocking of social pretension.[82] The participants were ridiculing whites, though the reference to Hayes suggests that they may have been poking fun at the black elite in big cities—at the posturing of their own race—as well.

Also arising from the demands of modern consumer culture, the black beauty contest offered African Americans another means to make a statement using black women's bodies. Organizers hoped to challenge the widely held view among whites—and among some blacks—that most black women were unattractive by exhibiting their forms and faces. Yet attempting to harness the possibilities of black beauty while showcasing the distinctiveness of black women was tricky. What version of black feminine beauty was best suited to contradict racist assumptions about black women? In the case of the black beauty contest, skin color and, to a lesser extent, hair texture proved the focal points.

Among the most enthusiastic sponsors of early competitions were African American newspapers and magazines, particularly the widely read urban periodicals with national audiences. Using photographic beauty competitions to increase circulation and occasionally to sell products, these publications pitted city against city in the search for the most beautiful black women, locating their contests at the nexus of commercialism and race pride. No doubt this emphasis on racial uplift made photo contests a relatively easy gimmick to swallow (as opposed to bathing beauty revues, for example), but so, too, did the medium of portrait photography, firmly established by the turn of the century as an acceptable and desirable trapping of bourgeois respectability.[83] Black southerners in cities read these periodicals and submitted photographs of local women, and rural southerners were privy to the contests, too. The poorest residents among them may have lacked the resources to submit photos, but articles about the contests and letters to the editor show that blacks in the rural South closely followed the competitions as they unfolded in each new issue.

*Half-Century*, Anthony Overton's magazine, ran a typical photograph contest in 1921 under the heading "Who Is the Prettiest Colored Girl in the United States?"[84] Soliciting photographs from readers all over the country, editors spoke directly to women themselves, especially to those who might think that they did not conform to accepted ideals of black beauty. The magazine insisted that all women should send in their photo. "Don't hesitate," it insisted, "because you do not consider yourself unusually good looking."[85] Six months into the magazine's effort to find the most beautiful colored woman in America, the publication began to justify the event in more pointed language: "Many white people are under the impression that there are no pretty Colored women. We want to show them that there are many Colored beauties of varying types. Let us show them that all beautiful hair is not straight, that all beautiful skin is not white, that all the pretty profiles do not belong to members of the white race, that all beautiful contours are not possessed by white women."[86] In the next several issues, editors printed a selection of photographs drawn randomly from the submissions. The majority of those featured were of light-skinned women, a function, perhaps, of the publication's middle-class sensibility, or of readers' own assumptions about what type of beauty would triumph in the end. Still, the contest reveals a concern of this black publication over the valuation of light skin and straight hair, reminding us that these issues were at the center of some black beauty contests from the beginning, long before Black Pride proponents in the 1960s criticized the rituals for being discriminatory.

The *Half-Century* contest also indicates the reach and influence of periodical-sponsored beauty competitions in the South.[87] Letters to the editor referencing the contest came from large cities such as New Orleans and Nashville, as well as from places such as Sugarnoochie, Mississippi, Dripping Springs, Texas, and Waycross, Georgia. The coterie of contestants was predominantly southern as well. Throughout 1921, the magazine included full-page updates with photos of hopefuls and information about their hometowns. Over half of the forty-four women whose pictures were randomly chosen hailed from southern states. The winner of the beauty contest was never announced in the pages of *Half-Century*. The reason for this odd omission is unclear. The last mention of the contest came in a letter from a male reader in Vicksburg, Mississippi. He complained that the magazine had ended its search for the most beautiful black woman too soon, failing to highlight the feminine pulchritude of his home state. "There are no prettier girls in the country than those in Mississippi," he asserted. "There are several in this town who are pretty enough to carry off a prize in any contest."[88]

Other national beauty competitions for black women followed *Half-Century*'s. These contests increasingly responded to black women's exclusion from the beauty competition whose title suggested it was the most national of all—the Miss America contest. In 1925, Madame Mamie Hightower of the Golden Brown Chemical Company, a cosmetics concern headquartered in Memphis, sponsored the Golden Brown National Beauty Contest. A photo contest advertised by the black press, it was not a bathing beauty revue, but the Miss America competition clearly informed its design. The Golden Brown competition culminated in Atlantic City. Awarding diamond rings to thirty state winners, including twelve women from southern states, organizers sent five finalists from among a total field of 1,400 hopefuls to the resort city, where a winner, Miss Josephine Leggett of Louisiana, was crowned and given the keys to a new car.[89]

The Golden Brown event melded racial uplift with business acumen. Helping to boost newspaper circulation numbers and her own company's bottom line, Hightower argued that in sponsoring the contest she wanted to "prove once and for all" that America boasted some of the most beautiful black women in the world. The ultimate goal in doing so, she insisted, was to foster "in every member of our group, that quality known as pride." Claiming to be a former beauty parlor owner in Memphis, Hightower followed other beauty culturists, such as Madam C. J. Walker and Annie Turnbo Malone, in linking female appearance to race pride. But Hightower ultimately diverged markedly from Walker and Malone, and she did not go nearly as far as the organizers at *Half-Century* had in opening up the criteria for what qualified as beautiful. Black women did not want to be white, "but," she added, "we do want that light, bright, velvety textured skin that is rightfully ours."[90] She could hardly have said otherwise, given that the skin preparation made by the Golden Brown company was, as the name suggests, a face bleach. The actual identity of Mamie Hightower further compromised the project. Hightower was, in fact, a fictional beauty culturist who had been modeled on the wife of a black custodial employee at the white-owned Golden Brown Chemical Company. The winner of the contest, Miss Leggett, not surprisingly, was light-skinned.

The black bathing beauty revue revealed similar tensions on the local level. Leading the way in removing the revue from the seaside and placing it in a new context where there was no practical reason to wear a swimsuit, black urban jazz clubs sponsored revues to drum up business. Harlem's Savoy Ballroom is generally credited with sponsoring the first bathing beauty revue for black women in 1926 as a ploy to attract customers to the six-month-old establishment, but the bathing beauty contest found a home in a few southern African American communities as well. The Pelican Roof Garden Club in New Orleans held its second annual bathing beauty contest in 1928, advertised as "one of the grandest and most elaborate affairs of its kind ever held [in the] South." The Miss America Pageant loomed large at this event, too, as the club was "landscaped into a big beach, the stage representing aristocratic Atlantic City, with sea, sand, beach parasols and lounging pillars."[91] Although the organizers of the New Orleans bathing beauty revue were less explicit about their goals than photograph contest sponsors, the event was a statement of pride, as well as of protest over black women's exclusion from all-white contests; the reference to Atlantic City was a clear indication of the latter. A publicity photograph of four contestants in the *Louisiana Weekly* shows three light-skinned women and one woman with darker skin.[92]

Press coverage of black bathing beauty revues declined in the mid-1920s, a fact that, for Shane White and Graham White, shows that their novelty was over.[93] Although the newness may have worn off, the bathing beauty revue was, arguably, a body ritual that some in the black community were simply less willing to sanction than the fashion show, which remained popular. Problematic for white southern women in the 1920s, the bathing beauty revue was potentially more disconcerting for black southerners worried about perceptions of black womanhood. While bathing beauty revues raised questions about the morality of white women, most black women struggled to prove their morality in the first place. The revue did provide an arena for the celebratory display of black female bodies, but it did not challenge the traditional association of unbridled sexuality with black women. Like conspicuous, gaudy, and revealing clothing, a contest in which participants drew attention to their legs and breasts highlighted a femininity that, at this date, was not yet the hallmark of respectability and was thus a dubious catalyst of racial progress.

Regardless, all of these early body and beauty contests were symbolically significant, providing forums for members of the southern black community to counter demeaning images. The timing of their emergence is worth noting as well. Interested in racial representation since emancipation, African Americans living in the 1920s were also living through the years of the Harlem Renaissance, whose intellectual and artistic luminaries debated how to create, as Martha Nadell has written, "an appropriate and useful racial aesthetic" to counter the array of racial stereotypes inherited from the nineteenth century.[94] These efforts to define the New Negro refuted older physical representations of African Americans, celebrating the black body in ways intended to defy caricature, pushing it into public view through the vehicle of art.

The impact of the visual and literary treatises of the Harlem Renaissance on most southern blacks is unclear, but this larger cultural project of displaying black bodies in new ways—this search for an appropriate and useful aesthetic—infused black culture throughout the decade. As we have seen, the search for a new body aesthetic in the South belittled the value of certain representational and performative styles and sometimes elevated a look that seemed a concession to white beauty standards. For young women who were to be race leaders, the search, and its consequences, defined their formative years.

BLACK SOUTHERN WOMEN participated in body rituals that were shaped by both rural and urban contexts. One of the most critical settings for debates over the meanings of black beauty, and eventually of rituals celebrating it, was an institution with a kind of hybrid quality: the black college. Southern black normal schools, seminaries, and colleges were spaces-in-between—in geographical, class, and generational terms. On the campuses of these institutions, poor students from the countryside and urban neighborhoods came under the supervision of more refined middle-class administrations, which were initially dominated by whites but gradually included middle-class blacks. Student tastes clashed with those of administrators and teachers, resulting in a continual battle to define the appropriate look for young black women.

Established by northern philanthropists, mission societies, the Freedmen's Bureau, and freedmen and -women themselves in the years after the Civil War, black southern colleges educated the individuals deemed the most capable of leading the race. As training grounds for preachers, teachers, and homemakers, these institutions were charged with a difficult job. They aimed to impart the knowledge that graduates would need to do their life's work. At the same time, schools were to transform their pupils into specimens of ideal manhood and womanhood, individuals who would stand as living testaments to black potential, black talent, and black virtue. This ambitious program was taxing in the early years, when the vast majority of students came from homes with meager resources—from the homes, quite often, of former slaves. Such deprivations weighed heavily on academic leaders. Institutional publications underscore administrators' determination to break students of the bad personal habits handed down by their slave forebears and magnified by contemporary poverty. Moreover, at institutions run by missionary associations—schools such as Fisk, Spelman, and Straight (later Dillard)—personal transformations were guided and supervised by whites. As James Anderson has noted, white administrators displayed "paternalistic tendencies" that were largely kept in check by a "principled liberalism," but some of the tensions between faculty and students must have been a product of complicated racial dynamics on campus.[95]

One of the most striking things about the literature published by black colleges is the degree to which the improvement of the body was the focal point at institutions ostensibly dedicated to the improvement of the mind. This fact resulted from a simple assumption. Administrators believed that their educational mission rested on the ability to control their students, which meant, ultimately, the ability to control their bodies.[96] Dress codes that prescribed detailed rules for dress and deportment were crucial, especially when it came to female students. Founded in 1865 by the Freedmen's Bureau and the American Missionary Association, Fisk University in Nashville offers a typical example. Although the school was interested in cultivating "the truest form of Christian manhood and womanhood," Fisk insisted in its 1893–94 catalog that the "highest interest of every race and community depends largely upon the intelligence, frugality, virtue, and noble aspirations of its women."[97] Administrators argued that this truth had "unusual force in its application to the future well-being of the colored people of the South," a widely held conviction in the late nineteenth century.[98] As black men were being systematically cut off from the body politic by disfranchisement and racial violence, many leaders were forced to conclude, according to Deborah Gray White, that "the uplift of women was the means of uplifting the race," and so focused on women as the race's saving grace.[99] Through their role as mothers, black women could go a long way toward raising the fortunes of the race at a time when black male political power was all but nonexistent. While southern black colleges had dress codes for their male and female students, they imbued the regulations for women with special import.[100] The consequences of black women failing to present themselves well seemed all the more serious during the nadir of southern race relations.

At the coeducational Fisk, women's appearance and conduct were "carefully guarded." In addition to shunning alcohol, tobacco, gambling, and profanity, women were to ensure that their clothing was not simply practical but also "becoming." Becoming clothing, however, meant plain clothing. "Those who bring extravagant and unnecessary finery," the college catalog announced, "will be required to lay it aside while in the University."[101] The emphasis on plainness, and the concurrent injunction against extravagance, dominated the dress codes of most black colleges in the late nineteenth and early twentieth centuries. Proscriptions against "showy or expensive dress" and pleas for "simplicity" were the most common refrains, though some schools felt compelled to spell out exactly what they meant. In anticipation of the 1885–86 school year, Atlanta University, also supported by the American Missionary Association, asserted that "silks, velvets and jewelry worn by girls are indicative neither of good taste nor good sense."[102]

Several concerns prompted the writing of these regulations. As institutions with religious as well as educational missions, black southern colleges hoped to instill in their female students a respect for the Christian virtues of modesty, sincerity, and thrift. The vanity, artifice, and sexuality promoted by modern consumer culture were considered inappropriate for young Christian women. This was especially true for those who were to shoulder the responsibility of race uplift. Teachers and administrators expected their pupils to exhibit neatness and cleanliness of person, then, but they did not want them to become obsessed with the intricacies of fashion, embody a false beauty, or raise questions about their virtue.

Permitting fine clothing and jewelry might have further undesirable consequences, encouraging noxious competition among female students. Schools envisioned their dress regulations as one way, according to Atlanta University, to "promote the interests of true democracy" and prevent conflicts between students from different class backgrounds.[103] Though some students could afford the latest fashions, many others could not. The daughters of Atlanta's growing black middle class, for example, attended the all-female Spelman Seminary, a Baptist school with elementary, high school, and college preparatory departments, but so, too, did women born into poverty. As late as 1905, fewer than half of the day students came from families that owned their own homes. In the 1920s, the majority of students were from rural or working-class families.[104] Spelman, which became a four-year liberal arts college in 1924, often felt compelled to remind its female students that their very presence on campus was the result of great financial sacrifice and that extravagant dressing habits only further burdened their families.

Finally, behind nearly every regulation governing how young women dressed was the goal of helping them rise above their rural or working-class origins. Requirements that clothing be "inconspicuous," "in good taste," and not "showy" reflected this interest. Many female students adorned their bodies in ways that betrayed both their meager backgrounds and their inability to follow accepted aesthetic norms. Their dressing habits proclaimed their race, in short, but not in the way school officials wanted. Spelman admonished students to avoid "loud, inharmonious colors, extreme styles, and inappropriate materials" and instead to embrace clothes that were "quiet in color, style and material."[105] At Spelman and other schools with large day-student populations, administrators also had to worry about students who did not spend all of their time on campus. Women who returned home to their families every day, and who were free to wander through the streets of Atlanta, could easily fall back into habits that were at odds with those the school was trying to inculcate. And these habits of self-presentation were directly related to habits of character. Spelman administrators, supervising their students only two miles away from Decatur Street, put the issue this way: cheap jewelry and "showy and immodest styles and materials will be carefully avoided by the cultured and virtuous."[106]

Respectable style bred virtuous behavior; virtuous behavior necessitated respectable style. And both had to be policed. Indeed, most southern black colleges closely linked dress regulations with conduct regulations. Proper dress meant little without good behavior, which turned on the disciplining of youthful black bodies. While schools such as Howard and Fisk also used military training to achieve the desired result in their male charges, most colleges relied on daily deportment regulations as their primary tactic for female students.[107] Spelman required women to practice obedience, courtesy, industry, and "good order," or bodily self-control.[108] The specter of the loud, promiscuous, working-class black woman haunted the men and women who ran these religious institutions. In their approach to molding models of Christian womanhood, morality, dress, and deportment were intimately intertwined. Administrators believed the Victorian tenet that a woman's inner virtue manifested itself in

Spelman Seminary High School graduates, Atlanta, 1887. These graduates embodied Spelman's emphasis on respectable black womanhood. Courtesy of the Photograph Collection, Spelman College, Atlanta, Ga.

her outward appearance and behavior. Spelman officials announced that they were focusing "all our energies toward developing the characters of our girls and we expect the result to reveal itself in the way a girl dresses and conducts herself."[109] But colleges could not guarantee that character alone would have the desired result, and so young women often received grades for their outward appearance to encourage conformity to acceptable standards. Presbyterian Stillman College in Tuscaloosa, Alabama, for example, graded students on deportment and required minimal proficiency in the subject for graduation.[110]

Photographs from black schools and colleges in the late nineteenth and early twentieth centuries show that female students fulfilled administration wishes, at least for these highly staged moments. Images of Spelman students in the 1880s feature assemblages of dignified young women holding hats and parasols, wearing attractive but modest dresses adorned with broaches and the occasional corsage. The appearance of these women was virtually indistinguishable from that of white coeds at other colleges in the North and South.[111] But this achievement came at a high price for the daughters of poor black families unschooled in the mores of respectability. A Baptist missionary reported in the 1890s that some Spelman women encountered resistance to their new style and behavioral patterns during their vacation trips home. Family members, the missionary wrote, called them "big-headed" or "too fine."[112] Seen to be turning their backs on rural folkways, Spelman women embodied the contradictions inherent in the strategy of racial self-representation pushed by black schools and suffered the consequences among their own families. White southerners, it seems, were not necessarily alone in feeling that black women should avoid trying to rise above their station by adopting new ways of dress and deportment. Such performances could be problematic on both sides of the color line.

These photographs also foreground an issue about which the text of college handbooks and student publications is silent—skin color. As sites where black class privilege and white assumptions about skin color met, black colleges could be brutal in honoring what Maxine Leeds Craig has called the "pigmentocracy."[113] Mamie Garvin Fields, as we have seen, chose not to attend the Avery Normal Institute in Charleston because she feared that her darker complexion would limit her social and educational horizons at the school. Her fears may have been well-founded, as reports of prejudice based on skin color were not uncommon at Avery and other black normal schools and colleges.[114] During her first week of classes as a freshman at North Carolina College for Negroes, Mary Mebane was called to a meeting by an English instructor who expressed surprise that she had earned the highest score on the English entrance exam. Mebane suspected the instructor doubted the results because of her dark complexion. "The faculty assumed that light-skinned students were more intelligent," Mebane later observed, "and they were always a bit nonplussed when a dark-skinned student did well, especially if she was a girl."[115]

No southern black college would have been so impolitic as to codify regulations regarding skin color as they did with rules of dress. But rumors that places such as Fisk and Spelman required successful applicants to pass a color test—even if they were not true—spoke to widely held perceptions about the kinds of women most likely to enroll.[116] In 1930 Alice Dunbar-Nelson visited South Carolina State College for Negroes, which, she had heard, required that prospective students submit a photograph with their application. "That is a joke," she wrote in her diary, "but from the looks of the student body it looks like a reality."[117] Howard University, long considered the "capstone of Negro education," did ask that students send a photo when they applied to the university in the early decades of the twentieth century.[118] The administration contended that the pictures were used to identify students after they enrolled. Still, well into the 1950s and 1960s, school lore held that prospective students with darker skin were disqualified on the basis of their photos and that the paper bag test—by which individuals with a complexion darker than a brown paper lunch bag were deemed too dark—determined one's social prospects on campus. "For the most part," one alumnus remembered, "if you were dark, you were not accepted."[119] Hair mattered, too. A Howard alumna said a friend who was dark felt she never fit in because of her hair. It was too short, so she wore a scarf to create the illusion of length. Over time, certain schools, such as Tuskegee and Bethune-Cookman, became known as refuges for young women with the "wrong" skin tone. The consequences of this kind of prejudice became self-fulfilling, as poorer, dark-complexioned women were more likely to pursue an industrial curriculum that prepared them for manual labor and domestic service.[120]

Regardless of the class status of their student bodies, in the years after World War I many of these schools saw tensions between students and administrators rise. As black coeds' access to consumer goods increased, college administrators attempted to crack down on the new flapper style, which undermined the decades of body work they had undertaken.[121] It was bad enough that their students were already partial to an aesthetic noteworthy for its inappropriate conspicuousness. The flapper positively exuded ostentatious consumption and, even more disconcertingly, modern sexuality. She personified the desire for bodily freedom, heightening its potential challenge to female virtue and racial integrity.

The new look forced colleges to formulate more intricate dress codes in an effort to assert the respectability of their female students. By the early 1920s, Atlanta University had devised a long list of dress regulations that detailed everything from what kinds of materials were acceptable to what kinds of jewelry were appropriate. "No georgette, net, chiffon, or similarly thin material can be worn; neither can silk, satin or velvet," one catalog read, adding that "shoes with French heels"—an essential accoutrement of the flapper—were also off-limits.[122] Nearby Spelman, according to one Atlanta University student, went further. To Lucy Rucker, Spelman women seemed more conservative in their dress than did her classmates. They were even required, she said, to wear white gloves every time they went into town.[123] At Fisk, discontent with these kinds of regulations— along with rules requiring chapel attendance, limiting mixed-sex socializing, and prohibiting dancing and listening to jazz—coalesced into a student strike in 1925. The clash crystallized the larger, generational struggle raging within black colleges, one that pitted, in Martin Summers's words, the "the exuberant body" against "the disciplined body." Within two years, a committee of faculty and students had devised a new dress code that, while still emphasizing female modesty, lacked strict rules against certain colors and materials.[124]

Proscriptions against showy dress did work at some institutions. Nannie Helen Burroughs imposed regulations on her students at the National Training School for Women and Girls in Washington, D.C., a Baptist secondary institution that offered occupational training. A dean of nearby Howard University noted after visiting the school in 1926 that they had the desired effect. Flappers were nowhere to be found. "[F]or this let us give thanks," Dean Kelly Miller declared. "You can never build womanhood of a strong and sterling race upon the basis of the flapper."[125] Pleased with Miller's pronouncement, and convinced that it could win over parents concerned about sending their daughters away to school, Burroughs used Kelly's remarks in promotional pamphlets for the institution.[126] Elsewhere struggles between students and administrators were intense. As a student at Shaw University in Raleigh, North Carolina, Ella Baker was asked by a group of her female peers in 1922 to lead a protest against the campus prohibition against silk stockings. Though not overly concerned with winning the freedom to wear such trendy items herself, Baker, known for her assertiveness, agreed. In response, the dean punished the petitioners with nightly chapel attendance. Baker was called in to the dean's office and forced to pray for forgiveness. She refused to admit any wrongdoing, causing the dean such distress that she actually fainted.[127]

Administrators at Spelman, too, had a hard time preventing their pupils from following the latest fashions. In 1927, two English artists visited the institution at the beginning of the academic year during their tour of the South, stopping in to give a lecture and later recording their observations for a published travelogue. The Englishwomen noted that Spelman students seemed to bristle under the administration's regulations and eagerly awaited the opening convocation to see if the school president had finally given in to the fashion for "high heels of extra height." The students were disappointed and "heaved a united sigh of resignation" once they saw her marching down the aisle in her traditional Oxfords. The observation suggests that Spelman women owned high heels, just as they must have owned other banned items that they donned surreptitiously in the city, within the privacy of their own dorm rooms, and on special occa-

Spelman College Senior Class, Atlanta, 1929. As the flapper look became popular in the 1920s, administrators at schools like Spelman increasingly struggled to dictate the clothing choices of students. Courtesy of the Photograph Collection, Spelman College, Atlanta, Ga.

sions. The foreign travelers also commented on the color choices of the assembled students, revealing that regulations may not have been as effective in erasing traditional tastes as school officials may have liked: "They did not know that, because the traditional Mammy wore bright colours, therefore bright colors were taboo; so they wore what colours they liked and made a pretty bouquet as they filed into chapel on a morning."[128] Some among the Spelman student body, which was still comprised of a significant number of working-class students, may have clung tenaciously to a look that felt comfortable and familiar or, alternatively, that they could little afford to abandon. The daughter of a poor black farmer in Arkansas who entered Spelman in the fall of 1937 reported having made much of her wardrobe before arriving on campus and having inherited certain items from her neighbors.[129] As a student at North Carolina College for Negroes, Mary Mebane had no choice but to wear the clothes her family's meager income allowed. One teacher reprimanded her nonetheless, criticizing an outfit that combined stripes and checks.[130] Mebane was humiliated, but for many female college students like her, conforming to an acceptable dress aesthetic was cost prohibitive.

Some schools, such as Spelman, seem to have taken an unusually hard line with their students, while many northern and southern colleges, white and black, slowly gave in to student desires.[131] Whatever the exact dynamics on black college campuses, the earliest body and beauty contests for female students were designed to encourage young women to conform to the school's ideals of dress and conduct—at ensuring that the exuberant body remained in check. Straight College in Tuscaloosa offered the Valena MacArthur Jones Prize throughout the 1920s and 1930s. Named for the wife of a Presbyterian bishop, the prize of ten dollars went to the young woman who that year had made "the best record for deportment." There were six requirements, including "simplicity in dress, neatness, tidiness as well as appropriateness," "moral integrity," and "lady-like bearing in relation to young men."[132] The expectations of Straight's young men seem to have been less exacting, as the men's prize went to the student who consistently kept his dorm room the neatest.

Spelman envisioned its May Day along the same lines. In the interwar years, Spelman women orchestrated the annual spring rite, inviting each dormitory to put forth a court with a queen and attendants. The event included a processional and dances, ending with the queens mounting their thrones to the applause of the excited audience. Finally, according to the Spelman *Messenger*'s account of the festivities in 1928, "The queens with their thrones and attendants were then judged on the basis of appropriateness, color harmony, simplicity and gracefulness."[133] The criteria for evaluating the young maidens reinforced the prescriptive tenets to which students were held. The way the participants in the May Day celebration moved and dressed demonstrated their internalization of body rules rooted in restraint and understatement, though not all students proved so tractable. That same year, Florence Read, Spelman president and dedicated Oxfords-wearer, assembled the younger students for a special meeting in which she pleaded with them to "dress more like sensible students with cultural tastes than like lilies of the field."[134]

The Spelman May Day celebration portended beauty contests at many southern black colleges. Embracing a ritual whose modern incarnations were indebted to the same consumer forces they condemned, administrators began to use the symbolic power of beauty contests for a variety of goals that constituted the college's raison d'être. At a host of black col-

Bennett College May Day court, Greensboro, North Carolina, ca. 1930. May Day celebrations at southern black colleges allowed female students to indulge their love of finery and still exude the kind of femininity administrations valued. Courtesy of the Thomas F. Holgate Library, Bennett College, Greensboro, N.C.

leges in the South, beauty contests emerged in the 1930s and 1940s as deft combinations of the themes that for decades had peppered administrative rhetoric regarding the ideal collegiate woman—the uplift of the race through finer womanhood, the disciplining of the female body, and the mastery of a respectable aesthetic.

Homecoming queen competitions were among the most prominent of this new breed of competition, receiving considerable publicity in publications on and off campus. Spelman's 1937 homecoming queen contest was typical. Selected by the men of nearby Morehouse, Spelman's brother college, the queen was held up as the embodiment of the highest ideals of black womanhood during the homecoming parade and at the football game. Crowned at halftime in front of a throng of admirers, she was not allowed, however, to participate in the highlight of the homecoming celebration. "Spelman was very strict, and I couldn't even go to the dance afterward," Eloise Ulcher Belcher recalled nearly seventy years after the event. "So after the football game, I went back to my dorm."[135] Belcher's beauty, and the respectable femininity to which it pointed, reflected well on the school, showcasing how it cultivated the character of young black

Dillard University homecoming court, New Orleans, 1950. The ensembles of the women on this homecoming court received more attention than the football game in the student newspaper. Courtesy of the Special Collections and Archives, Will W. Alexander Library, Dillard University, New Orleans, La.

women. But the beauty ritual also reinforced the bodily control she was to observe as a young lady. Belcher's participation in the queen coronation was, in fact, premised upon her not attending the dance, a setting in which the female body might enjoy too much freedom and flirt dangerously close to crossing the line separating moral from immoral. Celebrating her physical beauty but denying her sexuality, the contest furthered the school's body project. Her fellow classmates, presumably, were unable to attend the dance as well, and so Morehouse men likely enjoyed the company of female students from other nearby colleges. Six years later, Spelman women could at least go to Morehouse dances, but complaints about being forced "to march sedately" instead of being allowed to do any real dancing suggest the administration had come only so far.[136]

Like fashion shows, black college beauty rituals honed women's aesthetic sensibilities. Although they rewarded beauty and popularity, homecoming queen contests also rewarded good fashion sense. The dress of the homecoming queen and her attendants became the focus of annual events. Press coverage of the court members' wardrobes rivaled odes to their personal beauty and even eclipsed analysis of the football games. The student newspaper at Dillard ran a typical article about Miss Dillard Inez Lawrence and her court, devoting most of the space to what the young women wore to the game: "Her highness, Miss Inez Lawrence, the 'Homecoming Queen,' was presented a beautiful bouquet by President Dent. She was most charming in a navy blue velveteen suit-dress designed with a tiered skirt and a tight-fitting jacket set off with rhinestone buttons, and made with dolman sleeves and a wide collar. A white satin cloak, suede gloves, blue suede bag and sandals made her outfit complete." The suits of the four other young women on the court received equal attention. With their hair immaculately arrayed and topped with attractive hats, the young homecoming honorees, chosen by vote of the student body, projected the height of dignified womanhood in the accompanying photo. The ladies reportedly changed clothes for the dance, and their elegant evening ensembles were also described in detail by the paper. Other aspects of the homecoming festivities were less newsworthy. About the game, the writer noted briefly that it was "extremely well-contested."[137] Sanctioned by the administration, the competitions helped inculcate in female students a respect for the principles of style by elevating certain looks over those deemed unsuitable.

As the Dillard article also makes clear, the rituals allowed female students to indulge their love of fads and finery, an interest that colleges were unable to squelch despite the tradition of restrictive sartorial regulations. New cultural currents facilitated coeds' pursuit of fashion and beauty by the late 1940s and early 1950s. The emphasis on consumerism, and its crucial civic function to an economy recovering from years of Depression and war, removed some of the stigma associated with conspicuous consumption on campus.[138] Many Americans, white and black, enjoyed a newfound ability to consume during the postwar years. But that was not all. The concurrent conflation of consumption with democratic ideals offered opportunities to African Americans. By participating in mass consumption, middle-class blacks advanced their claim to full citizenship. For black women, buying fashionable clothes—constructing themselves as epitomes of femininity and middle-class status—was one way to support this larger goal.[139]

On black college campuses, a détente emerged. Administrators were now less likely to view their female students' fashion desires as problematic. Beauty contests of this era represented a kind of compromise between administrators and students—antagonists who had been at odds for decades over how much energy female students should spend trying to be fashionable, which was not the same thing, as we have seen, as being merely respectable. Miss Dillard and her attendants, while not exactly ostentatious or "showy" in their respective outfits, certainly did not pay homage at the altar of "simplicity," long the ideal for which young black women were to strive. Indeed, some colleges began to pay for homecoming queens' ensembles with student fees.[140] Campus publications also indicate that black college women followed fashion trends even more closely at midcentury than before. Newspapers and magazines ran regular ads for local dress shops and department stores, as well as lengthy fashion columns in which coeds dispensed fashion tips and commented on the style of their fellow female students. Fashion writers congratulated young women who kept up with the latest trends, singling out those who had done especially well each season. "Elaine Ziegler," the Dillard columnist wrote characteristically in the spring of 1949, "won't you ever run out of beautiful new suits? . . . Cynthia Butler, please give me your blue corduroy dress." She concluded with a nod to "Marcell Ray and Joy Whitefield [who] show us how to keep our hair long, beautiful and well-groomed and at the same time look fine in general."[141]

Young women seem to have balanced a love of fashion with middle-class restraint, but columnists stood ready to step in when necessary to remind them of the rules to which they should adhere. These student critics showed that they did, in fact, place greater weight on the aesthetic of respectability than earlier generations of college women had. When their peers failed to do their part, postwar fashion columnists took note. "[G]irls, watch the colors, watch the colors," the Dillard fashion commentator wrote caustically in 1948. "It's a good thing we live in New Orleans where flowers bloom the year round, because we certainly have some floral minded young maids."[142] The Kentucky State University fashion columnist chastised female students for sloppiness and for "weird color combinations of solid colors and plaid and striped twosomes," which revealed "bad taste." Dress appropriately, she intoned, for "when you leave your room for any occasion . . . [t]he eyes of Kentucky are upon YOU."[143]

The eyes of Louisiana were upon Dillard women, too. In a telling observation, the Dillard columnist announced that the women on campus "still have complaints" about the expectations for male dress. Dillard men, it seems, did not go to class in formal attire. "We think if the girls have to wear long dresses," she wrote, "the young men should at least wear dark suits."[144] While it is unclear whether official regulations or custom determined this disparity, women at Dillard conformed to a more formal dress standard than their male peers well into the twentieth century. They also received a tutorial on the principles of dress during freshman week and were encouraged to attend the school's "Charm Clinic," which sponsored sessions throughout the year.[145] The assumption that women still bore a unique bodily burden in representing the race resonated on black southern campuses. Dillard women may have resented that this responsibility fell to them, but acquiring fashionable clothes was a separate matter, and they did so with enthusiasm.

Midcentury beauty contests complemented these fashion columns, continuing to frame the black female body as a vessel for racial progress. The women who won homecoming and other beauty contest titles on college campuses almost always made a public promise to their peers that they would embody the values the school held dear. A Miss Stillman from the late 1950s, for example, announced that she would "forever uphold the ideals and qualities that 'Miss Stillman' should possess."[146] A queen of Dillard who was described by the campus paper, in routine fashion, as "attractive and gracious," said to her classmates, "I shall endeavor, with God as my guide, to live up to those standards that you have so faithfully entrusted to me."[147] A year's worth of exuding beauty and moral uprightness—of being widely recognized by all as "the fairest of the fair"—apparently was insufficient proof of success in certain places. So some queens reiterated their good intentions at the end of their reigns. "I have tried to the utmost of my capacity," one Stillman honoree avowed, "to uphold these traits and qualities that you think, and I, also think, Miss Stillman should possess."[148] Using language almost identical to that used by administrators, queens situated themselves as central players in colleges' efforts to raise the fortunes of the race and validated the importance of the female body in this endeavor.

Another high-profile system of black beauty contests in the South advanced the same argument in the post–World War II years. Founded in 1944 as a fund-raising organization for black higher education by forty-four historically black colleges and universities, the United Negro College Fund relied on the beauty of young college women in its primary fund-raising campaign each year. Sponsored at most member institutions, the Miss United Negro College Fund competition used beautiful coeds to raise money for scholarships. Miss UNCF competitions resembled a more traditional beauty contest in that they did not include a fashion component, but they did continue another practice embedded in black culture—commodifying the black female body for race uplift.

Campus winners of the Miss UNCF title usually rose to the top by succeeding at raising more money than their competitors and by doing well at a beauty pageant held during the fund-raising festivities. Local Miss UNCFs then traveled to the national contest where a national winner was crowned. Miss UNCF contests were occasionally construed as black analogues to the Miss America Pageant. The campus newspaper at Stillman College noted one year that the annual Miss UNCF beauty pageant had been anticipated in Tuscaloosa "with as much splendor and excitement as if it had been the Miss America Pageant," and that the "officials in Atlantic City, N.J. could not have worked any harder and more effectively" than had Stillman organizers and participants.[149] The veracity of these claims notwithstanding, it was true that Miss UNCF contests were seen to be providing much needed opportunities for the recognition of black southern women's beauty and of black womanhood more generally. Rivaling homecoming queen contests at black colleges—press coverage lasted for weeks and schools usually raised several thousand dollars for the fund—Miss UNCF contests honored beautiful women as the schools' ideal. Photographs of Miss UNCF winners feature radiant young women in beautiful evening gowns and tiaras, the very picture of feminine loveliness.

Not surprisingly, most of those same photos show black women with light or light-brown skin and straightened hair, as do images of black homecoming queens. In addition to all the other lessons taught by black colleges through the beauty contest from the 1930s to the early 1960s—lessons about dress and deportment, style and respectability—these same institutions seemed to be instilling another lesson as well. If young black women wanted to be recognized for their beauty, their chances would be much improved if they had skin that was not too dark and hair that was not too kinky. At many institutions, these attributes remained unspoken requisites for winning campus titles, but some schools did not shy away from acknowledging their importance. The newspaper at Kentucky State University, for example, stressed that the 1944 Campus Sweetheart contestants had fair skin and straight locks, celebrating hopefuls with "peaches and crème" complexions and "long, long, beautiful black hair."[150] As Karen Tice has noted, light-skinned women with pressed hair won beauty contests at Kentucky State until the 1970s.[151]

Publicly at least, few seemed to mind the veneration of these traits in campus beauty competitions. Soon, that complacency would disappear, as black students across the South questioned both the glorification of whiteness and the emphasis on respectable self-presentation that, they argued, supported it. Theirs was one of many challenges with which southerners would grapple in the coming years, a time that demonstrated how useful—how profoundly political—beautiful women's bodies, black and white, could be.

CHAPTER FIVE

# Bodies Politic

*Beauty and Racial Crisis
in the Civil Rights Era*

Lynda Lee Mead, a student at the University of Mississippi, was crowned Miss America in 1959 at the annual pageant in Atlantic City. Three months into her reign, having logged over 40,000 miles traveling around the United States and Europe, Mead returned to Mississippi for a homecoming celebration. Mississippians were proud to have her back. After a luncheon held in her honor in Jackson, an affair attended by "top state dignitaries," Mead paused to make an announcement to the press. During her three-month tour as the nation's top beauty, she had not once apologized for Mississippi. "And I won't," she concluded. "We have nothing to apologize for." The *Jackson Daily News* was happy to report that, as its headline read, "Lynda Lee Takes Up For Her State."

The article failed to say exactly why Mead felt compelled to defend her state's honor during visits to other states and countries, but the reason was clear enough. Mississippi had not, despite her claims to the contrary, shown itself to be a welcoming community of "wonderful people" in recent years.[1] A rash of racially motivated murders—including, most famously, the killing of fourteen-year-old Emmett Till in 1955 as well as a high-profile lynching just five months before her coronation—had rippled through the state. In response to the *Brown v. Board of Education* decision, Mississippi had also become home to the first Citizens' Councils, dedicated to fighting the Court's order to desegregate schools, and had even passed a constitutional amendment calling for the abolition of the public school system to prevent integration. Mississippi blacks, meanwhile, were on the offensive, attacking Jim Crow on all fronts. Seven months after Mead's victory at the Miss America Pageant, black protesters had led a "wade-in" in Biloxi

Anne Moody (seated, third from front) at a Jackson, Mississippi, sit-in, 1963. Homecoming queen and civil rights activist Anne Moody retreated to the safety and comfort of a beauty shop after being assaulted with food at a Jackson, Mississippi, sit-in. Courtesy of the photographer, Fred Blackwell.

to desegregate coastal beaches, the stomping ground of the state's white bathing beauties.[2]

Three years later, another beauty queen was in Jackson. She was black, not white, a participant in the movement to upend segregation in Mississippi. Anne Moody had been chosen her school's homecoming queen as an eighth grader, and in 1963, as a student at Tougaloo College, led a sit-in at the Woolworth's in downtown Jackson. Beaten and then thrown on the floor, Moody left the sit-in wondering if such efforts would ever bear fruit. Before returning to campus, with her hair and legs covered in the mustard, ketchup, and sugar that whites poured on her as she sat at the lunch counter, she stopped in at a beauty shop to see if the proprietor could wash her hair. "'My land, you were in the sit-in huh?'" the beautician exclaimed. She then moved her ahead of three women waiting in line and even, Moody wrote, "took my stockings off and washed my legs while my hair was drying."[3]

One woman had beamed beneath a sparkling tiara. The other, dirty and disheveled, retreated to a place where she could be made presentable again. Mead and Moody would likely have seen eye to eye on very little, but on one thing they might have agreed: beauty had a place in the civil rights movement. Chaos may have been raging in the streets of their home state, but appearances mattered. Given what had transpired during the preceding decades, it would be surprising to discover otherwise. Despite early misgivings over the propriety of modern beauty ideals and practices, female beauty had emerged over the course of the twentieth century as a private concern with public consequences. White southerners had turned to beauty for a variety of social and economic reasons, all of which, ultimately, served to sustain Jim Crow. Black southerners, conversely, had relied on their own pretty women as tools to tear it down.

Although some white southerners answered the siege of Jim Crow in the 1950s and 1960s with violence, others responded with massive resistance. The "respectable" form of opposition to desegregation, massive resistance encompassed a number of tactics, ranging from the legal to the extralegal, and from the political to the cultural. One of the most unusual fell into this last category—the use of female beauty. In response to African American demands for equality, white southerners turned to their beauty queens, especially to those affiliated with the Miss America Pageant. Showcased in the regional and national media, these beauties provided a genteel veneer to cover up the unsavory behavior some white southerners exhibited as they resisted black demands. Beauty queens also symbolized white supremacy and highlighted desegregation's threat to white female virtue.

That young white women would assume these functions followed logically from the problem. Since fears over their fate lay at the heart of anxieties over desegregation, white women, and the beauty that formed such a critical component of their racial identity, were bound to be a part of the solution. Examining white southern beauty queens during the civil rights era, then, shows how much white women's bodies undergirded massive resistance.[4] It ultimately widens our understanding of this larger campaign, allowing "the full textures and breadth of southern resistance to emerge," in George Lewis's words, rather than focusing on political responses to *Brown* or the major flashpoints, like Little Rock and Birmingham, of black activism and white defiance.[5]

Anne Moody's decision to seek out a beauty shop after suffering at the hands of an angry white mob made sense, too. Black beauticians had long presided over spaces of refuge, places where they labored to give confidence to black women forced to confront a hostile white public. During the tumultuous years of the civil rights movement, beauticians were poised to provide balm for emotionally and physically wounded activists. Even more significantly, they were well positioned to become civil rights activists themselves. Part of the beautician's job had always been to undermine Jim Crow by helping her clients and communities mitigate segregation's injustices. Using the shops over which they presided, and the institutional networks they had established, these independent business-women now sought to undo Jim Crow altogether. Throughout the South, they ranked among the most prominent grassroots activists during the civil rights movement.

By the mid-1960s, however, the very idea that their line of work held radical possibilities, that it was capable of promoting black equality and black welfare, came under attack. To younger black activists, the consumptive practices and aesthetic that beauticians championed were seen as impediments to progress, not catalysts. As the movement shifted away from its initial emphasis on integration and toward the separatist politics of Black Power, the aesthetic of respectability lost its appeal.[6] Defined by pressed hair, inconspicuous clothing, restraint, and its implicit valuation of lighter skin, this older conception of the black body struck some youth as a blind concession to white values, a holdover from an outdated and ineffective strategy for winning black rights.

The struggle to formulate a new look for black women (and men) revealed cleavages of politics and generation and represented one of the many ways black youth challenged the boundary between bourgeois values and revolutionary aesthetics.[7] Once again, the black college campus provided the backdrop for heated conversations about the appropriate appearance of black women. College students argued that "Black is Beautiful" and praised dark skin, unpressed hair, and bold, African-inspired clothing. They commandeered campus beauty contests to promote this new aesthetic among women, depriving administrators of one of the tools they had deployed for decades to control potentially wayward female students.

The very different responses of white and black southerners to the prospect of dismantling segregation and assimilating into the national mainstream thus relied on a common tactic. Both used female beauty to advance their case. In the pitched debate that played out during these years, beautiful black and white women were invoked as symbols of their race; indeed, they *were* their race, representing blackness and whiteness through face and form. This was hardly an unfamiliar role, of course, for either group. What was new was that a captive national audience increasingly paid attention to, and approved of, the way white southern women embodied their racial identity. For black southern women, what was new, by the mid to late 1960s, was the idea that they needed to change how they embodied theirs, that they needed to be more racially authentic than their forebears had been.

There was, finally, the degree to which the bodies of white and black southern women helped inform race during these years. The civil rights movement was in many ways the moment when this long-standing tradition reached its apex. It was the time when southern women did the most work on behalf of their race with their bodies. More than anything that had come before, the movement provoked a direct confrontation between southern whites and blacks, inspiring each group to explicitly defend and define its racial identity against the assaults of its antagonists. In heels and bathing suits, pretty white women of the South stood as evidence of racial integrity and superiority. In Afros and leopard-print dresses, pretty black women of the South did the same.

IN 1938, the *Southern Tobacco Journal*, the trade publication for the tobacco industry in the Southeast, reported that the young woman selected as Miss Tennessee, and thus the state's delegate to the Miss America Pageant, had chosen to skip the national contest. She wanted to enter the tobacco queen competition in South Boston, Virginia, instead. "South Boston's National Tobacco Festival outranks Atlantic City's beauty pageant in attraction," the journal bragged, "for at least one young lady."[8] The fact that she had entered the preliminary contest for the national title at all was significant, suggesting eroding opposition to a competition that had been forced to shut down ten years earlier because it was deemed indecent even by the civic leaders of New Jersey's summertime playground. The state contest was one thing, though; the national competition, quite another. Miss Tennessee preferred the quaint revelry of a tobacco warehouse to the bright lights of Atlantic City.

The Miss America Pageant had been resuscitated just three years before. Hoping to make the contest reputable and relevant, Atlantic City boosters had hired Lenora Slaughter to ensure that the right "class of girls," in her words, dreamed of becoming Miss America.[9] As a southerner herself, and a Southern Baptist at that, Slaughter must have known that reforming the pageant was essential if the daughters of Dixie were to see Miss America as the most desirable and most respectable beauty title in the country. Fresh on the heels of her success in St. Petersburg, Florida, where she had coordinated a "Festival of States Parade" that caught the attention of pageant officials in Atlantic City, Slaughter set out to burnish the image of the national contest.[10] During her first year as executive director, she added a voluntary talent component to the pageant. Designed to convince skeptics that contestants were more than just bathing beauties, the talent competition became mandatory in 1938, the same year that Slaughter altered the qualifying rules for entrants. From then on, young hopefuls had to be single, never married and never divorced, a regulation that imbued the contest with an aura of female virtue. So, too, did the requirement that contestants sign a pledge guaranteeing that they had not engaged in any acts of "moral turpitude." It was during this period that Slaughter also instituted the most infamous pageant regulation. Rule number seven stated that contestants must be "of good health and of the white race."[11] Although these changes failed to inspire Miss Tennessee to forgo the South Boston tobacco queen contest in 1938, the next few years represented a turning point for Slaughter and her pet project.

Slaughter's crusade to transform the Miss America Pageant was soon helped immeasurably by circumstances beyond her control. In 1941, when the United States entered World War II, female beauty suddenly became an issue of national import. The federal government, along with the American businesses that did its bidding, argued that looking beautiful was a duty. While obeying food rations and working in a factory assembling airplanes represented noble contributions to the war effort, advertisements, pulp fiction, newsreels, and recruitment posters insisted that glamour was essential, too. According to such literary and visual narratives, wearing cosmetics, painting nails, and grooming hair were patriotic actions in which all American women could engage and absolute necessities if one did, in fact, take a job in a traditionally male work environment or enter the armed services.[12] Rosie the Riveter was capable of filling a man's shoes, but she would never have dreamed of abandoning the accoutrements of femininity while she did so. Indeed, by maintaining their femininity during the war, women who did men's work and yet labored to be beautiful softened the threat to traditional gender roles their very employment represented. Just as important, American beauties, particularly the ubiquitous pinups of the era, symbolized the reason servicemen were fighting in the first place—they were defending American womanhood from the "yellow hand of lust."[13] The pinup also spoke directly to women, arguing for what Robert Westbrook has called a "reciprocity of obligation": American women had to prove themselves worth fighting for by being beautiful.[14]

Photos of pinups peppered newspapers and magazines, including those in the South, where local girls began to strike the pinup pose. Starting in the mid-1940s, for example, campus publications recruited coeds in bathing suits to grace their pages. The University of Alabama's *Rammer Jam-*

*mer* magazine appealed explicitly to the female student body for their photos, sending them overseas to lonely troops and using them on the cover of the magazine for the next ten years.[15] This emphasis on bathing-suited beauties resulted in what one scholar has identified as a nationwide "obsession with female legs," one in which appeals to patriotism muted the overt eroticism of female exhibitionism.[16]

Lenora Slaughter, for her part, saw an opportunity. Exploiting the heightened connection between beauty and civic duty, she spent the war years recasting Miss America as the embodiment of American loyalty. In exchange for financial support of the struggling contest, Slaughter and pageant officials proposed to the War Finance Department that the 1943 winner embark on a national tour to sell war bonds. The partnership worked for all involved. Jean Bartel, Miss America 1943, sold over $2.5 million in Series E bonds. Venus Ramey, Miss America 1944, was so successful that she won a citation from the Treasury Department for her efforts.[17] By the late 1940s, Slaughter had used this wartime momentum to raise money for college scholarships as pageant prizes and to secure the Junior Chambers of Commerce (Jaycees) as the sponsors of some state preliminaries. Along with strict new rules of behavior for contestants— contestants, for example, could not speak with any man, including their fathers, during their stay in Atlantic City—these innovations went a long way toward making the Miss America Pageant a magnet for the "class of girls" Slaughter had long hoped to attract. Southern women took note. A contestant from Chattanooga, who had gone on record with her opposition to posing in a swimsuit for pictures because, she said, "I don't think it's nice," had changed her mind by the time she arrived in Atlantic City in September 1946.[18] She submitted to the photographers on hand to document the festivities. According to A. R. Riverol, a Miss America Pageant historian, the contest had been transformed. It was "ready," as he has written, "to take its place with established American institutions."[19] By the middle of the 1950s, pageant officials were able to take a step that earlier sponsors and participants would likely have thought unimaginable.

On 11 September 1954, the Miss America Pageant televised its proceedings for the first time. Twenty-seven million viewers, or about 30 percent of the television viewing audience, tuned in. By 1956, the audience had reached forty million viewers. By 1958, it was sixty million. By 1964, ten years after the pageant's television debut, eighty million Americans, or about 70 percent of the evening's viewing audience, watched the contest. Throughout the 1960s, the Miss America Pageant rated as the first or second most popular show for eight of ten years.[20] The fifties through the mid-sixties were the "golden years," as pageant aficionados put it, a time when the contest achieved a degree of popularity and visibility that it would struggle to retain once the women's liberation movement emerged at the end of the sixties. Riverol summed up the attitude at headquarters in Atlantic City during these halcyon days: "Taking itself and its pristine image quite seriously . . . the Miss America Pageant seemed to have come a long way from the socially disdained cattle calls of the twenties to the respectability of social acceptance."[21] Hardly sex objects, he argued, Miss America contenders were more like debutantes.

It was also during these "golden years" that contestants from the South did remarkably well at the pageant. Before World War II, no contestant from a southern state had won the national title, not a surprising fact given that state preliminary winners might not even travel to Atlantic City to compete in the contest. During the war years, however, two southern women prevailed, and in 1947, Miss Memphis took home the honors, becoming the last woman representing a city, rather than a state, to win.[22] Beginning in 1950, the fortunes of contestants from the former Confederacy rose in a spectacular fashion. A southerner won in 1950 (Miss Alabama), in 1952 (Miss Georgia), in 1956 (Miss South Carolina), in 1958 (Miss Mississippi), in 1959 (Miss Mississippi again), in 1961 (Miss North Carolina), and in 1963 (Miss Arkansas). From 1947 to 1963, then, southerners captured the coveted tiara eight out of seventeen times, winning 47 percent of the titles while constituting only about 21 percent of the possible pool of winners, depending on the year.[23] Between 1954 and 1963, or during the first ten years of the pageant's highly popular televised broadcast, southern women emerged triumphant five times. Southern Miss Americas thus represented half of the decade's titleholders, while southern states provided just a quarter of the country's total population.[24]

If these years were golden for organizers of the pageant, and for the Miss America winners from the South, many Americans living in the former states of the Confederacy saw them quite differently. Miss Memphis's victory in 1947 heralded both the ascendancy of Dixie's women at the national beauty contest and a new day in Dixie's race relations. From the perspective of southern blacks and progressive southern whites, the immediate postwar years may have represented a season of hope. For the vast majority of southern whites, they represented a season of anxiety and uncertainty.[25] Their "way of life" was under attack.

The demands of returning black veterans and President Truman's new interest in civil rights sent a shock through the southern system. Advocating elimination of the poll tax, a federal antilynching bill, and desegregation of the military in the platform of 1948, Truman and the Democratic Party embarked upon a course that was an anathema to southern Democrats. The initiatives represented a betrayal to most white southerners and their legislators in Washington, D.C., a reneging on the terms of the political compromise that had governed national politics since the end of Reconstruction. The Dixiecrats' revolt in July 1948 set the region down a road of states' rights politics and revealed white intransigence on the issue of civil rights to be, potentially, formidable. Building on years of prewar activism, some southern blacks, meanwhile, fed this intransigence by pushing for the dismantling of the economic and legal foundations of Jim Crow. A spate of victories in the 1940s and early 1950s, such as the establishment of the Fair Employment Practices Commission and the end of the white primary, presaged the Supreme Court's 1954 *Brown* decision, which invalidated the legal justification for segregation and, largely as a result, crystallized white resistance to black civil rights.[26]

This opposition was fluid and expressed by a number of different constituencies in a number of different ways. Just two months after the Supreme Court rendered its decision, massive resistance found an institutional home in White Citizens' Councils, established in Indianola, Mississippi, and located in every former Confederate state by 1956.[27] Like many organizations and individuals that fought desegregation, the Citizens' Councils couched their actions within a framework of respectability, defending states' rights while publicly eschewing violence. Southern politicians registered their discontent in 1956 with the Southern Manifesto, the resolution condemning the Supreme Court's "clear abuse of judicial power" and pledging to fight desegregation at all costs.[28] Signed by 101 of the 128 U.S. senators and congressmen representing the South, the manifesto gave cover to southern legislators who simply ignored the mandate to desegregate, closed public schools, or created ineffective pupil placement and freedom of choice plans to satisfy demands for compliance.

Grassroots resistance was formidable, too. It reared its head in the hundreds of clashes that erupted throughout the South, as well as in more subtle and insidious ways long after interest in groups like the Citizens' Council had waned in the late 1950s. White flight to the southern suburbs, for example, represented a powerful tool of massive resistance that seemed, on its surface, a benign demographic shift rather than a race-conscious reaction to blacks moving into formerly white schools and neighborhoods.[29]

Largely absent from the formal halls of southern power, white women fought desegregation from within their own channels of grassroots activism, using white femininity and motherhood as justifications for their efforts. In Little Rock, Arkansas, the Mothers' League of Central High, in concert with the local Citizens' Council, organized to halt the desegregation of Central High School in 1957 by emphasizing the alleged danger to their daughters' virtue.[30] White women in Mississippi labored throughout the late 1950s and early 1960s to rid schools of textbooks they deemed subversive, pushed for history curricula that emphasized the advantages of segregation, and sponsored essay contests for white schoolchildren on topics such as "Why Separate Schools Should Be Maintained for the White and the Negro Races."[31] White mothers insisted they had a duty to protect their children, especially their daughters, from the threat of race mixing and to ensure the future of white supremacy.

The civil rights movement, which broke into the public consciousness in 1955 with the Montgomery bus boycott, further fueled the fires of southern white anger. By the next year, the region had assumed the dual identity it would maintain in the national imagination for the next decade—it was a breeding ground of heroism and horror, in almost equal measure. A newly assertive population of southern blacks bravely fought discrimination, while southern whites held their ground with the pen as well as the sword. The standard-bearers of massive resistance, even had they wanted to, could not contain the more radical elements of white southern society desperate to stop the beginnings of school desegregation. In the fall of 1956, several confrontations at southern schools anticipated the famous melee at Central High School in Little Rock a year later. In Clinton, Tennessee, an angry mob of stone-throwing rioters was met by the carbines, bayonets, and tear gas of national guardsman sent in to preserve order. More moderate southerners, such as the editors of city dailies, publicly shunned this violence but staked out an intractable position that was a tacit endorsement of such tactics. Shortly before the Clinton incident, an editorial in the Jackson, Mississippi, newspaper applauded the resolve of politicians and Citizens' Councils in thwarting change, insisting that "guts . . . and ramrod backbones is what we must have if we hope to win."[32]

Guts and ramrod backbones may have been part of what the white South needed in its struggle to maintain segregation, but it seems to have required the services of its pretty women, too. Resistance to desegregation was indeed varied and fluid, assuming the corporeal form of the southern white beauty queen: it is difficult to dismiss the connection between the unrest in the South and the region's success in Atlantic City as mere co-incidence. That southern contestants did so well in the years after 1954—the year that the *Brown* decision set off waves of protest across the region and that the Miss America Pageant was first televised—is particularly notable. Images featured in the print and visual media in the 1950s and 1960s captured a blend of white defiance and beauty, violence and grace, suggesting that the symbolic power of Dixie's white beauty queens had acquired new resonance for southerners and nonsoutherners alike. The ideal of white southern womanhood sold by the National Cotton Council in the early 1940s—and by manufacturers like the National Toilet Company before it—became the most salient component of the southern contestant's symbolic power. Although white womanhood had always been displayed along with the region's other natural resources in beauty contests, it now replaced crops as the region's most prized homegrown export, a commodity to be consumed by a national audience of television viewers in the comfort of their own living rooms.

The agricultural beauty contests that were so important in earlier decades did not disappear from the beauty contest scene. On the contrary, in the postwar years crop beauty queens traveled thousands of miles on promotional tours at home and abroad. Over time, furthermore, considerable overlap existed between contestants in agricultural beauty competitions and those beauty contests that sent winners to the state preliminaries for Miss America. The 1951 Miss North Carolina already had a Miss Brightleaf title under her belt and was slated to serve as the state's representative in the beauty contest at the Richmond Tobacco Festival later that year.[33] Miss South Carolina, who won in Atlantic City in 1956, had been a runner-up at the Pageland Watermelon Festival and the Farmer Queen of the Mullins Tobacco Festival, while a Miss Arkansas, who took home the Miss America crown in 1964, had been the Arkansas Forest Queen, the Arkansas Poultry Queen, and the National Cotton-Pickin' Queen in the early 1960s.[34]

Agricultural beauty contests, in fact, might serve as preliminary events at the local level, chosen by the Miss America organization as the contests that young women had to win before proceeding to the state level. During these years, southerners acknowledged the relationship between agriculture and their pageantry tradition. After Miss South Carolina's victory in Atlantic City, one South Carolina newspaper declared proudly that "[a]ll the world should know by now that when prettier girls are grown, South Carolina will grow them."[35] Lenora Slaughter, too, seems to have recognized the importance of the South's rural pageant tradition. In

1956, Slaughter told an Atlanta reporter that the South ran the best Miss America preliminaries, adding that she had taken the Georgia state preliminary away from Atlanta and given it to smaller Columbus, where there was more interest.[36]

The system of rural pageantry that was inaugurated in the 1930s in a climate of economic crisis served a new purpose in a climate of racial crisis. The timing of the Miss America Pageant on this point is revealing. Since its founding in 1921, the pageant had always been held in the first or second week of September, a function of the founders' desire to extend the summer tourist season in Atlantic City beyond Labor Day. The practical result was that the national contest either coincided with, or immediately followed, the beginning of the school year across the country. After 1954, this confluence was significant. Miss Americas were chosen as hostile confrontations raged in those parts of the South where schools were attempting to honor the Supreme Court's order to desegregate. And television cameras were there to capture the developments in both places—in the streets and schoolyards of the South, and in Convention Hall in Atlantic City.

During the first week of September 1956, Americans turned on the nightly news and saw effigies of blacks hanging above schoolhouses throughout the South and riots erupting over school desegregation in Clinton, Tennessee. That same week, forty million of them tuned in to watch as the region's first post-*Brown* winner was crowned. Marian McKnight, Miss South Carolina, was chosen as Miss America on 8 September 1956.[37] McKight's crowning also happened to come on the heels of the Southern Manifesto, a document that had significant ties to the Palmetto State. In February, South Carolina senator Strom Thurmond, the Dixiecrats' cofounder and their 1948 nominee for president, had helped write the initial draft of the resolution that put a "legal" stamp of approval on massive resistance.

Miss South Carolina's triumph in Atlantic City also spoke to recent events in Dixie but in a way that belied the apparent frivolity of a beauty contest. McKnight visually rebutted the charges being leveled against the South in the national media. As civil rights protests spread throughout the region, television reporters and cameramen funneled graphic images of violent resistance into the homes of millions of Americans, inciting indignation over the militancy of white southerners unwilling to grant blacks social and political equality. For this reason, the media, and television in particular, emerged as central weapons in the arsenal of civil rights demonstrators, facilitating their successes and ultimately forcing the federal government to intervene on their behalf. White southerners, however, also understood the power of print and visual media and attempted to control the image of the South being broadcast to the rest of the nation. Their efforts on this front often involved using the same tactics of intimidation against reporters as they used against blacks, which meant, ironically, that they did little to dissuade most Americans from believing that the white South had a fundamental penchant for brutality.

Broadcasts and photographs routinely showed how poorly the press fared at the hands of southern mobs. In September 1956, for example, *Time* magazine reported that the press was just as much the target of rioters' stones and clubs in the antidesegregation rallies throughout Tennessee as were blacks. The "chief danger," the magazine continued, was to photographers and newsreel men, as the white protesters understood that their pictures "would arouse public opinion—and action—against them."[38] An accompanying photograph suggests the protesters' fears were well-founded. A young white man, his face frenzied with anger, is shown ripping a photographer's equipment from his hands. In the background stands a cameraman recording the entire encounter on newsreel. The photograph that captured this assault is damning, to say the least, and yet just a few pages away, Miss South Carolina's countenance graced the "People" section of the magazine, reminding readers that the South was also home to a tradition of grace and gentility. In the war of images that raged in the post-*Brown* media, southern queens such as McKnight could serve as persuasive public relations agents for a region tarnished by its reactions to calls for racial justice.

The coverage surrounding the victories of McKnight and the two beauties from Mississippi is the best illustration of this fact. Mississippi's Miss America winners, both students at Ole Miss, were crowned in 1958 and 1959, four and five years after the *Brown* decision and in the midst of the state's continuing effort to ward off the forces of change beating on its doors. The University of Mississippi, itself, was a flashpoint of the state's struggles, hardly surprising, given that it was, in alumnus Curtis Wilkie's words, a "clearinghouse for the state's political power structure."[39] Ole Miss provided the backdrop for the most famous desegregation riot in the state when James Meredith attempted to enroll at the university in 1962, but resistance at the university had erupted much earlier. In 1948, the Confederate flag became an official university icon after students who had attended the Dixiecrats' convention in Birmingham returned to campus and made it "a symbol of the Mississippi spirit," explicitly expressing their allegiance to white supremacy and "the opposite of civil rights."[40]

For the next ten years, an "action-reaction" mentality reigned in Oxford.[41] In October 1950, the renegade editor of the campus newspaper came out in favor of admitting blacks to the university's law school. Furious, a group of students burned a cross in protest. A month later, students sponsored the first annual "Dixie Week," a weeklong celebration that opened with the reading of the state's Ordinance of Secession and included an Old South ball. In January 1954, five months before *Brown*, Medgar Evers did, in fact, apply to the University of Mississippi law school, only to find his application stymied by bureaucratic technicalities.[42] That fall, the Dixie Week festivities, evolving "ominously," as one historian of Ole Miss has written, were expanded to include a reenactment of the assassination of Lincoln, an appearance by the Ku Klux Klan, and a mock slave auction.[43] In short order, the marching band adopted the full dress uniform of the Confederate army as its official attire. Two events dominated the end of the decade, foreshadowing the response to Meredith's later desegregation effort. In May 1958, a black man attempted to gain acceptance as a graduate student in the history department, an action that eventually landed him, following the governor's request, in a state mental institution. The same year, a group of alumni led an investigation into the "apostasy" of the chancellor and several faculty members. In addition to appearing soft on segregation, some among them were allegedly espousing communism as well.[44] Though they had been officially cleared of all charges by the summer of 1959, the incident was nasty, and accusations continued into 1960.

Throughout these events, a multitude of Ole Miss beauty queens reigned on and off campus. Mary Ann Mobley and Lynda Mead, in fact, were both crowned Miss America as the apostates were busy defending their loyalty to Mississippi's way of life, adding beauty and decorum to an atmosphere that was nothing if not ugly. The number of beauty queens on campus during the period was dizzying. Ole Miss coeds competed as queens of the university, homecoming, May Day, Rebelee, the Parade of Favorites, and the nearby Memphis Maid of Cotton Contest, which recruited on campus. The Miss University Contest, the largest of the school's multiple beauty competitions, which Lynda Mead won in 1959, served as a preliminary for the Miss Mississippi Pageant. And between 1948 and 1961, eight Ole Miss students won the state title. These women did not make a habit of linking their Miss America victories, or their beauty, to the spirit of militant defiance that was gripping their university and their home state, though Mead came awfully close to doing so during her homecoming tour.

One did not have to look far, however, to find the connection. Like many state preliminaries for the Miss America Pageant, the Miss Mississippi Pageant was sponsored by the Jaycees, a business group that in Mississippi opposed desegregation and, in 1962, published an inflammatory defense of the university against the "tyranny" of the federal government for supporting the efforts of James Meredith.[45] What these young women did say, moreover, was suggestive in its own right. In the interview portion of the Miss America Pageant, for example, Mobley was asked by pageant emcee Bert Parks what made a man great. She announced to the 22,000 people gathered in Atlantic City's Convention Hall and to the sixty million viewers watching at home that a great man was one who "tries to respect other people's viewpoints."[46] It was an ambiguous, even empty platitude that may have carried a more particular meaning coming from a Mississippian than from, say, a Nebraskan. Some listeners may have heard an appeal to respect the "viewpoint" of the white South in its time of troubles. Just six years before, Miss Georgia, the eventual winner, had been asked to state briefly how she thought "democracy [might] be advanced in the United States." She made a similar plea for cordiality, stating that democracy would best be expanded through the Declaration of Independence, trust in the Lord, and "getting along with one another."[47]

South Carolina's Marian McKnight gave a pointed answer during her interview. Parks asked what winning the title would mean to her. "The winner," McKnight replied, "always carries the ideals of her city and state throughout the world," adding that those of her birthplace were "the finest ideals there are."[48] In the wake of her victory, South Carolinians applauded her answer. "We like the way she said it," declared the *Florence Morning News*, adding that she was "a beautiful Southern girl from a typical Southern community located in a typical Southern area of a typical Southern state."[49] McKnight's hometown newspaper, the *Manning Times*, was convinced that her answer had been "the deciding factor" in her victory.[50] In a telegram to the new Miss America, the South Carolina governor thanked her for publicly acknowledging "the responsibility of [her] South Carolina citizenship" and expressed confidence that she would represent "its traditions with dignity and honor."[51] Both the *Manning Times* and the *Charleston News and Courier* declared their state's intention to take the new Miss America—and Miss Alabama, the second runner-up—with them if the talk of secession bore fruit. As the *Manning Times* quipped, "What would the Supreme Court say of its handiwork then?"[52]

The Mississippi press explained what its Miss Americas stood for in similar terms. On Mobley's triumph in 1958, one newspaper posited a collective view shared by all white Mississippians: "[E]verybody knew what the Miss America victory was, and they cared a right smart. They cared all at one time because, through the magic of electronics, they had seen it all at one time. And somehow," the writer concluded, "it meant even more, just knowing that the rest of the world had also seen it."[53] The writer's point was clear: Mississippi was in conversation with the rest of the nation and the world. The "magic of electronics" had finally been harnessed in the service of Mississippi rather than in the service of "agitators" and "traitors." A defensive, in-your-face tone ran throughout the paper's comments. In winning Miss America, the state had done something right, and that something demonstrated that Mississippi was right about other things, too. The following year, marking only the second time a state boasted a consecutive repeat winner, Lynda Mead was crowned Mississippi's second Miss America. The Ole Miss newspaper was happy to report that she "spoke well of her Mississippi" throughout the week of competition and that her fellow students reveled in "their hour of triumph" after her name had been called on television.[54]

The Meridian newspaper lauded her achievement for its potential to sway public opinion: "She will be a first-rate goodwill ambassador for our state and will secure for us invaluable publicity. . . . Moreover, a triumph such as Miss Mead's helps 'sell' Mississippi to Mississippians." Mead's job was to sell a positive image of Mississippi to the nation and to her own state's citizens, some of whom, the paper lamented, accept "the slander that is directed against our state" and thus "tend to be apologetic about Mississippi." "This," the paper pleaded, "must NEVER be." The Meridian editorial staff had no doubt that the national press would toe its typical line, which was to condemn the state without reservation, even if the news there was good: "Nevertheless, we daresay that ALL is not joy over Miss Mead's victory. We must consider the feelings of Life and Time. What a gnashing of teeth there must be in the offices of these unhappy publications; what a frantic search for verbal vitriol strong enough to properly debunk Mississippi in her hour of triumph."[55] The Meridian newspaper was almost giddy with delight at the prospect of the media's consternation over the state's triumph at the national beauty pageant. Mead's winning seemed to prove that the national press's predilection for criticism was misplaced.

The paper's suspicion that the national media, or the nation more generally, were gnashing their teeth over the state's second Miss America title was completely off the mark. Jim Halley, editor of a small-town Mississippi newspaper, reported that while on vacation in New York City in 1959, a businessman told him that "that Mobley girl was worth millions in good value to Mississippi. You should never let her get away." Based on his time in the city, Halley concluded that it was "impossible to overestimate the good will value the two Miss America's [*sic*] have won for Mississippi."[56] Publications from *Life* to *Sports Illustrated* celebrated Lynda Mead's victory, just as they had celebrated southern contestants in the preceding years. The *Saturday Evening Post*, for example, had run a splashy feature on the Miss Arkansas preliminary just a few years earlier.[57] In his feature on football and beauty queens at Ole Miss after Mead's crowning, a *Sports Illustrated* writer did acknowledge that the university had "no reason to be proud" of the fact that it was all white. But he glossed over the problem by arguing that "segregation is simply a fact of life at Ole Miss, as indeed it is everywhere else in the state." Most of the article focused on the wonder that was the University of Mississippi, breeding ground of a strong football tradition and "dazzling Miss Americas."[58]

*Life* embraced Mississippi's beauty victories without qualification. In 1961, it published a pictorial essay on Ole Miss, which, as everyone recognized, possessed "a spectacular corner on beauty." With two titles under its belt, Ole Miss now had three of its own holding state titles—Miss Mississippi, Miss Tennessee, and Miss Missouri—and ready to compete in Atlantic City. The magazine reported that some observers believed that the university nurtured beauty in its students, while others felt beautiful women were simply lured to the university in the first place. Majorettes, known to be a "notoriously good-looking group"—Mobley was one—received university scholarships, the article noted.[59]

The university did, in fact, make the cultivation of feminine beauty and campus beauty queens an institutional priority. The university sponsored cheerleading and majorette camps, which, combined, drew 1,600 high school students to campus each summer, many of whom would enroll upon graduation.[60] In the mid to late 1950s, the registrar's office got involved in recruiting attractive young women, including future baton twirlers, to attend Ole Miss. William H. "Chubby" Ellis—an assistant university registrar, Citizens' Council member, and crusader against the communistintegrationists among the faculty and administration—led this initiative.[61] He invited young women to campus for the weekend, set them up on dates, and sent them to parties thrown by Chi Omega, a sorority renowned for its beauties (Mobley and Mead were members).

Thank-you notes his young recruits wrote after their on-campus visits suggest Ellis's deep and somewhat disturbing commitment to the project. One woman from Gulfport wrote that she had to attend a girls' school for her freshman year, but, she said, "When I come as a Sophomore, though, I want to be one of 'your girls.' You can take care of me just like you did last week-end!"[62] If his attention to their careers once they arrived on campus is any indication, Ellis did take care of "his girls." He kept a scrapbook detailing their successes—forty-eight pages of clippings, photos, and other memorabilia capturing the adventures of Ole Miss beauties on campus and in the national media. By 1961, the university had gone even further, hosting a "Young and Beautiful Charm Camp" at which hundreds of young girls learned the tricks to beauty, including "how to use makeup effectively."[63]

VALUED AS BOTH public relations ambassadors and symbols of defiance—in almost equal measure—beauty queens for white southerners held still more profound significance. They evoked deeply held assumptions about race and sexuality as well. The bodies of beauty queens answered desegregation's challenge to white supremacy. Given their indebtedness to better baby contests, which were always motivated, in part, by a eugenic concern with the health of the white race, southern bathing beauty contests encouraged the improvement of white womanhood, the literal strengthening of the white race, through the ritual of competition.

By the mid-1950s, the scientific racism inherent in these earlier body contests enjoyed a resurgence in popularity as southerners struggled to justify Jim Crow. Citizens' Councils all over the region invoked the long tradition of comparing the physical traits of whites and blacks, pointing to differences as evidence of black inferiority. Tracts published by the Citizens' Councils of America in the late 1950s and 1960s included long lists of black features—lips, noses, hair, cheekbones—that "proved" African Americans' lack of civilization, their innate inability to live like whites. In Louisiana, Virginia, and Mississippi, legislators even pushed for the major treatise of this pseudoscientific ideology, *Race and Reason*, to be required reading for all schoolchildren.[64] Undergirding this response to desegregation was white southerners' sensory understanding of racial difference.

Whites feared that desegregation represented, in Mark M. Smith's words, "a forced sensory folding or collapsing," which would require their smelling, seeing, hearing, touching, and maybe even tasting blackness.[65] The tactile dimensions of this threat were the most troubling. White southerners worried that white women would be touched, squeezed, and crowded by black men, physical acts of contamination that would inevitably lead to sex.

If the bodies of white southern women stood as proof of white superiority, then, they also embodied what was at stake in the battle over school desegregation: the possibility of "race mixing," "mongrelization," or "amalgamation." School desegregation posed a sexual threat to white women and thus the "purity" of the white race. Like their prodesegregation enemies, segregationists invoked the Bible in justifying their cause, citing ample evidence in the Old and New Testaments that racial mixing was the worst of all transgressions against God.[66] God had created different races, they asserted, and those races were to keep to themselves. At its core, segregationist ideology was rooted in this theological argument against miscegenation, a harbinger of the apocalypse or, as Jane Dailey has written, "the chief sin in the service of the anti-Christ."[67] Tom Brady, Mississippi circuit court judge and intellectual luminary of the Citizens' Councils in the state, invoked this theological prohibition against racial mixing in his infamous treatise against school desegregation, placing white women at the center of southerners' resistance to the nefarious scheme. In *Black Monday: Segregation or Amalgamation . . . America Has Its Choice*, penned just one month after the *Brown* decision, Brady paid tribute to the "loveliest and the purest of God's creatures, the nearest thing to an angelic being that treads this terrestrial ball." This creature was, of course, "a well-bred, cultured Southern white woman or her blue-eyed, golden haired little girl." The Jim Crow South had succeeded in protecting her, and therefore in fostering peaceful race relations, but its ability to do so was threatened by the meddling of the Supreme Court and its "Communist-front" sympathizers. Brady argued that white southerners had to defend the "inviolability of Southern Womanhood" if they hoped to avoid the inevitable result of amalgamation—"moral leprosy and degeneracy."[68] It was against God's will to do anything less.

While Brady, Citizens' Councils, and the Ku Klux Klan went about protecting this inviolability through a variety of legal and extralegal means, the region's beauty queens served as a very public, visual reminder of what was on the line. On the stage in Atlantic City, on millions of television sets, and in millions of newspapers, the loveliest of the region's loveliest bolstered the resolve of segregationists and facilitated the segregationist effort. Resplendent in all their royal glory, here were the southerners who would suffer most if schools were integrated. And schools were just the beginning. White women would become vulnerable in other public facilities as well, including, of course, swimming pools, which emerged as poignant spaces in the battles over desegregation given the type of interracial intimacy their use entailed. White women in swimsuits would, in effect, end up bathing with black men if desegregation won the day. In upholding Baltimore's segregation of its municipal swimming pools in 1954, despite the recent *Brown* ruling, one judge observed that for this very reason, pools were "more sensitive than schools."[69] Not surprisingly, some white southerners in the 1950s and 1960s abandoned newly desegregated pools in their communities, while in other places officials closed public pools rather than opening them up to black residents. In midcentury beauty contests, the bathing beauty became a symbol of what could happen, reminding viewers of the danger white women would encounter at this sexually charged leisure spot on the weekend, as well as in the classroom and on the bus during the week.

In paying homage to their beauty queens, white southerners were not simply pledging to support them in competition or during their post-victory reigns. They were pledging to protect them from the dangers of race mixing, from predatory black men. White southerners did not make a habit of rhetorically casting their queens as symbols of white women's vulnerability in a South transformed by desegregation and the civil rights movement, but they did not have to. The context for positioning the significance of these women was woven into the fabric of mid-twentieth-century civic life. Homecoming celebrations held in honor of Mary Ann Mobley and Lynda Mead, for example, recalled the massive resistance rallies sponsored by Citizens' Councils across the South during the same years, which themselves recalled Lost Cause celebrations from the early twentieth century. Photographs show that thousands of white Mississippians turned out for the events in the streets of Jackson, Natchez, and other towns. Just as United Daughters of the Confederacy sponsors had done decades before, Mobley and Mead stood onstage at their respective celebrations as state and town officials delivered odes to their loveliness. These midcentury beauties were then ushered through the throngs of adoring fans on the arms of men, presumably their fathers.[70] It does not require

Mary Ann Mobley at homecoming celebration, Jackson, Mississippi, 1959. A large crowd feted Mary Ann Mobley, the first of two consecutive Miss Americas from the state, at a celebration in Jackson after her win in Atlantic City. Courtesy of the Southern Media Archive, Special Collections, University of Mississippi Libraries, University, Miss.

a stretch of the imagination to assume that the marching bands in attendance played "Dixie" and that the speakers at the podiums waxed poetic about the South's many fine traditions.

The visual presentation of attractive women, especially seminude women in bathing suits, may seem difficult to reconcile with widespread fears about maintaining racial purity and preventing interracial sex. But the apparent paradox of this southern body project—of efforts to guard white women's sexuality while also celebrating the white bathing beauty— is not as baffling as it may seem. For one, Lenora Slaughter's efforts to transform the image of the contest in the minds of both the public and contestants had paid off. In addition to all the rules governing contestants' behavior, Slaughter had downplayed the significance of the swimsuit competition. By the postwar period, the bathing suit portion of the Miss America contest and its preliminaries was only one of several scored components. During much of the competition, contestants appeared in voluminous gowns and costumes as they showcased a talent or answered an interviewer's questions. Slaughter also ensured that the winner was crowned when she was in an evening gown, not a bathing suit, as had been the practice, and insisted that the term "bathing suit" itself be replaced with "swimsuit" to suggest athleticism rather than sexuality.

After 1950, moreover, the last time a winning Miss America would wear a swimsuit in connection with the contest was at the pageant in Atlantic City. For years, titleholders had been required to wear swimsuits at Miss America appearances, but Miss Alabama Yolande Betbeze, crowned Miss America in September 1950, challenged the tradition. The morning after the pageant, Betbeze announced that she would not don a swimsuit during her reign, arguing that she was a singer, not a beauty queen. A performer with the Mobile Opera Guild, and a product of a convent school, Betbeze insisted that she had not entered the competition to be a pinup. She hoped to escape the South and, as became quickly apparent, use the crown to earn money at appearances (which she did quite successfully). Slaughter would later maintain that Betbeze was a bit "onery"—and, indeed, this was just the first of several provocative pronouncements—but she backed Betbeze's swimsuit stance since it would further burnish the contest's image.[71] Angered by the decision, Catalina Swim Wear, a major pageant sponsor, withdrew its support and established the rival Miss USA and Miss Universe competitions, the latter of which, according to A. R. Riverol, "makes no bones as to what it really is."[72]

The sexuality that Miss America contestants did exude in the swimsuit competition was also of a certain kind. Some observed that it did not exist at all. Philip Roth, commenting on the television broadcast of the 1957 Miss America Pageant in the *New Republic*, noted with palpable regret that most of the contestants seemed more like prudes than like real live sex objects. In his estimation, it was the interview portion of the contest that gave them away. Miss Georgia, who Roth said had showed off "an exquisite pair of legs" during the swimsuit competition, diminished their allure with her answer to a query about what had helped her become a contestant for the Miss America title. "My faith in God," she had responded. Miss Oklahoma was asked what she wanted her first-born child to be like. She said she hoped he would be just like her father and brothers. Miss Oklahoma also spoke out against men wearing Bermuda shorts and, according to Roth, quickly added that she was opposed to women wearing them, too. In Roth's paraphrase, she stated that "girls *might* wear them in their own backyards." For her, wearing a swimsuit on national television was apparently an entirely different matter. For Roth, the whole spectacle was hardly worth watching. How disappointing it was, he concluded, "to find that all those lovely legs are really girls who play the Hammond organ . . . and who, when asked what they admire most, will talk to the flesh's distraction about their brothers and their Daddies."[73] Hoping to project a certain kind of fantasy on these Miss America contestants, Roth found that it would not stick.

Words reframed the images onstage, softening the danger of overt eroticism. Seven years earlier, South Carolina's Marian McKnight had done what *Life* magazine called a "hip-wiggling parody" of Marilyn Monroe for her talent.[74] But, as we have seen, she still managed to cast herself as the standard-bearer of virtuous citizenship during the interview portion. Mississippi's Mary Ann Mobley displayed a similarly remarkable agility during the 1958 pageant. Several bars into an aria from *Madame Butterfly*, Mobley stopped singing. She then announced that she wanted to "sing and dance to something that's solid and hot," ripped off her long gown to reveal a tight skirt below, and began a "torchy rendition" of a jazz song before removing the skirt and finishing the number in a short one-piece jumper.[75] All the while, she was wearing a gift from her Sunday school teacher: a charm bracelet with a Bible verse tucked inside, a fact that was advertised to and reported by the press. During her interview, moreover, Mobley epitomized the wallflower. When Bert Parks asked what topics she enjoyed discussing with members of the opposite sex, she stated that she had learned long ago to inquire about a boy's interests before saying anything about herself. "And if you can't get him to answer you," she concluded, ". . . you're just quiet for the rest of the evening."[76] Acts like Mobley's were entertaining because the contestants, as the personifications of rectitude, were so obviously adopting a performative, even artificial, sexuality. This was the same year that a *Time* reporter overheard a judge, bemused by the naïveté of the contestants, wonder aloud: "Do you think they're all certified virgins?"[77]

The swimsuit competition reinforced the impression of the contestants' collective virtue. The beauty queens did strut across stages and television screens wearing tight swimsuits that hugged their curves and exposed their arms and legs. But unlike earlier tobacco queen contests that asked contestants to radiate sexuality by moving freely in tobacco fields and handling a symbolic male phallus, later contests did away with freedom of movement and opportunities for sexual play. Clad in bathing suits that noticeably squeezed their breasts, hips, and thighs, contestants in Miss

America and agricultural beauty competitions alike conveyed bodily restraint as they glided across the stage in their high heels. Nothing moved, nothing jiggled. The art critic of the *New York Times* remarked that the typical Miss America contestant seemed "a girl-like product synthesized from fleshlike plastic."[78] Susan Bordo's observations about the bodily containment inherent in modern femininity are apt on the consequences of this fact. The women who participated in these beauty contests demonstrated that their bodies were "protected against eruption from within."[79]

The swimsuit competition was thus not so much about emphasizing sexuality as it was about drawing attention to a sexuality safely reined in, entirely under control. In a climate tinged with fears over black male sexuality—and over white women's own possible interest in black men—the cultural logic of the beauty contest therefore actually made a good deal of sense. It rendered contestants oddly asexual, devoid of desire. For decades, furthermore, many agricultural beauty contests had carefully tread the line separating overt sexuality and agrarian innocence, tempering the dangers of the former with images that called up the latter. White southerners had long connected beauty contestants' sexuality to rural virtue, drawing an association that effectively disciplined the body. The tradition of southern pageantry, in short, had operated to reconcile any contradiction between virtue and public displays of female flesh.

Contestants also did not speak as they walked across the stage to model their swimsuits before the judges and audience. The muting of female voices in this component of the contest, in the words of one pageant scholar, contains "the female body by reducing it to an isolated sexuality, one with no voice and no chance to talk back." The bathing beauty's body is "spoken for or on behalf of."[80] Whatever sexuality contestants do possess, in other words, is the exclusive property of men. In the South of the 1950s and 1960s, this visual statement supported the southern patriarchy. When contestants did speak during the interview portion of the contest, they strengthened the visual message. As Roth noted, the young women in Atlantic City went on "to the flesh's distraction" about their fathers and brothers. Press accounts reveal that boyfriends and future husbands were a common topic of conversation onstage as well. Mobley, for example, said that if she could spend an evening with anyone in the whole world, she would choose her "best beau."[81]

The promise of protection hung over these beauties like the red velvet robe that cloaked the eventual winner. Indeed, the Miss America Pageant and its preliminaries represented perfect forums for white men to reassert their paternal power, under assault not just from blacks demanding desegregation but from their own daughters.[82] As cracks in the façade of segregation began to appear in the postwar years, young white women became members of the first generation of southerners to display a collective interest in black culture and what it seemed to signify. They allowed black culture to inform their behavior as no southerners before them had.[83] In speech, in dress, and especially in music, young southerners of this era mimicked what they perceived to be the style of their black counterparts.

Even young Mississippi women were not immune. In 1960, on the heels of Mobley's and Mead's Miss America victories, native Mississippian Muddy Waters played at an Ole Miss dance where the female students enjoyed the latest craze, the twist. According to one Ole Miss student, black performers like Waters were always more popular than white ones, inciting behavior that she characterized as "very loose."[84] The Waters performance was no exception, as the young women in attendance danced so furiously that, in Waters's own words, "their little white panties [were] showing."[85] Alarmed at the scene before them, the organizers of the dance forced the band to stop playing, sending its members outside to wait for their money. Exhibiting their own brand of benign sexuality, southern beauty queens checked unacceptable displays of female sexuality such as this one and put it where it belonged—in the hands of white men, especially white fathers. The subtext of this father-daughter dynamic is hard to dismiss. The father of a southern beauty queen was both guardian and audience of his daughter's sexuality. In this way, southern beauty contests fed the eroticized father-daughter relationship that, as Rachel Devlin has shown, characterized the postwar period.[86]

In the mid-twentieth-century South, then, the rhetoric of purity and protection went hand in hand with the objectification of women. Placed on a public stage to parade around in swimsuits, southern women defended against the threat of black male sexuality. Through the vehicle of the beauty contest, they enacted a quiet form of massive resistance.[87] Compared to the irate southern men and women shouting on the nightly news, these pretty women seemed to be resisting nothing at all, a visual illusion that was the very source of their subtle but potent power. This power, moreover, flowed in many directions. Just because the beauty contests of this era objectified women and reinforced patriarchy, in other words, does not mean that women had no stakes in these rituals. Feminist critics of beauty contests were right to point out, as they later did, that the valorization of beauty queens bred an interest in female bodies that subjected women to ogling male eyes, demanding aesthetic standards, and crass commercialization. Using somewhat different language, some southerners themselves had criticized beauty contests for similar reasons since the 1920s. But in the mid-twentieth-century South, it is also true that contest sponsors, contestant chaperones, and participants all had much to gain.

Women who organized beauty contests throughout the region, or who traveled to Atlantic City as contestants' chaperones, shaped their civic cultures in ways that secured their privileged position in southern society. The celebration of the white beauty queen was a celebration of their own access to power and protection. Just as blocking the desegregation of a school or lobbying for a segregationist curriculum did, ensuring the success of these young beauties afforded southern matrons a tool to maintain the racial status quo. For participants, these benefits were even more tangible. They were heralded by the press and political leaders and given heroes' welcomes in their home states when they won the big prize in Atlantic City. Coverage of Marian McKnight, to take one example, dominated the first two sections of the *Manning Times* upon her victory in September and her homecoming a month later. The parade marking the latter was deemed "the biggest event in the history of the town."[88] Twenty-five thousand people descended upon Manning, population 3,000, to celebrate her feat.[89] Across the region, beauty queens like McKnight were held up as all that was good and honorable in southern society. Fulfilling that role—literally embodying the southern way of life—was an important act, indeed.

The beauty contest of the civil rights era provided young white women an arena for performing their racialized beauty. Offstage, this same demographic of women was doing the same thing in a more unusual way: they were putting on blackface. Although minstrelsy has traditionally been characterized as a male pastime, southern women were drawn to the practice more than we have previously appreciated.[90] A handful of United Daughters of the Confederacy members in the early twentieth century, for example, blacked up to prove their knowledge of enslaved women and thus establish themselves as a part of the region's aristocracy in a socially mobile New South.[91] In the 1950s and 1960s, as college yearbooks reveal, young female minstrels began to appear with frequency at sorority parties throughout the South. At Ole Miss, the Chi Omegas and the Tri Delts both blacked up in 1951, the latter spoofing *Snow White* with a performance of "Coal Black and the Seven Spades."[92] Two years later, the University of Alabama's Phi Mu chapter sponsored a Showboat party in which some of the group's members dressed as hoopskirted antebellum belles while

*The Tri Delts prove most useful as hostesses. (!)*

Delta Delta Delta sorority members, Southern Methodist University, 1956. These college women blacked up in 1956 and proved themselves "most useful hostesses" at the Kappa Alpha Old South Ball. Courtesy of the DeGolyer Library, Southern Methodist University, Dallas, Texas, SMU Archives, SMU *Rotunda*, 1956.

others were in loud, mismatched clothes and blackface.[93] The 1955 University of Alabama yearbook included a shot of a blacked-up sorority girl teaching her blacked-up charges at "Aunt Jemima's Pancake School." The page also showed an assemblage of sorority-girls-cum-southern-belles standing in front of a white-columned mansion.[94]

In the visual records of both Alabama events, the contrast between the white and black versions of femininity was stark. At the 1956 Old South Ball at Southern Methodist University (SMU), which included a secession reenactment by cannon-firing fraternity men, sorority women employed the same visual trick. Wearing aprons around their waists and bandanas on their heads, Tri Delts blackened their faces and proved themselves, as the yearbook caption read, "most useful as hostesses." A photo featured these "black" hostesses announcing, "Shut my mouf! We's integrated." On the same page were two more pictures. In one appeared a pair of fraternity men in Confederate uniforms, providing the backdrop to a group of exquisitely appointed Old South belles, "The real charm," according to the caption, "of Southern hospitality—ribbons, ruffles, and radiance." In the other were more fraternity men wearing Confederate uniforms and antebellum tuxedos.[95]

Discerning the intentions of these women (and men) is not easy, but it seems safe to speculate about the effect of their minstrel moments, which the SMU and University of Alabama photos reveal especially well. Juxtaposed against the elegant white belles, the made-up "black" women acted as their aesthetic foils. White women possessed beauty; black women did not. The latter could not escape the stereotype of the unattractive, menial mammy or the black sartorial aesthetic that had long struck white observers as a "'distortion' of the conventional."[96] Perhaps, too, these col-

Delta Delta Delta sorority members, Southern Methodist University, 1956. The women in this photograph, which was placed next to the photograph of their blacked-up sorority sisters in the yearbook, displayed "the real charm of Southern hospitality." Courtesy of the DeGolyer Library, Southern Methodist University, Dallas, Texas, SMU Archives, SMU *Rotunda*, 1956.

lege women were responding to the changing racial order of the South. It is difficult to ignore the timing of the uptick in female minstrelsy among young southern women, or in case of the SMU Old South Ball, the jocular reference to integration and the invocation of Confederate imagery, which white southerners routinely used in massive resistance efforts.[97]

Regardless of their motives, as these women shored up their racialized beauty within the cloistered spaces of college campuses, some of their peers—in tiaras and heels—did the same in the service of massive resistance, and in a very public manner. Southern beauty queens received a great deal of attention during these years, and not just by white southerners and the southern press. The regional effort to showcase beauty queens as ambassadors of the segregated South—to provide an appealing justification both for the southern way of life and for efforts to defy desegregation—was well-received by the nation as a whole. The dominance of southern women at the Miss America Pageant testifies to that fact, but it also begs for an explanation. Why were southern women allowed to dominate the most high-profile form for articulating a definition of American citizenship through the female body?[98]

Several factors seem to have made southern beauty queens especially attractive to the nation during the civil rights movement. Americans were arguably predisposed to seeing southern women as the natural heirs to the national beauty throne given the region's history of exporting beauty queens, and images of beauty queens. For decades, Americans had seen southern beauties pedaling tobacco, cotton, and other commodities. In advertising and marketing campaigns for items such as cosmetics, they had also been sold the idea that southern women, by virtue of their birth as southerners, were inherently and uniquely beautiful. Cosmetics manufacturers, it will be recalled, based ads on this claim beginning in the 1920s. In the process of consuming these images and products, Americans had also been buying the racialized beauty that underpinned marketing strategies. This beauty was part of the culture of segregation that seeped beyond the porous borders of the South and that, as Grace Hale has so persuasively argued, provided the cornerstone of an American conception of nationhood fundamentally rooted in whiteness.[99] Along with a host of cultural products exported by the Jim Crow South to the rest of the nation, then, this racialized southern beauty helped inform American identity. The degree to which this was true was often obscured by the sheer otherness of the South—its violence, its disregard for the rule of law, its backwardness. But the fact that southern beauty queens, time and again, were honored as the incarnation of American ideals in the 1950s and 1960s is suggestive at the very least.

Southern beauty queens, furthermore, may not have assuaged the fears of southerners alone. Although they were appalled by the images of white southern brutality on television, nonsouthern whites had their own misgivings about the move toward greater racial equality. The South bore the brunt of the bad publicity, given that it provided the setting for some of the era's most heinous acts of violence. But de facto and de jure segregation existed outside of the region as well, including, significantly, in Atlantic City. Until the 1960s, the host city of the Miss America Pageant was as rigidly segregated as any in the South. A Georgia native who moved to Atlantic City called it a "Jim Crow town for sure."[100] Many public spaces, such as the Boardwalk and beaches, were off-limits to African Americans. Black residents lived in crowded conditions away from the city's bustling center, where they worked as menial and service laborers—pushing the famous rolling chairs, for example—in the tourism industry. Segregation extended to the festivities surrounding the beauty contest itself, as blacks were prohibited from participating in the pageant's Boardwalk Festival of Floats. The pageant's hometown embodied the far-flung nature of both racism and resistance to change. White Americans everywhere had qualms about blacks attending their schools, about blacks moving into their neighborhoods, and about blacks eating in their restaurants. The effects of dismantling white privilege were disturbing to many Americans, not just to southerners. In the Miss America contest of the civil rights era, Americans could cope with their anxiety in a way that seemed to do no harm. Honoring beauties from the South as the incarnation of American ideals, they projected a fantasy that, unlike Philip Roth's, did stick—the American fantasy of white superiority and white supremacy.

The international tensions of the day provide another explanation for the national appeal of southern beauties. As the inquiry at the University of Mississippi attests, many white southerners construed the defense of segregation as a defense against communist forces. The effort to achieve social equality was damning enough. Revealing the affinities between anti-communism and massive resistance, segregationists also argued that de-segregation represented a Soviet-style invocation of federal power at the expense of states' rights.[101] According to this logic, the regional struggle to maintain racial apartheid was really a national struggle to defeat the communist enemy and defend Americanism. As one South Carolinian wrote in a typical screed against the communist-desegregationists, "nearly all the white people in the Southern States are one hundred percent American," suggesting, of course, that all the white people elsewhere—not to mention the black people—failed to measure up.[102] White women were especially vocal in contending that the South's fight against desegregation was a defense of the ideals on which the United States was founded. They insisted that their role as mothers demanded that they battle the unpatriotic forces in their midst and rescue their children from the un-American practice of race mixing.[103] While it is difficult to know exactly how the average American responded to this argument, in a national climate suffused with fears over communist subversion, southern assertions of "one hundred percent Americanism" may have, on some level, struck a chord. Southern beauty queens were perfectly poised to represent this claim in the national imagination.

The paradox of the southern Miss America, then, was that her appeal as an icon of regional distinctiveness coexisted with her equally forceful appeal as an icon of national patriotism. She was the perfect symbol of Americanism at a time when many Americans were anxious about racial change and communism. It was also a time when they could easily access and validate that ideal. Before 1954, unless they attended the event in person, Americans saw the Miss America Pageant only in the print media or on newsreels. After 1954, they could be privy to the glamour and intrigue in Atlantic City as it unfolded on their televisions. As William Goldman, a screenwriter who grew up in Chicago, remembers it, this was a very big deal: "[S]uddenly when television happened, here was this fabulous event . . . it was free, it was in your house, you could watch it. And it changed everything."[104]

Aside from the sheer excitement of watching the pageant live, televising the contest had further consequences, given the power of the new medium in shaping Americans' conceptions of themselves. Television altered the imagined community of American identity, transforming it into an embodied community. Performances on television, in other words, became central to how Americans viewed themselves.[105] In this new context, a show that overtly marketed its winner as the personification of American identity was bound to be profoundly appealing, especially at the height of the Cold War. The sheer ubiquity of television, moreover, meant that a remarkable number of Americans could participate in constructing the vision of national identity on its airwaves. Even if they could not cast a vote for the winner, Americans gained increased access to the process by simply turning on their television sets.

Geographical disparities in television ownership are illuminating. Take, for example, 1954, the year of *Brown* and the first televised Miss America Pageant. In most of the former states of the Confederacy, fewer than 40 percent of families owned television sets. In many midwestern states, the number was upward of 60 or 70 percent. In many New England and Middle Atlantic states, it was 70 or 80 percent.[106] The consistently high ratings of the pageant after 1954, and the home states of the women who won 50 percent of the titles for the next ten years, suggest that Americans living outside the South were content to have their national identity symbolized by beauties that hailed from the region. The mass media of the mid-twentieth century may have helped bring down Jim Crow, but it also perpetuated a seductive image of southern beauty that exerted an insidious influence well beyond the boundaries of the region.

ON ITS SURFACE, the *Brown* decision that helped increase the visibility and power of white southern beauty queens would seem to have little to do with the beauty of black women. Yet conceptions of black beauty had a deeper connection to *Brown* than may appear at first glance. In rendering its unanimous decision, the Supreme Court relied, in part, on arguments based on research about attitudes toward appearance and skin color.[107] In doing so, the Court was responding to the strategy pursued by the National Association for the Advancement of Colored People (NAACP), which had abandoned earlier attempts to force school districts to equalize school funding and facilities. Not only had such attempts proven costly and time-consuming, but they also did nothing to challenge the principle of separate but equal, which was, the NAACP argued, discriminatory by its very nature. By 1950, the head of the NAACP's Legal Defense Committee, Thurgood Marshall, had settled on a new approach—using recent data from the social sciences to show that separate but equal caused black students psychological harm. Chief Justice Earl Warren cited this body of scholarship in denouncing separate but equal as a violation of the Fourteenth Amendment, asserting that segregated schools bred "a sense of inferiority" among black children.[108]

The evidence that received the most attention, both then and now, came from a series of tests conducted by Kenneth and Mamie Clark, a husband-and-wife research team trained at Columbia.[109] In the doll test, the most famous of the experiments, the Clarks presented black children ranging in age from three to seven with four dolls. Two had white skin and blond hair; two had black skin and black hair. Then they asked the children to perform tasks designed to determine how the children identified themselves in racial terms and to show which race, white or black, they preferred. The majority of children recognized the racial classification of the dolls and thus showed an awareness of their race ("Give me the doll that looks like a colored child," "Give me the doll that looks like a white child") while expressing preference for the white dolls ("Give me the doll that looks bad," "Give me the doll that is a nice color"). Fifty-nine percent of the children said that the black doll looked bad; 17 percent said the white doll looked bad; 24 percent did not know or gave no response. Asked to choose the doll with the nice color, 38 percent chose the black doll; 60 percent chose the white doll; and 2 percent did not know or gave no response. As the Clarks concluded, the results highlighted "the development of racial concepts and attitudes" and their implications for "racial mental hygiene"—in other words, for self-esteem.[110] To Marshall and the Supreme Court, these findings proved why segregation had to be overturned. Because school segregation reinforced racial difference even when resources were equal, it damaged the psyches of black children, generating, in effect, racial self-hatred.

In subsequent decades, social scientists chipped away at the Clarks' research, challenging the connection between racial preference and self-esteem on methodological grounds.[111] Just because black children said that black dolls looked bad or that white dolls had a better skin color, in other words, did not mean that they suffered from feelings of inadequacy. Other critics took issue with the strategy of relying on social science research, rather than on legal or constitutional arguments, to invalidate separate but equal. Still, dismissing the significance of the doll test altogether seems misguided. That the NAACP used research about the politics of skin color to inform its campaign to end segregation is revealing, in and of itself, suggesting the widespread cultural currency of ideas about black skin tones and attractiveness. Legitimate or not, the approach was revolutionary for positing that conceptions of beauty could be grounds for establishing a violation of the Fourteenth Amendment's equal protection clause. And while the connection between the children's judgments of the dolls and their own self-esteem may be lacking, their choices, at the very least, highlight awareness of those ideas.[112] Children who were dark-skinned themselves, in fact, were even more cognizant of skin color than the medium- and light-skinned children in the study. They more accurately identified the black doll as black and more accurately chose it as the doll that looked most like them. Some participants also offered unsolicited explanations for their decisions, observing, for example, that they rejected the black doll "'cause it don't look pretty."[113]

Interestingly, the Clarks did find slight regional differences among the children in their study. Both northern and southern children said that they wanted to play with the white doll over the black doll; that the white doll was nicer than the black doll; that the colored doll looked bad; and that the white doll had a nice color. Despite these shared preferences, southern children were slightly less likely to conclude that the white doll had a nice color. At the same time, southern children were three times as likely to volunteer their reasons for choosing white dolls over black dolls and, when they did so, to explain their selection in terms of attractiveness. Thirty-two percent of southern children justified their choice in terms of the prettiness of the white doll and the ugliness of the black doll. Among northern children, only 10 percent did so. The Clarks speculated that children in the South had "a greater preoccupation" with such racial matters than did children in the North.[114]

Perhaps the Clarks were right. It is difficult to know why more southern children opted for a language of aesthetics in expressing their doll preferences, but clearly they had learned a thing or two about beauty in the South at an early age. By the 1950s, moreover, these lessons had migrated to a new and very public classroom, the annual Miss America Pageant, and some southern black adults, at least, had taken notice. North Carolinian Mary Mebane was one. In the fall of 1958, Mebane carpooled to her teaching job in Durham with a young man who spent each morning talking about the current Miss America contestants, a group which that year included Mary Ann Mobley, the eventual winner. "He discussed each one's attributes in loving detail with many whoops and hollers," Mebane recalled with palpable bitterness, continuing: "His eyes gleamed, and he had a big smile on his face. I listened in stunned surprise but said nothing. Perhaps, I thought . . . when the pageant was over, the subject would change. But I was wrong. This topic was discussed every morning. When he had exhausted the current crop of Miss America contestants, he went back to the past and started discussing former contestants one by one and in great detail." Mebane was amazed that her carpool companion expressed his interest in the beauties so freely, despite the taboo against interracial sex. She was more shocked, and indeed angry, at what his comments suggested about black women: "[H]e seemed totally oblivious of the implications of his conversation on the self-esteem of black women, for he never held up a single black woman as attractive."[115] Mebane found a new ride to work.

Mebane was not alone in seeing the Miss America Pageant as a forum for denigrating black women. Seven years later, another black woman from Durham penned an emotional column for the local black newspaper in which she condemned the competition for reinforcing a culture of self-hatred among black women. Titling her column "Contest Should Be Called 'Miss White America,'" Ruth Burnett noted that tears came to her eyes, just as they did for the winner that year, Miss Kansas, but not for the same reasons. "I wept for the little girls who must go to the beauty parlor to have their hair relaxed," Burnett wrote. "I wept because the cosmetic industry of America advertises its products on how to be beautiful and, in their eyes, every beautiful woman is white." Black women everywhere must wonder after watching such an event when their own beauty would be honored, as she put it, "for its sheer integrity." Burnett doubted that black women could soon look to the Miss America Pageant for what they most needed — validation that "their brown skins and curly hair and gay dancing brown or black eyes" were beautiful.[116] As black women living in the South, both

Burnett and Mebane would have been aware that white southern women had done especially well in Atlantic City in recent years. The assault on black female beauty must have felt all the more personal as a result.

The southern winners of the Miss America Pageant were silent on the contest's discriminatory practices, with one exception: Yolande Betbeze, the Alabaman crowned Miss America in 1950 who refused to pose in a swimsuit during her reign. Two years after her victory, Betbeze spoke out against the racism of the pageant in the wake of a decision by officials in South Dakota to prohibit Native American women from competing. She was joined by two other former Miss Americas, one of whom was Bess Myerson, the first Jewish American titleholder. "It is a humiliation to every girl who enters the contest," Betbeze proclaimed, "to feel that others just as pretty but of a different race are not free to compete with her."[117] The condemnation was noteworthy, particularly coming from a southern woman. In response to Betbeze's criticism, pageant headquarters passed the buck. The directors noted that women of all races were free to compete at the national level. This was true, as the pageant had eliminated the rule that contestants be "of the white race" in the years after World War II. Yet state organizations, the officials explained, could make their own eligibility rules. By 1960, Betbeze's opposition to the pageant's exclusionary rules had transformed into a frontal assault on segregation itself. She became active with the NAACP and Congress of Racial Equality (CORE), picketing F. W. Woolworth's in New York City to demonstrate her support of the student sit-ins sweeping the South. "I'm a Southern girl," she stated, "but I'm a thinking girl."[118] "Pageant officials weren't very happy about it," Betbeze later recalled.[119] Slaughter offered a blunt assessment of Betbeze's civil rights activism: "That was beneath her dignity."[120]

For most of the 1950s and 1960s, black southern women answered their exclusion from the Miss America Pageant by participating in all-black contests. As we have seen, beauty contests at historically black colleges and universities provided regular forums for the recognition of black beauty, often serving as tools by which administrators could transmit the school's ideals to the students who were the most likely to find themselves the target of whites' critical stares—women. While white southern women were busy shoring up their dominant presence in Atlantic City, black colleges continued their queen coronations at football games and United Negro College Fund events. Fisk crowned its 1966 homecoming queen at a football game in typical fashion, "acknowledging beauty, scholarship and finer womanhood" as a Fisk tradition and its bequest to all female students.[121]

Younger women participated in similar contests. A decade earlier, Anne Moody had relished her experience as homecoming queen as an eighth-grader in Centreville, Mississippi. The consequences of feeling attractive for the first time in her life reverberated beyond her segregated schoolhouse's door. Coiffed, made-up, and dressed in a long gown, Moody rode through downtown Centreville in a parade that blacks and whites came out to view. Spotting her white employer in the crowd, who seemed surprised at Moody's transformation, Moody recalls that she wanted to shout, "Yes, Linda Jean, it's me. Negroes can be beautiful, too." Her joy was cut short, however, when the band started playing "Dixie." "I thought I would die," Moody recalled, "especially when I saw some . . . familiar white faces bellowing out the lyrics."[122]

Although she did not manage to attract as much attention as the white bathing beauty, the black bathing beauty made a minor comeback during these years. The wartime emphasis on beauty had raised the fortunes of the black bathing beauty just as it had for the white. In keeping with patterns firmly established in the black community, the black bathing beauty made a claim for the attractiveness of black women, visually undermining white women's assertion of racial superiority. African American beauties also continued to provide communities economic benefits. Fraternal and benevolent organizations were the most enthusiastic sponsors of the events, combining bathing beauty contests with fund-raising. The Elks of Tuscaloosa, Alabama, for example, invited high school women to participate in their first annual competition in 1956.[123] The lure of a state title and then a trip to a national final seem to have drummed up minimal interest, however. By its second year, the Elks contest attracted only three contestants, and press accounts of this and similar contests waned thereafter.[124] Black beauty contests do not dominate the pages of southern black newspapers as white contests do the pages of white publications.

More newsworthy, though rarer, were black women who attempted to enter white competitions. For the most part, black women in the South shied away from this strategy, but the black press in southern cities reported when women successfully pursued it elsewhere. In 1959, the black newspaper in New Orleans featured a large picture of the new Miss Indiana University on its front page. Nancy Streets, "a sepia beauty" from South Bend, had beaten out fourteen white women to become the first black queen at the university.[125] She thus qualified for the state preliminary for Miss America. Calling her "sepia," however, overstated the matter considerably. The first black woman to integrate a Miss America preliminary in the Deep South did so seven years later. Cheryl Pride competed in the Miss Tampa contest in 1966, placing in the top ten. *Ebony* magazine, which ran a story on the event, remarked that she had "opened a long-barricaded door for other girls from that part of the country." Pride viewed her achievement in the same light: "I believe that the pageant will help me further convince myself and others that all individuals in this great city of Tampa have an equal opportunity to prove themselves acceptable in the community."[126] To Pride, her success in this competition was evidence that all blacks could do well in a world dominated by whites if they took advantage of opportunities to demonstrate their worthiness.

Black women such as Pride and Streets entered these contests for political reasons, hoping their participation would advance black civil rights in yet another area of American life closed to blacks. For some black contestants, the attempt to integrate white beauty contests was even a part of a broader personal commitment to the cause. After winning her title, for example, Streets attempted to integrate a whites-only skating rink but was prevented from doing so by the gun-wielding owner.[127] Throughout the civil rights movement, many black beauty queens wore their political loyalties on their sleeves, while white beauty queens offered platitudes about democracy and family that masked their political import. Black women who performed this race work with their bodies did little, of course, to challenge the belief that the beauty contest was a beneficial institution for women. Even as a strategy for advancing black civil rights, trying to integrate all-white beauty contests left something to be desired. Like all-black bathing beauty competitions, white contests that proved vulnerable to determined black women ultimately failed to have much cultural impact in the southern black community.

Pride's own interpretation of her breakthrough points to part of the problem. Framing her success in terms of personal effort and achievement, she suggested that equality was a matter of exploiting existing opportunities, of simply trying hard enough. Competing in an all-white beauty contest was a civil rights milestone but revealed itself to be a shallow victory once the celebration had died down. Although the brave beauty enjoyed momentary glory and temporary inclusion, her symbolic importance as a Deep South beauty "first" was ephemeral.[128] One woman's breakthrough did not alter the fortunes of most black women with dreams of winning Miss America. Contest sponsors did not suddenly dedicate themselves to recruiting black women to enter their competitions, nor did legions of black women line up to enter. In fact, in arguing that her action demonstrated that "all individuals" could gain acceptance in the Tampa community, Pride delivered a blow to the Florida pageant that lacked much punch. In stark contrast to how most queens at historically black colleges had always seen themselves, she cast her integration of the contest in individualistic, rather than racial, terms. Touted by the black press and civil rights activists, women such as Pride only cracked the long-barricaded door for black beauty queen hopefuls. To open it fully would take several decades. A black woman did not win Miss America until 1983. A black woman from the South did not win until 1993.[129]

The attempt to gain recognition for black female beauty by integrating an all-white contest had other shortcomings. A woman who attempted this feat garnered publicity and demonstrated that black women were "acceptable," but she did not change a pageant's evaluative criteria. As Elizabeth Boyd has argued about black contestants more generally, Pride succeeded because she blended in with the white contestants, because she engaged in what amounted to an act of racial passing.[130] A black woman in an all-white contest offered evidence of a pageant's commitment to diversity, certainly a politic move at a time when blacks were demanding inclusion. But ultimately her participation did "little or nothing to challenge the racial construction of femininity."[131] Her participation did not so much prove that black women were beautiful as it proved that black women could look and move like white women. These pathbreaking contestants used their pageant performances to announce that there were no aesthetic differences between white and black women, a debatable claim, as we have seen. Integrating white beauty contests did not change ways of seeing among white southerners and nonsoutherners, an already tall order given the conspicuousness of Dixie's white beauty queens. Trying hard enough in a competition designed and sponsored for white women was not, in the final count, enough. Over time, the strategy of integration lost its appeal, and opponents of segregated pageants opted for disruption instead.[132] Black activists in Mobile, Alabama, planned to stop the segregated Junior Miss Pageant in 1969, but local police made 100 arrests, rendering the protest futile.

IF ANY ASPECT OF the practice of beauty in the South was valuable in undermining the symbolic power of white beauty queens, it was the civil rights work of black beauticians. As Tiffany M. Gill has shown, beauticians built on what was, by the postwar period, a long tradition of business-based activism and embraced the civil rights movement with enthusiasm.[133] A perusal of any southern black newspaper reveals the centrality of beauticians in the movement. Free from economic entanglements with whites, beauticians fought the intransigence of white southerners by taking advantage of the opportunities their workplaces provided. Beauticians nurtured talk in their shops that could lead to action that would have proven dangerous, if not impossible, to carry out in other spaces in black communities.

Bernice Robinson's beauty parlor in her home in Charleston, South Carolina, for example, emerged as a vital center of civil rights activities in the city in the 1950s.[134] A local leader in the NAACP and its voter registration drives, Robinson began taking customers to the registration office in the early 1950s, leaving wet-haired women behind, under the dryer. "If you get too hot under there," she instructed them as she left her shop, "just cut her off and come out!" As her involvement intensified, sometimes women phoned to find out whether she would actually be doing hair. She also used her shop as a base to recruit new members of the NAACP. Because many of her recruits, who worked as teachers and nurses, feared their jobs would be in jeopardy if their white mailman noticed NAACP mailings, Robinson had their membership cards and other correspondence sent to her house. By virtue of Robinson's profession, she enjoyed both the economic independence to pursue and the space to discuss and plan civil rights activities. "I didn't have to worry about losing my job or anything because I wasn't a schoolteacher or a caseworker with the Department of Social Services or connected with anything I might be fired from," she observed. "I had my own business . . . so I didn't have to worry. Many people did."[135] Carolyn Daniels of Dawson, Georgia, said much the same thing. Though her activism did not go unnoticed—local authorities revoked her driver's license for three months—her work as an independent black beautician made all the difference in terms of her ability to sustain her involvement. "I was free to do what I chose," she stated.[136]

Ruby Parks Blackburn of Atlanta was free, too, and as her appointment books and personal papers illustrate, she took advantage of this fact. Blackburn ran her beauty shop while simultaneously pursuing a multipronged agenda designed to redress racial inequality in the city. The founder of three separate civic groups, Blackburn first launched the TIC ("To Improve Conditions") Club in the early 1930s, which undertook beautification projects in the neglected black neighborhoods of Atlanta, lobbied for and won the construction of two schools for black children, and convinced chain department stores in Atlanta at the height of the Depression to hire black clerks. Her efforts through the TIC Club inspired one African American newspaperman in the city, Martin Richardson of the Scott Newspaper Syndicate, to reevaluate his opinion of who would ultimately do the most for the race: "I . . . made one slight error," he confessed in a letter to Blackburn. "I had my sexes mixed. I had always felt that any salvation of the race would come through its alleged men. I am quite open on the subject now."[137] In the 1940s, Blackburn organized the Georgia League of Negro Women Voters, a group that sought to instill a "proper sense of civic duty and responsibility" in its members by fighting for the needs of the black community, such as bus service to black neighborhoods. Her Atlanta Cultural League, incorporated in 1945, provided training for Atlanta's black cooks, maids, waitresses, and janitors, while pushing white employers to offer "a fair day's pay for a fair day's work."[138] Finally, she headed membership drives for the Atlanta NAACP and fund-raising campaigns for the group's Defense Fund, which provided legal aid to African Americans.[139] Soliciting donations was not easy, but, as she reported to a Defense Fund committee meeting, "she wasn't tired of working . . . she was just beginning, and that funds were needed and that she and her helpers would not slacken until they were raised."[140] A former Atlanta branch president insisted, in fact, that "there is no harder worker in the organization than Mrs. Blackburn."[141] Blackburn's success owed much to her membership in a profession that gave her the time, space, and freedom necessary to move back and forth between the black community and the white power structure of Atlanta. Like Robinson, Blackburn became so involved in local campaigns that her work in beauty culture occasionally took a backseat. In 1956 and 1957, for example, Blackburn brought in close to sixty dollars some weeks. In others, her earnings were closer to ten dollars.[142]

Dedicated to the status of beauty culture as well as to the welfare of black communities, professional organizations harnessed the many possibilities of beauty shops as community centers. Local, state, and regional affiliates of the National Beauty Culturists' League (NBCL) undertook racial justice activities along with professionalization projects during these years. Durham, for instance, was home to numerous beauticians' associations in the middle decades of the twentieth century. DeShazor's Beauty College boasted alumnae chapters in Durham and the surrounding area. DeShazor graduates in these chapters did their fair share of socializing, but they also organized to use their shops in much the same way Robinson did, sponsoring fund-raising for local causes and recruiting customers to join the NAACP. DeShazor alumnae consistently outpaced other

Durham clubs and organizations in this effort, winning annual membership contribution awards in the 1950s.[143]

The annual conventions sponsored by the NBCL and its affiliates brought southern beauticians together on a regular basis, encouraging attendees to see their shops as vital community institutions. In Mississippi, the Mississippi Independent Beautician Association (MIBA) used its July 1954 gathering to advertise its support of the recent *Brown* decision. The 500 members in attendance drew up a declaration of principles—the first of which was that it wanted to "go on record as highly endorsing the decision"—and had the list printed in the state's largest black newspaper, the *Jackson Advocate*. The MIBA ended its public statement with a call to action. It urged other beauticians to do their share in easing the transition to desegregated schools so that future generations would not suffer from the "feeling of inferiority" caused by segregated education.[144] The Mississippi beauticians' stance reveals, quite clearly, the difference between the function of beauty in the black and white South during the civil rights era. White beauty queens provided both symbolic cover and motivation to a white South made anxious by the threat of desegregation. Black beauticians, utilizing the advantages afforded by their jobs, actively labored to hasten the desegregation project.

Similarly, the NBCL organized its 1955 convention in Washington, D.C., around the theme "Beauticians United for New Responsibilities" to help members become better attuned, the group's historian wrote, to "community economics and political affairs." Conference participants could attend the usual sessions on electrotherapy, hair tinting, and the coordination of hairstyles with hats. They could also attend panels titled "Beauticians United for Economic Security" and "Beauticians United for Political Action," which featured officials from the Defense Department, the Labor Department, and the NAACP, as well as prominent NBCL leaders such as Ella Martin of Atlanta, who headed the largest state delegation in attendance.[145] The following year the Alabama state convention adopted a similar theme, "Beauticians' Role in an Integrated World," placing beauticians and their businesses at the center of civil rights struggles throughout the state.[146] Officers of the 1957 NBCL meeting in New Orleans emphasized the symbiotic relationship between beauticians' own advancement and the progress of the race. They insisted that beauticians had a duty to improve the status of black women within the profession by voting for governors who would appoint black women to cosmetology boards. They were also to urge their patrons to oust southern legislators who, in their "last ditch fight" against the forces of change, opposed civil rights legislation and the desegregation of schools. "[W]e should interest ourselves enough," officers declared, "to see to it that every customer, every student that goes in and out of our doors, are taking an active part in their city, state and national governments."[147] Based on a solid foundation of business-driven activism that supported economic uplift and independence for black women, black beauticians fostered a network of professional organizations that facilitated their civic engagement.

It was this long-standing mix of professional independence, community activism, and interpersonal trust that propelled beauticians into the constituency of ministers, independent farmers, and funeral home directors who attended the Highlander Folk School to learn about organizing on the local level. Myles Horton, the director of the Tennessee school, had noticed their presence at the school's training workshops in the 1940s, he said, "just by sheer accident." But beauticians themselves, as well as the neighbors they served, would have well understood the skills they possessed and appreciated that these skills did not amount simply, as Horton once remarked, "to straightening hair or whatever the hell they do."[148] Throughout the civil rights movement, Highlander made concerted efforts to hone the abilities of these women. As Septima Clark, director of workshops, wrote in a 1960 invitation to a beauticians' workshop, beauty culture "is one of the professions which offer[s] to its members great freedom for leadership."[149]

Exploiting this freedom, Clark and her staff remained in close contact with beauticians' associations throughout the South, offering advice and the use of Highlander facilities to plan initiatives. Bernice Robinson's opening of the first citizenship school on Johns Island, South Carolina, is perhaps the most famous fruit of Highlander's relationship with beauticians, but there were many others.[150] Clark relied heavily on Vera Pigee, who attended Highlander workshops in 1960, for example, to shepherd the movement in the Mississippi Delta. The proprietor of a beauty salon in Clarksdale and a leader in the NAACP, Pigee was so successful in mobilizing locals that Clark decided to take out a lifetime membership in the NAACP through the Clarksdale chapter. By 1965, Pigee had overseen the operation of twenty citizenship schools, some of which were held in the tiny alcove discreetly located at the back of her shop. Pigee's salon eventually became known as "the birthing room for civil rights in Clarksdale," a fact highlighted by a 1963 photo of Pigee at work.[151] The image shows a poster on the wall that asks customers to stop police brutality by

Bernice Robinson (standing left) and Septima Clark (standing right) at a citizenship school training workshop, ca. 1961. Charleston beautician Bernice Robinson established citizenship schools to help southern blacks register to vote. Courtesy of the Avery Research Center for African American History and Culture, College of Charleston, Charleston, S.C.

electing Aaron Henry for governor. Pigee stands fixing a woman's hair, while the client prepares herself for the task of ousting resistant politicians and law enforcement, reading through a stack of voter registration forms. As Francoise N. Hamlin observes, the photograph captures how the serenity of this female space supported defiant political action in a violent time.[152] It is an incongruous image, in some ways, but it is not one that would have raised too many eyebrows in civil rights circles.

Beauticians from Jackson, Tennessee, to take another example of Highlander's cultivation of beautician activists, met at the school in 1961. They discussed how to build a health center for the black residents of "Tent City," a ramshackle encampment for black sharecroppers evicted from their homes for attempting to vote in the 1960 presidential election. In addition to placing boxes for donations in their own shops, they asked members of the State Beauticians' Association to donate the proceeds from one hairdo to their campaign.[153] Although disagreements and legal details slowed the project, the beauticians' leadership proved instrumental in the construction of the building, which began in 1962. After overhearing conversations about the effort, the local organizer told Clark that

Vera Pigee's beauty shop, Clarksdale, Mississippi, 1963. A patron at Pigee's beauty shop reads voter registration forms. A poster hanging above the mirror explains why voting matters. Courtesy of Charles Moore/Black Star.

she felt compelled, in fact, "to inform people that this is not confined to Beauticians only."[154]

In some cases, beauticians did see themselves as the front line of local activism. The declaration penned by the members of the Mississippi Independent Beautician Association in favor of the *Brown* decision revealed a concern that not all constituencies in the black South would do what was required of them. "[U]nder no circumstances," the members asserted, "will we cooperate with any group which has its objective the perpetuation of segregation in any form—voluntarily or otherwise."[155] This statement was directed as much at blacks who were reluctant to publicly fight for desegregation as it was at whites who feared for their way of life.[156] If two contests sponsored by Durham's black newspaper the *Carolina Times* in the spring of 1958 are any indication, beauticians rivaled ministers in central North Carolina in terms of their public profile, if not community involvement. The paper first sponsored a popularity contest for area beauticians, and then, a few weeks later, one for ministers. The top vote-getter in the former contest received an all-expense-paid trip to the annual NBCL convention in Miami; in the latter, the winner earned a trip to Bermuda. Both contests garnered front-page coverage for weeks on end and suggest that the black beautician was the female counterpart to the black minister.[157]

In Durham, however, some beauticians might have bristled at the comparison. Four years earlier in the *Carolina Times*, several beauticians had pointed to the exemplary nature of their own civil rights work while criticizing local ministers for not doing enough.[158] Septima Clark would likely have recognized the sentiments behind their critique. While attending the trial of white policemen for the beating of several black women in Oxford, Mississippi, Clark stayed with a woman in Holly Springs, over forty-five miles away. Given the distance, it was not her first choice. "I couldn't get any of the black people in Oxford to give me a room to stay there," she explained. For five days, she rode back and forth between the two towns because no one in Oxford wanted, or was able, to provide accommodations. But the woman in Holly Springs was a beautician, Clark noted years later, "so she wasn't afraid."[159]

Many beauticians were prominent community activists, just as dedicated to working for racial progress as they were to fixing hair. These two tasks, moreover, were neither mutually exclusive nor even just peripherally related. Rather, they were interwoven into the fabric of black beauty culture. Helping black southern women feel well-groomed was an enterprise with political consequences, one undertaken, in part, to confute whites' stereotypes about black womanhood. Beauticians' grooming services themselves might take on special meaning within the context of the civil rights movement. In a 1970 tribute to Montgomery, Alabama, poet Gwendolyn Brooks gave evidence of this fact. Paraphrasing a woman who fifteen years earlier had driven a car during the bus boycott and who had emphasized the importance of appearances to participants, Brooks wrote, "I told 'em, 'Look nice! / Straighten your hair! / Take a bath!'"[160] Anne Moody's retreat into a beauty salon after the Jackson sit-in testified, in turn, to the power of beauticians to undo the damage inflicted by white mobs, whose attacks were regularly aimed at the body.

BLACK BEAUTICIANS MUST have felt it keenly, then, when young black activists in the mid-1960s started to take the movement in a new direction, rejecting the strategies these women had long pursued. Frustrated with the pace of change and the integrationist program of black moderates and white liberals, younger activists embraced Black Power. Their more militant stance was predicated on the belief that blacks themselves had to control their destiny. For what the black beauty queen brought into sharp relief as she walked across the stage with a phalanx of white beauties, many activists knew from their own daily lives: attempting to assimilate into the existing system did not necessarily change white minds. Certainly it had not, despite the gradual demise of Jim Crow in the South, solved the more intractable problems of de facto segregation that plagued the entire country. The shift in thinking manifested itself in the changed tactics of organizations like the Student Nonviolent Coordinating Committee (SNCC), as well as in the establishment of newer organizations, like the Black Panther Party for Self-Defense in 1966.

These groups pursued a radical political agenda rooted in black autonomy and black nationalism. As numerous scholars have argued, however, this new concern with racial separatism was as much cultural in nature as it was political.[161] Black Power activists insisted that practices and ideals that smacked of whiteness had to be abandoned in favor of ones that denoted blackness, for only in this way could a new black consciousness—and effective political action—emerge. Within the context of this new cultural nationalism, the traditional aesthetic of respectability became a problem. How could someone be truly black, and thus a legitimate proponent of the advance of the race, if he or she mimicked whites?

The recollections of civil rights organizer Cleveland Sellers shed light on this dilemma, showing how black politics and aesthetics, which had always been intertwined, became more so even as their relationship was redefined in certain respects.[162] Entering Howard University in 1962, Sellers was disturbed by the appearance of most of his fellow classmates. As the "capstone of Negro education," Howard had worked for decades to inscribe the tenets of respectability onto the bodies of its students.[163] Sellers said that everyone—students, teachers, and administrators—went to great lengths to preserve *"the Howard image*, which," he argued, "was designed to create the impression that there were no substantial differences between Howard's students and those at elite white colleges."[164] To maintain the image, "young ladies wore skirts and stockings and heels. And the young men wore slacks and shirts and ties. I thought I was going to Howard University because it was going to be the hotbed of civil rights activities," he continued. "When I got there it was the reverse."[165] Whereas black colleges had long tied an aesthetic of respectability to racial progress,

Sellers severed the connection entirely. He regarded the "Howard image" as a sign of an indifference to, even the "reverse" of, civil rights. The color prejudice at Howard, which the Greek system, in particular, nurtured, played a role as well, reinforcing the perception of some students that the institution was a bastion of racial conservatism.[166]

Far from abandoning their appearance to whimsy, Sellers and other students who began to criticize the image adopted a new look, rejecting "respectable" wardrobes. Sellers, for example, opted for jeans, sweatshirts, and army jackets. Perhaps more importantly, they refused to straighten their hair, wearing an "Afro" or "natural," a hairstyle that has become almost synonymous in the American imagination with the Black Power movement. To a significant degree, these Howard students were pioneers, a small but influential group who took an early lead in experimenting with innovative grooming practices.[167] Their aesthetic choices represented the vanguard of a new cultural nationalism, one that would ultimately become one of Black Power's most influential and long-lasting contributions.[168]

But they were not the first to give up straightened hair. In the 1950s and early 1960s, a small group of intellectuals and artists in New York, female members of a kind of Black Bohemia, wore natural hairstyles.[169] Natural hair was healthier, they believed, and suggested sympathy with independence movements in Africa. The look became a fashion statement, accepted by white and black members of the cultural elite. Outside these rarified circles, other women might experiment with unstraightened hair, but they did so at great risk to their reputations. In 1943, ten years before natural hair became the vogue among some New Yorkers and twenty before it gained popularity among Black Power advocates, Annabelle Baker, a sophomore at the Hampton Institute in Virginia, let her hair go natural and endured years of pain and isolation as a result. She later stated that the decision had changed her life forever.[170] Since childhood, Baker had had a complicated relationship with the straightening process. At times it made her feel pretty; at still others, when the hot irons grazed her skin, it inflicted pain. Her studies at Hampton transformed this ambivalence into outright rejection. Studying the human form in her art classes, she began to appreciate a wide spectrum of physical traits as beautiful. Changing hairstyles seemed a logical outcome of this new way of seeing.

In a scenario that would play out among civil rights activists in the 1960s—and that recalled the experiences of the first women to bob their hair in the 1920s—Baker went to a black barbershop for help in achieving a natural look. Remembering this event decades afterward, Baker did not say why, but she did not have to. No beautician would have understood her request. Beauty shops were spaces dedicated to getting rid of natural hair, to processing it into something else. Barbershops, by contrast, dealt with natural hair on a daily basis since grooming for the majority of black men involved nothing more than a basic cut.[171]

Back on campus, Baker found that what she had considered "a simple step" represented a major offense to many of her classmates, who were shocked and subsequently hostile. The dean of women, Flemmie P. Kittrell, was angry, too, and insisted that Baker could not represent the school at an upcoming conference at Wellesley College. In retrospect, Baker realized, Kittrell "was under a lot of pressure" since female students were supposed to "go out into the world as standard-bearers of deportment and achievement." At the time, Baker found the intensity of the campaign against her intolerable, and while she eventually won permission to make the trip, her days at Hampton were numbered. After two expulsions for rules violations, which she attributed to continued opposition to her hair, Baker returned home to Jacksonville, Florida. This move did not solve her problem, however, since her aunts, with whom she lived, owned the largest beauty parlor in town. Recognizing the "shame" that her hairstyle caused her family, Baker left, finding acceptance, in her words, "among the illiterate or minimally educated working class."[172] With this one decision about her appearance, Baker violated the aesthetic of respectability, breaking a sacred social contract.

It was the women of the Student Nonviolent Coordinating Committee, though, who in the early 1960s played a major role in redefining the black body and laid the groundwork for the Black Power aesthetic that would become popular by the end of the decade.[173] From the organization's founding in 1960, female members recognized that their respectable clothing—dresses, petticoats, stockings, bobby socks—was not suited to the physical demands of demonstrations and sit-ins. Straightened hair, too, was difficult to maintain. Movement activities might make a visit to the beauty shop an unnecessary luxury in terms of both time and money, while a physical confrontation or a stint in a hot, crowded jail could undo a beautician's careful work in seconds. According to Debbie Amis Bell, a SNCC field secretary, the way black women adorned themselves was "totally unreasonable" for engaging in civil rights protests. Such practical considerations magnified as SNCC women traveled into the rural South to register voters beginning in 1961, but political considerations quickly emerged as the primary concern. Hoping to connect with the poor sharecroppers they sought to register, male and female members of SNCC wore work shirts and denim overalls and pants (or skirts) as a sign of their solidarity with the black working class. The gravity of their charge among this disenfranchised group, too, made things like pressed hair seem silly: "[W]e thought our message was the most important thing and not our looks," Bell asserts.[174]

The "SNCC uniform," as SNCC member Gwendolyn Zoharah Simmons has called the new style, or "SNCC skin," in the words of historian Tanisha C. Ford, represented a critique of the aesthetic of respectability that black women, especially, had been taught to embody.[175] As Ford argues, the plain work clothes and natural hair that together constituted SNCC skin offered a "beauty aesthetic for the new activist female body," an aesthetic that most women in the organization had adopted by 1963.[176] At the March on Washington in August 1963, when a group of Mississippi SNCC members were called onstage to sing freedom songs, Anne Moody "reluctantly" followed her fellow activists to the stage, but not because she was afraid to perform. "I think I was the only girl from Mississippi with a dress on," Moody remembered. "All the others were wearing denim skirts and jeans."[177] SNCC skin also became the style of choice for SNCC members in southern cities. Two Maryland sisters who traveled to a SNCC conference in Atlanta arrived, as one recalled, in "little white gloves and full-skirted summer dresses." "People in SNCC were looking at us like we were crazy," she said.[178]

Opinions about SNCC denim varied. Some movement leaders felt SNCC activists looked sloppy in their work clothes; other observers wondered why they would want to adopt a style that many impoverished blacks themselves likely yearned to abandon; some critics accused SNCC of romanticizing the poor rather than forging a genuine bond of respect. Ella Baker, who herself had protested the restrictive Shaw University dress code as an undergraduate back in 1922, nevertheless understood that the casual style might be off-putting to more urbane college students. She encouraged SNCC organizers to use it carefully in campus recruitment drives.[179]

SNCC women's unpressed hair made perhaps an even bigger impression than did their denim attire. For while denim work clothes were ubiquitous in the countryside, natural hair was not. Rural black women, including local civil rights organizers, had their hair pressed. When Howard University student Muriel Tillinghast arrived in Mayersville, Mississippi, in 1964 to deliver a speech about registering to vote, Unita Blackwell, a young woman in the audience, was taken aback. Tillinghast's natural seems to have been more striking than her message. Tillinghast, said the Mayersville native, "was the first black woman I saw with a nappy head smiling." Concerned that the SNCC organizer might not know where she could get her hair pressed in Mayersville, Blackwell offered to help. The organizer demurred. Blackwell was perplexed: "I didn't say any more about it and we went up to Greenville to a meeting and there were about five or six other women in there like that," she recalled, "and then I discovered that this was a style."[180]

Even in cities, the natural hair of SNCC women raised eyebrows. The startled reaction of one middle-aged visitor to the group's Atlanta headquarters captured this fact succinctly. "I ain't never seen nothin' like this," he exclaimed. "Y'all sho' are some new Negroes."[181] Juadine Henderson, an activist from Batseville, Mississippi, working near Washington, D.C., sought help from a barber in her effort to achieve a natural. Distressed by her request, he offered to give her money to get her hair done properly. She refused, and he acquiesced.[182] Mary Lovelace O'Neal was likely the first woman to don a natural at Howard University in 1961. But the decision diminished her social life and the esteem of her male peers, ruining her chance, rumored to be good, of being chosen the queen of Kappa Alpha Psi, a campus fraternity partial to women with fair skin and long hair.[183] O'Neal remembered that most students kept asking her, "Why don't you get your hair pressed?" After she refused, she recalled, she was "kind of ditched and couldn't be the Kappa queen."[184] Muriel Tillinghast, another early adopter of the natural at Howard, said that her unpressed hair had limited her circle of friends while at school.[185] Gwendolyn Zoharah Simmons, who entered Spelman in 1962, was called in to the dean of students' office after she let her hair go natural not that long after her arrival on campus. The dean called Simmons an "embarrassment" to the school, since all Spelman women were to be "well-groomed." Though she escaped punishment by the administration, many of her classmates were no more sympathetic. She only felt comfortable with her natural hair among fellow SNCC activists. "But other than that," Simmons remembered, "walking down the street in the black community, people just thought nothing of insulting you about it. Every day you girded up to go out and face the world."[186] Still, some were inspired by the bravery of women like Tillinghast, Simmons, and O'Neal. Having seen an activist with unpressed hair on television, one woman stole a fork from her college dining hall, using it to release her hair from its disciplined state.[187]

As the civil rights movement embraced the call of Black Power, these aesthetic choices were increasingly filtered through the lens of black nationalism. By 1964, when Unita Blackwell met Tillinghast and other SNCC activists in Mississippi, she understood that natural hair was a part of "what it means to be black."[188] These choices were also increasingly intertwined with the black student movement. Indeed, it was hardly coincidental that college students launched some of the earliest rejections of the aesthetic of respectability. Over time, some students involved in the civil rights movement began to view the black college as the handmaiden of the conservative, integrationist politics of civil rights leaders. Student suspicions of administrators at historically black colleges and universities had a long history, as we have seen. For decades, students had taken issue with efforts to mold them into perfect specimens of black manhood and womanhood. These conflicts erupted into full-blown rebellions at Fisk and Howard Universities in the 1920s, and though administrators there granted slightly more liberal regulations governing things like behavior, dress, and socialization, black colleges maintained firm control over their students. This was particularly the case for female students. Black coeds still had to adhere to dress and conduct codes. They were still subject to the disciplining function of beauty contests, as well as to the critical eye of fashion columnists.

But by the mid-1960s, the anti-authoritarian proclivities of contemporary youth culture, white and black, combined with the rising tide of Black Power to forge a potent challenge on black college campuses. Beginning in the spring of 1967, militant students railed against administrators and professors for promoting an elitist education indebted to white norms, detached from black community needs.[189] Ultimately, the black student movement would roil black campuses nationwide, often in violent ways. It was on southern black colleges that the movement began, however, a fact that belies the conservative image associated with these institutions.[190] From Howard to Tennessee State to Texas Southern, as one sympathetic professor wrote, students protested "an outmoded generation of Negro overseers" who dispensed a "chittlin' education."[191] Students demanded nothing less than a revolution on their campuses, pushing for better facilities, Black Studies curricula, less restrictive conduct rules, and a stronger student government to counter both "Uncle Tom" administrators and white trustees.[192] As William Van Deburg observes, and this list of demands suggests, it was on the college campus that Black Power's cultural concerns became most clearly manifest.[193] In transforming their universities into institutions rooted in racial solidarity and black culture, students simultaneously transformed them into laboratories for exploring the expressive possibilities of Black Power, including a new aesthetic of blackness. Helping to give birth to the mantra "Black is Beautiful," they challenged traditional ideals of fashion, conduct, skin color, and hair texture.

The change was not necessarily immediate, nor was it absolute. At Bennett College in Greensboro, North Carolina, which, like many historically black colleges for women, had fairly strict regulations, campus unrest began in the spring of 1968. Students questioned compulsory chapel attendance and early curfews, invited a Black Power activist to speak on campus, and attempted to create a Black Power group (a request denied by the administration). Yet "Bennett Belles," as the students were called, moved with caution in embracing the new aesthetic. Although the leader of the proposed Black Power organization wore a natural, the relatively dark-skinned 1968 May Day queen had straightened hair. The fashion columnist that year described the latest trends for "classroom dress" in typical language, moreover, registering no complaints about formal dress requirements for attending class.[194] The campus newspaper also ran a feature story on a brownskin Bennett student with pressed hair who had competed in the 1967 Miss Tan America pageant, a national contest for black women dating to 1965 that, given its name, seems to have struggled with the changing climate as well.

By the spring of 1969, however, Bennett's Miss United Negro College Fund titleholder sported a natural, and in an indication of how black nationalism had turned attention away from denim, the home economics department sponsored an African-themed fashion show. The Black Power speaker that Bennett Belles had asked to campus the year before made his visit, too, delivering a lecture that was well received by much of the student body. Howard Fuller, founder of the short-lived Malcolm X Liberation University in Durham, exhorted Bennett women to demand a black-oriented curriculum that would better serve their communities and themselves. Bennett, he proclaimed, needed to produce revolutionary sisters "committed toward helping their people rather than produce white-patterned 'Negro ladies.'"[195] Campus newspaper columnist Gladys Ashe agreed: "We no longer want to be 'lily-white young ladies,' but we want to be 'black soul-sisters.'"[196]

Such militant proclamations reflected a new political atmosphere at Bennett, but the more traditional body aesthetic coexisted with Black is

Beautiful as the decade came to a close. In the fall of 1969, the student newspaper published a poem lauding women who honored their blackness within and without: "You with your 'fro and your black & beautiful body au naturel / Can you dig that you don't need no / white-man-manufactured-hair-thing / No need to wear inferiority / on the inside / in your mind / on the outside / on your crowning glory."[197] The consensus on campus was that the "Bennett Ideal" had widened to encompass a "sister with a natural and a dashiki," yet of the multi-hued women on the 1969 May Day court, only one, the runner-up, had natural hair, and a straight-haired Bennett Belle competed in a preliminary for the Miss America Pageant that fall.[198] Despite the fashion columnist's new enthusiasm for "African prints," old dress codes and conduct regulations also died hard. "I've never heard of not wearing pants downtown," one freshman complained to a reporter, adding that "curfew hours are ridiculous," too.[199] No doubt some of her peers shared her desire to wear pants downtown, but by the early 1970s, the editorial board of the newspaper believed that Bennett Belles had gone too far in embracing more casual dressing habits. Still appealing to their peers as "Black women," some of whom continued to wear their hair naturally, the writers nevertheless criticized students for wearing hair rollers, bathrobes, and slippers beyond the privacy of their dorm rooms. They lamented that behavioral standards had declined as well. "We have become loud and boisterous in public," they wrote, "shedding the cloak of a woman."[200] As did the aesthetic of respectability, the new aesthetic required, though not quite in the same measure or same way, bodily discipline.

The remorse of Bennett women on the issues of dress and behavior seems an anomaly. At North Carolina College for Negroes, where Mary Mebane had endured the scolding of a teacher who found her striped and checked clothing distasteful, students attempted to change campus dress expectations in a variety of ways. The yearbook staff sponsored a fashion show that stressed "individuality," while one student argued in an op-ed that the administration wanted students to look, act, and smell like white people, and enforced its dress code to those ends.[201] The administration believed that most students "come from the backwoods," he observed, and that they did not understand "how to put on clothes, let alone dress appropriately for the white people."[202]

As to whether or not the new aesthetic penetrated campus culture, Bennett women were in good company. Dedication to blackness did not necessarily entail a new hairdo or wardrobe. Students sometimes cast blackness as a political or cultural position that stemmed from an inner conviction, not an outward style. Black means "soul," said one woman, which was more about "internal feelings" and less about wearing certain clothes or an Afro.[203] Indeed, these pronouncements were often paired with critiques of a superficial adoption of the aesthetic divorced from substantive personal change. Campus queens might also downplay the physical, choosing not to embody Black is Beautiful themselves while still employing the rhetoric of Black Pride. The 1968 queen of Elizabeth City State College, also in North Carolina, emphasized that she was a "Black American" who was "proud of her people" in a campus newspaper feature, which showed her posing in a demure dress and with pressed hair.[204]

*Ebony*'s August 1971 "Belles of the South" article, which opened the discussion in Chapter 4 and which profiled sixteen young beauties enrolled or recently graduated from historically black colleges, also reveals that the aesthetic of blackness was more appealing to some women than to others. The August issue of the magazine, devoted to "The South Today," was intended as a status report on the region, examining how the civil rights movement had changed the prospects of southern blacks in recent years. The cover illustration shows a South of black militancy. One man gives the Black Power salute; two women sport naturals, one wears leather, the other an animal-print dress. The Belles of the South profiled inside softened this image. Most of the campus beauties had medium to dark skin tones, though several were light. Half, meanwhile, had straightened hair.[205] None appeared in clothing designed to evoke Africa or radical politics.

Yet students at some black colleges did display a greater dedication to Black is Beautiful, which was best exemplified by their efforts to use campus beauty contests to forward the new look. In doing so, students coopted the ritual that administrators had employed for decades to enforce a conservative body aesthetic. It was also the ritual that had, of course, rewarded women with lighter skin more often than not. Occasional challenges to the tradition of choosing light-skinned women as queens had occurred, however, before militant students took aim at campus beauty contests in the mid- and late 1960s. Morehouse College freshmen in the early 1950s decided, for example, that a brownskin woman should be queen, and so bloc-voted to ensure her victory. Pleased with their achievement, the students were informed by the disapproving alumni association that they would have to hold their homecoming dance, at which the queen would be presented, off campus.[206] At Howard, younger members of a black fraternity voted for a brownskin woman to be their queen in 1952. In 1960, a brownskin woman herself lobbied to become Howard homecoming queen. Lacking the requisite grade point average to win the honor, she was widely admired by her classmates for attempting the feat, according to one of her female classmates. "It was a real grassroots operation," the woman stated, noting that the incident represented an early example of the kind of student resistance that would, in just a few short years, be unexceptionable.[207] Although not a widespread phenomenon at black colleges, these efforts to recognize the beauty of brownskin women in campus contests showed that a few students publicly questioned the veneration of lighter skin, at least, before the emergence of Black Power. Some students may have been ready, in other words, to accept the aesthetic challenge issued by Black Power advocates during the black student movement. For some, admiring "brown" may have been a stepping stone to admiring "black," in terms of both the color of a woman's skin and the texture of her hair.[208]

Still, turning the college beauty contest into an arena for celebrating blackness was not without difficulty. In 1966, four male Howard students active in civil rights struggles faced this reality when they tried to challenge the "blue-vein tradition" of the campus's homecoming queen contest. Deciding that a woman with a natural should be elected homecoming queen, they undertook a hard-fought battle to convince classmates that Robin Gregory, a SNCC member who had marched from Selma to Montgomery, deserved the honor. The Independents, as her proponents called themselves, paraded through campus holding signs imprinted with her photo, arranged informational meetings for skeptical students, and helped her write a skit about black culture in America. Not all students supported the idea. According to a story in *Jet*, Gregory had been an object of "derision" by some and was "not that well received" when she gave a speech to a group of upperclassmen.[209] The strategy of associating her natural hair and darker skin (described as brown, not black) with pride in black achievement, history, and beauty ultimately paid off. The *Jet* article actually suggested that Gregory's natural was the single most important qualification she brought to the contest. After she was proclaimed queen at the coronation ceremony, the applause lasted for fifteen minutes. In the wake of Gregory's victory, rumors appeared in the black press that a recount had been demanded, and that the dean of students had refused to place the crown on her head.[210] Though unsubstantiated, these reports suggest that her winning was no small matter, that it had rankled the leaders of the prestigious black university.

Women fought these battles on their own behalf, too, making the recognition of Afrocentric beauty standards a focus of their campaigns to become campus queens. Janet Lane Martin was a candidate for the Spelman College homecoming crown in 1970. She challenged her male classmates at Morehouse College, who decided who would be elected Miss Maroon and White, to live up to the high-flying rhetoric then circulating on both campuses. "Everyone was walking around saying, 'I'm black and I'm proud and black is beautiful,'" Martin told a reporter several decades later, "so I told them if they really believed that, it was time to prove it." Martin implied that it may have taken some prodding for male students to select contestants who fit the new ideal. After all, Gwendolyn Zoharah Simmons had earlier faced the condemnation of a dean and the reproachful stares of her peers on the very same campus for wearing a natural. Martin won her case, noting that being elected queen was "very empowering," both "for me and others who look like me."[211]

Most of the 1970 Spelman homecoming court embodied the standards of beauty for which Martin had demanded recognition. Of the sixteen women who served on the court, few had pressed hair. Most wore naturals, most had dark skin, and many wore clothing and jewelry intended to evoke associations with Africa—fabrics with bright, colorful patterns and animal prints. During part of the week's festivities, some of the women donned turbans, long seen by respectable blacks as an embarrassing symbol of black rural style. Beneath Martin's coronation photo in the yearbook, editors assessed her significance: "Here is the essence of Black pride, dignity and femininity. Here is a Black woman."[212] Photos from the football game testify to this blending of the new conception of feminine beauty with a defiant political stance. In one hand, court members hold their flower bouquets—an essential accoutrement of the beauty queens for decades—while they give the Black Power salute with the other. Several 1973 Kentucky State University queen contenders also wore their hair in its natural state and appeared in clothing with African motifs. They rejected the traditional dresses and white gloves worn by previous contestants since these items gave off "too much of a white image."[213] Although the director of the university's charm school for beauty queens, which honed

Miss Maroon and White court, 1970. Elected to the homecoming court by the men of Morehouse College, these Spelman women displayed a new, more militant brand of black beauty. From Spelman College yearbook, *Reflections*, 1971, Spelman College, Atlanta, Ga.

the skills of campus royalty, criticized their actions, women with naturals and dark skin won the queen contest more often than not in the years thereafter.[214]

On formerly all-white campuses, the black student movement raged, too. At these institutions, black students advocated for the new aesthetic as a part of their broader crusade to assert the legitimacy of black culture and black demands at institutions that had only recently been desegregated. Working through separatist black student organizations, they protested the marginalization of black students, argued for curricula that included black history and literature, organized black cultural events, and spent significant energy emphasizing the beauty of black women as a correlate to all of these goals.

The recognition of women's blackness, and its liberating power, represented a recurring motif in black student publications. The black woman's "beauty is her own," a female writer for the University of North Carolina's *Black Ink* declared, "not copied from her fair sister but divine in its own

Miss Maroon and White queen contestants giving the Black Power salute, 1970. From Spelman College yearbook, *Reflections*, 1971, Spelman College, Atlanta, Ga.

creation in the shadow of darkness."[215] The black woman was a queen, she continued, to be worshipped and adored, a woman whose physical and mental evolution made her different from her ancestors. At the University of North Carolina (UNC) and elsewhere, black students also chose their own queens in all-black campus contests, women who synthesized, with their bodies, the radical aesthetic and political commitments of their generation. The most important qualification for Miss Black Student Movement at UNC was that she "be Black and be proud of her Blackness."[216] Secondly, she had to serve as a spokesman for black students and motivate them to act on behalf of the black community. Crowned in 1971, the first annual winner was a dark-skinned beauty with a natural. She embraced her role, condemning the Vietnam War, defending black nationalist and communist Angela Davis, and even expressing reservations over the institution of marriage. This Carolina queen exuded the dual meaning of blackness as an inner stance and an outer style.

Black students at some white colleges set their sites on traditional homecoming queen contests. Most homecoming competitions relied heavily on voting by the student body, and as black students gained power, they took advantage of the divided loyalties of white students and bloc-voted to elect black beauties. *Jet* reported on the phenomenon in 1967.[217] Only one of the eight schools listed by the magazine to have elected a black queen—

Morehead State University, in Kentucky—was southern. The women pictured in the story, moreover, had light to medium skin, and all had pressed hair. Within the next several years, more homecoming contests at formerly white colleges in the South proved vulnerable to determined black students, and some of the winners embraced the aesthetic of blackness. At the University of South Carolina (USC), the Association of Afro-American Students sponsored the first "Black Week" in the fall of 1970, which culminated in the crowning of a Miss Black USC. Yet that same semester, a black woman, natural-haired Barbara Dixon, was runner-up for homecoming queen; the following year, Dixon won Miss Black USC.[218] There was a degree of irony in trying to get black women elected homecoming queens, as these contenders effectively integrated white contests. But students undertook such efforts within the framework of Black Power, proclaiming their racial solidarity at institutions that were not always hospitable to their presence on campus. These contests were also easy targets.[219] Convincing administrators to change the curriculum or to recruit minority faculty, by contrast, required more energy and resources than did a week-long get-out-the-vote campaign.

A black victory in a homecoming contest at a white college, however, might provoke white anger. Henry Walker, a former head of the USC Association of Afro-American Students, made a successful bid for student body president in 1971, becoming the university's first black president. Walker cited Dixon's solid showing in the homecoming contest the year before as the reason he decided to run, claiming that whites had supported her candidacy. "[T]here was a certain excitement among the whites in voting for her," he contended. "It was as though they thought they were going against tradition and the business of putting the white woman on the pedestal."[220] Although some white students may have relished participating in this tiny rebellion, or in electing a black student body president, Walker overestimated white support of black queens. In the fall of 1973, the Association of Afro-American Students threw its weight behind Gayle Ransom, who emerged from a field of eight semifinalists to become the university's first black homecoming queen.[221] When Ransom's name was called during halftime at the homecoming game, boos rang out from the student section, lasting, according to one campus reporter, for almost a minute. Already skeptical of homecoming festivities (seeing them as sophomoric and silly), this eyewitness wrote that as the booing continued, "the horrifying reality was slapping my face like an unclean and smelly glove . . . it was 1959 and again someone had not been careful with the cage doors."[222]

Gayle Ransom, University of South Carolina homecoming queen, 1973. When Ransom was crowned the university's first black homecoming queen, boos erupted from the student section. Courtesy of the South Caroliniana Library, University of South Carolina, Columbia.

Other students were neither shocked nor remorseful. "Well, this is the South, you know," overheard a yearbook staff member, who later explained why homecoming traditions still mattered to students. "[W]ith Home-coming in the air," he conjectured, "we can all close our eyes and pretend nostalgically that the good old days are still with us and everything is simple and good and as it should be."[223] In the yearbook, one photo of the halftime ceremony showed the new natural-haired homecoming queen smiling, but the other—of Ransom's coronation—was taken from behind, her face hidden from view.[224] The angle may have been accidental, a function of where the photographer was positioned during the coronation. But

Gayle Ransom, 1973, University of South Carolina homecoming queen. Included in the yearbook, this photograph of Ransom poignantly captures how the student body struggled to accept the school's first black winner. Courtesy of the South Caroliniana Library, University of South Carolina, Columbia.

as a record of this historic event, the image seems appropriate, capturing the reluctance of USC students to face their new black queen. Still, black students continued to use the contest as a display of racial unity. A black woman earned the homecoming queen title the following year and again in 1977 (both of whom, remarkably, were also named Gail).

The same year that Gayle Ransom was elected USC's first black homecoming queen, Terry Points became the first black woman to win the crown at the University of Alabama. Entering the contest on a lark—she thought the prospect of winning was "far-fetched" and never even told her parents she was a finalist—Points beat out eleven other women for the honor.[225] Just as momentous as her victory, perhaps, was the man on hand to crown her at the pep rally: Governor George Wallace, who ten years earlier had made his infamous "Stand in the Schoolhouse Door" at the university. Wallace performed his duty graciously, according to Points, who observed that the governor had not known in advance who would win the contest.[226] The following day, Wallace crowned Points again at the official coronation during halftime. As the crowd of 58,000 cheered, Points knelt in front of Wallace's wheelchair to receive her tiara (an assassination attempt had left him paralyzed the year before), "foregoing," one newspaper noted, "the usual kiss for a handshake."[227] If there was any opposition to Points's victory, it remained unspoken, at least publicly. The student newspaper celebrated the new black queen and praised the student body for its bravery and civility: "We are intensely proud of our university and feel that perhaps the light at the end of the proverbial tunnel is indeed in sight."[228]

Perhaps the light was in sight in Tuscaloosa. Accounting for the different reactions to the first black Alabama and South Carolina homecoming queens requires speculation. Race relations on the Alabama campus may have been better, or maybe it was Points herself. During her three years on campus, Points had been a member of the African American Association, but her campus activities were numerous and varied—she had marched with the band, served as the president of two dorms, and sat on the Student Government Association.[229] She may not have been connected with a more radical brand of black politics by her peers. Certainly she did not embrace Black Power's aesthetics. Unlike Gayle Ransom, Points had pressed hair, and thirty years after her coronation, she complained bitterly about the young man who was her date to the homecoming game. A "brother" she did not know that well, the man arrived at her dorm with an Afro, she said, adding, "and it was all messed up." He was also wearing a pair of jeans and an Alabama sweatshirt. "I was so upset," Points recalled, "just trying to keep myself away from him so nobody would know that I was with [him]."[230]

FIFTY YEARS EARLIER, editors at *Half-Century* had sponsored a beauty contest to make a statement. By publishing reader-submitted photos of black women with diverse physical characteristics, they would demonstrate that "all beautiful hair is not straight, that all beautiful skin is not white . . . that all beautiful contours are not possessed by white women."[231] As we have seen, *Half-Century* had a hard time honoring its intentions, featuring a slew of light-skinned, straight-haired beauties in its pages. Other contests often did the same. Resurrecting a goal that had been unattainable for most of the century—even impractical, as some might have said—beauty contests of the Black Power era were both products and catalysts of a reconceptualization of beauty. By 1970, Gwendolyn Brooks observed in her ode to Montgomery, Alabama, that the straight-haired women of the boycott days had disappeared from the streets of the city. She noted, instead, a "Real Cool" girl who "flicks a comb / through the short black wires of her hair / She examines tan sandals on feet / that were made to frolic through jungles."[232] Brooks's description of black Alabama women missed, of course, those like Terry Points who felt more comfortable with traditional hair and clothes.

Yet the new aesthetic was striking, and perhaps more than anything or anyone else, Angela Davis pushed it into the national consciousness. Aside from homecoming queen competitions at traditionally white colleges, after all, Black Power beauty contests drew mostly black audiences. A native of Birmingham, Davis sported what became the most famous Afro of the era when, in 1970, she went into hiding to avoid capture by the FBI. It was not just her look. Charged with kidnapping, conspiracy, and murder for her connection with a Marxist revolutionary cell at a California prison, Davis became the poster child of black radicalism—literally. FBI wanted posters featured Davis's face, surrounded by her huge natural. Davis became so associated with the natural that she was forced to wear wigs during her stint underground, one of which "was straight and stiff, with long bangs and elaborate spitcurls." "I doubted," she later wrote, "my own mother could have recognized me."[233]

Although her mother would likely have understood Davis's recourse to a straightened wig given the circumstances, it was the elder Davis woman who had paved the way for the daughter's adoption of the Afro. Unlike most young black girls from the segregated South of the 1940s and 1950s, Angela Davis had not grown up getting her hair pressed. A political activist herself, her mother criticized straightened hair long before doing so became a badge of commitment in civil rights circles. "I pleaded with my mother to let me get it straightened, like my friends," Davis recalled, but she continued "to fix the two big wavy plaits which always hung down my back." Davis loved to visit her cousins in Alabama where, freed from her mother's supervision, she could use a hot comb to make her hair "straight as a pin."[234] Despite her mother's early lessons, Davis still struggled with her desire to conform as her own activism took root during her college years. A student at Brandeis University in the early 1960s, Davis attended an eye-opening lecture by Malcolm X, who made her "feel good about myself," as she put it. Finally, she said, "I could celebrate my body (especially my nappy hair, which I always attacked with a hot comb in ritualistic seclusion)."[235]

By 1967 Davis had followed the lead of other Black Power proponents and let her hair go natural. Although she had trouble with black nationalism in theory as well as in practice—she questioned, in particular, its lack of interest in issues of class oppression and its tendency toward male chauvinism—Davis nevertheless felt compelled to identify herself as a black radical. Constructing a new appearance was central to that effort. "I needed to say 'Black is beautiful,'" she insisted. "I needed to explore my

African ancestry, to don African garb, and to wear my hair natural as much as the blinder-wearing male supremacist cultural nationalists." Davis felt Black is Beautiful capacious enough both for her and for her ideological opponents within the broader political movement. She had no sense at the time, however, that her own appearance would ultimately garner so much attention, that it "would achieve," she said, "its somewhat legendary status."[236]

Indeed, her natural became the most salient symbol of her identity, the locus of meaning to her enemies and sympathizers alike. From the perspective of the FBI and many white Americans, Davis's hair represented the look of a dangerous firebrand, an antiwhite and anti-American black nationalist bent on lawlessness. This view had ramifications beyond Davis's own plight, as hundreds of black women with natural hair were harassed and arrested by law enforcement officers during her two-month concealment.[237] Her supporters, meanwhile, showcased the same image as a sign of strength or, in Davis's words, "of a charismatic and raucous revolutionary ready to lead the masses into battle," which, while a more positive association, nevertheless made her feel that she was under pressure to live up to certain expectations.[238] Among some pockets of the black population, Davis's hair took on a life of its own. Her Afro became known as the "Angela Davis look" on the streets and among wigmakers, who attempted to re-create the hairstyle for their clients.

Davis's experience is noteworthy for what it suggests about the solutions Black is Beautiful offered to black women. In many respects, Black is Beautiful had widened narrow conceptions of black beauty by the early 1970s. As a bookend to the story of how southern black women experienced and pursued beauty during the Jim Crow and civil rights eras, it seems a triumph. But a new hairstyle did not change things, as Angela Davis discovered. To be sure, by the mid-1960s, the natural had begun to shed its suggestion of brazen rebelliousness and emerge as a more mainstream statement of racial pride among blacks.[239] No better illustration of this was the willingness of *Ebony*, a staid publication, to routinely celebrate the Afro and the "new breed of Negro women challenging white concepts of beauty by going 'natural.'"[240] Black women still encountered whites prone to sharp judgments about the black female body. To some whites—and even to some blacks—the aesthetic of blackness indicated not simply an inability to master the finer points of femininity but a commitment to a racial militancy that made them uncomfortable. Four years after Davis became infamous for her hair, for example, the University of

Georgia student newspaper reported that a nearby resort owner had developed a clear policy regarding black patrons: he welcomed blacks into his park if "they are nice and clean looking, but not if they have Afro's [*sic*] and not if they are agitators."[241] Davis had also found, moreover, that blacks themselves believed that she, as a woman, shouldered a unique burden with her body, one she did not necessarily relish. To sympathizers, her natural hair signaled her dedication to the race. Finally, Davis's hair was quickly transformed into a fashion statement, a development that threatened to loosen the style from its political moorings. Black is Beautiful, in short, posed a host of questions even as it answered others.

# Conclusion

On 7 September 1968, the day of the Miss America Pageant, members of the women's liberation movement gathered outside of Convention Hall in Atlantic City, where they staged a demonstration that quickly became one of the era's most iconic.[1] As contestants and officials completed last-minute preparations inside for the annual beauty ritual, protesters on the Boardwalk outside hurled false eyelashes, curlers, girdles, and bras into a "freedom trash can." Contrary to legend, bras were not burned. Instead, the can's contents were denounced as symbols of women's "enslavement" to modern beauty standards.[2] Protesters also carried a huge bathing beauty puppet clad in a red, white, and blue bathing suit, decorated with chains; sang antipageant songs in three-part harmony; ripped up a *Playboy* magazine; and crowned a ram, festooned in yellow and blue ribbons, as the new Miss America.

The ram, in fact, represented part of the much broader protest motif. Attacking the pageant for promoting "The Degrading Mindless-Boob-Girlie Symbol," the women's liberationists located the origins of this symbol not within the world of the pinup or pornography, as the phrase might suggest, but within the culture of agricultural judging. The first on the ten-point protest list they distributed announced that "[t]he Pageant epitomizes the roles we are all forced to play as women. The parade down the runway blares the metaphor of the 4-H Club county fair, where the nervous animals are judged for teeth, fleece, etc., and where the best 'specimen' gets the blue ribbon."[3] In terms of describing what beauty contests did—and particularly by identifying the institutions that nurtured them—theirs was an accurate assessment, one illustrated on the posters the protesters carried. "Welcome to the Miss America Cattle Auction," read one, while another showed a naked woman's body sectioned, with magic marker, into different cuts of meat. It was ready, like the body of a cow, to be slaughtered and sold at market.

The pageant demonstration was a provocative bit of guerrilla theater that conveyed a serious message about how beauty oppressed American women. In taking aim at the contest, women's liberationists targeted the

Miss America Pageant protest, 1968. Women's liberationists, throwing instruments of women's oppression into a "freedom trash can." Courtesy of the Alix Kates Shulman Papers, David M. Rubenstein Rare Book and Manuscript Library, Duke University, Durham, N.C.

country's most conspicuous forum for the perpetuation of female beauty standards. In 1968, the pageant was still wildly popular, capturing over 60 percent of the television viewing audience on the night that it aired for the previous three years.[4] The showcase for wholesome American womanhood, it was the only television program Tricia Nixon, the soon-to-be-president's daughter, was allowed to stay up to watch.[5] Not surprisingly, the protesters on the Boardwalk found that most of the 650 onlookers disapproved of their demonstration and dismissed their critique. According to the *New York Times*, one man shouted that the women should throw themselves in the trash can because "it would be a lot more useful."[6] Before long, a small counterprotest—led by the runner-up to Miss America in 1967, a young woman wearing a Nixon-for-President button, appropriately enough—emerged.

The press helped spread this spirit of opposition well beyond Atlantic City. The claim that the media invented the charge of bra-burning "to avoid presenting the real reasons for the growing discontent of women," as protest organizer Robin Morgan claimed in 1968, was not entirely true, though versions of what happened vary.[7] Some recall that protesters had planned to burn a bra but backed down at the request of the mayor. A female reporter from the *New York Post*, who covered the demonstra-

Miss America Pageant protester, 1968. Protesters argued that the pageant judged women like farm animals and crowned a ram as the new Miss America, tying the contest to the tradition of evaluation at the agricultural fair. Courtesy of the photographer, Bev Grant.

tion, later said she was responsible for the falsehood, having used "bra-burning" in her article to give the protest "moral weight" by linking it to draft-card-burning.[8] Either way, once the rumor of bra-burning started, the effect was the same: the protesters were cast as whiny women given to silly theatrics for no apparent reason. The *New Pittsburgh Courier*, one of the preeminent black papers in the country, offered a typical take on the protest, topping its coverage of the demonstration and the alleged burning with the headline: "Women with Gripes Lured to Picket 'Miss America.'"[9]

The civil rights movement, the antiwar movement, the student movement, and now a nascent women's movement—all challenged the status quo, and the Miss America Pageant, like many established institutions, found itself in the crosshairs of change. Pageant officials were not pleased. Albert Marks, chairman of the Miss America organization, made this fact clear in the wake of the women's liberation demonstration. Appealing to Nixon's Silent Majority before the president made the phrase famous, Marks announced, "We stand for the great American middle class, the nonvocal middle class, for normal, average, young American womanhood." "We are for normalcy," he continued. "We have no interest in minorities or causes. SDS [Students for a Democratic Society] has its thing. We have no thing. If that is a crime in today's society, so be it. Our youngsters are interested in plain American idealism."[10] Marks's attempt to distance the contest from politics was futile, for it had always been a political affair. Case in point: the pageant did not, to use Marks's own words, have much of an interest in minorities, a fact that the women's liberationists drove home as they marched around the Boardwalk. Although they condemned the very idea of a beauty contest as degrading to women, women's liberationists, many of whom had been active in the civil rights movement and a handful of whom were black, complained that the Miss America Pageant had never had a black finalist. Item number two on their protest list called the contest "racism with roses."[11]

In response to this habit of honoring only white women, a second protest was brewing that night in Atlantic City. Down the Boardwalk at the Ritz-Carlton Hotel, the NAACP was set to sponsor the first annual Miss Black America Pageant at midnight, a time chosen so that the media might stop by after the Miss America Pageant had concluded. Organizers touted the black beauty contest as a "positive protest" against the pageant's history of excluding black women.[12] Local African Americans had actually attacked the discriminatory practices of both the pageant and the city for years, occasionally using the former as a weapon to gain concessions from the latter. The local branch of the NAACP, for example, had pressured pageant officials to open up the segregated Boardwalk Festival of Floats, in which contestants paraded around in their finery, since the early 1960s. The campaign succeeded, and in 1966, integrated floats made their first appearance. In 1967, one activist called for the relocation of the Miss America Pageant, arguing that Convention Hall, a municipal space, was an inappropriate venue for an event that claimed to represent all of America but that, in reality, did not. The same year, the Afro-Unity Movement announced that unless certain demands were met—such as the implementation of rent control and the hiring of a black principal at a local school—it would cut off access to the roads leading into town during the pageant.[13]

The 1968 Miss Black America Pageant represented the logical outcome of this local struggle and, at the same time, of the larger civil rights movement. Indeed, the contest testified to the NAACP's own affirmation of the changing cultural and political climate. "We're not protesting against beauty," an organizer of the black competition insisted. "We're protesting because the beauty of the black woman has been ignored. . . . We'll show black beauty for public consumption—herald her beauty and applaud it."[14] His statement reflected a central element of the Black is Beautiful campaign. Its proponents never lost faith in the power of black female beauty as an effective tool in achieving racial progress.

The NAACP was not interested in issuing a blanket condemnation of the beauty contest as a ritual. By contrast, many of the feminists down the Boardwalk were, criticizing both contests "as part of the system" despite recognizing that Miss Black America was a response to discrimination.[15] The African American women among them were more conflicted. Asked about the Miss Black America Pageant, one black women's liberationist said, "I'm for beauty contests. But then again maybe I'm against them. I think black people have a right to protest."[16] Her words suggest the conundrum in which black feminist women found themselves as these two rival protests unfolded. While they, too, criticized beauty contests as rituals that harmed women, they were mindful of the long history of denying black women's beauty. It is not surprising, then, that a few might let the Miss Black America Pageant off the hook, preferring to see it as a "positive protest" against the racism, but not the sexism, of beauty contests.

At 2:45 A.M., Saundra Williams was crowned Miss Black America. A young woman with a natural whose talent consisted of performing the "Fiji"—a "frenetic African dance"—Williams reiterated the goal of this new breed of competition after the ceremony. "With my title," she stated, "I can show black women that they too are beautiful, even though they do have large noses and thick lips." Williams also directly tied her beauty and her participation in the beauty contest to political activism. A native of Philadelphia, Miss Williams attended college in Princess Anne, Maryland. "I never experienced a bit of discrimination," she told the press, "until I got to Maryland State College." Once there, she decided to fight Jim Crow and organize a boycott of a segregated restaurant. "The restaurant," she boasted to reporters, "is integrated now."

Her white counterpart—Judith Ann Ford, a college student in Louisiana, the Miss Illinois titleholder, and the junior national trampoline champion (she jumped for her talent)—said nothing about the Miss Black America Pageant. A Miss America official had instructed her to remain silent about the NAACP contest. After some prodding by reporters, she

Saundra Williams (middle), the first Miss Black America. Williams won the other big contest in Atlantic City on 7 September 1968 — the Miss Black America Pageant, billed as a "positive protest" against the Miss America Pageant. Courtesy of the Associated Press.

did discuss the possibility that a black woman might one day win Miss America. Ford said she felt it would be acceptable for a black woman to be crowned, as long as she was really the prettiest. Not that she was impervious to significant moments in beauty pageant history. Informed during the exchange that she was the first blonde to win the crown in eleven years, the new Miss America was thrilled. "I'm so glad," she announced. "I feel like it's a breakthrough."[17]

THE PROCEEDINGS IN Atlantic City on 7 September 1968 seem an appropriate end to the history recounted in these pages. The Miss America Pageant demonstration and the Miss Black America Pageant were highly charged symbols of the two biggest ideological challenges to the pursuit of beauty in the twentieth century — second-wave feminism and the Black is Beautiful movement. Thrust into the national consciousness by way of America's most famous celebration of beautiful women, both events raised questions about female beauty and its role in the lives of American women. Both, moreover, owed their origins to frustrations with the civil rights movement. Black Power proponents criticized the movement's integrationist tactics and white aesthetics; feminists protested its sexism. That female beauty would end up being a casualty of a movement for racial justice might have surprised early activists, though perhaps not. The connection between race and beauty had been forged at the dawn of southern segregation—even before—informing Jim Crow culture in ways that many would have well understood. The *Brown* decision, which helped spark the movement, was based, after all, on the recognition that this very link harmed the self-esteem of black children.

What did these two challenges mean for southern women pursuing beauty during segregation's waning years? The way in which the two events in Atlantic City differed sheds some light. Unlike the women's liberation protest, the Miss Black America Pageant institutionalized an aesthetic that had already touched the lives of black southern women. As we have seen, some black women in the South, such as SNCC workers, had jettisoned what they perceived to be white beauty standards in the years before the contest. Their actions, furthermore, built on an earlier tradition of scrutinizing the meaning of beauty in black women's lives, a tradition that dated back to the birth of black beauty culture in the 1910s and 1920s. By the post–World War II period, there was, to be sure, a consensus among black southerners about the acceptability of practices like pressing hair. Even as the civil rights movement gained momentum in the 1950s, few asserted that a black woman with straightened hair was a traitor to her race.[18] Still, the pursuit of beauty had always been a proposition fraught with more difficulties for black southern women than it had been for white southern women. For this very reason, Black is Beautiful resonated among black women in the South, as it did elsewhere. The Miss Black America Pageant stood as testament to this fact.

Despite the fact that Black is Beautiful had already made more waves in the South than had second-wave feminism, it would be a mistake to overstate its acceptance. According to a 1969 *Newsweek* poll, a majority of blacks in the North approved of the natural, but only 40 percent of blacks in the South did.[19] And approval, of course, did not necessarily translate into adoption. Black Power enjoyed stronger support in urban areas and on college campuses, but not all students who shared its political goals, as the previous chapter showed, were taken with its aesthetics. Outside of activist circles, Black is Beautiful had an even more muted effect. Catherine Cardozo Lewis, the owner of a beauty shop in Washington, D.C., with her two sisters, told an interviewer in 1980 that the new hairstyle of the late sixties had seemed for her personally an inappropriate choice.

This was the case not just because she had once helped run a beauty shop, an institution endangered by a style that did not require the services of a beautician. There was much more. "When the Afro was first started," she remembered, "I would never have assumed that hairdress because I just felt that it was an affectation. Particularly in view of my color."[20] Deemed the more "natural" style by many of its proponents, the Afro seemed an affectation to Lewis because she had light skin. It did not, in her mind, "match" the rest of her physical features.

Equally significant was that the Afro did not match her politics. Lewis conceded that the hairstyle made an ideological statement with which she disagreed. Many blacks, she said, "assumed [the Afro] as a symbol of racial consciousness and," she insisted, "racial division," by which she meant a divisiveness within the African American community. Lewis wanted to distance herself from the Black Power movement "because they wanted everything." She argued that for Black Power activists, "you didn't have to do anything else, you didn't have to exert yourself. You didn't have to exert any self-discipline. You were simply black, and that was it, that was the important thing."[21] Expressing sympathy for a moderate, integrationist approach to civil rights work, Lewis viewed the young men and women of the Black Power movement as lackadaisical troublemakers. To her, they seemed to make unjustified demands based on a shallow appeal to blackness, failing to show the discipline, hard work, and respect that were prerequisites for gaining concessions from whites.

Lewis was a generation older than the young college activists she criticized and, moreover, shaped by her elite status. As we have seen, the Cardozo sisters worked hard to ensure that their beauty salon reflected the class values they shared with their clientele, emphasizing professionalism and discouraging shop talk that elsewhere might nurture more direct activism. Lewis viewed the Afro and the Black is Beautiful movement more generally as an affront to the political and aesthetic strategies that for decades had served her well. Especially in the wake of the Angela Davis manhunt, someone like Lewis probably saw the natural as beyond the pale. Writer Lawrence Otis Graham, who grew up a member of the black elite, remembered that his conservative grandmother was dismissive of the look, too. "I don't see anything civil about a bunch of nappy-headed Negroes screaming and marching around in the streets," she told him.[22]

Though some younger women dismissed the conservative politics of this older generation, they occasionally echoed Cardozo's argument that simply celebrating blackness was not enough. Gladys Ashe, the Bennett

College student who declared that she and her peers no longer wanted to be "lily-white young ladies," asked her classmates point-blank: "Do you really want to be black or do you just want to look black?"[23] Ashe insisted that blackness was first and foremost an identity. Outward manifestations of blackness were fine, if adopted in the right spirit. Disconnected from a political commitment to blackness, they were meaningless. Young men and women who competed over "who can wear the biggest 'fro," said another group of students, operated under an "illusion of Blackness."[24] Criticisms like these revealed a skepticism of cultural nationalism and its power to effect change. The Black Panthers, among others, agreed, arguing that an emphasis on style, rather than substance, distracted from the real racial problems plaguing American society.[25]

Even for those willing to embrace it, Black is Beautiful did not represent a panacea. The new aesthetic was an imperfect resolution of the tensions that underscored black women's pursuit of beauty. In 1969, the NAACP opted to forgo a second annual contest—perhaps suggestive in its own right—so Asbury Park, New Jersey, sponsored its own national black beauty pageant.[26] Organizers of a preliminary competition in New Orleans employed language typical of such contests, lamenting that black women traditionally "have been ignored as to possessing any beauty." "The 'Black is Beautiful' Movement," according to the contest program, "has made the Black Woman come alive. It has made her realize that she . . . must have pride and carry herself with dignity." The New Orleans event, it continued, "acclaims, stages and applauds Black Beauty."[27] Despite this rhetoric, the bathing beauty competition did not feature an assemblage of dark-skinned beauties with natural hair. Of twenty-three contestants, only two had Afros; almost all had light skin. Perhaps organizers were simply paying lip service to the new call to celebrate blackness. Or perhaps their efforts were fruitless. New Orleans was, after all, home to a large population of African Americans of Creole descent, men and women with significant white ancestry. Finding interested women who had what was now considered the "right" look—dark skin and curly hair—may have been challenging for the contest sponsors.

When taken to its logical conclusion, Black is Beautiful represented a judgment against black women with features that seemed too white. One Bennett College student bemoaned this reality in 1969. "A sister with a natural and a dashiki who discriminates against another sister who has none," she wrote, "is just as bad as a fair sister discriminating against her darker sister."[28] In the hands of its most enthusiastic supporters, then, the aesthetic simply reordered the old black beauty hierarchy, relegating some black women to the category of unattractive. At the same time, given the close connection between the physical markers of blackness and racial authenticity, someone without a dashiki, dark skin, and an Afro, as one North Carolina woman complained, was not considered "true to the black race."[29] This assessment had, of course, a familiar ring. In the early twentieth century, some critics of modern beauty products believed that black women who used them wanted to get whiter. In doing so, the argument went, these women forfeited their authentic racial identity. By reviving this critique, and leaving intact the belief that black women had a special duty to the race to be attractive, Black is Beautiful placed some black women in an uncomfortable position. The message was that they could not be devoted to the race if they did not look the part. Ironically, the aesthetic also reinforced the supposedly natural difference that had sustained Jim Crow, since race was seen to manifest itself in particular physical features.

The relationship between Black is Beautiful and the black beauty salon was problematic as well. Catherine Cardozo Lewis's sister Margaret recalled that black beauticians were fearful that clients would stop patronizing their shops once the natural became popular. The best defense, they concluded, was a good offense. Thus, even though Catherine herself did not wear a natural because she opposed the politics of Black Power, the Cardozo sisters nevertheless added the care of the natural to the services they offered. Black beauticians like the Cardozos contended that the new natural hairstyle required a maintenance regime just as pressed hair did. Women could not just let their hair go and be done with it. (The bob, it will be recalled, had elicited a similar response from beauticians back in the 1920s.) We were "quick to adapt and modify the natural style," Margaret said, a step that may have helped save their business.[30] What such a move undoubtedly did is lead to the commodification of the Afro, a development that the trajectory of Angela Davis's famous hair—by becoming a model for wig makers—highlighted in vivid terms.[31] Manufacturers of beauty products also furthered the trend. Both black- and white-owned companies, including the Madam C. J. Walker Company and Clairol, marketed creams and conditioners for use on natural hair.

On the one hand, the assimilation of the natural into black beauty culture represented a betrayal of the style's politics. The whole point of rejecting straightened hair had been to renounce the artificial manipulation of the hair and all that it symbolized—white beauty standards and racial self-hatred, as well as the accommodationist and integrationist strategies of those female entrepreneurs who made pressing hair their life's work. Yet by the late 1960s, the Afro increasingly represented just one style among many, a choice that could be adopted or abandoned at whim. In 1969, *Ebony* observed, "As recently as three years ago, it was almost possible to determine the degree of a woman's militance [*sic*] by the state of her hair." Not so anymore, it concluded, as the Afro was now an "item of fashion."[32] Evidence of this transformation could already be seen on college campuses in the South. The same year, a student artist at Tuscaloosa's Stillman College sketched a series of women with naturals and African clothing for the campus newspaper's fashion page. The layout, titled "Fashion for the Afro-Amer.[*sic*] Ball," made no mention of politics, offering, instead, cues on how to play dress-up for the forthcoming event.[33] The Bennett College fashion columnist welcomed the convenience of the Afro wig for affording women "a change of pace."[34]

Dark skin, too, could be separated from politics. At the University of Georgia, a 1970 promotion for a life insurance company in the student newspaper pictured babies of four ethnicities (black, Native American, white, and Asian) with the caption: "Black Is Beautiful, Red Is Beautiful, White Is Beautiful, Yellow Is Beautiful."[35] In a particularly arresting example of this phenomenon, *Ebony* carried an ad for Nadinola bleaching cream in 1968 that announced "Black Is Beautiful."[36] The spot praised "naturally beautiful skin" and made no mention of Nadinola's bleaching attributes. The product promised, instead, "a smooth, glowing skin tone." Despite this rhetorical evasion, tying the Black is Beautiful mantra to a face bleach ultimately emptied it of meaning.

On the other hand, the commodification of Black is Beautiful followed a well-worn path. Certainly it was not the first or last time an aesthetic developed in defiance of commercial and political systems was co-opted by those very same interests.[37] As Susannah Walker has argued, moreover, some black beauticians themselves "saw no conflict between supporting racial causes and making money caring for black women's hair, no matter what style they chose."[38] The nexus between business activism and racial uplift was as old as the profession itself. Black beauticians emphasized this connection with renewed vigor in the wake of the natural, but their business declined, at least in the short term. In 1970, the National Beauty Culturists' League found in a survey of members that profits had decreased by

20 percent.[39] For those women who wore naturals to show their solidarity with a more militant civil rights agenda, the appeals of beauticians to continue to patronize their shops fell flat.

But for some, abandoning straight hair was bittersweet. Willi Coleman, who, from the vantage point of adulthood and academia, fondly remembered the moments when her mother would press her and her sisters' hair, was one of these. In a poem titled "Among the Things That Used to Be," Coleman bemoaned the loss of intimacy and camaraderie that came with the adoption of natural hair. "Lots more got taken care of than hair . . . we came together to share and share and share," she wrote, but no longer: "Cause with a natural / there is no natural place / for us to congregate."[40] bell hooks, too, expressed regret at forgoing the straightening ritual, though she viewed the development through a different lens. Once the vogue for straight hair returned after the decline of Black Power, hooks argued, it was corporations, which increasingly made relaxers to straighten the hair chemically, that undermined "a real space of black women bonding through ritualized, shared experience." "Gone was the context of ritual," she wrote, "of black women bonding. . . . [They] lost a space for creative talk."[41] hooks combined her nostalgic ode to the past with a healthy dose of critical distance. She acknowledged that the desire for straight hair owed much to white standards. Yet, as she saw it, it was the coupling of straightening with female bonding that kept the racism of the ritual in check. Unleashed from its setting by the ease and convenience of chemicals, artificially straightened hair had no redeeming qualities.

Black beauty shops recovered from the early slump caused by the introduction of the natural, which did, as hooks observed, wane in popularity by the mid-1970s. But in other ways, these spaces never again assumed the same role in black communities. In an irony that played out in other black institutions in the South, the civil rights movement spelled the end of the golden era of the black beauty shop. It is difficult to imagine that black beauticians would have begrudged the gains of the movement. Still, with the organized crusade to end Jim Crow went a major component of their professional identity. Gone, too, was the prestige granted to black beauticians during segregation.[42] For decades, black women who aspired to professional status, particularly those with limited means, acquired it with a diploma from a black beauty school, but the civil rights movement opened up new educational and employment opportunities. As increasing numbers of young black women opted for career paths made possible by the desegregation of higher education, training in black beauty culture became the purview of technical and vocational schools. Although beauty parlors would emerge as key centers for the dissemination of public health information in subsequent years, their political and professional import was changed.

PUBLICLY, AT LEAST, white southerners did not have much to say about the Miss Black America Pageant. As for the women's liberation protest, they were dismissive. Many decried the event as further evidence that the wave of unrest sweeping the country was ripping apart the very fabric of American society and, in the process, undermining the femininity of its women. One Methodist minister in South Carolina, representing those who were "getting fed up with rioting in the streets," railed against "uncouth women in dirty bluejeans, with uncombed hair and a dangling cigarette."[43] Fresh on the heels of the protests at the Democratic National Convention in Chicago, which had occurred just a week before, the Miss America demonstration revealed, according to the *Charleston News and Courier*, the "emotional imbalance" plaguing the country.[44] The paper pleaded with Americans to pull it together, though it did go on record as a supporter of the Miss Black America Pageant, if in subdued tones. As the editors wrote, the black beauty contest was an event "that in our judgment is not open to reasonable objection," and its organizers had shown "commendable enterprise in staging their own contest at the same time in the same city." Suggesting that such a contest was fine so long as it was kept separate from the main event—a sentiment with which Black is Beautiful proponents would have agreed, but for different reasons—the editors found nothing redeeming about the Miss America protest. They could not fathom the need for the "liberation" of women—a word they deliberately put in quotation marks—deeming such a desire "curious," and wondered what kind of women would want to burn their bras. "If the question has been answered by the protest in Atlantic City," they concluded, "we shall withhold our own opinion in the interest of chivalry."[45]

The *Dallas Morning News* was similarly incredulous at the idea that beauty contests served as agents of women's oppression, deeming such a claim a function of "syncopated logic." Its tongue-in-cheek response was to award the women's liberationists its annual protest prize for injecting a little creativity into a year of protest otherwise lacking in originality and artistry. The ingenuity of the feminists' method—the alleged bra-burning—even warranted, it quipped, a rechristening of the movement itself: "The National Front Liberation."[46]

Cloaked in the mantle of humor, these comments betrayed a deep attachment to the Miss America Pageant in the white South. As the women's liberationists were planning their attack in the days before the pageant, one small town in Georgia, for example, was asserting its rightful claim to the state's representative to the national contest. The *Atlanta Constitution* had featured a photo of Miss Georgia in late August, incorrectly asserting that she hailed from Macon. Several residents of Warner Robbins wrote in to the paper to express their unhappiness, including one woman who said they were "terribly upset" by the mistake. "Warner Robbins is very proud and honored," she proclaimed, "to be the 'Home of Miss Georgia.'"[47] Many southern newspapers still sent correspondents to Atlantic City to report on every move of their state delegate throughout competition week. The sense that southern contestants were noteworthy, deserving of special attention at home and in New Jersey, was palpable. "Some contestants at the Pageant capture people's hearts more than others," the *Jackson Daily News* declared the day before the contest that year, concluding, "Miss Mississippi is one of these."[48] The day after the pageant and protest, the Jackson paper reminded readers of the state's venerable Miss America history. The lead story in its "Pages from the Past" feature was about Mary Ann Mobley's victory in Atlantic City ten years before.[49] In Mississippi, the future envisioned by women's liberationists, one in which women did not aspire to be beauty queens, was answered with nostalgia for a past in which they did.

Unlike the Miss Black America Pageant, the Miss America Pageant demonstration issued an aesthetic and political challenge with which white southerners were loath to grapple. Certainly, white southerners, like black southerners, had harbored doubts about the propriety of modern beauty products and rituals when they were first introduced. And these early misgivings about cosmetics and beauty contests stemmed from convictions that, while they might have seemed overly moralistic to women's liberationists, would nevertheless have struck a chord politically. By the 1960s, however, few white southerners had an interest in probing what the pursuit of beauty meant for women. No widespread southern assault on beauty emerged in the years when many black women and northern white women began to question the role of beauty in their lives. Part of this had to do with how white southern women's beauty was entangled with white racial identity. Indeed, in contrast to black southerners during these years, white southerners never doubted that racial identity could be expressed with the body. The symbiotic relationship between whiteness and the female body was so well established, so seemingly natural—and so useful—that it was almost invisible. The appeal of feminism, and its indictment of beauty, was also largely limited in the South to those associated with the New Left and the civil rights movement.[50] The demonstration revealed this well. A few women's liberationists from Gainesville, Florida, a college town that was a hotbed of activism in the 1960s, were among the protesters on the Boardwalk. But the protest—and the many conversations about beauty and women's oppression that gave rise to it—was the brainchild of the New York Radical Women, a feminist group in New York City.

On the southern beauty contest circuit, feminism registered in subtle ways in the years that followed. As they waved, sang, and danced their way toward glory, beauty contestants might appropriate the language of feminism, emphasizing personal achievement and career goals, while still offering up their bodies as objects for public consumption.[51] A 1971 candidate for homecoming queen at Ole Miss pursued this strategy in typical fashion. Her ad in the campus newspaper announced, "We've come a long way," a nod to the Virginia Slims marketing campaign that celebrated women's new power while playing up their sexuality: "Yes, a choice for a change has come, Debbie Pace . . . something new for Homecoming Queen." Next to the photograph of Debbie, showing off her short shorts, made-up face, and styled hair, the text emphasized that she was a "beautiful girl," but one who cared about student government and doing well in her pre-med courses.[52]

Still, this embrace of "change" in the South did not dim the allure of Atlantic City. It is true that southern women's dominance of the Miss America Pageant declined slightly, a logical development, given that the most turbulent years of the civil rights movement were over. But southern contestants continued to do well at the national contest. They won a third of the titles in the thirty years after the passage of the Civil Rights Act of 1964, with Mississippi home to four Miss Americas by 1985.[53] (The first southern black woman to win was South Carolina's Kimberly Aiken, in 1993.) After spending 1970 interviewing pageant aficionados and hopefuls, Frank Deford observed what can only be called a kind of southernization of the contest, a recognition that contestants from the South had come to dominate the event. "Atlantic City," he remarked, "is south of the Mason-Dixon Line, and every day of the Pageant it drifts farther into Dixie."[54] Three sociologists at the University of Southern Mississippi confirmed this drift. Studying data from the Miss America Pageant and its preliminaries nationwide, they concluded that southern contestants did outperform women from other regions, mainly because of expectations that they would and because of strong southern state pageant systems.[55]

Deford went so far as to argue that now southern contestants were determining what pageant judges looked for in a Miss America. The beauty of the white southern woman was hardly in doubt or danger—it was being copied, emulated, and then honored at the nation's premier contest. This development, too, seems a logical outcome, given all that had transpired during the preceding years. As an image with a national profile for much of the twentieth century, the white southern beauty queen was ripe for imitation, though imitation was, in a sense, not quite the dynamic in play. If the previous twenty years of activity in Atlantic City had proved anything, it was that American beauty was, to a large extent, southern beauty. Since World War II, Americans had chosen white southern women to represent their identity time and again.

NO ONE BETTER embodied the future, and the history, of beauty in the white South than Mary Kay Ash, best known for the fleet of pink Cadillacs that she unleashed on southern roadways beginning in 1969. Just six years before, in 1963, Ash had founded her cosmetics company, Beauty by Mary Kay—or "Mary Kay," as it is colloquially known—in Dallas, Texas. That was the same year, of course, in which Betty Friedan published *The Feminine Mystique*, the trenchant critique of modern American womanhood that would culminate in, among other things, the women's liberation demonstration at the Miss America Pageant.

At just the moment, then, that Friedan was giving voice to the vague sense of unease that haunted women who were taught that "the highest value and the only commitment for women is the fulfillment of their own femininity," Ash was starting a business rooted in that very commitment.[56] Armed with her company's skincare and cosmetic products, her independent beauty consultants were charged with helping other women look more beautiful, which was, Ash contended, their divinely ordained duty. "I truly believe [God] made us feminine for a reason," she stated, "and we should always strive to maintain our femininity."[57] Yet underlying this entire aesthetic project was a feministic politics that Friedan and women's liberationists would have recognized. Mary Kay Ash was a study in contradictions, a perfectly manicured and made-up symbol of white female beauty in a region resistant to most—but not all—of what second-wave feminists had to say.

Mary Kay Ash, 1978. Pictured here with her cosmetics company's signature pink Cadillac, Ash promised women that selling her brand of southern beauty could bring economic liberation. © Graham Bezant/Toronto Star/ZUMA Press.

Ash had gotten her start in business back in the 1940s in Dallas by necessity rather than by choice. A divorced mother with young children, she went to work for Stanley Home Products, a direct sales company whose organization and operation her cosmetics company would later emulate. Sales representatives hosted home parties where they sold products—in this case, home cleaning products—and recruited other representatives, a percentage of whose sales they received. Ash excelled at Stanley and attributes her success to the company's incentive program. During her early years as an employee, this program included a contest that she could not resist. Stanley Home Products announced one week that the representative who recruited the most new salespeople would be crowned "Miss Dallas." "I decided that was the only way I would ever be 'Miss Dallas,'" she remembered, "so I was determined to win." She did, and while her sales figures were impressive thereafter, she later learned that a man she had trained had been named to a management position. After quitting, Ash signed on with another direct sales company and eventually became its national training director, only to discover that the men she was teaching were earning double her salary. By the early 1960s, she had decided to start her own company, one that would "give women all the opportunities I had never had."[58]

Ash's various memoirs almost read like manifestos, replete with bold declarations of women's equality and thoughtful ruminations on the employment obstacles they faced in the decades after World War II. "It was a period," she wrote, "when women were often being paid fifty cents on the dollar that men received for the same work. It disturbed me that men were paid more 'because they have families to support.'"[59] Ash knew many women like herself—single, divorced, widowed—who shouldered the burden of supporting their families alone. Even those who supplemented their husband's incomes, she insisted, wanted higher pay and greater flexibility. And the cash-strapped were not the only women who needed options. She believed that those with sufficient financial resources should have the chance to pursue careers outside the home and reap their just emotional and financial rewards.

Many beauty consultants who worked at Mary Kay in the early years recalled that it was the promise of a life beyond the domestic sphere that drew them to the company. One Texas woman spoke of "a void in her life" and wanting something "that was my very own."[60] Another woman from Louisiana appreciated her beautiful house and loving family but was nevertheless "restless." "I felt," she remembered, "that all my potential wasn't being used."[61] Still another Texan claimed that while she did not necessarily want a career, she was "going nutsy from staying at home."[62] The similarities between these sentiments and those of Friedan's interviewees in *The Feminine Mystique* are striking. So, too, are the solutions both women proposed, at least in one respect. Both Friedan and Ash urged women to realize that they could pursue goals outside the home and that they did not have to be dependent on their husbands for financial support. Ash was clear on this point. "I'm working for the economic liberation of women," she once stated.[63] It is difficult to imagine, however, that Ash and many second-wave feminists would have seen eye to eye on the issue of personal appearance. For her, the path to women's economic liberation was paved with lipstick and rouge. Embracing certain components of the mainstream liberal feminist agenda, she rejected the position of cultural feminists like the Miss America protesters who wanted to reenvision conceptions of gender.

Beauty consultants who worked at Mary Kay in the late 1960s said as much about their boss, arguing she did more to liberate women than many

activists of the era. But, as one put it, "she was no women's libber."[64] Looking back years later on this period, Ash did not mince words. "That was the
time when women burned their bras, put on their low-heeled shoes, cut
their hair short like a man and took off all their makeup and went around
trying to act just like a man, lowered their voices, etc. They found out fairly
quickly it did not work." She was grateful that the "foolishness" was over.[65]
The rejection of femininity—of bras and makeup and all that went with
it—made women mannish in Ash's eyes. How different her view was from
that of John W. Porter, the minister who, in the 1920s, had railed against
the feminist embrace of cosmetics and the "masculinization" of women
that would surely result.

Ash found a receptive audience for both her products and her vision
of women's economic advancement. By 1975, annual sales at Mary Kay
totaled $32 million, and her sales force had grown to about 30,000, up
from the 9 who started with the company twelve years before.[66] By 1983,
the company brought in over $300 million and boasted 200,000 beauty
consultants, about 750 of whom had won the right to drive a pink Cadillac for a year.[67] Mary Kay also employed 166 sales directors, beauty consultants who had reached certain recruiting and sales targets, who earned
over $50,000 annually.[68] The top fifty of that group each brought in over
$150,000. Mary Kay claimed, not unjustly, to be the best company in
America for women who wanted to make money, though becoming a top
seller was not easy. Excluding all 5,000 sales directors, the average income
of a Mary Kay beauty consultant in 1983, most of whom sold part-time,
was $1,655.[69]

If the dream of financial independence failed to materialize for many
Mary Kay consultants, the allure of working for the cosmetics tycoon out-
weighed any disappointment. At the heart of the Mary Kay corporation
lay the promise that success was just around the corner, and nothing more
vividly put this possibility on display than the annual meeting of consultants, called Seminar. Part business convention, part pep rally, Seminar
brought thousands of Mary Kay consultants to Dallas for a three-day
opportunity to bask in the wisdom and enthusiasm of their company's
founder. For Ash, the idea was to energize her sales force by recognizing
their hard work while also making them feel glamorous. The culminating
event of Seminar, awards night, combined these goals into an extravaganza
of sequined evening gowns, fur coats, and diamonds (the latter two given
as prizes). "[Consultants] may never make their debut; they may never be a
prom queen; they may never be Miss America," Ash once remarked. "So on

our awards night, we try to put all that together for one great, big wonderful moment."[70] Until declining health prevented her from participating in the mid-1990s, Ash personally crowned her queens of sales and recruiting. As at the Miss America Pageant, tears flowed freely.

It is easy to dismiss Ash and her experiment in using beauty products to achieve the economic liberation of women. Like many direct marking companies run by men or women, Mary Kay built a cult of personality around its founder and nurtured dreams in its employees about the ease of striking it rich. The pink Cadillacs, the tiaras, the rah-rah spirit that infused corporate culture—all have motivated plenty of observers to write off Mary Kay consultants as purveyors of an outdated femininity and members of a hokey adult sorority. But that critique seems facile and unfair, disparaging of Ash's goal to help women improve their financial situations. The same motivation, after all, underscored the work of black beauty culturists in the early twentieth century. Annie Turnbo Malone, Madam C. J. Walker, and scores of less famous entrepreneurs who recruited agents to work for their companies argued that selling beauty could provide black women a source of income. Although black beauty culturists received their fair share of criticism, most of it resulted from concerns that they pedaled an ideal of beauty too beholden to white standards. As we have seen, black beauty culturists so successfully countered this charge that few blacks expressed reservations about their services by the 1940s. African Americans in the South had only to look around their neighborhoods and business districts to see the proof of beauty culture's promise. To be sure, some black women discovered that beauty culture did not pay in the way they had hoped. But for others, like Mamie Garvin Fields, Bernice Robinson, and Ruby Parks Blackburn, it did. They found a way to make money at a time when employment opportunities for black women in the South were limited, and even to use their jobs to engage in political activism. Ash was working in a different time and under different circumstances, but her economic vision for her consultants was nevertheless very much the same. Yet it is striking, if not surprising, that Ash never publicly acknowledged her debt to these black pioneers. In none of the interviews she gave, in none of the half dozen books she authored, did she mention the long line of black beauty entrepreneurs who had come before her. Perhaps she was reluctant to concede that her plan was not completely original. Perhaps she was simply unaware of its precursors.

In other respects, Ash's sense of history was acute. When Mary Kay opened an office in Atlanta in 1971, the celebration surrounding the event had an antebellum theme. Employees dressed in hoopskirts, channeling their inner Scarlett O'Haras.[71] At the Seminar that commemorated the twenty-fifth anniversary of the company in 1988, the same motif reigned. On awards night, Ash was ushered onto the stage in a carriage as a stream of hoopskirted belles and tuxedo-clad gentlemen gathered to greet her.[72] By 1988, Mary Kay's sales force was still well represented in the South, but the company boasted consultants all over the country and in nine foreign countries, including some in South America and Asia.

Still, Mary Kay draped itself in the iconography of the Old South, holding up the southern lady as the paragon of beauty, suggesting that she was the wellspring of what Ash and her consultants had to offer to women who wanted to look more attractive. Indeed, despite the company's increasingly global reach, Mary Kay also struggled to diversify its sales force and product line at home. Not until the late 1970s and early 1980s, when greater employment opportunities began to thin the ranks of the company's consultants, did Mary Kay make an effort to recruit black women in the United States. Not until the late 1990s, moreover, did the company introduce a line of cosmetics in a full range of shades and tones appropriate for women of color.[73] That Mary Kay, like dozens of beauty companies before it, opted to explicitly associate itself with an antebellum ideal of white southern beauty fit within this narrow aesthetic view. And in summoning this image from the past, Mary Kay buttressed the assumptions that went with it: that beauty was both the privilege and duty of white southern women.

Of course, by the 1970s and 1980s, few, if any, white southerners would have questioned a woman's recourse to cosmetics as they did when the strategy of invoking a uniquely southern ideal was first introduced. Mary Kay, the woman and the company, were at once testaments to how much things had changed and yet how much things remained the same in the post–civil rights South. Mary Kay Ash talked about women's economic independence in a way that would have bewildered her southern forebears, but she honored one of the most important southern traditions of all—selling the beauty of the white South to women within the region and beyond.

# Notes

ABBREVIATIONS

ARC Amistad Research Center, Tulane University, New Orleans, Louisiana

AUCA Atlanta University Center Archives, Robert W. Woodruff Library, Atlanta University Center, Atlanta, Georgia

BTV Behind the Veil: Documenting African-American Life in the Jim Crow South Records, Rare Books, Manuscripts, and Special Collections Library, Duke University, Durham, North Carolina

CESR Cooperative Extension Service Records, University Archives, D. H. Hill Library, North Carolina State University, Raleigh, North Carolina

CMJC The Dr. R. Q. and Ethyl H. Venson Cotton Makers Jubilee Collection, Memphis and Shelby County Room, Memphis Public Library, Memphis, Tennessee

DNCC North Carolina Newspapers, Digital NC Collection, North Carolina Heritage Center, University of North Carolina at Chapel Hill, http://www.digitalnc.org/collections/newspapers

FSMCS Field Studies in the Modern Culture of the South Records, Southern Historical Collection, Wilson Library, University of North Carolina at Chapel Hill

JDWL Department of Archives and Special Collections, J. D. Williams Library, University of Mississippi, Oxford, Mississippi

JWTA J. Walter Thompson Company Archives, John W. Hartman Center for Sales, Advertising, and Marketing History, Rare Books, Manuscripts, and Special Collections Library, Duke University, Durham, North Carolina

MCJWP Madam C. J. Walker Papers, Indiana Historical Society, Indianapolis, Indiana

NCC North Carolina Collection, Wilson Library, University of North Carolina at Chapel Hill, Chapel Hill, North Carolina

NCDCDC North Carolina Department of Conservation and Development Collection, Division of Archives and Records, State Archives of North Carolina, Raleigh, North Carolina

RPBP Ruby Parks Blackburn Papers, Archives Division, Auburn Avenue Research Library, Atlanta, Georgia

SCHS South Carolina Historical Society, Charleston, South Carolina

SCRBC Schomburg Center for Research in Black Culture, New York Public Library, New York, New York

SHC    Southern Historical Collection, Wilson Library, University of North
       Carolina at Chapel Hill, Chapel Hill, North Carolina
SHSW   State Historical Society of Wisconsin, Madison, Wisconsin
WHSL   University Archives, William H. Sheppard Library, Stillman College,
       Tuscaloosa, Alabama
WSHSC  W. S. Hoole Special Collections Library, University of Alabama,
       Tuscaloosa, Alabama
WWAL   Archives and Special Collections, Will W. Alexander Library, Dillard
       University, New Orleans, Louisiana

## INTRODUCTION

1. The incident described here occurs on pp. 151–71 and 195–205 of Crafts, *Bondwoman's Narrative*. Debate over the true identity of Hannah Crafts swirled after the publication of her novel in 2002 by Henry Louis Gates Jr., who had acquired the manuscript at a 2001 auction. Some scholars did not accept Gates's and Crafts's own contention that she was a fugitive slave, arguing that she was a free black or white woman. Gates and Robbins, *In Search of Hannah Crafts*, contains several essays that explore these possibilities (see pp. 315–416). Others posited that Crafts was actually a white woman (see Bernier and Newman, "*Bondwoman's Narrative*"). In 2013, Gregg Hecimovich of Winthrop University announced that he had definitively determined that Crafts was, in fact, a slave woman named Hannah Bond. Before her escape, she lived on a Murfreesboro, North Carolina, plantation owned by John Hill Wheeler. Wheeler's wife, the impulsive mistress who, at least in the narrative, fell victim to the chemist's powder, was Ellen. After her escape, Bond took refuge with an upstate New York family named Crafts, which likely accounts for the pseudonym she chose. See Hecimovich, "The Life and Times of Hannah Crafts: The True Story of *The Bondwoman's Narrative*," unpublished book manuscript.

2. Seidel, *Southern Belle in the American Novel*, 11.

3. Hentz, *Eoline; or, Magnolia Vale*, 22–23.

4. Jordan, *White Over Black*, 248.

5. Jefferson, *Notes on the State of Virginia*, 138.

6. For an early survey of this voluminous field, see Hall and Scott, "Women in the South." For a more recent one, see Turner, "Women in the Post–Civil War South."

7. Scott, *Southern Lady*; White, *Ar'n't I a Woman?*, 27–61. For investigations of southern femininity in more recent decades, see McPherson, *Reconstructing Dixie*, and Boyd, "Southern Beauty."

8. Examples include Banner, *American Beauty*; Steele, *Fashion and Eroticism*; Thesander, *Feminine Ideal*; and Mulvey and Richards, *Decades of Beauty*.

9. Peiss, *Hope in a Jar*. Also see Willett, *Permanent Waves*.

10. Gill, *Beauty Shop Politics*; Craig, *Ain't I a Beauty Queen?*; Walker, *Style and Status*; Rooks, *Hair Raising*.

11. See Hale, *Making Whiteness*; Ayers, *Promise of the New South*; Ownby,

*American Dreams in Mississippi*; Hall et al., *Like a Family*, esp. 237–88; Singal, *War Within*; and Kirby, *Rural Worlds Lost*.

12. Barlow et al., "Modern Girl around the World"; Weinbaum et al., *Modern Girl around the World*. Also see Conor, *Spectacular Modern Woman*, and Felski, *Gender of Modernity*.

13. Barlow et al., "Modern Girl around the World," 245.

14. Cahn, *Sexual Reckonings*, 7–8.

15. This book also adds to the literature on women, gender, and massive resistance. See Elizabeth Gillespie McRae, "White Womanhood, White Supremacy, and the Rise of Massive Resistance," and Karen S. Anderson, "Massive Resistance, Violence, and Southern Social Relations," in Webb, *Massive Resistance*; Anderson, *Little Rock*; and Godfrey, "Bayonets, Brainwashing, and Bathrooms."

16. Boyd, "Southern Beauty."

17. Stewart, *Put Down and Ripped Off*; Brownmiller, *Femininity*; Lakoff and Scherr, *Face Value*; Wolf, *Beauty Myth*; Bordo, *Unbearable Weight*; Brumberg, *Body Project*; Jeffreys, *Beauty and Misogyny*.

18. Bordo, "Body and the Reproduction of Femininity," 14.

19. Collins, *Black Feminist Thought*; Morton, *Disfigured Images*; hooks, *Black Looks*; Jewell, *From Mammy to Miss America and Beyond*. On the image of "mammy," see Manring, *Slave in a Box*.

20. Barlow et al., "Modern Girl around the World," 267. Liz Coner makes a similar point about the flapper, arguing that she "complicated the woman-object's traditional inability to attain subject status" (*Spectacular Modern Woman*, 13).

21. Mark M. Smith has pioneered the sensory history of the South. See *How Race Is Made*. For a take on the field more broadly, see his "Producing Sense, Consuming Sense, Making Sense."

22. Alison Piepmeier convincingly argues that victimization and agency should not be seen "as mutually exclusive but as interpenetrating." "The question," she asserts, "becomes not whether . . . women . . . are victims or agents, but how does agency—or how do *acts* of agency and resistance—emerge within a social, cultural, and perhaps a personal context of disempowerment and even oppression?" (*Out in Public*, 9). Two recent studies provide the kind of nuanced interpretation I hope to achieve here. See Banet-Weiser, *Most Beautiful Girl in the World*, and Black, *Beauty Industry*.

## CHAPTER ONE

1. Bickett, "How to Be Beautiful," in Bickett, *Public Letters and Papers*, 221, 222, 223, 226. I would like to thank Sarah Thuesen for bringing this speech to my attention.

2. Greeley, *Food and Drugs Act, June 30, 1906*, 73.

3. Peiss, *Hope in a Jar*, 24.

4. Douglas and Isherwood, *World of Goods*, xxii.

5. This strategy thus fits into the much broader project of constructing white

racial identity and the culture of segregation discussed by Grace Hale, though here I'm emphasizing how white racial identity in the South was made manifest in the body. In this sense, then, whiteness takes on a more literal meaning. See Hale, *Making Whiteness*. For critical appraisals of whiteness studies in general, see Arnesen, "Whiteness and the Historians' Imagination," and Kolchin, "Whiteness Studies."

6. On this transformation, see Peiss, *Hope in a Jar*, 37–60.

7. Ibid., 19.

8. Ibid., 9–31, 37–41, 53–54.

9. Anne Firor Scott's analysis of the southern lady remains the classic exploration of the image and its power. See Scott, *Southern Lady*, esp. 4–21. For an examination of the lady in twentieth-century popular culture, see McPherson, *Reconstructing Dixie*, 39–94.

10. Holmes, *Diary of Miss Emma Holmes*, 39.

11. Ibid., 210.

12. Ripley, *Social Life in Old New Orleans*, 114.

13. Ibid., 115.

14. Felton, *Country Life*.

15. Chesnut, *Mary Chesnut's Civil War*, 380.

16. Peiss, *Hope in a Jar*, 9–10, 14–15, 35–36, and 40.

17. Ibid., 44–50.

18. Susman, "'Personality' and the Making of Twentieth-Century Culture," 280. An early study of women in Topeka, Kansas, conducted by J. Walter Thompson, for example, hoped that women were learning to see the cosmetic routine as "a part of their personality" and not something that was "artificial." See "Analysis of Women Interviewed in Topeka, Kansas," September 1923, 8, microfilm reel 59, Research Reports, JWTA.

19. Peiss, *Hope in a Jar*, 44, 49, 59.

20. Ibid., 39.

21. Ibid., 97.

22. Willett, *Permanent Waves*, 26–27.

23. *Columbia (S.C.) Daily Union*, 28 February 1873, n.p.

24. Richard von Krafft-Ebing, quoted in Duberman, Vicinus, and Chauncey, *Hidden from History*, 269.

25. Garden, "Why I Bobbed My Hair," 8.

26. Willett, *Permanent Waves*, 30.

27. "Economic Effects of Hairbobbing," 74.

28. In 1920, the census defined urban areas as those with a population of 2,500 or more. The percentage of southerners living in rural areas in 1920 was roughly 73 percent. See Bureau of the Census, *Fourteenth Census, 1920*, vol. 1.

29. Hale, *Making Whiteness*, 169. Statistic from Ayers, *Promise of the New South*, 81.

30. Carson, *Old Country Store*, 235.

31. On the heavy consumption of these medicines among southerners, see Clark, *Pills, Petticoats, and Plows*, 236–40.

32. Ibid., 228.

33. *Griffin (Ga.) Evening Call*, 12 April 1901, 1.

34. Peiss, *Hope in a Jar*, 17.

35. John Branch Account Book, vol. 2, Branch Family Papers, SHC; J. W. Dennis Drugstore Journal, 1867–68, WSHSC.

36. See, for example, the appendix of store inventories from North Carolina, Virginia, and Maryland in Hanson, "Home Sweet Home," 312.

37. Inventory, 1929, Pierce and Company Papers, SHC.

38. Daybook, 1939, W. L. Bruce Collection, WSHSC.

39. "Outstanding Facts on Investigation in Small Towns in Indiana," *J. Walter Thompson News Bulletin*, no. 9, April 1917, JWTA.

40. Hagood, *Mothers of the South*, 64.

41. Sharpless, *Fertile Ground*, 93.

42. Tyler, "Ideal Rural Southern Woman," 326.

43. Letter, quoted in Tyler, "Ideal Rural Southern Woman," 327.

44. Inez Folley, quoted in Sharpless, *Fertile Ground*, 95.

45. Evelyn Petree Lewellyn, quoted in Walker, *Country Women Cope with Hard Times*, 129.

46. Hagood, *Mothers of the South*, 41.

47. Ownby, *American Dreams in Mississippi*, esp. 7–32.

48. Hale, *Making Whiteness*, 171.

49. "The Small Town Paper," *J. Walter Thompson News Bulletin*, 24 October 1916; "Country Weeklies," *J. Walter Thompson News Bulletin*, 28 November 1916; "What is the Farm Market?," *J. Walter Thompson News Bulletin*, 4 February 1926, JWTA.

50. On the general store as public space, see Jones, *Mama Learned Us to Work*, 27–34, and Ownby, *American Dreams in Mississippi*, 7–32.

51. Dickins, "Clothing and Houselinen Expenditures of 99 Rural Families," 4.

52. Hagood, *Mothers of the South*, 160.

53. Jones, *Mama Learned Us to Work*, 33.

54. Information about the number of white beauticians in each southern state was gathered from 1920 census data. Per capita numbers were calculated based on the total number of white females living in each state regardless of age. Bureau of the Census, *Fourteenth Census, 1920*, vol. 3, and *Fourteenth Census, 1920*, vol. 4.

55. Sally Carter, "Out of Miss Dixie's Bandbox—How Shall I Wear My Hair?," *Progressive Farmer*, 1 December 1928, 28. Also see F. M. Register, "Woman's Crown of Glory: A Little Sermon on Good Health," *Progressive Farmer*, 31 August 1929, 17.

56. Sally Carter, "Hair Styles for Fall," *Progressive Farmer*, October 1937, 41.

57. Willett, *Permanent Waves*, 41–46.

58. On white women's expanded job opportunities during the Depression, see Jones, *Labor of Love*, 199–200, and Kessler-Harris, *Out to Work*, 250–72.

59. Bureau of the Census, *Sixteenth Census, 1940*, vol. 3.

60. Ibid.; Bureau of the Census, *Sixteenth Census, 1940*, vol. 2.

61. "The Lilac Beauty Shop," folder 222, Federal Writers' Project Papers, SHC.

62. "Clothing" notecard, folder 21, box 1, subseries 1.1, FSMCS, SHC.

63. Bureau of the Census, *Fifteenth Census, 1930*, vol. 1.

64. Durr, *Outside the Magic Circle*, 49.

65. "Woodbury's Facial Soap Investigation among Southern Debutantes," 25 September 1925, 1, Research Reports, microfilm reel 45, JWTA.

66. On the development of youth culture on college campuses in the 1920s, see Fass, *Damned and the Beautiful*.

67. Montgomery native Zelda Fitzgerald, to many the embodiment of flapperdom, wrote about the importance of cosmetics to the flapper look in several essays. See Fitzgerald, "Eulogy on the Flapper" and "Paint and Powder." On the enthusiasm for and meaning of flapperdom in the South more generally, see Cahn, *Sexual Reckonings*, 16–18.

68. For more on this migration, see Kirby, *Rural Worlds Lost*, 286–99, and Hall et al., *Like a Family*, 41–43.

69. Abbott, *Womenfolks*, 171.

70. See Cahn, *Sexual Reckonings*, 129–55, for a discussion of how these southern girls used consumer goods to forge their identity.

71. Cahn also discusses the humiliation working-class girls suffered because of their wardrobes in *Sexual Reckonings*, 135–39.

72. "Bonnie, the Hairdresser," folder 377, Federal Writers' Project Papers, SHC.

73. Woodward, *Strange Career of Jim Crow*, 116; Willett, *Permanent Waves*, 44. The full text of the ordinance can be found in Murray, *States' Laws on Race and Color*, 627.

74. Bureau of the Census, *Fourteenth Census, 1920*, vol. 4, 1055.

75. According to Julie A. Willett, some barbers believed that women patronized their shops because of the "thrill" of having a young, good-looking barber cut their hair. See *Permanent Waves*, 43–44.

76. Nannie Pharis, interview by Allen Tullos, transcript, 8 and 30 January 1979, Southern Oral History Program, SHC.

77. Scott, *Southern Lady*, 221–26.

78. "Should Women Paint?," *Baltimore Sun*, 25 August 1912, sec. 4, p. 6.

79. On this issue, see Kasson, *Rudeness and Civility*, 100, and Hall, "Private Eyes, Public Women," 255–56.

80. "Should Women Paint?," *Baltimore Sun*, 25 August 1912, sec. 4, p. 6.

81. Ed Angly, "Beauties Concur in Resolutions," *Daily Texan*, 4 May 1918, 1, University Archives, Dolph Briscoe Center for American History, University of Texas at Austin.

82. *Forester*, November 1923, Texas and Dallas History Collection, Dallas Public Library.

83. *Rammer Jammer*, n.d. 1927, 130, University Archives, WSHSC.

84. A 1909 poem titled "The U. of A. Co-Ed," for example, heralded her as "the fairest flower of all" (*Crimson-White*, 20 October 1919, 1, University Archives, WSHSC).

85. McCandless, *Past in the Present*, 84, 99.

86. Porter, "Menace of Feminism," 24, 28.

87. Milford, *Zelda*, 22.

88. Fitzgerald, "Eulogy on the Flapper," 391.

89. Fitzgerald, "Paint and Powder," 415, 416.

90. I am drawing heavily on the portrait of the modernist worldview outlined by Singal in "Toward a Definition of American Modernism," 7–26, and on Christine Stansell's discussion of sexual modernism in *American Moderns*, 225–72.

91. Singal, "Toward a Definition of American Modernism," 15.

92. Cahn, *Sexual Reckonings*, 20, 44.

93. See, for example, "A Trim Hair Arrangement," *Progressive Farmer*, 31 May 1924, 20.

94. F. M. Register, "Care of the Hair and Scalp," *Progressive Farmer*, 14 June 1924, 19; "Hair, Beautiful and Otherwise," *Progressive Farmer*, 25 February 1928, 17.

95. Rice noted that the most spiritual of Christian women "cannot go to the extremes that worldly women follow in painting the face" even if they did choose to use cosmetics, but he insisted that the Bible "expressly teaches that a woman should have long hair" as a sign of her submission. See *Bobbed Hair, Bossy Wives, and Women Preachers*, 66–68.

96. Peiss, *Hope in a Jar*, 101.

97. F. D. Aley to James Allan, 12 February 1919, James Allan Papers, SCHS.

98. Sample advertisement, quoted in James Allan to H. H. Baynard, 12 February 1919, James Allan Papers, SCHS.

99. Ibid.

100. James Allan to F. D. Aley, 25 July 1919, James Allan Papers, SCHS.

101. Ibid., 26 May 1921.

102. Peiss, *Hope in a Jar*, 40–41, 149–50.

103. Abbott, *Womenfolks*, 6.

104. "Sex Typing" notecard, folder 21, box, 5, subseries 1.5, FSMCS.

105. Ripley, *Social Life in Old New Orleans*, 108.

106. Gilmore, *Gender and Jim Crow*, 72.

107. *Progressive Farmer*, 15–31 March 1931, 35.

108. *Wisconsin State Journal*, 9 September 1913, n.p.

109. Southern Flowers Face Powder Advertisement, 1924, Nadine Cosmetics 1924–1926, folder 10, box 4, U.S. Series: Advertising, Dorothy Dignam Papers, SHSW.

110. Cox, *Dreaming of Dixie*. Also see Gerster and Cords, "Northern Origins of Southern Mythology."

111. Nadine Face Powder Advertisements, 1924, Nadine Cosmetics 1924–1926, folder 10, box 4, Dorothy Dignam Papers, SHSW.

112. Nadinola Bleaching Cream Advertisements, 1924, Nadine Cosmetics 1924–1926, folder 10, box 4, Dorothy Dignam Papers, SHSW.

113. Cox, *Dreaming of Dixie*, 3.

114. Barlow et al., "Modern Girl around the World," 246, 249, 251, 265, 286.

115. Statistics for the 1930s are from Tyler, "Ideal Rural Southern Woman," 315. For the 1950s, see *Readership of 16 Selected Magazines in the Rural South*, 10, 22.

116. Hagood, *Mothers of the South*, 70.

117. *Readership of 16 Selected Magazines in the Rural South*, 14. *Readership of 16 Selected Magazines in the Rural South* was a study of rural southern reading habits sponsored by the *Progressive Farmer*. The research company that conducted the study for the magazine defined the rural South as "that part of 16 Southern states generally outside of urbanized areas as defined by the U.S. Census Bureau and outside of towns of 2,500 or more people" (p. 5). The sixteen states included were Texas, Oklahoma, Louisiana, Arkansas, Mississippi, Georgia, Alabama, Florida, Kentucky, Tennessee, West Virginia, North Carolina, South Carolina, Virginia, Maryland, and Delaware. While it is possible that some black farm families subscribed to the *Progressive Farmer*, its content was clearly aimed at white southerners. The results of the readership study reflect this fact (see p. 62).

118. *Progressive Farmer*, 14 April 1923, cover.

119. *Progressive Farmer*, 15–30 April 1931.

120. Carter, "Out of Miss Dixie's Bandbox—What to Do About Your Freckle Crop," *Progressive Farmer*, 15–31 October 1930, 28.

121. Carter, "Out of Miss Dixie's Bandbox—For Sun Kissed Dixie Belle," *Progressive Farmer*, 1–14 June 1932, 12.

122. Carter, quoted in Tyler, "Ideal Rural Southern Woman," 326.

123. Carter, "Out of Miss Dixie's Bandbox—The Romance of Beauty," *Progressive Farmer*, 1–14 July, 1931, 15.

124. Carter, "Out of Miss Dixie's Bandbox—What the Book of Charms Told," *Progressive Farmer*, 15–31 July, 1931, 22.

125. Carter, "Out of Miss Dixie's Bandbox—The Romance of Beauty," *Progressive Farmer*, 1–14 July 1931, 15.

126. *Progressive Farmer*, 1–15 March 1931, 26.

127. McKimmon, *When We're Green We Grow*, 280, 281.

128. Carter, "Out of Miss Dixie's Bandbox—Making Friends with Make-Up," *Progressive Farmer*, 15–28 February 1931, 23.

129. Carter, "Out of Miss Dixie's Bandbox," *Progressive Farmer*, February 1937, 55.

130. Carter, "Quickies for School Day Beauty," *Progressive Farmer*, October 1941, 39.

131. Carter, "Out of Miss Dixie's Bandbox—Would You Dye for Beauty's Sake?," *Progressive Farmer*, October 1939, 30.

132. See, for example, "Keeping the Color of the Hair," *Progressive Farmer*, 1 August 1925, 11.

133. Carter, "Out of Miss Dixie's Bandbox—Glamour for Christmas," *Progressive Farmer*, December 1939, 30.

134. McEuen, *Making War, Making Women*, 45.

135. Ibid.

136. This statistic excludes toilet soaps. See "Cosmetics Output Spirals," 68. Government regulation of the cosmetics market during the war was, relative to other industries, somewhat lax due to the protests of both manufacturers and consumers. See "Cosmetics Output Spirals" and McEuen, *Making War, Making Women*, 45–47.

137. "Cosmetics Output Spirals," 68. This was true for poorer, working women in cities as well. See Zolotow, "Boom in Beauty," 22.

138. Walker, *All We Knew Was to Farm*, 285. Pete Daniel discusses the way in which the war raised consumer expectations among rural southerners in "Going among Strangers," 895.

139. Carter, "Fall Make-Up Trends," *Progressive Farmer*, November 1945, 53.

140. "American Women Spend $8.59 on Cosmetics," 72. By contrast, women in the top-ranking state, New York, spent $18.20.

141. "Women's Business and Professional Club" notecard, folder 52, box 3, subseries 1.3, FSMCS.

142. "Family Description" notecard, folder 48, box 4, subseries 1.4, FSMCS.

143. Peiss, *Hope in a Jar*, 152.

144. Carter, "Out of Miss Dixie's Bandbox," *Progressive Farmer*, June 1935, 29.

145. Carter, "Summer Make-Up Bows to Fashion," *Progressive Farmer*, August 1936, 33.

146. Carter, "Suntan vs. Sunburn," *Progressive Farmer*, July 1945, 34.

147. Mixon, "Resistance to Industrialization," 251.

148. Morland, *Millways of Kent*, 190.

149. For more on pool construction during these years, see Wiltse, *Contested Waters*, 87–120.


CHAPTER TWO

1. Julia Lucas, interview by Leslie Brown, transcript, 21 September 1995, BTV.

2. On class, the NAACP, and the teachers' salary controversy in Durham, see Brown, *Upbuilding Black Durham*, 312–22.

3. Julia Lucas, interview by Leslie Brown, transcript, 21 September 1995, BTV.

4. For a discussion of studies that posit consumption as a political category, see Glickman, "Toward a History of Consumer Culture, Women, and Politics." A number of scholars have turned their attention to the political possibilities of femininity for black women, as well as to the political importance of beauty parlors and beauty culture in African American communities. In addition to more fully exploring these two issues, I hope to go further, demonstrating that they were intricately connected. See Rooks, *Hair Raising*; Bundles, *On Her Own Ground*; Blackwelder, *Styling Jim Crow*; Walker, *Style and Status*; Davarian L. Baldwin, "From the Washtub to the World: Madam C. J. Walker and the 'Re-creation' of Race Womanhood, 1900–1935," in Weinbaum et al., *Modern Girl around the World.*; Gill, "'I Had My Own Business'"; and Gill, *Beauty Shop Politics*. For a study of the beauty parlor as female space in contemporary film, see Scanlon, "'If My Husband Calls, I'm Not Here.'"

5. Byrd and Tharps, *Hair Story*, 1–7.

6. White and White, *Stylin'*, 39.

7. Ibid., 55.

8. Ibid., 55–56.

9. Willett, *Permanent Waves*, 17; Walker, *History of Black Business in America*, 182. For more on Potter, see Santamarina, *Belabored Professions*, 103–38, and Potter's own memoir, *A Hairdresser's Experience in High Life*.

10. Fox-Genovese, *Within the Plantation Household*, 216.

11. *Savannah Tribune*, 4 February 1899, 1.

12. *Colored American*, 11 August 1894, 7.

13. *Report of the Thirteenth Annual Convention of the National Negro Business League*, 65, 67.

14. Spelman Seminary Catalogue, 1892–93, AUCA.

15. Atlanta University Catalogue, 1885–86, AUCA.

16. Armstrong, *On Habits and Manners*, 31.

17. Fields, *Lemon Swamp*, 219.

18. Mebane, *Mary, An Autobiography*, 35.

19. Bundles, *On Her Own Ground*, 61–62; Byrd and Tharps, *Hair Story*, 136.

20. Fields, *Lemon Swamp*, 218.

21. Rooks, *Hair Raising*, 42–50.

22. Walker, quoted in Rooks, *Hair Raising*, 63; Bundles, *On Her Own Ground*, 20.

23. Marie Cane to Madam C. J. Walker, 21 May 1918, MCJWP.

24. Peiss, *Hope in a Jar*, 225–26.

25. Coclanis, "What Made Booker T. Wash(ington)?," 81.

26. For a discussion of racial uplift and black club women's efforts in this arena, see White, *Too Heavy a Load*, chaps. 1 and 2, and Hunter, *To 'Joy My Freedom*, esp. chaps. 7 and 8. On black Baptist women, see Higginbotham, *Righteous Discontent*, esp. chap. 7. Gaines discusses the problems and limitations of uplift ideology in *Uplifting the Race*.

27. Higginbotham, *Righteous Discontent*, 195.

28. Bundles, *On Her Own Ground*, 122.

29. Gill, "'I Had My Own Business,'" 178.

30. Booker T. Washington to Frederick Randolph Moore, 18 December 1911, in Harlan and Smock, *Booker T. Washington Papers*, 420.

31. Burroughs, "Not Color but Character," 278.

32. Wolcott, "'Bible, Bath, and Broom,'" 94.

33. Cornelia Bowen, quoted in Young, *Your St. Louis and Mine*, 52.

34. Walker, *Style and Status*, 51, 64–70.

35. See Gaines, *Uplifting the Race*, 3, and Higginbotham, *Righteous Discontent*, 185–229.

36. Tiffany M. Gill uses the phrase "racial authenticity" in her study of black beauty culture. See *Beauty Shop Politics*, 4. In her examination of light-skinned blacks and Mexicans in more recent decades, Margaret Hunter opts for "ethnic legitimacy." See *Race, Gender, and the Politics of Skin Tone*, 93–110.

37. Craig, "Color of an Ideal Negro Beauty Queen," 87.

38. Powdermaker, *After Freedom*, 176.

39. Walker ad, quoted in Rooks, *Hair Raising*, 64.

40. See Rooks, *Hair Raising*, 51–74, for more on how early black beauty culturists reconfigured images of working-class black women. Beauty culturists demonstrate well Victoria W. Wolcott's contention that black working-class women's concern with respectability was "part of a pre-existing working-class culture" and not something that was simply imposed by elite black female reformers. See "'Bible, Bath, and Broom,'" 89.

41. Fields, *Lemon Swamp*, 188.

42. Catherine Cardozo Lewis, interview by Marcia Greenlee, in Hill, *Black Women Oral History Project*, 259.

43. Fields, *Lemon Swamp*, 187. Actually, Annie Turnbo Malone began her career in beauty culture earlier, but the two rivals were both popularly associated with the new pressing regimen.

44. Higginbotham, *Righteous Discontent*, 187–88.

45. *Walker News*, September 1928, n.p., MCJWP.

46. Nannie Helen Burroughs, "Address at Apex Commencement," *Apex News*, January–February–March 1938, 27, SCRBC.

47. Gill, "'I Had My Own Business,'" 173.

48. Walker, *Style and Status*, 4; Willett, *Permanent Waves*, 19.

49. Nannie Helen Burroughs, "Address at Apex Commencement," *Apex News*, January–February–March 1938, 27, SCRBC.

50. *Dallas Express*, 14 January 1928, 6.

51. *Report of the Thirteenth Annual Convention of the National Negro Business League*, 154.

52. Ibid.

53. Madam C. J. Walker to Booker T. Washington, 13 March 1914, container 815, Booker T. Washington Papers, Manuscript Division, Library of Congress, Washington, D.C.

54. Booker T. Washington to Madam C. J. Walker, 25 March 1914, ibid.

55. Malone, quoted in Peiss, *Hope in a Jar*, 51.

56. Peiss, *Hope in a Jar*, 280.

57. Rooks, *Hair Raising*, 48, 53.

58. Bundles, *On Her Own Ground*, 92.

59. F. B. Ransom to Mrs. A. C. Burnett, 10 September 1918, MCJWP.

60. See, for, example, Clarke, *Tupperware*.

61. Fields, *Lemon Swamp*, 189.

62. Peiss, *Hope in a Jar*, 112–13.

63. Armstrong, *On Habits and Manners*, 31.

64. Joyner, quoted in Walker, *Style and Status*, 65.

65. Dunbar-Nelson, *Give Us Each Day*, 91.

66. "Rouge and Progress," 10.

67. Rose Doggett, "Make Me Beautiful," *Apex News*, April–May–June 1938, 8, SCRBC.

68. "Beauty and Romance," *Carolina Times*, 5 February 1938, 2.

69. Nannie Helen Burroughs, "Address at Apex Commencement," *Apex News*, January–February–March 1938, 27, SCRBC.

70. "Beauty and Romance," *Carolina Times*, 26 February 1938, 2.

71. Ibid., 5 February 1938, 2.

72. Brown, *Correct Thing*, 62.

73. Peiss, *Hope in a Jar*, 221 (quote), 220–21.

74. William Gordon, interview by John Egerton, transcript, 19 January 1991, Southern Oral History Program, SHC.

75. Mebane, *Mary, An Autobiography*, 105, 118.

76. *Helena (Ark.) Reporter*, 1 February 1900, 2.

77. "An Unscdrupulous [*sic*] Concern," 17. Paris, Tennessee, was home to several cosmetic manufacturers in the early twentieth century, so it is difficult to know whether the *Half-Century* correspondent was referring to the National Toilet Company, whose ads are discussed in Chapter 1 and later in this chapter, or one of the other concerns. Nadinola, the company's bleaching cream, did contain enough ammoniated mercury (10 percent) to damage the skin. In response to customer complaints, the company lowered the amount of this ingredient in the late 1930s and again in the early 1940s. See Peiss, *Hope in a Jar*, 212.

78. "Safer to Patronize Your Own," 17.

79. Mebane, *Mary, Wayfarer*, 79.

80. *Walker News*, July 1930, n.p., MCJWP.

81. Ibid. (quote); Walker, *Style and Status*, 65.

82. Peiss, *Hope in a Jar*, 113; Walker, *Style and Status*, 22–23.

83. Company records did not include information on sales by product until the 1950s. See Sales by Dealer Records and Sales Distribution Records, MCJWP.

84. *Walker News*, September 1928, n.p., MCJWP. The Atlanta and New Orleans women placed first and third. An agent from Detroit placed second.

85. Holsey, "Negro Business," 321.

86. Information about his distribution channels and business philosophy can be found in *Report of the Thirteenth Annual Convention of the National Negro Business League*, 99.

87. See, for example, High-Brown Sample Envelope.

88. Mary Beckwith operated the company with her husband James. The 1923 Cleveland City Directory lists her as president and James as secretary-treasurer. See *Cleveland City Directory, 1923*, Western Reserve Historical Society, Cleveland, Ohio.

89. *Columbia (S.C.) Southern Indicator*, 2 July 1921, 1 and 3.

90. Peiss, *Hope in a Jar*, 110; Walker, *Style and Status*, 20–26.

91. *Columbia (S.C.) Southern Indicator*, 27 January 1923, 3.

92. *Pittsburgh Courier*, 6 June 1925, 2.

93. *Louisiana Weekly*, 5 May 1934, 2.

94. Peiss, *Hope in a Jar*, 224–26.

95. Dunbar-Nelson, "People of Color in Louisiana," 361. For more on Dunbar-

Nelson's understanding of race, see Alexander, *Lyrics of Sunshine and Shadow*, esp. chap. 2.

96. Dunbar-Nelson, *Give Us Each Day*, 91, 385–86, 430, 434.

97. For more on color prejudice in the African American community, see Hunter, *Race, Gender, and the Politics of Skin Tone*; Russell, Wilson, and Hall, *Color Complex*; Craig, *Ain't I a Beauty Queen?*, 37–43; Gatewood, *Aristocrats of Color*, 149–81; Haidarali, "'Vampingest Vamp Is a Brownskin'"; and Keith and Herring, "Skin Tone and Stratification."

98. Gatewood, *Aristocrats of Color*, 153.

99. Fields, *Lemon Swamp*, 13.

100. Julia Lucas, interview by Leslie Brown, transcript, 21 September 1995, BTV.

101. The Institute for Research in Social Science at the University of North Carolina, for example, sent teams of doctoral students to counties in North Carolina, South Carolina, and Alabama. Morton Rubin's *Plantation County* and Hylan Lewis's *Blackways of Kent* resulted from this project. Other important monographs from this research impulse include Powdermaker, *After Freedom*, and Dollard, *Caste and Class in a Southern Town*. Black sociologists like Lewis were especially prolific during these years. The American Council on Education commissioned several studies by black scholars on racial prejudice, including Frazier's *Negro Youth at the Crossways*; Johnson's *Growing Up in the Black Belt*; and Davis and Dollard's, *Children of Bondage*. Also see Davis, Gardner, and Gardner, *Deep South*.

102. Davis, Gardner, and Gardner, *Deep South*, 21.

103. Dollard, *Caste and Class in a Southern Town*, 69–71.

104. Davis, Gardner, and Gardner, *Deep South*, 247.

105. The four other choices were "brown," picked by 6.6 percent of boys and 12.1 percent of girls; "light-brown," picked by 6.5 percent of boys and 9.7 percent of girls; "yellow," picked by 10.8 percent of boys and 11.5 percent of girls; and "white," picked by 10.5 percent of boys and 8.7 percent of girls. See Johnson, *Growing Up in the Black Belt*, 261.

106. Davis, Gardner, and Gardner, *Deep South*, 41.

107. Powdermaker, *After Freedom*, 179.

108. Johnson, *Growing Up in the Black Belt*, 265.

109. Dollard, *Caste and Class in a Southern Town*, 70.

110. Odum and Johnson, *Negro Workaday Songs*, 146.

111. Jaxon, "It's Heated."

112. Oliver, *Blues Fell This Morning*, 77.

113. Davis and Dollard, *Children of Bondage*, 153.

114. See Zanger, "Tragic Octoroon," and Raimon, *"Tragic Mulatta" Revisited*.

115. Horne and Schickel, *Lena*, 31–32. See also Powdermaker, *After Freedom*, 176.

116. Powdermaker, *After Freedom*, 178.

117. Johnson, *Growing Up in the Black Belt*, 262.

118. Frazier, *Negro Youth at the Crossways*, 53.

119. Parrish, "Color Names and Color Notions," 18.

120. "I'm Going 'Way," quoted in Tracy, *Write Me a Few of Your Lines*, 151; Levine, *Black Culture and Black Consciousness*, 286.

121. Wallace, "I'm So Glad I'm Brownskin."

122. Levine, *Black Culture and Black Consciousness*, 287.

123. Johnson, *Growing Up in the Black Belt*, 269.

124. Parrish, "Color Names and Color Notions," 18.

125. Frazier, *Negro Youth at the Crossways*, 181.

126. Ibid., 182.

127. Haidarali, "'Vampingest Vamp Is a Brownskin,'" 97–161. Also see Craig, "Color of an Ideal Negro Beauty Queen," 87.

128. Haidarali, "'Vampingest Vamp Is a Brownskin,'" 155, 102.

129. Davis, Gardner, and Gardner, *Deep South*, 246–47; Lewis, *Blackways of Kent*, 10, 56.

130. Haidarali, "'Vampingest Vamp Is a Brownskin,'" 160.

131. Johnson, *Growing Up in the Black Belt*, 256.

132. "Safer to Patronize Your Own," 17.

133. "An Unscdrupulous [*sic*] Concern," 17.

134. *Pittsburgh Courier*, 6 June 1925, 2; *Louisiana Weekly*, 5 May 1934, 2; Peiss, *Hope in a Jar*, 226.

135. Johnson, *Growing Up in the Black Belt*, 9. Craig makes the same observation in *Ain't I a Beauty Queen?*, 26.

136. Johnson, *Growing Up in the Black Belt*, 259, 265.

137. Lewis, *Blackways of Kent*, 46–57.

138. *Dallas Express*, 11 January 1919, 3.

139. *Dallas Express*, 18 January 1919, n.p.

140. Black populations were larger in Mississippi (47.7 percent white and 52.2 percent black) and South Carolina (48.6 percent white and 51.4 percent black). Data about the number of beauticians in South Carolina and North Carolina in 1920 is missing from the census. Given the available information from nearby states, however, it is safe to assume that the same patterns described here would have applied to them as well. Ratios were calculated based on the total number of black females living in each state regardless of age. See Bureau of the Census, *Fourteenth Census, 1920*, vol. 3, and Bureau of the Census, *Fourteenth Census, 1920*, vol. 4.

141. Willett, *Permanent Waves*, 29.

142. The nonsouthern states examined for a sense of comparison were Illinois, Indiana, New Jersey, New York, Ohio, and Pennsylvania.

143. Bundles, *On Her Own Ground*, 277.

144. Blackwelder, *Styling Jim Crow*, 8. In the early 1930s, for example, in 230 southern counties where blacks made up 12.5 percent or more of the total population, there were no high school facilities for black students, while 195 counties with the same population breakdown offered one or two years of high school. See Anderson, *Education of Blacks in the South*, 188.

145. Johnson, *Growing Up in the Black Belt*, 215–16.

146. "Registration of Beauty Schools," folder 81, box 13, MCJWP.

147. Willett, *Permanent Waves*, 57.

148. "Business Directory for Atlanta, 1944," typescript, folder 5, box 9; "Business Directory for Louisville," typescript, folder 9, box 9; and "Business Directory for Durham," typescript, folder 8, box 9, Project to Study Business and Business Education Among Negroes, 1944–1946, AUCA.

149. Mark, *National Beauty Culturists' League*, 21.

150. "The Atlanta Beauty Culturists League Constitution and By-Laws," n.d., folder 3, box 7, RPBP.

151. Ella Martin, quoted in Kuhn, Joye, and West, *Living Atlanta*, 108.

152. Blanche Scott, interview by Beverly Jones, transcript, 11 July 1979, 26, Southern Oral History Program, SHC.

153. Ibid., 27.

154. Emily Fletcher, quoted in Wolcott, "'Bible, Bath, and Broom,'" 102.

155. Mary Elizabeth Roberts, interview by Rhonda Mawhood, tape recording, 2 August 1993, BTV.

156. Helen Fisher Dunson, interview by Rhonda Mawhood, tape recording, 4 August 1993, BTV.

157. Bernice Robinson, quoted in Wigginton, *Refuse to Stand Silently By*, 180, 182.

158. Alice Adams, quoted in Kuhn, Joye, and West, *Living Atlanta*, 119.

159. Appointment Book, 1956–57, folder 2, box, 6, RPBP.

160. Elizabeth Cardozo Barker, interview by Marcia Greenlee, in Hill, *Black Women Oral History Project*, 101.

161. "The Poro Beauty Shoppe," folder 194, Federal Writers' Project Papers, SHC.

162. Rosa Grantham, interview by Sonya Ramsey, tape recording, 5 August 1993, BTV.

163. Using the *Historical Statistics of the United States*, Gill says the number increased from 9,700 to 16,300 during that twenty-year time period. *Historical Statistics* uses a 1950 census scheme to classify occupations and draws distinctions only between "white" and "non-white" workers. For the calculations in this section, I am relying instead on 1920 and 1940 census data, which offers statistics for female beauticians as they were classified at the time, for white and "Negro" beauticians, and for beauticians on a state-by-state basis. (Comparisons for South Carolina and North Carolina from 1920 to 1940, however, cannot be made because the 1920 census does not include the number of women occupied as beauticians in either state). See Gill, *Beauty Shop Politics*, 66; *Historical Statistics of the United States*, table Ba3082–3125; Bureau of the Census, *Fourteenth Census, 1920*, vol. 3; Bureau of the Census, *Fourteenth Census, 1920*, vol. 4; Bureau of the Census, *Sixteenth Census, 1940*, vol. 2; and Bureau of the Census, *Sixteenth Census, 1940*, vol. 3.

164. Gill, *Beauty Shop Politics*, 62, 66. Robert L. Boyd makes the case for black beauticians and the disadvantage theory of business enterprise in "Survi-

valist Entrepreneurship." Significantly, he argues that the theory was born out by black beauticians in the northern cities that he examined but not by black beauticians in southern cities.

165. There was an increase in the number of black beauticians throughout the United States as a whole, and a sampling of nonsouthern states—Illinois, New Jersey, New York, Ohio, and Pennsylvania—reveals that the number of black beauticians went up in those locations as well.

166. Walker, "'Independent Livings'?," 65.

167. The exception was the border state of Maryland, where blacks were roughly 16 percent of the population but black beauticians constituted about 19 percent of the state's beauticians. The highest numbers of per capita black beauticians, in fact, were in Upper South states such as Maryland, Tennessee, Virginia, and Kentucky, as well as in Texas and Florida.

168. On this question, Boyd argues that black women in the urban South were likely unmotivated to become beauticians during the Depression because "jobless blacks in the South, unlike their counterparts in the North, could readily find work in agriculture and thus were not intensely pressured to become self-employed in urban occupations" ("Survivalist Entrepreneurship," 981). Boyd's hypothesis is unconvincing, however, given the long-term trend of tenant and sharecropper displacement, which was hastened by New Deal programs that supported crop reduction and mechanization. In 1920, 27 percent of black women in the national labor force worked in agriculture. In 1940, it was down to 16 percent. More black women in the South, in short, were moving to urban areas for non-agricultural work during these years. See Jones, *Labor of Love*, 200–201.

169. Erickson, *Employment Conditions in Beauty Shops*, 37, 39 (quote).

170. Powdermaker, *After Freedom*, 180.

171. For more on efforts to regulate the black and white beauty industries during the Depression, see Willett, *Permanent Waves*, 87–120.

172. National Recovery Administration, *Code of Fair Competition*; Gill, *Beauty Shop Politics*, 69–70; Erickson, *Employment Conditions in Beauty Shops*, 38.

173. Blackwelder, *Styling Jim Crow*, 27, 28 (quote), 68.

174. "City Merchants to Aid Beauty Parlor Operators," *Dallas Express*, 14 January 1939, 3.

175. Mark, *National Beauty Culturists' League*, 127, 137, 146, 180, 190; Gill, *Beauty Shop Politics*, 101.

176. Business Directory typescripts, folders 5–14, box 9, Project to Study Business and Business Education Among Negroes, 1944–1946, AUCA.

177. Gill, *Beauty Shop Politics*, 105.

178. Willett, *Permanent Waves*, 128–29.

179. Ibid., 148. See pp. 121–52 for more on how and why beauty shops changed after World War II.

180. In most southern states for which comparative data is available, the number of black beauticians per capita in 1960 exceeded 1920 levels. See Bureau

of the Census, *Fourteenth Census, 1920*, vol. 3; Bureau of the Census, *Fourteenth Census, 1920*, vol. 4; and Bureau of the Census, *Eighteenth Decennial of the United States, 1960*, vol. 1.

181. Erickson, *Employment Conditions in Beauty Shops*, 39; Rosa Grantham, interview by Sonya Ramsey, tape recording, 5 August 1993, BTV.

182. "The Poro Beauty Shoppe," folder 194, Federal Writers' Project Papers, SHC.

183. Business Directory typescripts, folders 5–14, box 9, Project to Study Business and Business Education Among Negroes, 1944–1946, AUCA.

184. Julia Lucas, interview by Leslie Brown, transcript, 21 September 1995, BTV.

185. *Madam C. J. Walker Beauty Manual*, quoted in Rooks, *Hair Raising*, 64.

186. *Madam C. J. Walker Beauty Manual*, 287, MCJWP.

187. Ada McWilliams, interview by Rhonda Mawhood, tape recording, 29 June 1993, BTV.

188. Powdermaker, *After Freedom*, 180.

189. Fields, *Lemon Swamp*, 188.

190. Billie Parks Douglas, quoted in Byerly, *Hard Times Cotton Mill Girls*, 104.

191. Marie Cane to Madam C. J. Walker, 21 May 1918, MCJWP.

192. Gates, *Colored People*, 40, 41.

193. Horne and Schickel, *Lena*, 31.

194. Mebane, *Mary, An Autobiography*, 36.

195. Harris, *Summer Snow*, 128.

196. Anabelle Baker, "Severed," in Harris and Johnson, *Tenderheaded*, 16.

197. Barbershops can elicit similar responses in men. Bryant Keith Alexander has written about his childhood memories of going to a barbershop in Louisiana. As an adult, he writes, the "aroma of hair oils and pomades" transports him back "not to Mr. Brown's barbershop, or even to my mother's kitchen, but to a place of comfort and familiarity that is exclusive not to the site but to the occasion." For Alexander, as for some southern black women, it was not the physical space but the ritual of grooming itself that was the source of comfort. See *Performing Black Masculinity*, 150.

198. Dunbar-Nelson, *Give Us Each Day*, 314.

199. bell hooks, "Straightening Our Hair," in Harris and Johnson, *Tenderheaded*, 111, 112.

200. Coleman, "Closets and Keepsakes."

201. Harriet Vail Wade, interview by Rhonda Mawhood, tape recording, 1 August 1993, BTV.

202. Julia Lucas, interview by Leslie Brown, transcript, 21 September 1995, BTV.

203. Ada McWilliams, interview by Rhonda Mawhood, tape recording, 29 June 1993, BTV.

204. Helen Fisher Dunson, interview by Rhonda Mawhood, tape recording, 4 August 1993, BTV.

205. Lewis, *Blackways of Kent*, 60.

206. Harriet Vail Wade, interview by Rhonda Mawhood, tape recording, 1 August 1993, BTV.

207. Elizabeth Cardozo Barker, interview by Marcia Greenlee, in Hill, *Black Women Oral History Project*, 114.

208. Ibid.

209. Barnes, "Black Beauty Parlor Complex," 152, 153.

210. Higginbotham, *Righteous Discontent*, 7.

211. Ibid., 11. See also Fraser, "Rethinking the Public Sphere."

212. Gill frames beauty parlors in a similar way in *Beauty Shop Politics*, 3.

213. Hamlin, "Vera Mae Pigee (1925–)," 291. Also see Hamlin, *Crossroads at Clarksdale*, 60–70. Evelyn Newman Phillips draws parallels between beauticians and nurses, both of which, she suggests, helped black women in the segregated South feel "emotionally and physically healthy" ("Doing More Than Heads," 39).

214. Alexander makes a similar case for the barbershop, which encourages customers to engage "in the negotiation of culture and community." "The protean and cultural act of manipulating hair," he writes, "occasions the nature of their engagement" (*Performing Black Masculinity*, 150).

215. Hall et al., *Like a Family*, 170–71.

## CHAPTER THREE

1. A portion of this chapter was previously published under the title "A New Cure for Brightleaf Tobacco: The Origins of the Tobacco Queen during the Great Depression," in *Southern Cultures* 12, no. 2 (Summer 2006), www.southern cultures.org. I thank the journal for allowing me to republish this material here.

2. The Miss America Pageant began this tradition of postdating titleholders in 1950 (the woman crowned in 1950 became Miss America 1951, and so on) because the majority of the winner's appearances and responsibilities fell in the calendar year after the September pageant. For the sake of clarity and consistency, throughout this book I describe Miss America contestants and winners from before and after 1950 by talking about the year in which they competed or were crowned.

3. Contestant, quoted in Deford, *There She Is*, 82.

4. Ibid., 80.

5. In many respects, Deford and the former Miss America offer a more satisfactory explanation than the few academics who have studied beauty contests in the region. See Boyd, "Southern Beauty," chap. 3, and Wilson, "Cult of Beauty," 17–26.

6. I am building on Mary Louise Roberts's distinction between "woman-as-commodity" and "woman-as-consumer" in "Gender, Consumption, and Commodity Culture."

7. See Banet-Weiser, *Most Beautiful Girl in the World*, esp. 1–21, for a succinct discussion of feminism, race, and beauty pageants. The women's liberation movement is widely understood to have begun when feminists protested the

Miss America Pageant in 1968 for its history of objectifying women. For more on this event and the critique at its core, see the conclusion to this book.

8. Banet-Weiser writes that women who participate in beauty pageants today are "neither complete victims nor entirely free agents," an observation that I think applies to southern beauty contests during this time period, too. See *Most Beautiful Girl in the World*, 23.

9. Tani E. Barlow et al. make a similar point about cosmetics in "Modern Girl around the World," 267.

10. Banner, *American Beauty*, 249–50.

11. Ibid., 253.

12. On pageantry during this era, see Glassberg, *American Historical Pageantry*.

13. For more on San Antonio's Fiesta, see Haynes, *Dressing Up Debutantes*, and Hernandez-Ehrisman, *Inventing the Fiesta City*.

14. On the Lost Cause, see Blight, *Race and Reunion*; Foster, *Ghosts of the Confederacy*; and Wilson, *Baptized in Blood*.

15. Ring tournaments, in fact, were sometimes held in conjunction with these early commemorative activities as a way to raise money for the reburial of Confederate soldiers in local cemeteries. See Crooks and Crooks, *Ring Tournament in the United States*, 151–52.

16. For the definitive study of the UDC and its activities on this front, see Cox, *Dixie's Daughters*.

17. Elizabeth Lumpkin, quoted in Hall, "'You Must Remember This,'" 451.

18. *Confederate Veteran*, quoted in Cox, *Dixie's Daughters*, 63 64. The UDC included Kentucky and Missouri among the states of the Confederacy.

19. Cox, *Dixie's Daughters*, 12, 37.

20. Pearson, "'Infantile Specimens,'" 341. Pearson is the first scholar to provide an analysis of this important yet underappreciated precursor to the modern beauty contest. I am drawing heavily on her analysis of the ritual here.

21. *(Savannah) Daily News and Herald*, quoted in ibid., 355.

22. Pearson, "'Infantile Specimens,'" 356.

23. Allen, *Horrible Prettiness*, 50.

24. Ibid., 225.

25. Banner, *American Beauty*, 255.

26. Comettant, *Trois ans aux Etats-Unis*, 32.

27. Banner, *American Beauty*, 259.

28. Kasson, *Amusing the Million*, 24.

29. Clarkson, "Atlanta's Beauty Show," 390.

30. On the Rehoboth Beach contest, see Deford, *There She Is*, 108–10, and Latham, *Posing a Threat*, 89–90.

31. For more on the decline of the corset, see Fields, *Intimate Affair*, 17–78.

32. For a sample of beach regulations, see "Bathing-Suits and Bathing-Beach Regulations." A Newport Beach, California, censor measured the distance between a young woman's hemline and her knee in much the same way that horses are measured—by placing his hands on her thigh and calculating the distance in

"hands." Local women's clubs were reported to be working for his recall, as they were "shocked by his method." See "After His Job," *Wilson (N.C.) Daily Times*, 21 July 1924, 2.

33. "Modesty for Bathers," *Chicago Daily News*, 22 March 1922, 11.

34. Porter, "Menace of Feminism," 25–26.

35. Raymonde Allain, quoted in Savage, *Beauty Queens*, 29.

36. R. H. Wynn, letter to the editor, *Lake Charles (La.) American Press*, 7 June 1928, reprinted in *American Press*, 7 June 2003, sec. B, p. 6.

37. Savage, *Beauty Queens*, 21.

38. Raymond Hunt to John J. Blair, 1 May 1925, box P.C. 249.1, folder 249.1, John J. Blair Papers, Division of Archives and Records, State Archives of North Carolina, Raleigh.

39. Latham, *Posing a Threat*, 82–87. Just five days before the first contest in 1921, an Atlantic City policeman had arrested a Miss Louise Rosine on the beach for refusing to roll her stockings up over her knees. Rosine was in violation of local decency regulations that prohibited bare limbs.

40. "Gorgeous Beauty Feature of Climaxing Spectacles in City's Great Pageant," *Atlantic City Daily Press*, 9 September 1921, quoted in Latham, *Posing a Threat*, 90.

41. "Monks Corner Girl Chosen for 'Miss South Carolina,'" *Charleston News and Courier*, 11 July 1926, 14.

42. "Bishop Condemns Beauty Pageant," *New York Times*, 30 November 1927, 10.

43. Marti, *Historical Directory of American Agricultural Fairs*, 13–14.

44. On the somewhat complicated and contentious relationship between the cooperative extension service and farm bureaus, see Rasmussen, *Taking the University to the People*, 78–80.

45. Western North Carolina Agricultural and Mechanical Fair Association Sixth Annual Fair Program, 1876, 23, NCC.

46. For more on how the better baby contest supplanted the baby show, see Pearson, "'Infantile Specimens,'" 362–63. On better baby contests in general, see Pearson, "Making Babies Better"; Dorey, *Better Baby Contests*; Holt, *Linoleum, Better Babies, and the Modern Farm Woman*, 95–123; Stern, "Better Babies at the Indiana State Fair"; Pernick, "Taking Better Baby Contests Seriously"; and Pernick, *Black Stork*, 22 and 136.

47. Some county agents sponsored entire "Better Baby Clinics" for farm women, offering nutrition and childrearing classes and bringing doctors in to examine children in areas with no medical care. See Rieff, "'Rousing the People of the Land,'" 84, 127–28.

48. People's Agricultural Fair Association Program, 1914, 83–84, NCC.

49. On eugenics in the South, see Larson, *Sex, Race, and Science*, and Pippa Holloway, *Sexuality, Politics, and Social Control*, esp. 21–51.

50. There are exceptions to this pattern, including Indiana, where better baby contests flourished through the mid-1930s. See Stern, "Better Babies at the Indiana State Fair."

51. Dorey, *Better Baby Contests*, 211–12; Pearson, "Making Babies Better," 36–39.

52. The 4-H motto asked members to pledge their "head to greater thinking," their "heart to greater loyalty," their "hands to larger service," and their "health to better living."

53. Circular 14, January 1941, South Carolina Extension Service, Clemson Agricultural College of South Carolina and Winthrop College, Subject Files, 4-H Youth Development Files, CESR.

54. "Health Pageant Held at College," *Raleigh News and Observer*, 8 August 1930, n.p, in Southeastern District Scrapbook, 1921–1937, North Carolina Homemaker's Association Records, 1923–1995, CESR.

55. "King and Queen of Health," unidentified newspaper clipping, in Southeastern District Scrapbook, 1921–1937, North Carolina Homemaker's Association Records, 1923–1995, CESR.

56. McKimmon, *When We're Green We Grow*, 224.

57. *Charlotte News* clipping, n.p., 8 July 1937, in 1937 Scrapbook, North Carolina Homemaker's Association Records, 1923–1995, CESR.

58. Willie H. Hunter, quoted in Ruth Current, "What Home Demonstration Work Means to the Farm Home and Family," North Carolina Homemaker's Association Records, 1923–1995, CESR.

59. Gay B. Shepperson, quoted in Jones, *Mama Learned Us to Work*, 173.

60. Mason, *Clear Springs*, 83.

61. "Color for the Individual," Club Series No. 7, June 1936, Green 'N' Growing: The History of 4-H and Home Demonstration in North Carolina Online Collection, Special Collections, D. H. Hill Library, North Carolina State University, http://www.lib.ncsu.edu/resolver/1840.6/142.

62. "Mill Children in Town HS" notecard, folder 495, box 5, subseries 1.5, FSMCS.

63. McKimmon, *When We're Green We Grow*, 103.

64. Olson, "Annual Report of Cooperative Extension Work," 42.

65. "Farm Women's Short Course, July 24–29, 1933," North Carolina Homemaker's Association Records, 1923–1995, CESR.

66. McKimmon, *When We're Green We Grow*, 103.

67. McClearly, "Shaping a New Role for the Rural Woman," 140.

68. Edna Hulvey Garber, quoted in ibid., 145. McClearly recounts the story of Garber, Jamison, and the dress revues on pp. 141–45.

69. 1924 Report, County Club Collection, 4-H Youth Development Files, CESR.

70. Eunice Whitley, "My 4-H Club Achievements," County Club Collection, 4-H Youth Development Files, CESR.

71. "Farm Women Tell How Home Demonstration Agents Waked Them Up," *Raleigh News and Observer*, 1 August 1923, n.p., in Scrapbook, 1923–1929, North Carolina Homemaker's Association Records, 1923–1995, CESR.

72. "Daughters of Eve," 27, North Carolina Homemaker's Association Records, 1923–1995, CESR.

73. "Nor an Ear-Bob nor Plucked Eyebrow Seen at Convention," *Raleigh News*

*and Observer*, 1 August 1923, n.p., in Scrapbook, 1923–1929, North Carolina Homemaker's Association Records, 1923–1995, CESR.

74. Mrs. W. N. Hutt, "Girls' Work Should Be Woman-Led," *Progressive Farmer*, 29 October 1927, n.p., in Scrapbook, 1923–1929, North Carolina Homemaker's Association Records, 1923–1995, CESR.

75. McClearly, "Shaping a New Role for the Rural Woman," 131. On corsets, see Fields, *Intimate Affair*, 47–78.

76. "Beauties in Burley," 9.

77. On the growing and selling of tobacco in the Southeast before and after the New Deal, see Daniel, *Breaking the Land*, chaps. 2 and 6.

78. Ibid., 35. Nannie May Tilley discusses some of these marketing techniques in *Bright Tobacco Industry*, 225–31.

79. Washington Duke, quoted in Bowman, "Questionable Beauty," 72.

80. On "woman-as-commodity," see Roberts, "Gender, Consumption, and Commodity Culture."

81. *The Columbia (S.C.) State*, 16 July 1938, n.p.

82. John G. Thomas, "Neptune Directs Wilson Carnival," *Raleigh News and Observer*, 17 August 1938, 1.

83. Wilson Tobacco Festival Photograph, n.d., NCDCDC.

84. Wilson Tobacco Festival Photograph, n.d., NCDCDC.

85. Wilson Tobacco Festival Photograph, n.d., NCDCDC.

86. Wilson Tobacco Festival Photograph, ca. 1940, NCDCDC.

87. Daniel, *Breaking the Land*, 207.

88. *Carolina Times*, 14 August 1937, 1.

89. Daniel, *Breaking the Land*, 37–38.

90. "Tobacco Markets in South America 'Best Potentiality for Recovering Export Trade,'" *Progressive Farmer*, February 1941, 81.

91. Tobacco Girl and Union Jack Photograph, 1941, NCDCDC.

92. Gastonia Cotton Festival Photograph, n.d., NCDCDC.

93. Wallace Strawberry Festival Photograph, n.d., NCDCDC.

94. Edenton Peanut Festival Photograph, n.d., NCDCDC.

95. For more on Carnival, see Rushing, *Memphis and the Paradox of Place*, 153–86; McLean, "Cotton Carnival and Cotton Makers Jubilee"; and Magness, *Party with a Purpose*.

96. Dunn, *Mr. Oscar*, 70–77; Russell, *U.S. Cotton and the National Cotton Council*, 1–8.

97. Russell, *U. S. Cotton and the National Cotton Council*, 20.

98. Maid of Cotton Advertisement, *New York Herald Tribune*, 18 May 1941, 4, Lever Brothers Advertisements, 1933–1941, box 32, JWTA.

99. Bowman, "Questionable Beauty," 70–80. Bowman provides a succinct history of opposition to female smoking and women's efforts to overcome it before 1930.

100. Bertha Miller, quoted in Byerly, *Hard Times Cotton Mill Girls*, 48.

101. Tate, *Cigarette Wars*, 106.

102. Roberts, "Gender, Consumption, and Commodity Culture," 820.

103. For more on the Samarcand incident and the role that the girls' sexual modernity played in their trial, see Cahn, *Sexual Reckonings*, 43–67.

104. Tice, *Queens of Academe*, 55–56.

105. Maid of Cotton Advertisement, *New York Herald Tribune*, 18 May 1941, 4, Lever Brothers Advertisements, 1933–1941, box 32, JWTA.

106. Russell, *U.S. Cotton and the National Cotton Council*, 63. An informational flyer from a later Maid competition promised contestants that the event could completely change their lives: "Winning the Maid of Cotton Selection is earning the experience of a lifetime. Suddenly you find yourself in the midst of a grand tour . . . dressing in elegant cotton fashions . . . being honored at banquets and receptions . . . making personal calls on international dignitaries, ambassadors, and government officials . . . holding press conferences with newspaper and magazine editors . . . making speeches to national organizations . . . and giving spectacular cotton fashion shows." According to the flyer, the winner would take home a designer wardrobe, a brand new Ford, and a $1,500 scholarship. See 1975 Maid of Cotton Flyer.

107. The crowning of the Wilson queen eventually moved to the Municipal Auditorium, presumably because the event had become so well attended.

108. Maid of Cotton Advertisement, *New York Herald Tribune*, 18 May 1941, 4, Lever Brothers Advertisements, 1933–1941, box 32, JWTA.

109. Rushing, *Memphis and the Paradox of Place*, 179.

110. Russell, *U.S. Cotton and the National Cotton Council*, 19. An ad in the 1 May 1949 issue of *Agricultural Review* invited farm women to write the NCC for a booklet containing thirty-two of the latest patterns for transforming cotton sacks into clothing.

111. Kidd, "Dissonant Encounters," 26.

112. F. Roy Stryker, quoted in Gordon, "Dorothea Lange," 718. John Raeburn contends that FSA photographs were not as widely circulated in the 1930s as we have come to believe. See *Staggering Revolution*, 143–45.

113. Stryker, quoted in Gordon, "Dorothea Lange," 718.

114. Marion Post Wolcott, quoted in Kidd, "Dissonant Encounters," 29. I'm also using Kidd's emphasis on dissemblance here.

115. Statistics on pool construction are from Wiltse, *Contested Waters*, 90–93, 229 n. 4, and "Nation-Wide Survey of WPA Pool and Beach Development," 52–56.

116. Wiltse, *Contested Waters*, 89.

117. William C. Pryor, "Carbon Hill, Alabama," October 1938, Miscellaneous Records of the Photography Division, RG 69, E 696, box 2, National Archives and Records Administration, New Deal Network, http://newdeal.feri.org/carbonhill/06.htm.

118. Wiltse, *Contested Waters*, 90.

119. "Raleigh Elects Three Beauty Queens," *Raleigh News and Observer*, 7 July 1938, 12.

120. Walker, *All We Knew Was to Farm*, chaps. 4 and 7; Jones, *Mama Learned Us to Work*.

121. McClearly, "Shaping a New Role for the Rural Woman," 150.

122. Walker, *All We Knew Was to Farm*, 240.

123. Sally Carter, "Out of Miss Dixie's Band Box—Rearing Prize-Winning Daughters—A Quizzical Quiz on How to Make Daughters Beautiful," *Progressive Farmer*, May 1940, 47.

124. "Feed Bags Now Holding Bathing Girls," *Raleigh News and Observer*, 1 May 1949, n.p, in Scrapbook, 1947–1950, North Carolina Homemaker's Association Records, 1923–1995, CESR.

125. Lumberton Tobacco Queen Photograph, 1947, NCDCDC.


CHAPTER FOUR

1. "Belles of the South," 159.

2. On the politics of respectability, see Higginbotham, *Righteous Discontent*; Gaines *Uplifting the Race*; Shaw, *What a Woman Out to Be and to Do*; Wolcott, *Remaking Respectability*; Mitchell, *Righteous Propagation*; and Haidarali, "'The Vampingest Vamp Is a Brownskin.'" In particular, I am building on the work of Michele Mitchell, who has argued that authors of black etiquette manuals in the late nineteenth and early twentieth centuries believed in "public performances of morality and character," and of Katharine Capshaw Smith, who similarly frames their view of the black child's behavior as a "performance of racial character." See Mitchell, *Righteous Propagation*, 108–40, and Smith, "Childhood, the Body, and Race Performance," 796. I am also drawing on Hazel Carby's discussion of the way middle- and upper-class blacks policed urban black women's bodies in the early twentieth century in "Policing the Black Woman's Body in an Urban Context."

3. Mitchell, *Righteous Propagation*, 115.

4. Hale, *Making Whiteness*, 121–97.

5. On the history of Aunt Jemima, see Manring, *Slave in a Box*, and McElya, *Clinging to Mammy*, 15–37.

6. "History of the Chatham County Colored Agricultural Fair, Inc." (North Carolina, c. 1980), n.p., NCC.

7. For various versions of this story, see Sanders Duke Williams, "The Cotton Makers Jubilee Interview with Mrs. Ethyl Venson," 2–3, Special Collections, Ned R. McWherter Library, University of Memphis, Memphis, Tenn.; the 1940 Program of the Memphis Cotton Makers Jubilee, CMJC; and McLean, "Cotton Carnival," 48–49. For more on Jubilee through the years, see McLean, "Cotton Carnival"; Rushing, *Memphis and the Paradox of Place*, 170–86; and Magness, *Party with a Purpose*, 176–84.

8. Despite her role in Jubilee's founding, Ethyl Venson is often not credited for her work, which was undoubtedly less high-profile than that of her husband. One reason may also be because her name was not included in the organization's initial paperwork since, as she put it, "the men did not think that a woman's name should be on the charter" (Sanders Duke Williams, "Cotton Makers Jubilee Interview with Mrs. Ethyl Venson," 7, Special Collections, Ned R. McWherter Library, University of Memphis, Memphis, Tenn.).

9. 1937 Program of the Memphis Cotton Makers Jubilee, CMJC.

10. Ethyl H. Venson, quoted in McLean, "Cotton Carnival," 53, 55.

11. Sanders Duke Williams, "Cotton Makers Jubilee Interview with Mrs. Ethyl Venson," 21, Special Collections, Ned R. McWherter Library, University of Memphis, Memphis, Tenn.

12. "'Spirit of Cotton' Wins Hearts of Orleanians," *Louisiana Weekly*, 19 April 1950, 1.

13. Press Release, 30 March 1953, and Mrs. Edna Owens to Mrs. R. Q. Venson, 15 April 1953, folder 7, CMJC.

14. Sandra Duke Williams, "Cotton Makers Jubilee Interview with Mrs. Ethyl Venson," 8, Special Collections, Ned R. McWherter Library, University of Memphis, Memphis, Tenn.

15. Handcox, "King Cotton," 192.

16. 1947 Program of the Memphis Cotton Makers Jubilee, CMJC.

17. Franklin S. Kimbrough, letter to the editor, *Time*, 17 June 1946, 4–5. The story that elicited Kimbrough's response was "Ring-Tailed Tooter," *Time*, 27 May 1946, 20–23.

18. Southern Interstate Immigration Bureau Poster, 1891, NCC.

19. Jones, "Role of Tuskegee in the Education of Black Farmers," 265.

20. Jones, *Mama Learned Us to Work*, 19, 141.

21. Rieff, "'Rousing the People of the Land,'" 115.

22. Ibid., 114. In some instances, Jeanes teachers working in rural black schools acted in a capacity that was similar to that of a demonstration agent, organizing clubs and giving lessons in things like sanitation. In still others, Jeanes teachers might be hired as home demonstration agents. See Reid, *Reaping a Greater Harvest*, 65–66, and Gilmore, *Gender and Jim Crow*, 197–98.

23. Smith, *Sick and Tired*, 24; Jones, *Mama Learned Us to Work*, 154.

24. Smith, review of *Formative Years*, 678; Smith, *Sick and Tired*, 56.

25. On the subversive uses of eugenics among black reformers, see Mitchell, *Righteous Propagation*, 80–81, 95–105.

26. Dazelle Foster Lowe, quoted in Jones, *Mama Learned Us to Work*, 168.

27. White and White, *Stylin'*, 23. Also see Foster, *"New Raiments of Self."*

28. White and White, *Stylin'*, 17.

29. Ibid.

30. Rawick, *American Slave*, 240.

31. Reid, *After the War*, 80, 81.

32. "Education of the Freedmen," 95.

33. See Chapter 2 for a list of these academics and the works they published.

34. "Clothing" notecard, folder 21, box 7, subseries 1.7, FSMCS.

35. Lewis, *Blackways of Kent*, 53; "Dress and Adornment" notecard, folder 21, box 6, subseries 1.6, FSMCS.

36. Lewis, *Blackways of Kent*, 54–55; "Dress and Adornment" notecard, folder 21, box 6, subseries 1.6, FSMCS.

37. Beam, *He Called Them by the Lightning*, 39–40.

38. "Dress and Adornment" notecard, folder 21, box 6, subseries 1.6, FSMCS.

39. Powdermaker, *After Freedom*, 70.

40. "Dress and Adornment" notecard, folder 21, box 6, subseries 1.6, FSMCS.

41. Susan Brownmiller goes so far as to argue that "to be truly feminine is to accept the handicap of restraint and restriction, and to come to adore it" (*Femininity*, 86).

42. Harris, "Grace Under Pressure," 216.

43. Guilford County Agent, quoted in Jane S. McKimmon, Annual Report, 1927, 69, in Green 'N' Growing.

44. Lewis, *Blackways of Kent*, 60.

45. Harris, "Grace Under Pressure," 211.

46. Olson, "Annual Report of Cooperative Extension Work," 50–51.

47. Reid, *Reaping a Greater Harvest*, 104–10.

48. Smith, *How Race Is Made*, 81. Smith offers a thorough analysis of the ways in which blacks' perceived filth informed white racism on pp. 80–89.

49. Davis, Gardner, and Gardner, *Deep South*, 16.

50. Hale, *Making Whiteness*, 190–91.

51. Annette Jones White, "Finding Form for the Expression of My Discontent," in Holsaert et al., *Hands on the Freedom Plow*, 101.

52. Baker, *Following the Colour Line*, 40; Smith, *How Race Is Made*, 85.

53. Davis, Gardener, and Gardener, *Deep South*, 16. John Dollard found that in one rural Mississippi store, black women were more likely to buy clothing that was cheaper than that bought by white women. Because of this, the store reported few problems with black women trying on clothes. See *Caste and Class in a Southern Town*, 353.

54. Holmes, *Diary of Miss Emma Holmes*, 428.

55. Ibid., 428.

56. Fields, *Lemon Swamp*, 63, 71, 72.

57. Lewis, *Blackways of Kent*, 54.

58. Dollard, *Caste and Class in a Southern Town*, 91.

59. Lewis, *Blackways of Kent*, 54.

60. For more on this phenomenon, see Hunter, *To 'Joy My Freedom*, 182–83; Hunter, "'Work That Body,'" 84–85; Carby, "Policing the Black Woman's Body"; Hunt, "Clothing as an Expression of History"; Hunt, "Struggle to Achieve Individual Expression"; and Rooks, *Ladies' Pages*.

61. Hunter, "'Work That Body,'" 84.

62. Alice Adams, quoted in Hunter, *To 'Joy My Freedom*, 182.

63. Lee, *Beale Street*, 64.

64. Harrison, *Black Pearls*, 37.

65. Mamie Smith, quoted in ibid., 46.

66. Hunter, "'Work That Body,'" 84.

67. Edwards, *Southern Urban Negro as a Consumer*, 58–59, 80.

68. Kytle, *Willie Mae*, 141.

69. Virginia Broughton, quoted in Higginbotham, *Righteous Discontent*, 200.

70. *Ringwood's Journal*, quoted in Rooks, *Ladies' Pages*, 52.

71. Anthony Binga, quoted in Hunter, *To 'Joy My Freedom*, 182.

72. Hunter, "'Work That Body,'" 79.

73. Woods, *Negro in Etiquette*, 48.

74. Charlie Love, quoted in Stearns and Stearns, *Jazz Dance*, 21, 24.

75. Hunter "'Work That Body,'" 85.

76. Woods, *Negro in Etiquette*, 49.

77. White and White, *Stylin'*, 212–13.

78. "Motion Pictures of the Style Show to Be Made," *Louisiana Weekly*, 20 March 1996, 1; "Style Show," *Louisiana Weekly*, 6 March 1926, 1.

79. "Style Show," *Louisiana Weekly*, 6 March 1926, 1.

80. *Louisiana Weekly*, 23 March 1927, 5.

81. Powdermaker, *After Freedom*, 282, 283.

82. Cahn, *Sexual Reckonings*, 150.

83. On the rise of portrait photography in nineteenth-century America, see Trachtenberg, *Reading American Photographs*.

84. "Who Is the Prettiest Colored Girl in the United States?" (May–June 1921). On Overton and his magazine, see Rooks, *Ladies' Pages*, 108–11, and Peiss, *Hope in a Jar*, 109.

85. "Who Is the Prettiest Colored Girl in the United States?" (September 1921).

86. "Do You Know a Beauty?," 8.

87. On southern readership of black national newspapers and magazines, see Edwards, *Southern Urban Negro as a Consumer*, 169–84.

88. "More Beauties," 21.

89. On the Golden Brown contest and the history of the sponsoring company, see White and White, *Stylin'*, 198–201.

90. Advertisement, *Pittsburgh Courier*, 6 June 1925, 8.

91. "Beauties Enter Pelican Show," *Louisiana Weekly*, 30 June 1928, 4.

92. The local newspaper never announced the winner of the Pelican's bathing beauty revue.

93. White and White, *Stylin'*, 205.

94. Nadell, *Enter the New Negroes*, 10.

95. Anderson, *Education of Blacks in the South*, 241. The racial profile of teachers and administrators did begin to change in the 1910s. Beginning in 1910, for example, Spelman started hiring more African American professors. By 1937, the ratio of black to white instructors was two to one. See Lowe, *Looking Good*, 107.

96. Summers, *Manliness and Its Discontents*, 244.

97. Fisk University Catalogue, 1882–83, folder 16, box 172 (first quote), and Fisk University Catalogue, 1893–94, folder 17, box 172 (second quote), American Missionary Association Archives (Addendum), ARC. See also Shaw, *What a Woman Ought to Be and to Do*, 68–103.

98. Fisk University Catalogue, 1893–94, folder 17, box 172, American Missionary Association Archives (Addendum), ARC.

99. White, *Too Heavy a Load*, 24.

100. Summers, *Manliness and Its Discontents*, 256.

101. Fisk University Catalogue, 1882–83, folder 16, box 172, American Missionary Association Archives (Addendum), ARC.

102. Atlanta University Catalogue, 1885–86, AUCA.

103. Ibid., 1919–20.

104. Higginbotham, *Righteous Discontent*, 33; Lowe, *Looking Good*, 6.

105. Quote in Shaw, *What a Woman Ought to Be and to Do*, 89.

106. Spelman Seminary Catalogue, 1921–22, AUCA.

107. Summers, *Manliness and Its Discontents*, 251–55.

108. Spelman Seminary Catalogue, 1905–6, AUCA.

109. Ibid., 1921–22.

110. Stillman College Catalogue, 1924–25, WHSL.

111. A photograph of Smith College students in 1888 situated next to one of Spelman women in 1887 in Lowe's *Looking Good*, 84–85, demonstrates this point well.

112. Baptist missionary, quoted in Higginbotham, *Righteous Discontent*, 38.

113. Craig, *Ain't I a Beauty Queen?*, 43.

114. For a discussion of color prejudice at Avery in the late nineteenth and early twentieth centuries, see Drago, *Initiative, Paternalism, and Race Relations*, 68–70 and 132–34.

115. Mebane, *Mary, An Autobiography*, 209.

116. The authors of *The Color Complex* report that students at Howard, Fisk, Atlanta, and Spelman allegedly had to pass such a test. See Russell, Wilson, and Hall, *Color Complex*, 28.

117. Dunbar-Nelson, *Give Us Each Day*, 350.

118. For a detailed account of the lore of skin color tests at Howard, see Kerr, *Paper Bag Principle*, 88–102.

119. Dr. Daniel, quoted in ibid., 91.

120. Russell, Wilson, and Hall, *Color Complex*, 29.

121. For more on this new collegiate look at Spelman, see Lowe, *Looking Good*, 103–33.

122. Atlanta University Catalogue, 1921–22, AUCA.

123. Lowe, *Looking Good*, 127.

124. Summers, *Manliness and Its Discontents*, 244 (quote). See pp. 262–70 and 275–78 for more on the Fisk strike. Howard University students also went on strike in 1925, and although they had always been allowed more leeway when it came to dress, their protest was nevertheless similarly aimed at overthrowing "the vestiges of late-Victorian moral education" (ibid., 270).

125. Kelly Miller, quoted in Wolcott, "'Bible, Bath, and Broom,'" 100.

126. Simmons, "African Americans and Sexual Victorianism," 61.

127. Ransby, *Ella Baker and the Black Freedom Movement*, 59–60.

128. Hornsby, *In the Cage*, 75.

129. Olivier, "Stony Path to Learning," 22.

130. Mebane, *Mary, An Autobiography*, 224–25.

131. Lowe, *Looking Good*, 127–28.

132. Straight College Bulletin, 1924, WWAL.

133. Spelman *Messenger*, July 1928, 22, AUCA.

134. Florence Read, quoted in Lowe, *Looking Good*, 128.

135. Eloise Ulcher Belcher, quoted in Dahleen Glanton, "A History of Crowning Glories," *Chicago Tribune*, 1 November 2004, 1.

136. Myrene Gray, "An Introduction to the Male Shortage or Freshman Week at Spelman College," *Campus Mirror*, October 1943, 3, Southern Pamphlets Collection, Rare Books Collection, Wilson Library, University of North Carolina at Chapel Hill.

137. "'Homecoming'—The Big Weekend," *Courtbouillon*, December 1950, 12, WWAL.

138. On postwar mass consumption, see Cohen, *Consumers' Republic*.

139. Laila Haidarali traces the rise of a consumerist ethos among black women after World War II, examining its effects on self-presentation, specifically in modeling. She argues that black women during these years used consumerism to construct beauty ideals as a strategy for racial advancement. See "'Vampingest Vamp Is a Brownskin,'" 222–75.

140. Dahleen Glanton, "A History of Crowning Glories," *Chicago Tribune*, 1 November 2004, 30.

141. "Who's Wearing What?," *Courtbouillon*, May 1949, 9, WWAL.

142. "Fads and Fashions," *Courtbouillon*, February 1948, 10, WWAL.

143. Gwen Sherard, "Correct, Collegiate, and Casual," quoted in Tice, *Queens of Academe*, 46.

144. "Fads and Fashions," *Courtbouillon*, February 1948, 10, WWAL.

145. 1941 Dillard Freshman Week Handbook, n.p., WWAL.

146. Katie Kelley, "Open Letter to Students," *Tiger's Paw*, May 1959, 2, WHSL.

147. "Loyce Vincent Will Be Crowned Miss Dillard '59," *Courtbouillon*, October 1959, 1, WWAL.

148. "An Open Letter from the Outgoing Miss Stillman," *Tiger's Paw*, March 1961, 2, WHSL.

149. "UNCF Beauty-Talent Pageant Held," *Tiger's Paw*, 7 December 1963, 1, WHSL.

150. *Kentucky Thoroughbred*, quoted in Tice, *Queens of Academe*, 50, 51.

151. Tice, *Queens of Academe*, 51.


CHAPTER FIVE

1. Lynda Mead, quoted in Bonita Appleton, "Lynda Lee Takes Up For Her State," *Jackson Daily News*, 15 December 1959, Miss University/Miss America Clipping File, University Archives, JDWL.

2. For a summary of these and other events in Mississippi in the mid-1950s and early 1960s, see Dittmer, *Local People*, and Bolton, *Hardest Deal of All*, 68–72.

3. Moody, *Coming of Age in Mississippi*, 268.

4. On women, gender, and massive resistance, see Elizabeth Gillespie McRae, "White Womanhood, White Supremacy, and the Rise of Massive Resistance," and

Karen S. Anderson, "Massive Resistance, Violence, and Southern Social Relations," in Webb, *Massive Resistance*; Anderson, *Little Rock*; and Godfrey, "Bayonets, Brainwashing, and Bathrooms."

5. Lewis, *Massive Resistance*, 12. On this point, see also Webb, *Massive Resistance*, 8–9. Recent studies that seek to capture the complexity of massive resistance include Webb's volume, as well as Lassiter and Lewis, *Moderates' Dilemma*; Moye, *Let the People Decide*; Kruse, *White Flight*; Sokol, *There Goes My Everything*; and Walker, *Ghost of Jim Crow*.

6. Studies of Black Power that have informed this chapter include Van Deburg, *New Day in Babylon*; Lazerow and Williams, *In Search of the Black Panther Party*; Ogbar, *Black Power*; Joseph, *Waiting 'Til the Midnight Hour*; Joseph, *Black Power Movement*; and Joseph, "Black Power Movement." On the search for a new representational style/aesthetic during the Black Power era, see Watkins, *Black Power, Yellow Power*; Martin, *No Coward Soldiers*, 82–131; Ogbar, *Black Power*, 116–22; and Van Deburg, *New Day in Babylon*, 192–202.

7. Martha Biondi frames the challenge they issued in this way in *Black Revolution on Campus*, 13. Although she does not discuss how black college students attempted to forge a new bodily aesthetic, her book offers the most comprehensive analysis of the effects of Black Power on college campuses.

8. "South Boston Outranks Atlantic City."

9. Lenora Slaughter, quoted in Banet-Weiser, *Most Beautiful Girl in the World*, 41.

10. For more on Slaughter's campaign to change the image of the contest, see Riverol, *Live from Atlantic City*, 31–33, 40, and Banet-Weiser, *Most Beautiful Girl in the World*, 37–40.

11. Miss America By-Laws, quoted in Watson and Martin, *"There She Is, Miss America,"* 5.

12. Melissa McEuen offers the most thorough examination of this wartime emphasis on beauty in the United States. See *Making War, Making Women*. See also Honey, *Creating Rosie the Riveter*, 114–16; Mary Anne Schofield, "Miss America, Rosie the Riveter, and World War II," in Watson and Martin, *"There She Is, Miss America"*; and Rupp, *Mobilizing Women for War*, 145–52.

13. Westbrook, "'I Want a Girl,'" 592.

14. Ibid., 603.

15. See *Rammer Jammer*, February 1945, 5, University Archives, WSHSC.

16. McEuen, *Making War, Making Women*, 73.

17. Schofield, "Miss America, Rosie the Riveter, and World War II," in Watson and Martin, *"There She Is, Miss America,"* 59–60.

18. *Hendersonville (N.C.) Times-News*, 6 September 1946, 3.

19. Riverol, *Live from Atlantic City*, 41.

20. For statistics on television viewership of the pageant, see ibid., 56, 87; Deford, *There She Is*, 308; and the Miss America Pageant website, http://www.missamerica.org/our-miss-americas/1950/review.aspx.

21. Riverol, *Live from Atlantic City*, 41.

22. Women who represented dozens of "key cities" could compete in Miss America until 1949, at which point key city representation was restricted to New York, Chicago, Philadelphia, Washington, D.C., Canada, and U.S. territories. With the exception of Washington, D.C., key city representation was eliminated altogether in 1963. Margaret Gorman, the first Miss America, crowned in 1921, competed as Miss Washington, D.C., and could therefore be considered southern. See Riverol, *Live from Atlantic City*, 40, 56. The southern women who won during World War II were Jo-Carroll Dennison, Miss Texas, and Kentuckian Venus Ramey, who entered as Miss Washington, D.C. In 1950, the pageant began the tradition of postdating Miss Americas (the woman crowned in 1950 was Miss America 1951, and so on). I identify women by the year in which they competed or won, for the sake of clarity and consistency.

23. Because city title holders could compete in the national pageant until 1963, and because full-state participation was not achieved until 1959, the number of contestants varied from year to year but averaged around fifty-two. See Deford, *There She Is*, 319–21.

24. U.S. Department of Commerce, *Statistical Abstract of the United States, 1964*, 11.

25. Goldfield, *Black, White, and Southern*, 45.

26. I am drawing here on the concept of the "long civil rights movement," which Jacquelyn Dowd Hall, among others, has posited as a necessary corrective to the traditional narrative of the movement, which stresses its "classical phase" from 1954 to 1965 (or 1968). She argues, for example, that the labor activism that came out of the New Deal and peaked in the 1940s was the civil rights movement's "decisive first phase." I am also persuaded by the argument that massive resistance has a longer history than we have previously appreciated, that a segregationist opposition movement hostile to black demands predated *Brown*. Nevertheless, I would contend that the increased publicity that the post-*Brown* resistance received in print and visual media—and that the post-1954 civil rights movement received for that matter—made it different from what had come before, a point that is important for my argument about the function of southern white beauty queens during this period. See Hall, "Long Civil Rights Movement," 1245. For a study of the long history of massive resistance, see Ward, *Defending White Democracy*. For a recent challenge to the long civil rights movement framework that stresses the "distinct context and character" of the classical phase of the movement, see Lawson, "Long Origins," 9–38 (quote on 14).

27. Lewis, *Massive Resistance*, 10. On the Citizens' Councils, see also McMillen, *Citizens' Council*, and Bartley, *Rise of Massive Resistance*.

28. *Congressional Quarterly Almanac, 84th Congress*, 416.

29. Kruse, *White Flight*, 8.

30. Godfrey, "Bayonets, Brainwashing, and Bathrooms," 46; Jacoway, *Turn Away Thy Son*, 82; Anderson, *Little Rock*, 73–76.

31. Elizabeth Gillespie McRae, "White Womanhood, White Supremacy, and the Rise of Massive Resistance," in Webb, *Massive Resistance*, 189–91.

32. *Jackson Daily News*, quoted in Goldfield, *Black, White, and Southern*, 86.

33. *Raleigh News and Observer*, 2 September 1951, n.p., Clipping File through 1975, NCC.

34. "Manning's Marian McKnight Chosen Miss South Carolina at Sun Fun Fest," *Manning (S.C.) Times*, 12 June 1956, 1.

35. "When Prettier, Finer Girls Are Grown, It'll Be South Carolina to Grow Them," *Florence (S.C.) Morning News*, reprinted in *Manning (S.C.) Times*, 12 September 1956.

36. Rebecca Franklin, "South Carolina Beauty May Be the Most Popular Miss America," *Manning (S.C.) Times*, 17 October 1956.

37. See the 17 September 1956 issues of *Time* and *Newsweek* for more on the incidents that occurred across the region that week.

38. "Southern Front," 73.

39. Wilkie, *Dixie*, 82.

40. 1948 University of Mississippi "M" Book, quoted in Thornton, "Symbolism at Ole Miss," 258. The song "Dixie" was added to the campus's "traditions" the next year.

41. For a detailed history of Ole Miss during these years, see Eagles, *Price of Defiance*, 9–180, and Sansing, *University of Mississippi*, 269–80.

42. Evers was not the first African American to apply to the law school. Two others had applied in 1952 and 1953. See Eagles, *Price of Defiance*, 70–71.

43. Thornton, "Symbolism at Ole Miss," 261.

44. The university's board of trustees formed the Special Committee on Charges of Apostasy at the University of Mississippi to investigate. It eventually cleared the chancellor and several faculty members of the charges against them, though the Jackson newspaper reported that they had to sign an oath stating that Mississippi was sovereign and that intermarriage often followed racial integration. See Sansing, *University of Mississippi*, 279. Also see Eagles, *Price of Defiance*, 167.

45. "Oxford: A Warning for Americans" (Jackson, Miss.: Mississippi State Junior Chamber of Commerce, 1962), 23, Ed King Collection, JDWL.

46. McCarthy, "Ordeal of Miss America," 107.

47. Bert Wilson, "Neva Langley Succeeds to Colleen's Title," *Press of Atlantic City*, n.d. 1952, n.p.

48. "SC Beauty Stunned by Big Victory," *Manning (S. C.) Times*, 12 September 1956; "When Prettier Girls Are Grown, It'll Be South Carolina to Grow Them," *Florence (S.C.) Morning News*, reprinted in *Manning (S.C.) Times*, 12 September 1956.

49. "When Prettier Girls Are Grown, It'll Be South Carolina to Grow Them," *Florence (S.C.) Morning News*, reprinted in *Manning (S.C.) Times*, 12 September 1956.

50. Lola Clark, "Miss America of 1957—Her Story," *Manning (S.C.) Times*, 17 October 1956.

51. "What Others Are Saying," *Manning (S.C.) Times*, 12 September 1956.

52. John Temple Graves, "South Claims Miss America Even If Apart from

Union," *Manning (S.C.) Times*, 17 October 1956. Graves quotes the *Charleston News and Courier* in his op-ed.

53. Unidentified Mississippi newspaper, quoted in Don Lee Keith, "A Walk Down the Runway, *Mississippi* (July/August): 20, Scrapbook, William H. "Chubby" Ellis Collection, University Archives, JDWL.

54. "Ole Miss Sorority Sisters Add Southern Charm and Beauty to Miss America Contest in Atlantic City," *The Mississippian*, n.d., 5; and "Our Gals Wow 'Em; It's Two in a Row," *The Mississippian*, 13 September 1959, 1, University Archives, JDWL.

55. "Proud of Mississippi," *Meridian Star*, 15 September 1959, n.p., Miss University/Miss America Clipping File, University Archives, JDWL.

56. "Miss Americas' Impact Is Strong in New York," *Meridian Star*, 17 January 1960, n.p., Miss University/Miss America Clipping File, University Archives, JDWL.

57. "Candidates for the Crown," 18–19.

58. Brown, "Babes, Brutes and Ole Miss," 117, 118.

59. "Beauty Queens to Spare," 59, 64.

60. Eagles, *Price of Defiance*, 14.

61. For more on Ellis's role in the campaign to root out communists on campus, see ibid., 165–66.

62. Helen Barber to Chubby Ellis, 19 March 1957, Scrapbook, William H. "Chubby" Ellis Collection, University Archives, JDWL.

63. Eagles, *Price of Defiance*, 14.

64. McMillen, *Citizens' Council*, 167.

65. Smith, *How Race Is Made*, 116.

66. Dailey, "Sex, Segregation, and the Sacred after *Brown*," 122–26.

67. Ibid., 123.

68. Brady, *Black Monday*, 45, 64.

69. Judge Roszel Thomsen, quoted in Wiltse, *Contested Waters*, 156.

70. Homecoming Celebration Photographs, Southern Media Archive, JDWL.

71. Lenora Slaughter, quoted in Deford, *There She Is*, 180.

72. Riverol, *Live from Atlantic City*, 41.

73. Roth, "Coronation on Channel Two," 21.

74. "Sitting Symphony of Beauties," 60. In 1952, Marilyn Monroe, at the invitation of pageant organizers, had served as the grand marshal of the annual Boardwalk parade that featured the contestants. She wore a low-cut dress—the winner that year said that it "was cut down to her navel"—and was not asked to reprise her role again. See *American Experience: Miss America*.

75. Mary Ann Mobley, quoted in *American Experience: Miss America*; "Miss America '59 Dazed by Victory," *New York Times*, 8 September 1958, 22.

76. Mary Ann Mobley, quoted in *American Experience: Miss America*

77 "Summit."

78. John Canaday, "What Miss America Is Made Of," *New York Times*, 18 September 1965, SM 124.

79. Bordo, *Unbearable Weight*, 190.

80. Banet-Weiser, *Most Beautiful Girl in the World*, 75, 76.

81. McCarthy, "Ordeal of Miss America," 107.

82. For more on the adolescent challenges to paternal authority during this era, see Cahn, *Sexual Reckonings*, 241–68, 269–303.

83. Bertrand, *Race, Rock, and Elvis*, 227. Pete Daniel also discusses the convergence of white and black culture during the 1950s. See *Standing at the Crossroads*, 179–89, and *Lost Revolutions*, 165–75.

84. Sandra Scarbrough, quoted in Daniel, *Lost Revolutions*, 169.

85. Muddy Waters, quoted in Daniel, *Lost Revolutions*, 169. Similarly, in 1955 at a Louis Armstrong performance at Ole Miss, one audience member—the secretary of the Mississippi Citizens' Council—expressed displeasure at hearing "the co-eds shriek when the yellow boy soloed on his slide trombone" (Daniel, *Lost Revolutions*, 169).

86. Devlin, *Relative Intimacy*.

87. Elizabeth Boyd uses the term "passive resistance" in her brief analysis of southern beauty contests during this period. See "Southern Beauty," 81.

88. "Homecoming Parade for Miss America Biggest Event in History of Town," *Manning (S.C.) Times*, 17 October 1956, sec. D, p. 1.

89. Kathleen Wheeler, "Homecoming for Marian Celebrated with Pomp and Grandeur Thursday," *Manning (S.C.) Times*, 17 October 1956, 1.

90. Lott, *Love and Theft* and "White Like Me."

91. McElya, *Clinging to Mammy*, 68–69, 71–72. During the same years, it was also not unheard of for younger white women to engage in minstrelsy. One Dallas-area high school, for example, sponsored a minstrel show in the early 1920s at which a minstrel queen was crowned, sometimes in blackface. See *Forester*, 1918–22, Texas and Dallas History Collection, Dallas Public Library.

92. Eagles, *Price of Defiance*, 59.

93. *Corolla*, 1952, n.p., University Archives, WSHSC.

94. Ibid., 1955, n.p.

95. *Rotunda*, 1956, 198–99, University Archives, DeGolyer Library, Southern Methodist University, Dallas, Tex.

96. Lewis, *Blackways of Kent*, 53.

97. Women at Southern Methodist University and the University of Alabama blacked up well into the 1970s. The Chi Omegas at the University of Mississippi appeared in blackface at a sorority party as late as 1979. See *Rotunda*, 1970, 284, University Archives, DeGolyer Library, Southern Methodist University, Dallas, Tex.; *Rammer Jammer* 2, no. 1 (1976): 12, WSHSC; and Boyd, "Southern Beauty," 58. John M. Coski discusses the use of the Confederate battle flag in massive resistance efforts in *Confederate Battle Flag*, 98–160.

98. Sarah Banet-Weiser provides the most thorough examination of how the Miss America Pageant fulfills this function in the United States in *Most Beautiful Girl in the World*.

99. See Hale, *Making Whiteness*.

100. James Usry, quoted in Simon, *Boardwalk of Dreams*, 15.

101. For more on this point, see Lewis, *White South and the Red Menace*.

102. S. J. Thompson, quoted in Lewis, "White South, Red Nation," in Webb, *Massive Resistance*, 122.

103. Elizabeth Gillespie McRae, "White Womanhood, White Supremacy, and the Rise of Massive Resistance," in Webb, *Massive Resistance*, 188–89. This line of argument was already well established in southern women's civic culture by the 1950s. Since the turn of the century, women's organizations such as the United Daughters of the Confederacy had insisted that the South, in seceding from the Union, was the true champion of the nation's founding principles. This assertion had also long found a receptive national audience, as the desire for sectional reconciliation after the Civil War proved stronger than objections to the South's actions on constitutional grounds or to its devotion to slavery on moral grounds. For southern women's role in furthering this process of reconciliation, and northern women's reception of it, see Morgan, *Women and Patriotism in Jim Crow America*, esp. 19–55.

104. William Goldman, quoted in *American Experience: Miss America*.

105. Invoking Benedict Anderson's conception of the imagined community, Banet-Weiser discusses the role of television in altering how Americans conceived of their national identity and how that identity was informed by the newly televised Miss America Pageant. She does not, however, examine the South's domination of the event in the years immediately following its television debut or what it might suggest about American identity during that time. See Banet-Weiser, *Most Beautiful Girl in the World*, 165.

106. *Broadcasting, Telecasting Yearbook*, 48.

107. See Bergner, "Black Children, White Preference," 304–8, for a summary of this strategy.

108. *Brown v. Board of Education of Topeka*.

109. Mamie Clark conducted the initial versions of these tests in the 1930s. She and her husband further honed them in the early 1940s and published their findings in a number of articles between 1939 and 1950. In addition to the doll test, the Clarks employed line drawing and coloring tests, as well as questionnaires, to elicit information about black children's racial identification and racial preferences. See Clark, "Effect of Prejudice and Discrimination on Personality Development," which the Supreme Court directly referenced in a footnote of the *Brown* decision, as well as Clark and Clark, "Development of Consciousness of Self"; Clark and Clark, "Emotional Factors in Racial Identification and Preference"; and Clark and Clark, "Racial Identification and Preference in Negro Children."

110. The children were told to perform eight separate tasks altogether: 1) "Give me the doll that you like to play with—(a) like best." 2) "Give me the doll that is a nice doll." 3) "Give me the doll that looks bad." 4) "Give me the doll that is a nice color." 5) "Give me the doll that looks like a white child." 6) "Give me the doll that looks like a colored child." 7) "Give me the doll that looks like a Negro child." 8) "Give me the doll that looks like you." The first four tasks were meant

to determine racial preference; the latter four were intended to determine racial identification. See Clark and Clark, "Racial Identification and Preference in Negro Children," 602, 608.

111. Bergner provides the most recent critique of the Clarks' research in "Black Children, White Preference." On earlier reappraisals, also see ibid., 300–301, 309, 310–11, and Craig, *Ain't I a Beauty Queen?*, 37–39.

112. In her own critique of the Clarks' findings about black children and self-esteem, Bergner concedes this point, acknowledging that "white preference behavior may indicate a subjective split or double consciousness stemming from children's understanding that African Americans are denigrated by the dominant culture" ("Black Children, White Preference," 302).

113. Clark and Clark, "Racial Identification and Preference in Negro Children," 611; Clark and Clark, "Emotional Factors in Racial Identification and Preference," 348.

114. Clark and Clark, "Emotional Factors in Racial Identification and Preference," 347.

115. Mebane, *Mary, Wayfarer*, 61.

116. Ruth Burnett, "Contest Should Be Called 'Miss White America,'" *Carolina Times*, 2 October 1965, sec. B, p. 1. The title for this article and another on the same page were mistakenly switched. Burnett's piece was printed with the title "Asks High Court to Reverse Death Sentence."

117. "Beauty Queens Hit Bias in 'Miss America' Contest."

118. "Bias Foes Picket Woolworth Here," *New York Times*, 16 June 1960.

119. Yolande Betbeze, quoted in Osborne, *Miss America*, 101.

120. Lenora Slaughter, quoted in Deford, *There She Is*, 184.

121. *Liaison: Fisk University Quarterly Newsletter*, October 1966, folder 11, box 174, American Missionary Association Archives (Addendum), ARC.

122. Moody, *Coming of Age in Mississippi*, 108.

123. "Beauty Pageant Dance April 12," *Alabama Citizen*, 14 April 1956, 1.

124. "Elks' District Won by Miss D. Vails," *Alabama Citizen*, 27 April 1957, 1.

125. "A Campus Beauty," *Louisiana Weekly*, 30 May 1959, 1.

126. "Brown Beauty with Courage," 104.

127. Craig, *Ain't I a Beauty Queen?*, 69.

128. Ibid., 72.

129. Vanessa Williams, Miss New York, was crowned Miss America in 1983, though she relinquished the title to the runner-up after *Penthouse* published nude photographs of her. In 1993 Kimberly Aiken, Miss South Carolina, became the first black winner from the South. The first black woman to win a state title and thus enter the Miss America Pageant was Cheryl Brown of Iowa, in 1970.

130. Boyd, "Southern Beauty," 87.

131. Ibid.

132. Craig, *Ain't I a Beauty Queen?*, 71.

133. Gill, *Beauty Shop Politics*, 98–120.

134. Gill provides a lengthy discussion of Robinson's civil rights activities in Charleston and at the Highlander School, convincingly demonstrating that she

was "the consummate beauty activist." See *Beauty Shop Politics*, 109–20 (quotation p. 108).

135. Bernice Robinson, quoted in Wigginton, *Refuse to Stand Silently By*, 245.

136. Carolyn Daniels, "We Just Kept Going," in Holsaert et al., *Hands on the Freedom Plow*, 152.

137. Martin Daniel Richardson to Ruby Blackburn, 10 October 1933, folder 1, box 4, RPBP.

138. Ninth Anniversary of the Atlanta Cultural League, Inc., Program, n.d., folder 2, box 4, RPBP.

139. "NAACP Membership Drive Officially Opens Tonight," unidentified newspaper clipping, n.d., n.p., folder 9, box 12; and "Mrs. Blackburn Leads Defense Fund Campaign," unidentified newspaper clipping, n.d., n.p., folder 9, box 12, RPBP.

140. "Register and Vote, Walden Tells Group," unidentified newspaper clipping, n.d., n.p., folder 9, box 12, RPBP.

141. Ibid.

142. Appointment Book, 1956–57, folder 2, box, 6, RPBP.

143. Chafe, "'Gods Bring Threads to Webs Begun,'" 1541; *Carolina Times*, 9 March 1957, 4.

144. "State Beauticians Praise Supreme Court Decision," *Jackson Advocate*, 24 July 1954, 3.

145. Mark, *National Beauty Culturists' League*, 38.

146. "Alabama Beauticians Meet in Selma," *Alabama Citizen*, 19 May 1956, 1.

147. Mark, *National Beauty Culturists' League*, 40.

148. Myles Horton, quoted in Morris, *Origins of the Civil Rights Movement*, 145, 146.

149. Septima Clark to Saliama Odums, 12 December 1960, folder 2, box 2, Highlander Folk School Collection, Tennessee State Library and Archives, Nashville.

150. For more on the Johns Island Citizenship School, see Charron, *Freedom's Teacher*, 247–63.

151. Hamlin, *Crossroads at Clarksdale*, 65 (quote). The photo is on p. 66. Hamlin discusses Pigee, her shop, and this photo on pp. 59–70.

152. Ibid., 67.

153. Charron, *Freedom's Teacher*, 280.

154. Septima Clark to Eva Bowman, n.d.; handwritten response on Eva Bowman to Co-Worker, 19 April 1961; and Eva Bowman to Septima Clark, 26 May 1961, 2, folder 4, box 2, Highlander Folk School Collection, Tennessee State Library and Archives, Nashville.

155. "State Beauticians Praise Supreme Court Decision," *Jackson Advocate*, 24 July 1954, 3.

156. Gill, *Beauty Shop Politics*, 102–3.

157. See, for example, "Ashford, Steele Finish 2d and 3d," *Carolina Times*, 19 April 1958, 1, and "Last Chance for Ministers," *Carolina Times*, 26 April 1958.

158. Gill, *Beauty Shop Politics*, 103.

159. Septima Clark, interview by Eugene Walker, 30 July 1976, transcript, folder 9, box 1, Septima Poinsette Clark Papers, Avery Research Center for the Study of African American History and Culture, College of Charleston, Charleston, S.C.

160. Brooks, "In Montgomery," 45.

161. Biondi, *Black Revolution on Campus*, 4; Van Deburg, *New Day in Babylon*, 9–10; Ogbar, *Black Power*, 93–94; Martin, *No Coward Soldiers*, 3–4; Street, *Culture War in the Civil Rights Movement*, 123. Also see Brown, *Fighting for Us*, and Guillory and Green, *Soul*. On the problem of overemphasizing the cultural side of Black Power at the expense of the political, see Joseph, "Black Power Movement," 758.

162. Waldo E. Martin Jr. observes that "[i]n cultural politics generally and in black cultural politics specifically, the boundary between the aesthetic and the political is more apparent than real" (*No Coward Soldiers*, 4).

163. For more on Howard's efforts to shape its female students, see Haidarali, "'Vampingest Vamp Is a Brownskin,'" 162–221.

164. Sellers, *River of No Return*, 58.

165. Cleveland Sellers, quoted in Craig, *Ain't I a Beauty Queen?*, 81.

166. Kerr, *Paper Bag Principle*, 88–102.

167. Craig, *Ain't I a Beauty Queen?*, 81.

168. Van Deburg, *New Day in Babylon*, 10.

169. Kelley, "Nap Time," 343.

170. Annabelle Baker, "Severed," in Harris and Johnson, *Tenderheaded*, 16.

171. Conking, a process by which hair was straightened with a lye-based cream and then manipulated into waves, was popular among certain populations of black men in the early to mid-twentieth century, mostly those outside the middle-class mainstream. "Depending upon one's perspective," Maxine Craig has written, "a conk marked a man as hip, sexy, dangerous, or low-class" ("Decline and Fall of the Conk," 404). In his autobiography, Malcolm X offers one of the most famous descriptions of the conking process and of the pain that it entailed. See Malcolm X and Haley, *Autobiography of Malcolm X*, 52–54.

172. Annabelle Baker, "Severed," in Harris and Johnson, *Tenderheaded*, 16, 18, 19.

173. Tanisha C. Ford provides a compelling discussion of this underappreciated link in "SNCC Women, Denim, and the Politics of Dress," 625–58. I am indebted to her analysis here. Ford argues that the emphasis on female activists' respectability—shared by both the media and many movement leaders, who believed presenting women favorably was crucial to the movement's success—has largely erased SNCC women's revolutionary aesthetic choices from the historical record (pp. 654–58).

174. Debbie Amis Bell, quoted in ibid., 636, 650.

175. Gwendolyn Zoharah Simmons, "From Little Memphis to Mississippi Amazon," in Holsaert et al., *Hands on the Freedom Plow*, 15; Ford, "SNCC Women, Denim, and the Politics of Dress," 626–27, 654.

176. Ford, "SNCC Women, Denim, and the Politics of Dress," 648.

177. Moody, *Coming of Age in Mississippi*, 307.

178. Gloria Richardson Dandridge, "The Energy of the People Passing through Me," in Holsaert et al., *Hands on the Freedom Plow*, 279.

179. Ford, "SNCC Women, Denim, and the Politics of Dress," 643–46.

180. Unita Blackwell, quoted in Crawford, "Beyond the Human Self," 22.

181. Llorens, "Natural Hair," 141.

182. Craig, *Ain't I a Beauty Queen?*, 124.

183. Kerr, *Paper Bag Principle*, 92.

184. Mary Lovelace O'Neal, quoted in Craig, *Ain't I a Beauty Queen?*, 82.

185. Muriel Tillinghast, "Depending on Ourselves," in Holsaert et al., *Hands on the Freedom Plow*, 250.

186. Gwendolyn Zoharah Simmons, "From Little Memphis to Mississippi Amazon," in Holsaert et al., *Hands on the Freedom Plow*, 15.

187. Craig, "Decline and Fall of the Conk," 416.

188. Unita Blackwell, quoted in Crawford, "Beyond the Human Self," 22.

189. Van Deburg, *New Day in Babylon*, 70; Biondi, *Black Revolution on Campus*, 5, 8.

190. Biondi, *Black Revolution on Campus*, 29–30.

191. Hare, "Behind the Black College Student Revolt," 58.

192. Van Deburg, *New Day in Babylon*, 71; Biondi, *Black Revolution on Campus*, 30.

193. Van Deburg, *New Day in Babylon*, 65. Also see Biondi, *Black Revolution on Campus*; Williamson, *Black Power on Campus*; and Glasker, *Black Students in the Ivory Tower*.

194. Darwin Prioleau, "Knits Are Big This Year," *Bennett Banner*, 20 February 1968, 4, DNCC.

195. Winona Griffin, "Fuller . . . Black School Curriculum Should Be Oriented to Blacks," *Bennett Banner*, 27 February 1969, 2 (quote); Winona Griffin, "Fuller Talks Spur Idea Exchange Here," *Bennett Banner*, 5 March 1969, 3, DNCC.

196. Gladys Ashe, "A Black Sister Speaks," *Bennett Banner*, 27 February 1969, 5, DNCC.

197. George Stevens, "Message for Sisters," *Bennett Banner*, 4 November 1969, 3, DNCC.

198. Darwin Prioleau, "Meet the New Bennett Ideal," *Bennett Banner*, 4 November 1969, 4, DNCC.

199. Dianne Dawson, "The Roving Reporter," *Bennett Banner*, 4 November 1969, 5, DNCC.

200. "Discipline and Self-Respect," *Bennett Banner*, 23 September 1972, 2, DNCC.

201. Andre Tally, "Eagle Staff Gives Fashion Show," *Campus Echo*, 20 December 1968, 7, DNCC; Alvin Rush, "NCC Viewed as Negro UNC," *Campus Echo*, 31 October 1968, DNCC.

202. Alvin Rush, "NCC Viewed as Negro UNC," *Campus Echo*, 31 October 1968, DNCC.

203. Emma Walker, "Be Natural," *Campus Echo*, 3 October 1969, 2. See also

Gladys Ashe, "A Black Sister Speaks" and "Get Serious With Your Minds," *Black Ink*, December 1971, 2, DNCC.

204. "The Royalty of ECSC," *Compass*, 8 November 1968, 1, DNCC.

205. Cover illustration and "Belles of the South," 158–62.

206. Kerr, *Paper Bag Principle*, 28.

207. Ibid., 92.

208. In tracing the rise of brownskin womanhood from 1920 to 1954, Laila Haidarali writes, "In many ways, African American women (and men, to some degree) needed to become 'Brown' before they became 'Black'" ("'Vampingest Vamp Is a Brownskin,'" 28). On the contestation of color prejudice within the black community before (and during) the 1960s, also see Craig, "Color of an Ideal Negro Beauty Queen."

209. Granton, "Pride in Blackness and Natural," 50.

210. Craig, *Ain't I a Beauty Queen?*, 73–74.

211. Dahleen Glanton, "A History of Crowning Glories," *Chicago Tribune*, 1 November 2004, 30.

212. Spelman Yearbook 1971, AUCA.

213. Cathy Ferguson, quoted in Tice, *Queens of Academe*, 52.

214. Ibid.

215. Mitzi Bond, "The Black Woman of Today," *Black Ink*, 20 October 1971, 4, DNCC.

216. Willie L. Wilson, "Miss BSM: Challenge for Black Women," *Black Ink*, September 1972, 6, DNCC.

217. Reid, "Black Beauty Queens at White Schools."

218. "Big Man on Campus," 108; "Barbara Dixon is Miss Black USC," *Gamecock*, 8 November 1971, 1, University Archives, South Caroliniana Library, University of South Carolina, Columbia.

219. Craig, *Ain't I a Beauty Queen?*, 71.

220. "Big Man on Campus," 108.

221. Lesesne, *History of the University of South Carolina*, 257; 1974 Garnet and Black yearbook, 383.

222. Bob Craft, "Bourbon 'N' Goobers," *Gamecock*, 22 October 1971, 7, University Archives, South Caroliniana Library, University of South Carolina, Columbia.

223. 1974 Garnet and Black yearbook, 23.

224. Ibid., 386.

225. Terry Points Boney, interview by Samory Pruitt, in Pruitt, "Reflection of Student Desegregation," 461.

226. Ibid., 466; James M. Evans, "Wallace Not Ungracious—Black Coed," unidentified Birmingham newspaper clipping, 21 November 1973, Information Services News Clippings, University Archives, WSHSC.

227. James M. Evans, "Wallace Not Ungracious—Black Coed," unidentified Birmingham newspaper clipping, 21 November 1973, Information Services News Clippings, University Archives, WSHSC.

228. "Acceptance May Be Just Ahead," *Crimson-White*, 3 December 1973, n.p., University Archives, WSHSC.

229. Terry Points Boney, interview by Samory Pruitt, in Pruitt, "Reflection of Student Desegregation," 471.

230. Ibid., 469, 470.

231. "Do You Know a Beauty?"

232. Brooks, "In Montgomery," 48.

233. Davis, *Angela Davis*, 10.

234. Ibid., 96, 97.

235. Davis, "Black Nationalism," 319.

236. Ibid., 320. Davis reflects upon the long-term consequences, and depoliticization, of her legendary hair in "Afro Images," 87–91.

237. Davis, "Afro Images," 89.

238. Ibid., 88.

239. Craig, "Decline and Fall of the Conk," 416.

240. Garland, "Natural Look," 143.

241. Ed Kimble, "Black Claims Resort Owner Guilty of Discrimination," *Red and Black*, 23 May 1974, 1, in *Red and Black* archive.

## CONCLUSION

1. Estimates on the number of demonstrators vary. The *New York Times* reported there were 100 women protesters. Robin Morgan, who organized the demonstration, states in her 1977 chronicle that there were 200 participants. Interviewed for a later documentary about the Miss America Pageant, Morgan said 400 women had been there. See Charlotte Curtis, "Miss America Pageant Is Picketed by 100 Women," *New York Times*, 8 September 1968, 81; Robin Morgan, *Going Too Far*, 64; and Morgan, quoted in *American Experience: Miss America*.

2. Charlotte Curtis, "Miss America Pageant Is Picketed by 100 Women," *New York Times*, 8 September 1968, 81.

3. "No More Miss America," in Bloom and Breines, *Takin' It to the Streets*, 405.

4. Deford, *There She Is*, 308.

5. Simon, *Boardwalk of Dreams*, 114.

6. Charlotte Curtis, "Miss America Pageant Is Picketed by 100 Women," *New York Times*, 8 September 1968, 81.

7. Morgan, *Going Too Far*, 65. For other interpretations that chalk up the myth to the media's desire to discredit the protesters' goals, see Kennedy, *Color Me Flo*, 62, and "No More Miss America," in Bloom and Breines, *Takin' It to the Streets*, 404. Alice Echols argues that feminists who push this view are "disingenuous" because they did initially hope to set fire to the trash can. See *Daring to Be Bad*, 94. Charlotte Curtis also reported that such a plan had been in the works. See "Miss America Pageant Is Picketed by 100 Women," *New York Times*, 8 September 1968, 81.

8. Van Gelder, "Truth About Bra-Burners," 81.

9. "Women with Gripes Lured to Picket 'Miss America,'" *New Pittsburgh Courier*, 21 September 1968, 3. This article reveals how quickly bra-burning became a part of the lore of the protest.

10. Albert Marks, quoted in Ryan, "There She Is, Miss America," 72.

11. "No More Miss America," in Bloom and Breines, *Takin' It to the Streets*, 405.

12. Charlotte Curtis, "Miss America Pageant Is Picketed by 100 Women," *New York Times*, 8 September 1968, 81.

13. Simon, *Boardwalk of Dreams*, 117.

14. Charlotte Curtis, "Miss America Pageant Is Picketed by 100 Women," *New York Times*, 8 September 1968, 81.

15. "Women with Gripes Lured to Picket 'Miss America,'" *New Pittsburgh Courier*, 21 September 1968, 3.

16. Charlotte Curtis, "Miss America Pageant Is Picketed by 100 Women," *New York Times*, 8 September 1968, 81.

17. Charlotte Curtis and Judy Klemesrud, "Along with Miss America, There's Now Miss Black America," *New York Times*, 9 September 1968, 54.

18. Gill, *Beauty Shop Politics*, 105.

19. Walker, *Style and Status*, 185.

20. Catherine Cardozo Lewis, interview by Marcia Greenlee, in Hill, *Black Women Oral History Project*, 262.

21. Ibid.

22. Graham, *Our Kind of People*, 3.

23. Gladys Ashe, "A Black Sister Speaks," *Bennett Banner*, 27 February 1969, 5, DNCC.

24. "On Pseudo Blackness," *Black Ink*, October 1972, 2, DNCC. Also see "How Do I Know How Black I Am?," *Black Ink*, October 1972, 7, DNCC.

25. Ogbar, *Black Power*, 115.

26. Western Union Telegram, Phillip H. Savage, Tri-State Director NAACP, to Evan Dessasau, 15 August 1969, Miss Black America Beauty Pageant Scrapbook, 1969, ARC. A rival Miss Black America Pageant was sponsored by the National Association of Women's Clubs in nearby New York City in 1969, though Evan Dessasau, organizer of the Asbury Park event, argued that his group was "the original organization and is not connected with any other competition" ("'Miss Black America Beauty Pageant' Picks 'Miss Essex County,' June 29th," *Afro-American*, n.d., n.p., Miss Black America Beauty Pageant Scrapbook, 1969, ARC). On the New York contest, see "Colored Women to Sponsor 'Miss Black America,'" *Jet*, 10 April 1969, 58.

27. Miss New Orleans–Miss Louisiana Black America Beauty Pageant Program 1969, WWAL.

28. Darwin Prioleau, "Meet the New Bennett Ideal," *Bennett Banner*, 4 November 1969, 4, DNCC.

29. Emma Walker, "Be Natural," *Campus Echo*, 3 October 1969, 2, DNCC.

30. Margaret Cardozo Holmes, interview by Marcia Greenlee, in Hill, *Black Women Oral History Project*, 58.

31. For more on the commodification of black cultural nationalism generally, see Ogbar, *Black Power*, 93–122. On the commodification of Black is Beautiful,

see Walker, *Style and Status*, 169–203. Two recent essays on this development include Feitz, "Creating a Multicultural Soul," and Gumbs, "Black (Buying) Power."

32. "Natural Look—Is It Here to Stay?," 104.

33. *Tiger's Paw*, 23 October 1969, n.p., WHSL.

34. "Fashions," *Bennett Banner*, 9 October 1968, 2, DNCC.

35. *Red and Black*, 23 April 1970, in *Red and Black* archive.

36. Nadinola "Black Is Beautiful" ad, *Ebony*, October 1968, 215. Walker discusses this ad, calling it "by far the most radical of the ads for facial cosmetics in terms of its overt reference to racial pride" (*Style and Status*, 178). An ad for Dr. Fred Palmer's skin whitener in the same *Ebony* issue, by contrast, makes no reference to changing aesthetic ideals, promising that a "lighter complexion can be yours" (*Ebony*, October 1968, 38).

37. See, for example, Frank, *Conquest of Cool*.

38. Walker, *Style and Status*, 191.

39. Gill, *Beauty Shop Politics*, 123.

40. Coleman, "Among the Things That Used to Be," 221–22.

41. bell hooks, "Straightening Our Hair," in Harris and Johnson, *Tenderheaded*, 112, 113. hooks argues that it was white corporations that developed these products "[i]n keeping with the move to suppress black consciousness and efforts to be self-defining." While white-owned companies did make inroads into the black beauty market during the 1960s, black-owned companies continued to make many of the same straightening products they had manufactured for years and also introduced chemical hair relaxers. See Walker, *Style and Status*, 192–93.

42. For more on the changes in black beauty culture during these years, see Gill, *Beauty Shop Politics*, 125–26.

43. "Fed Up with the Destroyers," *Charleston News and Courier*, 18 September 1968, sec. A, p. 10.

44. "Waves of Emotion," *Charleston News and Courier*, 13 September 1968, sec. A, p. 12.

45. "Burning the Bra," *Charleston News and Courier*, 12 September 1968, sec. A, p. 12.

46. Jim Wright, "NFL Wins Annual Protest Prize," *Dallas Morning News*, 12 September 1968, n.p.

47. Mrs. Robert D. Parris, letter to the editor, *Atlanta Constitution*, 11 September 1968, sec. A, p. 4.

48. "Miss Mississippi Is Pageant Pleaser," *Jackson Daily News*, 7 September 1968, sec. A, p. 1.

49. "Pages from the Past," *Jackson Daily News*, 7 September 1968, sec. H, p. 2.

50. On feminism in the South, see Spruill, "Mississippi 'Takeover.'"

51. For more on this pattern in post-1960s beauty contests, see Banet-Weiser, *Most Beautiful Girl in the World*, 24–25.

52. *The Mississippian*, 19 October 1971, n.p., University Archives, JDWL.

53. Miss America History, Miss America Pageant website, http://www .missamerica.org/our-miss-americas/miss-america-history.aspx.

54. Deford, *There She Is*, 220.

55. Phyllis Ten Elshof, "Picking a Winner," *Jackson Clarion-Ledger*, 15 October 1986, sec. C, pp. 1 and 4.

56. Friedan, *Feminine Mystique*, 43.

57. Ash, *Mary Kay*, 108.

58. Ibid., 8, 18.

59. Ash, *Mary Kay on People Management*, xvii.

60. Wynne Lou Ferguson, quoted in *There's Room at the Top*, 91.

61. Carolyn Ward, quoted in *There's Room at the Top*, 27.

62. Rena Tarbet, quoted in Joyce Senz Harris, "For Consultants, Mary Kay Ash Exuded the Power of Pink," *Dallas Morning News*, 27 November 2001, sec. C, p. 2.

63. Mary Kay Ash, quoted in Elizabeth Kastor, "Mary Kay, in the Pink, the Cosmetics Tycoon, Determinedly Feminine," *Washington Post*, 24 November 1984, sec. F, p. 9.

64. Johnette Shealy, quoted in Independent National Sales Directors, *Paychecks of the Heart*, 299.

65. Mary Kay Ash, quoted in Elizabeth Kastor, "Mary Kay, in the Pink, the Cosmetics Tycoon, Determinedly Feminine," *Washington Post*, 24 November 1984, sec. F, p. 9.

66. "Doors to Executive Suite Were Closed, So She Started Her Own Company," *Chemical Week*, 6 August 1975, 40.

67. Ash, *Mary Kay on People Management*, xv; Thomas C. Hayes, "Retrenchment at Mary Kay," *New York Times*, 31 March 1984, 33.

68. Ash claimed that "business analysts report that we have more women earning more than $50,000 per year than any other company in the nation" (*Mary Kay*, 106).

69. Thomas C. Hayes, "Retrenchment at Mary Kay," *New York Times*, 31 March 1984, 33. On this issue in more recent years, see Virginia Sole-Smith, "Pink Pyramid Scheme: How Mary Kay Cosmetics Preys on Desperate Housewives," *Harper's Magazine* (August 2012): 26–32+.

70. Mary Kay Ash, quoted in Joe Simnacher, "Cosmetics Icon Mary Kay Ash Dies; Pink Empire Changed the Face of Business for Women," *Dallas Morning News*, 23 November 2001, sec. A, p. 33.

71. Docent, Mary Kay Museum, interview.

72. Photograph, Mary Kay Museum (visited January 2003).

73. Kreydatus, "'Enriching Women's Lives.'"

# Bibliography

### MANUSCRIPT SOURCES

*Atlanta, Georgia*
Auburn Avenue Research Library, Archives Division
   Ruby Parks Blackburn Papers
Robert W. Woodruff Library, Atlanta University Center
   Atlanta University Center Archives
   Project to Study Business and Business Education Among Negroes,
      1944–46

*Austin, Texas*
Dolph Briscoe Center for American History, University of Texas at Austin
   University Archives

*Chapel Hill, North Carolina*
North Carolina Collection, Wilson Library, University of North Carolina at
      Chapel Hill
   "History of the Chatham County Colored Agricultural Fair, Inc.," ca. 1980
   North Carolina Collection Clipping File through 1975
   People's Agricultural Fair Association Program, 1914
   Southern Interstate Immigration Bureau Poster, 1891
   Western North Carolina Agricultural and Mechanical Fair Association
      Sixth Annual Fair Program, 1876
Rare Books Collection, Wilson Library, University of North Carolina at
      Chapel Hill
   Southern Pamphlets Collection
Southern Historical Collection, Wilson Library, University of North Carolina
      at Chapel Hill
   Branch Family Papers
   Federal Writers' Project Papers
   Field Studies in the Modern Culture of the South Records
   Pierce and Company Papers
   Southern Oral History Program

*Charleston, South Carolina*
Avery Research Center for African American History and Culture, College of
      Charleston
   Septima Poinsette Clark Papers
   Mamie E. Garvin Fields Papers

South Carolina Historical Society
  James Allan Papers

*Cleveland, Ohio*
  Western Reserve Historical Society
    City Directories

*Columbia, South Carolina*
  South Caroliniana Library, University of South Carolina
    University Archives

*Dallas, Texas*
  Dallas Public Library
    Texas and Dallas History Collection
  DeGolyer Library, Southern Methodist University
    University Archives
  Mary Kay Museum, Mary Kay World Headquarters

*Durham, North Carolina*
  Rare Books, Manuscripts, and Special Collections Library, Duke University
    Behind the Veil: Documenting African-American Life in the Jim Crow
      South Records
    J. Walter Thompson Company Archives, John W. Hartman Center for
      Sales, Advertising, and Marketing History

*Indianapolis, Indiana*
  Indiana Historical Society
    Madam C. J. Walker Papers

*Madison, Wisconsin*
  State Historical Society of Wisconsin
    Dorothy Dignam Papers

*Memphis, Tennessee*
  Memphis and Shelby County Room, Memphis Public Library
    The Dr. R. Q. and Ethyl H. Venson Cotton Makers Jubilee Collection
  Ned R. McWherter Library, University of Memphis
    Special Collections

*Nashville, Tennessee*
  Tennessee State Library and Archives
    Highlander Folk School Collection (microfilm)

*New Orleans, Louisiana*
  Will W. Alexander Library, Dillard University
    Archives and Special Collections
  Amistad Research Center, Tulane University
    American Missionary Association Archives (Addendum)
    Miss Black America Beauty Pageant Scrapbook, 1969

*New York, New York*
  Schomburg Center for Research in Black Culture, New York Public Library
    *Apex News*

*Oxford, Mississippi*
  Department of Archives and Special Collections, J. D. Williams Library,
      University of Mississippi
  Ed King Collection
  Southern Media Archive
  University Archives
      William H. "Chubby" Ellis Collection
      Miss University/Miss America Clipping File
      Photograph Collection

*Raleigh, North Carolina*
  State Archives of North Carolina, Division of Archives and Records
    John J. Blair Papers
    North Carolina Department of Conservation and Development Collection
  University Archives, D. H. Hill Library, North Carolina State University
    Cooperative Extension Service Records
      4-H Youth Development Files
      North Carolina Homemaker's Association Records, 1923–95

*Tuscaloosa, Alabama*
  W. S. Hoole Special Collections Library, University of Alabama
  W. L. Bruce Collection
  J. W. Dennis Drugstore Journal, 1867–68
  University Archives
  William H. Sheppard Library, Stillman College
    University Archives

*Washington, D.C.*
  Manuscript Division, Library of Congress
    Booker T. Washington Papers

INTERVIEWS, ONLINE SOURCES,
OR SOURCES IN AUTHOR'S POSSESSION

Docent, Mary Kay Museum, Mary Kay World Headquarters, telephone interview
  by author, August 2011.
Felton, Rebecca Latimer. *Country Life in Georgia in the Days of My Youth.*
  Atlanta: Index Printing Company, ca. 1919, http://docsouth.unc.edu/fpn
  /felton/felton.html. October 2010.
Garnet and Black Yearbooks, University of South Carolina Libraries Digital
  Collections, http://library.sc.edu/digital/collections/yearbook.html. October
  2012.
Green 'N' Growing: The History of 4-H and Home Demonstration in North

Carolina Online Collection, D. H. Hill Library, North Carolina State University, http://www.lib.ncsu.edu/resolver/1840.6/142. October 2010.
High-Brown Sample Envelope, Illinois Digital Archives, http://www.idaillinois .org/cdm/ref/collection/lakecou02z/id/3503. October 2012.
Miscellaneous Records of the Photography Division, RG 69, E 696, Box 2, National Archives and Records Administration, New Deal Network, http:// newdeal.feri.org/carbonhill/06.htm. December 2009.
Miss America Pageant Website, http://www.missamerica.org/our-miss-americas /miss-america-history.aspx. August 2010.
1975 Maid of Cotton Flyer, Maid of Cotton Collection [unprocessed and unorganized as of December 2009], National Museum of American History Smithsonian Institution, Washington, D.C. Copy in author's possession.
North Carolina Newspapers, Digital NC Collection, North Carolina Heritage Center, University of North Carolina at Chapel Hill, http://www.digitalnc.org /collections/newspapers. October 2012.
*The Red and Black*, An Archive of the University of Georgia's Student Newspaper, http://redandblack.libs.uga.edu/xtf/search. October 2012.

## NEWSPAPERS AND JOURNALS

| | |
|---|---|
| *Alabama Citizen* | *Jackson Clarion-Ledger* |
| *Atlanta Constitution* | *Jackson Daily News* |
| *Baltimore Sun* | *Lake Charles (La.) American Press* |
| *Carolina Times* | *Louisiana Weekly* |
| *Charleston News and Courier* | *Manning (S.C.) Times* |
| *Chicago Daily News* | *New Pittsburgh Courier* |
| *Colored American* | *New York Times* |
| *Columbia (S.C.) Daily Union* | *Pittsburgh Courier* |
| *Columbia (S.C.) Southern Indicator* | *Press of Atlantic City* |
| *Dallas Express* | *Progressive Farmer* |
| *Dallas Morning News* | *Raleigh News and Observer* |
| *Ebony* | *Savannah Tribune* |
| *Griffin (Ga.) Evening Call* | *Washington Post* |
| *Helena (Ark.) Reporter* | *Wilson (N.C.) Daily Times* |
| *Hendersonville (N.C.) Times-News* | *Wisconsin State Journal* |
| *Jackson Advocate* | |

## PUBLISHED PRIMARY SOURCES

Abbott, Shirley. *Womenfolks: Growing Up Down South*. New Haven, Conn.: Ticknor and Fields, 1983.
*American Experience: Miss America*. PBS Home Video, 2002; DVD, 2006.
"American Women Spend $8.59 on Cosmetics." *Sales Management: The Magazine of Marketing*, 15 July 1949, 72.

Armstrong, Mrs. M. F. *On Habits and Manners*. Hampton, Va.: Normal School Press, 1888.

Ash, Mary Kay. *Mary Kay: The Success Story of America's Most Dynamic Businesswoman*. 3rd ed. New York: Harper Perennial, 1994.

——. *Mary Kay on People Management*. New York: Warner, 1984.

Baker, Ray Stannard. *Following the Colour Line: An Account of Negro Citizenship in the American Democracy*. New York: Doubleday, Page, 1908.

"Bathing-Suits and Bathing-Beach Regulations." *The American City*, June 1923, 569–70.

Beam, Lura. *He Called Them by the Lightning: A Teacher's Odyssey in the Negro South, 1908–1919*. Indianapolis: Bobbs-Merrill, 1967.

"Beauties in Burley." *Southern Tobacco Journal*, October 1939, 9.

"Beauty Queens Hit Bias in 'Miss America' Contest." *Jet*, 22 May 1952, 5.

"Beauty Queens to Spare." *Life*, 25 August 1961, 58–64.

"Belles of the South." *Ebony*, August 1971, 158–62.

"Better Babies in the South." *Woman's Home Companion*, July 1913, 5.

Bickett, Thomas Walter. *Public Letters and Papers of Thomas Walter Bickett*. Raleigh: Edward and Broughton, 1923.

"Big Man on Campus." *Ebony*, August 1971, 106–12.

Bloom, Alexander, and Wini Breines, eds. *Takin' It to the Streets: A Sixties Reader*. New York: Oxford University Press, 2003.

Brady, Tom P. *Black Monday: Segregation or Amalgamation . . . America Has Its Choice*. Winona, Miss.: Association of Citizens' Councils, 1954.

*Broadcasting, Telecasting Yearbook: Marketbook Issue 1954*. Washington, D.C.: Broadcasting Publications, 1954.

Brooks, Gwendolyn. "In Montgomery." *Ebony*, August 1971, 42–48.

Brown, Charlotte Hawkins. *The Correct Thing: To Do, To Say, To Wear*. Boston: Christopher Publishing House, 1941; Sedalia, North Carolina: Charlotte Hawkins Brown Historical Foundation, 1990.

Brown, Joe David. "Babes, Brutes, and Ole Miss." *Sports Illustrated*, 19 September 1960, 117–27.

"Brown Beauty with Courage." *Ebony*, October 1966, 102–5.

*Brown v. Board of Education of Topeka*, 74 Sup. Ct. 686 (1954).

Burnett, Ruth. "Contest Should Be Called 'Miss White America.'" *Carolina Times*, 2 October 1965.

"Burning the Bra." *Charleston News and Courier*, 12 September 1968.

Burroughs, Nannie Helen. "Not Color but Character." *Voice of the Negro*, July 1904, 277–79.

Byerly, Victoria. *Hard Times Cotton Mill Girls: Personal Histories of Womanhood and Poverty in the South*. Ithaca: ILR Press, Cornell University, 1986.

"Candidates for the Crown." *Saturday Evening Post*, 1 September 1956, 18–19.

Chesnut, Mary Boykin. *Mary Chesnut's Civil War*. Edited by C. Vann Woodward. New Haven: Yale University Press, 1981.

Clark, Kenneth B. "Effect of Prejudice and Discrimination on Personality

Development." Midcentury White House Conference on Children and Youth, 1950.

Clark, Kenneth B., and Mamie P. Clark. "The Development of Consciousness of Self and the Emergence of Racial Identification in Negro Preschool Children." *Journal of Social Psychology, S.P.S.S.I. Bulletin* 10 (1939): 591–99.

———. "Emotional Factors in Racial Identification and Preference in Negro Children." *Journal of Negro Education* 19 (Summer 1950): 341–50.

———. "Racial Identification and Preference in Negro Children." In *Readings in Social Psychology*, edited by Eleanor E. Maccoby, Theodore M. Newcomb, and Eugene L. Hartley, 602–11. 3rd ed. New York: Henry Holt and Co., 1958.

Clarkson, Elmer Vance. "Atlanta's Beauty Show." *Metropolitan Magazine* 2 (December 1895).

Coleman, Willi. "Among the Things That Used to Be." In *Home Girls: A Black Feminist Anthology*, edited by Barbara Smith, 221–22. New York: Kitchen Table, 1983.

———. "Closets and Keepsakes." *Sage* (Fall 1987): 34.

"Colored Women to Sponsor 'Miss Black America.'" *Jet*, 10 April 1969, 58.

Comettant, Oscar. *Trois ans aux Etats-Unis*. Paris: Pagnerre, 1857.

*Congressional Quarterly Almanac, 84th Congress, Second Session, 1956*. Washington, D.C.: Congressional Quarterly News Features, 1956.

"Cosmetics Output Spirals." *Business Week*, 24 August 1946, 68–70.

Crafts, Hannah. *The Bondwoman's Narrative*. Edited by Henry Louis Gates Jr. New York: Warner Books, 2002.

Davis, Allison, and John Dollard. *Children of Bondage: The Personality Development of Negro Youth in the Urban South*. Washington, D.C.: American Council on Education, 1940.

Davis, Allison, Burleigh B. Gardner, and Mary R. Gardner. *Deep South: A Social Anthropological Study of Caste and Class*. Chicago: University of Chicago Press, 1941.

Davis, Angela. "Afro Images: Politics, Fashion, and Nostalgia." In *Names We Call Home: Autobiography on Racial Identity*. New York: Routledge, 1996.

———. *Angela Davis: An Autobiography*. New York: Random House, 1974.

———. "Black Nationalism: The Sixties and the Nineties." In *Black Popular Culture: A Project by Michele Wallace*, edited by Gina Dent, 317–24. Seattle: Bay Press, 1992.

Dickins, Dorothy. "Clothing and Houselinen Expenditures of 99 Rural Families of Mississippi during 1928–29." *Mississippi Agricultural Experiment Station Bulletin*, no. 294 (September 1931): 1–39.

Dollard, John. *Caste and Class in a Southern Town*. New Haven: Yale University Press, 1937.

"Doors to Executive Suite Were Closed, So She Started Her Own Company." *Chemical Week*, 6 August 1975, 40.

"Do You Know a Beauty?" *Half-Century*, November 1921, 8.

Dunbar-Nelson, Alice. *Give Us Each Day: The Diary of Alice Dunbar-Nelson*. Edited by Gloria Hull. New York: W. W. Norton, 1984.

———. "People of Color in Louisiana." *Journal of Negro History* 1 (October 1916): 361–76.

Durr, Virginia Foster. *Outside the Magic Circle: The Autobiography of Virginia Foster Durr.* Edited by Hollinger F. Barnard. Tuscaloosa: University of Alabama Press, 1985.

Echols, Alice. *Daring to Be Bad: Radical Feminism in America, 1967–1975.* Minneapolis: University of Minnesota Press, 1989.

"Economic Effects of Hairbobbing." *Literary Digest,* 26 September 1925, 74.

"Education of the Freedmen." *DeBow's Review,* After the War Series, 2 (July 1866): 95.

Edwards, Paul K. *The Southern Urban Negro as a Consumer.* New York: Prentice-Hall, 1932.

Erickson, Ethel. *Employment Conditions in Beauty Shops: A Study of Four Cities.* Washington, D.C.: Government Printing Office, 1935.

Fields, Mamie Garvin. *Lemon Swamp and Other Places: A Carolina Memoir.* New York: Free Press, 1983.

Fitzgerald, Zelda. "Eulogy on the Flapper." In *Zelda Fitzgerald: The Collected Writings,* edited by Matthew J. Bruccoli, 391–93. New York: Charles Scribner's Sons, 1991.

———. "Paint and Powder." In *Zelda Fitzgerald: The Collected Writings,* edited by Matthew J. Bruccoli, 415–17. New York: Charles Scribner's Sons, 1991.

Floyd, Silas X. *Floyd's Flowers or Duty and Beauty for Colored Children.* Atlanta: Hudgins, 1905.

Frazier, E. Franklin. *Negro Youth at the Crossways: Their Personality Development in the Middle States.* Washington, D.C.: American Council on Education, 1940; New York: Schocken Books, 1967.

Friedan, Betty. *The Feminine Mystique.* 1963; reprint, with an introduction by Anna Quindlen. New York: W. W. Norton, 2001.

Garden, Mary. "Why I Bobbed My Hair." *Pictorial Review,* April 1927, 8.

Garland, Phyl. "The Natural Look." *Ebony,* June 1966, 143–44+.

Gates, Henry Louis, Jr. *Colored People: A Memoir.* New York: Alfred A. Knopf, 1994.

"Get Serious with Your Minds." *Black Ink,* December 1971.

Graham, Lawrence Otis. *Our Kind of People: Inside America's Upper Class.* New York: Harper Perennial, 2000.

Granton, E. Fannie. "Pride in Blackness and Natural." *Jet,* 10 November 1966, 48–53.

Greeley, Arthur P. *The Food and Drugs Act, June 30, 1906: A Study with Text of the Act, Annotated, the Rules and Regulations for the Enforcement of the Act, Food Inspection Decisions and Official Food Standards.* Washington, D.C.: John Byrne, 1907.

Hackely, Azalia. *The Colored Girl Beautiful.* Kansas City: Burton Publishing, 1916.

Hagood, Margaret. *Mothers of the South: Portraiture of the White Tenant Farm Woman.* Chapel Hill: University of North Carolina Press, 1939.

*Hair Stories.* New York: Washington Square Press, 2001.

Handcox, John. "King Cotton." In *The Black Worker from the Founding of the CIO to the AFL-CIO Merger, 1936–1955.* Vol. 7 of *The Black Worker: A Documentary History from Colonial Times to the Present.* Edited by Philip S. Foner and Ronald L. Lewis, 192. Philadelphia: Temple University Press, 1983.

Hare, Nathan. "Behind the Black College Student Revolt." *Ebony,* August 1967, 58–61.

Harlan, Louis R., and Raymond W. Smock, eds. *The Booker T. Washington Papers.* Vol. 11. Urbana: University of Illinois Press, 1981.

Harris, Juliette, and Pamela Johnson, eds. *Tenderheaded: A Comb-Bending Collection of Hair Stories.* New York: Washington Square Press, 2001.

Harris, Trudier. *Summer Snow: Reflections from a Black Daughter of the South.* Boston: Beacon Press, 2003.

Hentz, Caroline Lee. *Eoline; or, Magnolia Vale.* Philadelphia: T. B. Peterson, 1852.

Hill, Ruth Edmunds, ed. *The Black Women Oral History Project.* Westport, Conn.: Meckler, 1991.

*Historical Statistics of the United States, Earliest Times to the Present: Millennial Edition.* Cambridge: Cambridge University Press, 2006.

Holmes, Emma. *The Diary of Miss Emma Holmes, 1861–1866.* Edited by John F. Marszalek. Baton Rouge: Louisiana State University Press, 1979.

Holsaert, Faith, et al., eds. *Hands on the Freedom Plow: Personal Accounts by Women in SNCC.* Urbana: University of Illinois Press, 2010.

Holsey, Albon L. "Negro Business: Its Real Test Is Still Ahead." *The Messenger* 9 (November 1927): 321.

Horne, Lena, and Richard Schickel. *Lena.* Garden City, N.Y.: Doubleday & Co., 1965.

Hornsby, Alton, Jr., ed. *In the Cage: Eyewitness Accounts of the Freed Negro in Southern Society, 1877–1919.* Chicago: Quadrangle Books, 1971.

Independent National Sales Directors. *Paychecks of the Heart.* Dallas: Mary Kay, 2000.

Jaxon, Frankie "Half-Pint." "It's Heated." 1929.

Jefferson, Thomas. *Notes on the State of Virginia.* Edited by William Peden. Chapel Hill: Published for the Omohundro Institute of Early American History and Culture by the University of North Carolina Press, 1955.

Johnson, Charles S. *Growing Up in the Black Belt: Negro Youth in the Rural South.* Washington, D.C.: American Council on Education, 1941.

Kennedy, Flo. *Color Me Flo: My Hard Life and Good Times.* Englewood Cliffs, N.J.: Prentice-Hall, 1976.

Kimbrough, Franklin S. Letter to the editor. *Time,* 17 June 1946, 4–5.

Kuhn, Clifford M., Harlon E. Joye, and Bernard West, eds. *Living Atlanta: An Oral History of the City, 1914–1948.* Athens: University of Georgia Press, 1990.

Kytle, Elizabeth. *Willie Mae.* New York: Alfred A. Knopf, 1958.

Lee, George W. *Beale Street: Where the Blues Began.* New York: Robert O. Ballou, 1934.

Lewis, Hylan. *Blackways of Kent.* Chapel Hill: University of North Carolina
Press, 1955.

Llorens, David. "Natural Hair: New Symbol of Race Pride." *Ebony*, December
1967, 139–44.

Lumpkin, Katharine du Pre. *The Making of a Southerner.* New York: A. Knopf,
1947; Athens: University of Georgia Press, 1981.

*The Madam C. J. Walker Beauty Manual: A Thorough Treatise Covering All
Branches of Beauty Culture.* 3rd ed. Indianapolis, Ind.: The Madam C. J.
Walker Manufacturing Company, 1940.

Mason, Bobbie Ann. *Clear Springs: A Memoir.* New York: Random House, 1999.

McCarthy, Joe. "The Ordeal of Miss America." *Holiday*, September 1959, 78–80+.

McKimmon, Jane Simpson. *When We're Green We Grow.* Chapel Hill: University
of North Carolina Press, 1945.

Mebane, Mary. *Mary, An Autobiography.* 1981. Reprint, Chapel Hill: University
of North Carolina Press, 1999.

———. *Mary, Wayfarer.* New York: Viking Press, 1976.

Moody, Anne. *Coming of Age in Mississippi.* New York: Dell, 1968.

"More Beauties." *Half-Century*, March 1922, 21.

Morgan, Robin. *Going Too Far: The Personal Chronicle of a Feminist.* New York:
Random House, 1977.

Morland, John Kenneth. *Millways of Kent.* Chapel Hill: University of North
Carolina Press, 1958.

Murray, Pauli, ed. *States' Laws on Race and Color and Appendices.* Cincinnati,
Ohio: Woman's Division of Christian Service, Board of Missions and Church
Extension, The Methodist Church, 1951.

National Recovery Administration. *Code of Fair Competition for the Beauty
Parlor Concessionaires Industry, As Submitted on August 22, 1933.*
Washington, D.C.: Government Printing Office, 1933.

"Nation-Wide Survey of WPA Pool and Beach Development." *Swimming Pool
Data and Reference Annual* (1937): 52–56.

"The Natural Look—Is It Here to Stay?" *Ebony*, January 1969, 104–9.

Odum, Howard W., and Guy B. Johnson. *Negro Workaday Songs.* New York:
Negro Universities Press, 1969.

Olivier, Warner. "Stony Path to Learning." *Saturday Evening Post*, 14 April 1945,
22–23+.

Olson, L. A. "Annual Report of Cooperative Extension Work in Agriculture and
Home Economics, 1932." *Mississippi State College Extension Department
Bulletin*, August 1932.

Parrish, Charles H. "Color Names and Color Notions." *Journal of Negro
Education* 15 (Winter 1946): 13–20.

Porter, John W. "The Menace of Feminism." In *Feminism: Woman and Her
Work.* Louisville, Ky.: Baptist Book Concern, 1923.

Potter, Eliza. *A Hairdresser's Experience in High Life.* 1859. Reprint, edited and
with an introduction by Xiomara Santamarina. Chapel Hill: University of
North Carolina Press, 2009.

Powdermaker, Hortense. *After Freedom: A Cultural Study in the Deep South.* New York: Viking Press, 1939.

Rawick, George P., ed. *The American Slave: A Composite Autobiography.* Vol. 3. Westport, Conn.: Greenwood Publishing Company, 1972.

*Readership of 16 Selected Magazines in the Rural South.* Birmingham, Ala.: Progressive Farmer, 1956.

Reid, Leahmon L. "Black Beauty Queens at White Schools." *Jet,* 30 November 1967, 42–46.

Reid, Whitelaw. *After the War: A Tour of the Southern States, 1865–1866.* 1866. Reprint, with an introduction by C. Vann Woodward. New York: Harper Torchbooks, 1965.

*Report of the Thirteenth Annual Convention of the National Negro Business League Held at Chicago, Illinois.* Washington, D.C., 1912.

Rice, John R. *Bobbed Hair, Bossy Wives, and Women Preachers: Significant Questions for Honest Christian Women Settled by the Word of God.* Wheaton, Ill.: Sword of the Lord Publishers, 1941.

Ripley, Eliza. *Social Life in Old New Orleans, Being Recollections of My Girlhood.* New York: D. Appleton, 1912.

Roth, Philip. "Coronation on Channel Two." *The New Republic,* 23 September 1957, 21.

"Rouge and Progress." *Half-Century,* May–June 1921, 10.

Rubin, Morton. *Plantation County.* Chapel Hill: University of North Carolina Press, 1951.

Ryan, Pat. "There She Is, Miss America." *Sports Illustrated,* 6 October 1969, 70–82.

"Safer to Patronize Your Own." *Half-Century,* February 1920, 17.

Sellers, Cleveland. *The River of No Return: The Autobiography of a Black Militant and the Life and Death of SNCC.* New York: William Morrow, 1973.

"Sitting Symphony of Beauties." *Life,* 1 October 1956, 60–61.

"South Boston Outranks Atlantic City." *Southern Tobacco Journal,* September 1938, 6.

"The Southern Front." *Time,* 17 September 1956, 73–74.

"Summit." *Time,* 15 September 1958, 46.

*There's Room at the Top: The Success Stories of Some of America's Leading Businesswomen.* Dallas: Mary Kay, 1987.

Tracy, Steven C. *Write Me a Few of Your Lines: A Blues Reader.* Amherst: University of Massachusetts Press, 1999.

"An Unscdrupulous [*sic*] Concern." *Half-Century,* April 1920, 17.

U.S. Bureau of the Census. *Fourteenth Census of the United States, 1920.* Vol. 1, *Population 1920, Number and Distribution of Inhabitants.* Washington, D.C.: Government Printing Office, 1921.

———. *Fourteenth Census of the United States, 1920.* Vol. 3, *Population 1920, Composition and Characteristics of the Population by States.* Washington, D.C.: Government Printing Office, 1922.

———. *Fourteenth Census of the United States, 1920.* Vol. 4, *Population 1920, Occupations.* Washington, D.C.: Government Printing Office, 1923.

———. *Fifteenth Census of the United States, 1930.* Vol. 1, *Retail Distribution.* Washington, D.C.: Government Printing Office, 1931–34.

———. *Sixteenth Census of the United States, 1940.* Vol. 2, *Characteristics of the Population.* Washington, D.C.: Government Printing Office, 1943.

———. *Sixteenth Census of the United States, 1940.* Vol. 3, *The Labor Force.* Washington, D.C.: Government Printing Office, 1943.

———. *Eighteenth Decennial of the United States, 1960.* Vol. 1, *Characteristics of the Population.* Washington, D.C.: U.S. Bureau of the Census, 1961.

U.S. Department of Commerce. *Statistical Abstract of the United States, 1921.* Washington, D.C.: U.S. Department of Commerce, 1922.

———. *Statistical Abstract of the United States, 1964.* Washington, D.C.: U.S. Department of Commerce, 1964.

Van Gelder, Lindsy. "The Truth About Bra-Burners." *Ms.*, September/October 1992, 80–81.

Walker, Melissa, ed. *Country Women Cope with Hard Times: A Collection of Oral Histories.* Columbia: University of South Carolina Press, 2004.

Wallace, Sippie. "I'm So Glad I'm Brownskin." *Sippie Wallace: Complete Recorded Works in Chronological Order.* Vol. 1. Document Records, 1995.

"Who Is the Prettiest Colored Girl in the United States?" *Half-Century*, May–June 1921, 15.

"Who Is the Prettiest Colored Girl in the United States?" *Half-Century*, September 1921, 9.

Wigginton, Elliot, ed. *Refuse to Stand Silently By: An Oral History of Grassroots Social Activism in America, 1921–1964.* New York: Doubleday, 1991.

Wilkie, Curtis. *Dixie: A Personal Odyssey through Events That Shaped the Modern South.* New York: Scribner, 2001.

Woods, E. M. *The Negro in Etiquette: A Novelty.* St. Louis: Buxton and Skinner, 1899.

X, Malcolm, and Alex Haley. *The Autobiography of Malcolm X.* New York: Ballantine Books, 1965.

Young, Nathan B. *Your St. Louis and Mine.* St. Louis: Nathan B. Young, 1937.

Zolotow, Maurice. "Boom in Beauty." *Saturday Evening Post*, 25 December 1943, 22–23+.

## PUBLISHED SECONDARY SOURCES

Alexander, Bryant Keith. *Performing Black Masculinity: Race, Culture, and Queer Identity.* Lanham, Md.: Alta Mira Press, 2006.

Alexander, Eleanor. *Lyrics of Sunshine and Shadow: The Tragic Courtship and Marriage of Paul Laurence Dunbar and Alice Ruth Moore: A History of Love and Violence among the African American Elite.* New York: New York University Press, 2002.

Allen, Robert C. *Horrible Prettiness: Burlesque and American Culture*. Chapel Hill: University of North Carolina Press, 1991.

*American Experience: Miss America*. PBS Home Video, 2002; DVD, 2006.

Anderson, James D. *The Education of Blacks in the South, 1860–1935*. Chapel Hill: University of North Carolina Press, 1988.

Anderson, Karen S. *Little Rock: Race and Resistance at Central High School*. Princeton: Princeton University Press, 2012.

Arnesen, Eric. "Whiteness and the Historians' Imagination." *International Labor and Working-Class History*, no. 60 (Fall 2001): 3–32.

Ayers, Edward L. *The Promise of the New South: Life After Reconstruction*. New York: Oxford University Press, 1992.

Banet-Weiser, Sarah. *The Most Beautiful Girl in the World: Beauty Pageants and National Identity*. Berkeley: University of California Press, 1999.

Banks, Ingrid. *Hair Matters: Beauty, Power, and Black Women's Consciousness*. New York: New York University Press, 2000.

Banner, Lois. *American Beauty*. New York: Alfred A. Knopf, 1983.

Barlow, Tani E., et al. "The Modern Girl around the World: A Research Agenda and Preliminary Findings." *Gender and History* 17 (August 2005): 245–94.

Barnes, Annie S. "The Black Beauty Parlor Complex in a Southern City." *Phylon* 36 (1975): 149–54.

Bartley, Numan. *The Rise of Massive Resistance: Race and Politics in the South during the 1950s*. 2nd ed. Baton Rouge: Louisiana State University Press, 1999.

Bergner, Gwen. "Black Children, White Preference: *Brown v. Board*, the Doll Tests, and the Politics of Self-Esteem." *American Quarterly* 61 (June 2009): 299–332.

Bernier, Celeste-Marie, and Judie Newman. "*The Bondwoman's Narrative*: Text, Paratext, Intertext and Hypertext." *Journal of American Studies* 39 (2005): 147–65.

Bertrand, Michael T. *Race, Rock, and Elvis*. Urbana: University of Illinois Press, 2000.

Biondi, Martha. *The Black Revolution on Campus*. Berkeley: University of California Press, 2012.

Black, Paula. *The Beauty Industry: Gender, Culture, Pleasure*. London: Routledge, 2004.

Blackwelder, Julia Kirk. *Styling Jim Crow: African American Beauty Training during Segregation*. College Station: Texas A&M University Press, 2003.

Blight, David W. *Race and Reunion: The Civil War in American Memory*. Cambridge: Harvard University Press, 2001.

Bolton, Charles C. *The Hardest Deal of All: The Battle Over School Integration in Mississippi, 1870–1980*. Jackson: University Press of Mississippi, 2005.

Bordo, Susan. "The Body and the Reproduction of Femininity: A Feminist Appropriation of Foucault." In *Gender/Body/Knowledge: Feminist Reconstructions of Being and Knowing*, edited by Alison M. Jaggar and Susan Bordo, 13–33. New Brunswick: Rutgers University Press, 1989.

———. *Unbearable Weight: Feminism, Western Culture, and the Body*. Berkeley: University of California Press, 1993.

Bowman, Nancy. "Questionable Beauty: The Dangers and Delights of the Cigarette in American Society, 1880–1930." In *Beauty and Business: Commerce, Gender, and Culture in Modern America*, edited by Philip Scranton, 52–86. New York: Routledge, 2001.

Boyd, Robert L. "Survivalist Entrepreneurship among Urban Blacks during the Great Depression: A Test of the Disadvantage Theory of Business Enterprise." *Social Science Quarterly* 81 (December 2000): 972–84.

Brown, Leslie. *Upbuilding Black Durham: Gender, Class, and Black Community Development in the Jim Crow South*. Chapel Hill: University of North Carolina Press, 2008.

Brown, Scot. *Fighting for Us: Maulana Karenga, the Us Organization, and Black Cultural Nationalism*. New York: New York University Press, 2003.

Brownmiller, Susan. *Femininity*. New York: Simon and Schuster, 1984.

Brumberg, Joan Jacobs. *The Body Project: An Intimate History of American Girls*. New York: Vintage, 1997.

Bundles, A'Lelia. *On Her Own Ground. The Life and Times of Madam C. J. Walker*. New York: Washington Square Press, 2001.

Butler, Judith. *Bodies that Matter: On the Discursive Limits of "Sex."* New York: Routledge, 1993.

———. *Gender Trouble: Feminism and the Subversion of Identity*. New York: Routledge, 1990.

Byrd, Ayana D., and Lori L. Tharps. *Hair Story: Untangling the Roots of Black Hair in America*. New York: St. Martin's Griffin, 2001.

Cahn, Susan K. *Sexual Reckonings: Southern Girls in a Troubling Age*. Cambridge: Harvard University Press, 2007.

Carby, Hazel V. "Policing the Black Woman's Body in an Urban Context." *Critical Inquiry* 18 (Summer 1992): 738–55.

Carson, Gerald. *The Old Country Store*. New York: Oxford University Press, 1954.

Chafe, William H. "'The Gods Bring Threads to Webs Begun.'" *Journal of American History* 86 (March 2000): 1531–51.

Charron, Katherine Mellen. *Freedom's Teacher: The Life of Septima Clark*. Chapel Hill: University of North Carolina Press, 2009.

Clark, Thomas. *Pills, Petticoats, and Plows: The Southern Country Store*. Norman: University of Oklahoma Press, 1964.

Clarke, Alison J. *Tupperware: The Promise of Plastic in 1950s America*. Washington, D.C.: Smithsonian Institution Press, 1999.

Clinton, Catherine. *Tara Revisited: Women, War, and the Plantation Legend*. New York: Abbeville Press, 1995.

Coclanis, Peter. "What Made Booker T. Wash(ington)?: The Wizard of Tuskegee in Economic Context." In *Booker T. Washington and Black Progress: Up from Slavery 100 Years Later*, edited by W. Fitzhugh Brundage, 81–106. Gainesville: University of Florida Press, 2003.

Cohen, Colleen Ballerino, Richard Wilk, and Beverly Stoeltje, eds. *Beauty*

*Queens on the Global Stage: Gender, Contests, and Power.* New York: Routledge, 1996.

Cohen, Lizabeth. *A Consumers' Republic: The Politics of Mass Consumption in Postwar America.* New York: Alfred A. Knopf, 2003.

Collins, Patricia Hill. *Black Feminist Thought: Knowledge, Consciousness, and the Politics of Empowerment.* New York: Routledge, 1991.

Conor, Liz. *The Spectacular Modern Woman: Feminine Visibility in the 1920s.* Bloomington: Indiana University Press, 2004.

Cooper, Wendy. *Hair: Sex, Society, Symbolism.* New York: Stein and Day, 1971.

Coski, John M. *The Confederate Battle Flag: America's Most Embattled Emblem.* Cambridge: Belknap, 2005.

Cox, Karen L. *Dixie's Daughters: The United Daughters of the Confederacy and the Preservation of Confederate Culture.* Gainesville: University Press of Florida, 2003.

———. *Dreaming of Dixie: How the South Was Created in American Popular Culture.* Chapel Hill: University of North Carolina Press, 2011.

Craig, Maxine Leeds. *Ain't I a Beauty Queen? Black Women, Beauty, and the Politics of Race.* New York: Oxford University Press, 2002.

———. "The Color of an Ideal Negro Beauty Queen." In *Shades of Difference: Why Skin Color Matters,* edited by Evelyn Nakano Glenn, 81–94. Stanford: Stanford University Press, 2009.

———. "The Decline and Fall of the Conk; or, How to Read a Process." *Fashion Theory* 1 (December 1997): 399–420.

Crawford, Vicki. "Beyond the Human Self: Grassroots Activists in the Mississippi Civil Rights Movement." In *Women in the Civil Rights Movement: Trailblazers and Torchbearers, 1941–1965,* edited by Jacqueline Anne Rouse and Barbara Woods, 13–26. Brooklyn: Carlson, 1990.

Crooks, Esther J., and Ruth W. Crooks. *The Ring Tournament in the United States.* Richmond, Va.: Garrett and Massie, 1936.

Dailey, Jane. "Sex, Segregation, and the Sacred after *Brown.*" *Journal of American History* 91 (June 2004): 119–44.

Daniel, Pete. *Breaking the Land: The Transformation of Cotton, Tobacco, and Rice Cultures since 1880.* Urbana: University of Illinois Press, 1985.

———. "Going among Strangers: Southern Reactions to World War II." *Journal of American History* 77 (December 1990): 886–911.

———. *Lost Revolutions: The South in the 1950s.* Chapel Hill: University of North Carolina Press, 2000.

———. *Standing at the Crossroads: Southern Life since 1900.* New York: Hill and Wang, 1986.

Deford, Frank. *There She Is: The Life and Times of Miss America.* New York: Viking Press, 1971.

Devlin, Rachel. *Relative Intimacy: Fathers, Adolescent Daughters, and Postwar American Culture.* Chapel Hill: University of North Carolina Press, 2005.

Dittmer, John. *Local People: The Struggle for Civil Rights in Mississippi.* Urbana: University of Illinois Press, 1994.

Dorey, Annette K. Vance. *Better Baby Contests: The Scientific Quest for Perfect Childhood Health in the Early Twentieth Century*. Jefferson, N.C.: McFarland, 1999.

Douglas, Mary. *Natural Symbols*. New York: Pantheon Press, 1982.

Douglas, Mary, and Baron Isherwood. *World of Goods: Towards an Anthropology of Consumption*. New York: Basic Books, 1979; New York: Routledge, 1996.

Drago, Edmund L. *Initiative, Paternalism, and Race Relations: Charleston's Avery Normal Institute*. Athens: University of Georgia Press, 1990.

Duberman, Martin, Martha Vicinus, and George Chauncey. *Hidden from History: Reclaiming the Gay and Lesbian Past*. New York: Meridian, 1990.

Dunn, Read P., Jr. *Mr. Oscar: A Story of the Early Years in the Life and Times of Oscar Johnston and of His Efforts in Organizing the National Cotton Council*. Memphis: National Cotton Council of America, 1991.

Eagles, Charles W. *The Price of Defiance: James Meredith and the Integration of Ole Miss*. Chapel Hill: University of North Carolina Press, 2009.

Fass, Paula S. *The Damned and the Beautiful: American Youth in the 1920s*. New York: Oxford University Press, 1977.

Feitz, Lindsey. "Creating a Multicultural Soul: Avon, Corporate Social Responsibility, and Race in the 1970s." In *The Business of Black Power: Community Development, Capitalism, and Corporate Responsibility in Postwar America*, edited by Laura Warren Hill and Julia Rabig, 116–54. Rochester: University of Rochester Press, 2012.

Felski, Rita. *The Gender of Modernity*. Cambridge: Harvard University Press, 1995.

Fields, Jill. *An Intimate Affair: Women, Lingerie, and Sexuality*. Berkeley: University of California Press, 2007.

Ford, Tanisha C. "SNCC Women, Denim, and the Politics of Dress." *Journal of Southern History* 79 (August 2013): 623–58.

Foster, Gaines M. *Ghosts of the Confederacy: Defeat, the Lost Cause, and the Emergence of the New South, 1865 to 1913*. New York: Oxford University Press, 1987.

Foster, Helen Bradley. *"New Raiments of Self": African American Clothing in the Antebellum South*. New York: Oxford University Press, 1997.

Fox, Richard Wrightman, and T. J. Jackson Lears, eds. *The Culture of Consumption: Critical Essays in American History, 1880–1920*. New York: Pantheon Books, 1983.

Fox-Genovese, Elizabeth. *Within the Plantation Household: Black and White Women of the Old South*. Chapel Hill: University of North Carolina Press, 1988.

Frank, Thomas. *The Conquest of Cool: Business Culture, Counterculture, and the Rise of Hip Consumerism*. Chicago: University of Chicago Press, 1997.

Fraser, Nancy. "Rethinking the Public Sphere: A Contribution to the Critique of Actually Existing Democracy." *Social Text* 8 (1990): 56–80.

Gaines, Kevin. *Uplifting the Race: Black Leadership, Politics, and Culture in the Twentieth Century*. Chapel Hill: University of North Carolina Press, 1996.

Gates, Henry Louis, Jr., and Hollis Robbins, eds. *In Search of Hannah Crafts: Critical Essays on the Bondwoman's Narrative.* New York: Basic Books, 2004.

Gatewood, Willard B. *Aristocrats of Color: The Black Elite, 1880–1920.* Bloomington: Indiana University Press, 1990.

Gerster, Patrick, and Nicholas Cords. "The Northern Origins of Southern Mythology." In *Myth and Southern History.* Vol. 2. Urbana: University of Illinois Press, 1989.

Gill, Tiffany M. *Beauty Shop Politics: African American Women's Activism in the Beauty Industry.* Urbana: University of Illinois Press, 2010.

———. "'I Had My Own Business So I Didn't Have to Worry': Beauty Salons, Beauty Culturists, and the Politics of African-American Female Entrepreneurship." In *Beauty and Business: Commerce, Gender and Culture in Modern America,* edited by Philip Scranton, 169–93. New York: Routledge, 2001.

Gilmore, Glenda Elizabeth. *Gender and Jim Crow: Women and the Politics of White Supremacy in North Carolina, 1896–1920.* Chapel Hill: University of North Carolina Press, 1996.

Glanton, Dahleen. "A History of Crowning Glories." *Chicago Tribune,* 1 November 2004, 1.

Glasker, Wayne. *Black Students in the Ivory Tower: African American Student Activism at the University of Pennsylvania, 1967–1990.* Amherst: University of Massachusetts Press, 2002.

Glassberg, David. *American Historical Pageantry: The Uses of Tradition in the Early Twentieth Century.* Chapel Hill: University of North Carolina Press, 1990.

Glickman, Lawrence. "Toward a History of Consumer Culture, Women and Politics." *Reviews in American History* 28 (December 2000): 584–93.

Godfrey, Phoebe. "Bayonets, Brainwashing, and Bathrooms: The Discourse of Race, Gender, and Sexuality in the Desegregation of Little Rock's Central High." *Arkansas Historical Quarterly* 62 (Spring 2003): 42–67.

Goldfield, David R. *Black, White, and Southern: Race Relations and Southern Culture, 1940 to the Present.* Baton Rouge: Louisiana State University Press, 1990.

Gordon, Linda. "Dorothea Lange: The Photographer as Agricultural Sociologist." *Journal of American History* 93 (December 2006): 698–727.

Graham, Allison. *Framing the South: Hollywood, Television, and Race during the Civil Rights Struggle.* Baltimore: Johns Hopkins University Press, 2001.

Guillory, Monique, and Richard C. Green, eds. *Soul: Black Power, Politics, and Pleasure.* New York: New York University Press, 1998.

Gumbs, Alexis Pauline. "Black (Buying) Power: The Story of *Essence* Magazine." In *The Business of Black Power: Community Development, Capitalism, and Corporate Responsibility in Postwar America,* edited by Laura Warren Hill and Julia Rabig, 95–115. Rochester: University of Rochester Press, 2012.

Gunn, Fenja. *The Artificial Face: A History of Cosmetics.* London: David and Charles, 1973.

Hale, Grace Elizabeth. *Making Whiteness: The Culture of Segregation in the South, 1890–1940*. New York: Vintage Books, 1998.

Hall, Jacquelyn Dowd. "The Long Civil Rights Movement and the Political Uses of the Past." *Journal of American History* 91 (March 2005): 1233–63.

———. "Private Eyes, Public Women: Images of Class and Sex in the Urban South, Atlanta, Georgia, 1913–1915." In *Work Engendered: Toward a New History of American Labor*, edited by Ava Baron, 243–72. Ithaca: Cornell University Press, 1991.

———. "'You Must Remember This': Autobiography as Social Critique." *Journal of American History* 85 (September 1998): 439–65.

Hall, Jacquelyn Dowd, and Anne Firor Scott. "Women in the South." In *Interpreting Southern History: Historiographical Essays in Honor of Sanford W. Higginbotham*, edited by John B. Boles and Evelyn Thomas Nolen, 454–509. Baton Rouge: Louisiana State University Press, 1987.

Hall, Jacquelyn Dowd, James L. Leloudis, Robert Rodgers Korstad, Mary Murphy, Lu Ann Jones, and Christopher B. Daly. *Like a Family: The Making of a Southern Cotton Mill World*. 1987. Chapel Hill: University of North Carolina Press, 2000.

Halttunen, Karen. *Confidence Men and Painted Women: A Study of Middle-Class Culture in America, 1830–1870*. New Haven: Yale University Press, 1982.

Hamlin, Francoise N. *Crossroads at Clarksdale: The Black Freedom Struggle in the Mississippi Delta after World War II*. Chapel Hill: University of North Carolina Press, 2012.

———. "Vera Mae Pigee (1925–): Mothering the Movement." In *Mississippi Women: Their Histories, Their Lives*. Vol. 1, edited by Martha H. Swain, Elizabeth Anne Payne, and Marjorie Julian Spruill, 281–98. Athens: University of Georgia Press, 2003.

Harris, Carmen. "Grace Under Pressure: The Black Home Extension Service in South Carolina, 1919–1966." In *Rethinking Home Economics: Women and the History of a Profession*, edited by Sarah Stage and Virginia B. Vicenti, 203–28. Ithaca: Cornell University Press, 1997.

Harris, Michael D. *Colored Pictures: Race and Visual Representation*. Chapel Hill: University of North Carolina Press, 2003.

Harrison, Daphne Duval. *Black Pearls: Blues Queens of the 1920s*. New Brunswick: Rutgers University Press, 1988.

Haynes, Michaele Thurgood. *Dressing Up Debutantes: Pageantry and Glitz in Texas*. New York: Oxford University Press, 1998.

Hernandez-Ehrisman, Laura. *Inventing the Fiesta City: Heritage and Carnival in San Antonio*. Albuquerque: University of New Mexico Press in cooperation with the William P. Clements Center for Southwest Studies, Southern Methodist University, 2008.

Herron, Caolivia. *Nappy Hair*. New York: Alfred A. Knopf, 1997.

Higginbotham, Evelyn Brooks. *Righteous Discontent: The Women's Movement in the Black Baptist Church, 1880–1920*. Cambridge: Harvard University Press, 1993.

Holloway, Pippa. *Sexuality, Politics, and Social Control in Virginia, 1920–1945*. Chapel Hill: University of North Carolina Press, 2006.

Holt, Marilyn Irvin. *Linoleum, Better Babies, and the Modern Farm Woman*. Albuquerque: University of New Mexico Press, 1995.

Honey, Maureen. *Creating Rosie the Riveter: Class, Gender, and Propaganda during World War II*. Amherst: University of Massachusetts Press, 1984.

hooks, bell. *Black Looks: Race and Representation*. Boston: South End Press, 1992.

Horton, Myles. *The Origins of the Civil Rights Movement: Black Communities Organizing for Change*. New York: Free Press, 1984.

Hunt, Patricia K. "Clothing as an Expression of History: The Dress of African-American Women in Georgia, 1880–1915." *Georgia Historical Quarterly* 86 (Summer 1992): 459–71.

———. "The Struggle to Achieve Individual Expression through Clothing and Adornment: African American Women under and after Slavery." In *Discovering the Women in Slavery: Emancipating Perspectives on the American Past*, edited by Patricia Morton, 227–40. Athens: University of Georgia Press, 1996.

Hunter, Margaret. *Race, Gender, and the Politics of Skin Tone*. New York: Routledge, 2005.

Hunter, Tera. *To 'Joy My Freedom: Southern Black Women's Lives and Labors after the Civil War*. Cambridge: Harvard University Press, 1997.

———. "'Work That Body': African American Women, Work, and Leisure in Atlanta and the New South." In *The Black Worker: Race, Labor, and Civil Rights Since Emancipation*, edited by Eric Arnesen, 72–93. Urbana: University of Illinois Press, 2007.

Jacoway, Elizabeth. *Turn Away Thy Son: Little Rock, the Crisis That Shook the Nation*. New York: Free Press, 2007.

Jeffreys, Sheila. *Beauty and Misogyny: Harmful Cultural Practices in the West*. London: Routledge, 2005.

Jewell, K. Sue. *From Mammy to Miss America and Beyond: Cultural Images and the Shaping of U.S. Social Policy*. New York: Routledge, 1993.

Jones, Allen W. "The Role of Tuskegee in the Education of Black Farmers." *Journal of Negro History* 60 (April 1975): 252–67.

Jones, Anne Goodwyn. *Tomorrow Is Another Day: The Woman Writer in the South, 1859–1936*. Baton Rouge: Louisiana State University Press, 1981.

Jones, Jacqueline. *Labor of Love, Labor of Sorrow: Black Women, Work, and the Family, from Slavery to the Present*. New York: Vintage, 1985.

Jones, Lu Ann. *Mama Learned Us to Work: Farm Women in the New South*. Chapel Hill: University of North Carolina Press, 2002.

Jordan, Winthrop D. *White Over Black: American Attitudes toward the Negro, 1550–1812*. Chapel Hill: Published for the Omohundro Institute of Early American History and Culture by the University of North Carolina Press, 1968.

Joseph, Peniel E., ed. "The Black Power Movement: A State of the Field." *Journal of American History* 96 (December 2009): 751–76.

———. *The Black Power Movement: Rethinking the Civil Rights–Black Power Era*. New York: Routledge, 2006.

———. *Waiting 'Til the Midnight Hour: A Narrative History of Black Power in America*. New York: Holt, 2006.

Kasson, John F. *Amusing the Million: Coney Island at the Turn of the Century*. New York: Hill and Wang, 1978.

———. *Rudeness and Civility: Manners in Nineteenth-Century Urban America*. New York: Hill and Wang, 1990.

Keith, Verna M., and Cedric Herring. "Skin Tone and Stratification in the Black Community." *American Journal of Sociology* 97 (November 1991): 760–78.

Kelley, Robin D. G. "Nap Time: Historicizing the Afro." *Fashion Theory* 1 (December 1997): 339–51.

Kerr, Audrey Elisa. *The Paper Bag Principle: Class, Colorism, and Rumor and the Case of Black Washington, D.C.* Knoxville: University of Tennessee Press, 2006.

Kessler-Harris, Alice. *Out to Work: A History of Wage-Earning Women in the United States*. New York: Oxford University Press, 2003.

Kidd, Stuart. "Dissonant Encounters: FSA Photographers and the Southern Underclass, 1935–1943." In *Reading Southern Poverty between the Wars, 1918–1939*, edited by Richard Godden and Martin Crawford, 25–47. Athens: University of Georgia Press, 2006.

Kirby, Jack Temple. *Rural Worlds Lost: The American South, 1920–1960*. Baton Rouge: Louisiana State University Press, 1987.

Kitch, Carolyn. *The Girl on the Magazine Cover: The Origins of Visual Stereotypes in American Mass Media*. Chapel Hill: University of North Carolina Press, 2001.

Kolchin, Peter. "Whiteness Studies: The New History of Race in America." *Journal of American History* 89 (June 2002): 154–73.

Kreydatus, Beth. "'Enriching Women's Lives': The Mary Kay Approach to Beauty, Business, and Feminism." *Business and Economic History On-Line* 3 (2005), http://h-net.org/~business/bhcweb/publications/BEHonline/2005/beh2005.html. May 2011.

Kruse, Kevin M. *White Flight: Atlanta and the Making of Modern Conservatism*. Princeton, N.J.: Princeton University Press, 2005.

Lakoff, Robin Tolmach, and Raquel L. Scherr. *Face Value: The Politics of Beauty*. Boston: Routledge and Kegan Paul, 1984.

Larson, Edward J. *Sex, Race, and Science: Eugenics in the Deep South*. Baltimore: Johns Hopkins University Press, 1995.

Lassiter, Matthew D., and Andrew B. Lewis, eds. *The Moderates' Dilemma: Massive Resistance to School Desegregation in Virginia*. Charlottesville: University of Virginia Press, 1998.

Latham, Angela L. *Posing a Threat: Flappers, Chorus Girls, and Other Brazen Performers of the American 1920s*. Hanover, Conn.: Wesleyan University Press, 2000.

Lawson, Steven F. "Long Origins of the Short Civil Rights Movement." In

*Freedom Rights: New Perspectives on the Civil Rights Movement*, edited by Danielle L. McGuire and John Dittmer, 9–38. Lexington: University Press of Kentucky, 2011.

Lazerow, Jama, and Yohuru Williams, eds. *In Search of the Black Panther Party: New Perspectives on a Revolutionary Movement*. Durham: Duke University Press, 2006.

Lears, T. Jackson. *Fables of Abundance: A Cultural History of Advertising in America*. New York: Basic Books, 1994.

Lesesne, Henry H. *A History of the University of South Carolina, 1940–2000*. Columbia: University of South Carolina Press, 2001.

Levine, Lawrence W. *Black Culture and Black Consciousness: Afro-American Folk Thought from Slavery to Freedom*. New York: Oxford University Press, 1977.

Lewis, Arthur H. *Carnival*. New York: Trident Press, 1970.

Lewis, George. *Massive Resistance: The White Response to the Civil Rights Movement*. London: Hodder Education, 2006.

———. *The White South and the Red Menace: Segregationists, Anticommunism, and Massive Resistance*. Gainesville: University Press of Florida, 2004.

Lott, Eric. *Love and Theft: Blackface Minstrelsy and the American Working Class*. New York: Oxford University Press, 1993.

———. "White Like Me: Racial Cross-Dressing and the Construction of American Whiteness." In *Cultures of United States Imperialism*, edited by Amy Kaplan and Donald E. Pease, 474–95. Durham: Duke University Press, 1993.

Lowe, Margaret A. *Looking Good: College Women and Body Image, 1875–1930*. Baltimore: Johns Hopkins University Press, 2003.

Lowry, Beverly. *Her Dream of Dreams: The Rise and Triumph of Madam C. J. Walker*. New York: Alfred A. Knopf, 2003.

Magness, Perre. *The Party with a Purpose: 75 Years of Carnival in Memphis, 1931–2006*. Jonesboro, Ark.: Pinpoint Printing, 2006.

Manring, M. M. *Slave in a Box: The Strange Career of Aunt Jemima*. Charlottesville: University of Virginia Press, 1998.

Mark, Vernice. *The National Beauty Culturists' League History, 1919–1994*. Detroit: Harlo, 1994.

Marti, Donald B. *Historical Directory of American Agricultural Fairs*. Westport, Conn.: Greenwood Press, 1986.

Martin, Richard, and Harold Koda. *Splash! A History of Swimwear*. New York: Rizzoli International Publications, 1990.

Martin, Waldo E. *No Coward Soldiers: Black Cultural Politics and Postwar America*. Cambridge: Harvard University Press, 2005.

McCandless, Amy Thompson. *The Past in the Present: Women's Higher Education in the Twentieth-Century South*. Tuscaloosa: University of Alabama Press, 1999.

McElya, Micki. *Clinging to Mammy: The Faithful Slave in Twentieth-Century America*. Cambridge: Harvard University Press, 2007.

McEuen, Melissa A. *Making War, Making Women: Femininity and Duty on the American Home Front, 1941–1945.* Athens: University of Georgia Press, 2011.

McKennon, Joe. *Pictorial History of the American Carnival.* Vol. 1. Sarasota, Fla.: Carnival Publishers, 1971.

McMillen, Neil R. *The Citizens' Council: Organized Resistance to the Second Reconstruction, 1954–1964.* Chicago: University of Chicago Press, 1971.

McPherson, Tara. *Reconstructing Dixie: Race, Gender, and Nostalgia in the Imagined South.* Durham: Duke University Press, 2003.

Milford, Nancy. *Zelda: A Biography.* New York: Harper and Row, 1970.

Mitchell, Michele. *Righteous Propagation: African Americans and the Politics of Racial Destiny after Reconstruction.* Chapel Hill: University of North Carolina Press, 2004.

Mixon, Wayne. "Resistance to Industrialization." In *The New Encyclopedia of Southern Culture.* Vol. 11. Edited by Melissa Walker and James C. Cobb. Chapel Hill: University of North Carolina Press, 2008.

Morgan, Francesca. *Women and Patriotism in Jim Crow America.* Chapel Hill: University of North Carolina Press, 2005.

Morris, Aldon D. *The Origins of the Civil Rights Movement: Black Communities Organizing for Change.* New York: Free Press, 1984.

Morrow, Willie. *400 Years without a Comb.* San Diego, Calif.: Black Publishers of San Diego, 1973.

Morton, Patricia. *Disfigured Images: The Historical Assault on Afro-American Women.* New York: Greenwood, 1991.

Moye, J. Todd. *Let the People Decide: Black Freedom and White Resistance Movements in Sunflower County, Mississippi, 1945–1986.* Chapel Hill: University of North Carolina Press, 2004.

Mulvey, Kate, and Melissa Richards. *Decades of Beauty: The Changing Image of Women, 1890s–1990s.* New York: Facts on File, 1998.

Nadell, Martha Jane. *Enter the New Negroes: Images of Race in American Culture.* Cambridge: Harvard University Press, 2004.

Norton, Robert E. *The Beautiful Soul: Aesthetic Morality in the Eighteenth Century.* Ithaca: Cornell University Press, 1995.

Ogbar, Jeffrey O. G. *Black Power: Radical Politics and African American Identity.* Baltimore: Johns Hopkins University Press, 2004.

Oliver, Paul. *Blues Fell This Morning: Meaning in the Blues.* Cambridge: Cambridge University Press, 1960.

Osborne, Angela Saulino. *Miss America: The Dream Lives On—A 75 Year Celebration.* Dallas: Taylor Publishing and the Miss America Organization, 1995.

Ownby, Ted. *American Dreams in Mississippi: Consumers, Poverty, and Culture, 1830–1998.* Chapel Hill: University of North Carolina Press, 1999.

Pearson, Susan J. "'Infantile Specimens': Showing Babies in Nineteenth-Century America." *Journal of Social History* 42 (Winter 2008): 341–70.

Peiss, Kathy. *Cheap Amusements: Working Women and Leisure in New York City, 1880 to 1920.* Philadelphia: Temple University Press, 1985.

———. *Hope in a Jar: The Making of America's Beauty Culture*. New York: Metropolitan Books, 1998.

Pernick, Martin S. *The Black Stork: Eugenics and the Death of "Defective" Babies in American Medicine and Motion Pictures Since 1915*. New York: Oxford University Press, 1996.

———. "Taking Better Baby Contests Seriously." *American Journal of Public Health* 92 (May 2002): 707–8.

Phillips, Evelyn Newman. "Doing More Than Heads: African American Women Healing, Resisting, and Uplifting Others in St. Petersburg, Florida." *Frontiers: A Journal of Women's Studies* 22 (2001): 25–42.

Piepmeier, Alison. *Out in Public: Configurations of Women's Bodies in Nineteenth-Century America*. Chapel Hill: University of North Carolina Press, 2004.

Probert, Christina. *Swimwear in Vogue since 1910*. New York: Abbeville Press, 1981.

Raeburn, John. *A Staggering Revolution: A Cultural History of Thirties Photography*. Urbana: University of Illinois Press, 2006.

Raimon, Eve Allegra. *The "Tragic Mullata" Revisited: Race and Nationalism in Nineteenth-Century Antislavery Fiction*. New Brunswick: Rutgers University Press, 2004.

Ransby, Barbara. *Ella Baker and the Black Freedom Movement: A Radical Democratic Vision*. Chapel Hill: University of North Carolina Press, 2003.

Rasmussen, Wayne D. *Taking the University to the People: Seventy-Five Years of Cooperative Extension*. Ames: Iowa State University Press, 1989.

Reid, Debra A. *Reaping a Greater Harvest: African Americans, the Extension Service, and Rural Reform in Jim Crow Texas*. College Station: Texas A&M University Press, 2007.

Riverol, A. R. *Live from Atlantic City: The History of the Miss America Pageant Before, After, and in Spite of Television*. Bowling Green, Ohio: Bowling Green State University Popular Press, 1992.

Roberts, Blain. "A New Cure for Brightleaf Tobacco: The Origins of the Tobacco Queen during the Great Depression." *Southern Cultures* 12, no. 2 (Summer 2006): 30–52.

———. "The Ugly Side of the Southern Belle." *New York Times*, 16 January 2013, A-21.

Roberts, Mary Louise. "Gender, Consumption, and Commodity Culture." *American Historical Review* 103 (June 1998): 817–44.

Rooks, Noliwe M. *Hair Raising: Beauty, Culture, and African-American Women*. New Brunswick: Rutgers University Press, 1996.

———. *Ladies' Pages: African American Women's Magazines and the Culture That Made Them*. New Brunswick: Rutgers University Press, 2004.

Rupp, Leila J. *Mobilizing Women for War: German and American Propaganda, 1939–1945*. Princeton: Princeton University Press, 1978.

Rushing, Wanda. *Memphis and the Paradox of Place: Globalization in the American South*. Chapel Hill: University of North Carolina Press, 2009.

Russell, Albert R. *U.S. Cotton and the National Cotton Council*. Memphis: National Cotton Council, 1987.

Russell, Kathy, Midge Wilson, and Ronald Hall. *The Color Complex: The Politics of Skin Color among African Americans*. New York: Harcourt Brace Jovanovich, 1992.

Sansing, David G. *The University of Mississippi: A Sesquicentennial History*. Jackson: University Press of Mississippi, 1999.

Santamarina, Xiomara. *Belabored Professions: Narratives of African American Working Womanhood*. Chapel Hill: University of North Carolina Press, 2005.

Savage, Candace S. *Beauty Queens: A Playful History*. New York: Abbeville Press, 1998.

Scanlon, Jennifer. "'If My Husband Calls, I'm Not Here': The Beauty Parlor as Real and Representational Female Space." *Feminist Studies* 33 (Summer 2007): 308–34.

Scott, Anne Firor. *The Southern Lady: From Pedestal to Politics, 1830–1930*. Chicago: University of Chicago Press, 1970.

Seidel, Kathryn Lee. *The Southern Belle in the American Novel*. Tampa: University of South Florida Press, 1985.

Sharpless, Rebecca. *Fertile Ground, Narrow Choices: Women on Texas Cotton Farms, 1900–1940*. Chapel Hill: University of North Carolina Press, 1999.

Shaw, Stephanie. *What a Woman Ought to Be and to Do: Black Professional Women Workers during the Jim Crow Era*. Chicago: University of Chicago Press, 1996.

Simmons, Christina. "African Americans and Sexual Victorianism in the Social Hygiene Movement, 1910–1940." *Journal of the History of Sexuality* 4 (1993): 51–75.

Simon, Bryant. *Boardwalk of Dreams: Atlantic City and the Fate of Urban America*. New York: Oxford University Press, 2004.

Singal, Daniel Joseph. "Toward a Definition of American Modernism." *American Quarterly* 39 (Spring 1987): 7–26.

———. *The War Within: From Victorian to Modernist Thought in the South, 1919–1945*. Chapel Hill: University of North Carolina Press, 1982.

Smith, Katharine Capshaw. "Childhood, the Body, and Race Performance: Early 20th-Century Etiquette Books for Black Children." *African American Review* 40 (2006): 795–811.

Smith, Mark M. *How Race Is Made: Slavery, Segregation, and the Senses*. Chapel Hill: University of North Carolina Press, 2006.

———. "Producing Sense, Consuming Sense, Making Sense: Perils and Prospects for Sensory History." *Journal of Social History* 40 (Summer 2007): 841–58.

Smith, Susan L. Review of *Formative Years: Children's Health in the United States, 1880–2000*, edited by Alexandra Minna Stern and Howard Markel. *Journal of American History* 90 (September 2003): 678.

———. *Sick and Tired of Being Sick and Tired: Black Women's Health Activism in America, 1890–1950*. Philadelphia: University of Pennsylvania Press, 1995.

Sokol, Jason. *There Goes My Everything: White Southerners in the Age of Civil Rights, 1945–1975*. New York: Alfred A. Knopf, 2006.

Sole-Smith, Virginia. "The Pink Pyramid Scheme: How Mary Kay Cosmetics Preys on Desperate Housewives." *Harper's Magazine* (August 2012): 26–32+.

Spruill, Marjorie Julian. "The Mississippi 'Takeover': Feminists, Antifeminists, and the International Women's Year Conference of 1977." In *Mississippi Women: Their Histories, Their Lives.* Vol. 2, edited by Elizabeth Anne Payne, Martha H. Swain, and Marjorie Julian Spruill, 287–313. Athens: University of Georgia Press, 2010.

Stallybrass, Peter, and Allon White. *The Politics and Poetics of Transgression.* London: Methuen Press, 1986.

Stansell, Christine. *American Moderns: Bohemian New York and the Creation of a New Century.* New York: Metropolitan Books, 2000.

Stearns, Marshall, and Jean Stearns. *Jazz Dance: The Story of American Vernacular Dance.* New York: Macmillan, 1968.

Steele, Valerie. *Fashion and Eroticism: Ideals of Feminine Beauty from the Victorian Era to the Jazz Age.* New York: Oxford University Press, 1985.

Stern, Alexandra Minna. "Better Babies at the Indiana State Fair: Child Health, Scientific Motherhood, and Eugenics in the Midwest, 1920–1935." In *Formative Years: Children's Health in the United States, 1880–2000,* edited by Alexandra Minna Stern and Howard Markel, 121–52. Ann Arbor: University of Michigan Press, 2002.

Stewart, Nora. *Put Down and Ripped Off: The American Woman and the Beauty Cult.* New York: Crowell, 1977.

Street, Joe. *The Culture War in the Civil Rights Movement.* Gainesville: University Press of Florida, 2007.

Summers, Martin. *Manliness and Its Discontents: The Black Middle Class and the Transformation of Masculinity, 1900–1930.* Chapel Hill: University of North Carolina Press, 2004.

Susman, Warren. "'Personality' and the Making of Twentieth-Century Culture." In *Culture as History: The Transformation of American Society in the Twentieth Century.* New York: Pantheon Books, 1984; Washington D.C.: Smithsonian Institution Press, 2003.

Tate, Cassandra. *Cigarette Wars: The Triumph of the "Little White Slaver."* New York: Oxford University Press, 1999.

Thesander, Marianne. *The Feminine Ideal.* London: Reaktion Books, 1997.

Thornton, Kevin Pierce. "Symbolism at Ole Miss and the Crisis of Southern Identity." *South Atlantic Quarterly* 86 (Summer 1987): 254–68.

Tice, Karen W. *Queens of Academe: Beauty Pageantry, Student Bodies, and College Life.* New York: Oxford University Press, 2012.

Tilley, Nannie M. *The Bright Tobacco Industry, 1860–1929.* Chapel Hill: University of North Carolina Press, 1948.

Trachtenberg, Alan. *Reading American Photographs: Images as History, Mathew Brady to Walker Evans.* New York: Hill and Wang, 1989.

Turner, Elizabeth Hayes. "Women in the Post–Civil War South." In *A Companion to the American South,* edited by John B. Boles, 348–68. Malden, Mass.: Blackwell Publishers, 2002.

Tyler, Pamela. "The Ideal Rural Southern Woman as Seen by *Progressive Farmer* in the 1930s." *Southern Studies* 2 (Fall/Winter 1981): 315–33.

Van Deburg, William L. *New Day in Babylon: The Black Power Movement and American Culture, 1965–1975.* Chicago: University of Chicago Press, 1992.

Walker, Anders. *The Ghost of Jim Crow: How Southern Moderates Used* Brown v. Board of Education *to Stall Civil Rights.* New York: Oxford University Press, 2009.

Walker, Juliet E. K. *The History of Black Business in America: Capitalism, Race, Entrepreneurship.* Vol. 1. Chapel Hill: University of North Carolina Press, 2009.

Walker, Melissa. *All We Knew Was to Farm: Rural Women in the Upcountry South, 1919–1941.* Baltimore: Johns Hopkins University Press, 2000.

Walker, Susannah. "'Independent Livings' or 'No Bed of Roses'?: How Race and Class Shaped Beauty Culture as an Occupation for African American Women from the 1920s to the 1960s." *Journal of Women's History* 20 (Fall 2008): 60–83.

———. *Style and Status: Selling Beauty to African American Women, 1920–1975.* Lexington: University Press of Kentucky, 2007.

Ward, Jason Morgan. *Defending White Democracy: The Making of a Segregationist Movement and the Remaking of Racial Politics, 1936–1965.* Chapel Hill: University of North Carolina Press, 2011.

Warner, Marina. *Monuments and Maidens: The Allegory of the Female Form.* London: Vintage, 1985.

Watkins, Rychetta. *Black Power, Yellow Power, and the Making of Revolutionary Identities.* Jackson: University Press of Mississippi, 2012.

Watson, Elwood, and Darcy Martin, eds. *"There She Is, Miss America": The Politics of Sex, Beauty, and Race in America's Most Famous Pageant.* New York: Palgrave Macmillan, 2004.

Webb, Clive, ed. *Massive Resistance: Southern Opposition to the Second Reconstruction.* Oxford: Oxford University Press, 2005.

Weinbaum, Alys Eve, et al., eds. *The Modern Girl around the World: Consumption, Modernity, and Globalization.* Durham: Duke University Press, 2008.

Westbrook, Robert B. "'I Want a Girl, Just Like the Girl that Married Harry James': American Women and the Problem of Political Obligation in World War II." *American Quarterly* 42 (December 1990): 587–614.

White, Deborah Gray. *Ar'n't I a Woman? Female Slaves in the Plantation South.* New York: W. W. Norton, 1985.

———. *Too Heavy a Load: Black Women in Defense of Themselves.* New York: W. W. Norton, 1999.

White, Shane, and Graham White. *Stylin': African American Expressive Culture from Its Beginnings to the Zoot Suit.* Ithaca: Cornell University Press, 1998.

Willett, Julie A. *Permanent Waves: The Making of the American Beauty Shop.* New York: New York University Press, 2000.

Williamson, Joy Ann. *Black Power on Campus: The University of Illinois, 1965–1975.* Urbana: University of Illinois Press, 2003.

Wilson, Charles Reagan. *Baptized in Blood: The Religion of the Lost Cause.*
Athens: University of Georgia Press, 1980.
———. "The Cult of Beauty." In *The New Encyclopedia of Southern Culture.*
Vol. 4. Edited by Charles Reagan Wilson. Chapel Hill: University of North
Carolina Press, 2006.
Wiltse, Jeff, *Contested Waters: A Social History of Swimming Pools in America.*
Chapel Hill: University of North Carolina Press, 2007.
Wolcott, Victoria W. "'Bible, Bath, and Broom': Nannie Helen Burroughs's
National Training School and African-American Racial Uplift." *Journal of
Women's History* 9 (Spring 1997): 88–110.
———. *Remaking Respectability: African American Women in Interwar Detroit.*
Chapel Hill: University of North Carolina Press, 2001.
Wolf, Naomi. *The Beauty Myth: How Images of Beauty Are Used against Women.*
New York: William Morrow, 1991.
Woodward, C. Vann. *The Strange Career of Jim Crow.* 3rd rev. ed. New York:
Oxford University Press, 1974.
Zanger, Jules. "The Tragic Octoroon in Pre–Civil War Fiction." *American
Quarterly* 18 (Spring 1966): 63–70.

## UNPUBLISHED SECONDARY SOURCES

Boyd, Elizabeth Bronwyn. "Southern Beauty: Performing Femininity in an
American Region." Ph.D. diss., University of Texas at Austin, 2000.
Haidarali, Laila. "'The Vampingest Vamp Is a Brownskin': Colour, Sex, Beauty
and African American Womanhood, 1920–1954." Ph.D. diss., York University,
2007.
Hanson, Susan Atherton. "Home Sweet Home: Industrialization's Impact on
Rural Households, 1865–1925." Ph.D. diss., University of Maryland, 1986.
McClearly, Ann Elizabeth. "Shaping a New Role for the Rural Woman: Home
Demonstration Work in Augusta County, Virginia, 1917–1940." Ph.D. diss.,
Brown University, 1996.
McLean, Robert Emmett. "Cotton Carnival and Cotton Makers Jubilee:
Memphis Society in Black and White." Master's thesis, George Mason
University, 1994.
Pearson, Susan J. "Making Babies Better: Motherhood and Medicalization in the
Progressive Era." Master's thesis, University of North Carolina at Chapel Hill,
1999.
Pruitt, Samory. "A Reflection of Student Desegregation at the University of
Alabama as Seen through the Eyes of Some Pioneering African American
Students: 1956–1976." Ph.D. diss., University of Alabama, 2003.
Rieff, Lynne Anderson. "'Rousing the People of the Land': Home Demonstration
Work in the Deep South, 1914–1950." Ph.D. diss., Auburn University, 1995.

# Index

Italicized page numbers refer to illustrations and illustration captions.

the Politics of Self-Esteem" (Bergner), 314 (n. 112)

Black college dress codes, 177–85, *184*, 187–89, 237–38, 243–45

Black colleges and universities: aesthetic of respectability, 14–15, 180–82, 185–86, 189–91, 195, 237–38, 242–44; black ideal of beauty, 14, 62, 180–82, *186*, 190–91, 226–27, 241, *248*; Black Power movement, 242–46; mission, 150–51, 176–78, 185–88, 242, 305 (n. 95)

Black culture, 215–16, 243, 316 (n. 162)

Blackface, 217–19, *218*, 312 (nn. 91, 97)

Black hair care: conking, 316 (n. 171); cultural and emotional significance, 23, 31–32, 59, *61*, 84–85, 99–100, 268, 316 (n. 171); hair texture, 84, 172–73, 182; natural hair and Afro, 11, 238–42, 246, 254–56, 263–64, 266–67, 319 (n. 236); slaves, 59–60; straightening, 61–70, *64*, *67*, 84–85, 98–99, 191

Black ideal of beauty: political significance, 11, 56, *248*, 248–49, 254–56; politics of skin color, 222–24; rural black women, 160–61; and white beauty standards, 67–70, 81, 172, 263. *See also* Black is Beautiful movement; Black skin color

*Black Ink* (University of North Carolina), 249

Black is Beautiful movement, 11, 63, 69–70, 195, 243–46, 254–56, 261–69

*Black Monday: Segregation or Amalgamation . . . America Has Its Choice* (Brady), 210

Black nationalism, 237–38, 242–45, 254–55

Blackness: aesthetics, 3–4, 11, 161, 243–50, 255; political implications, 15, 68, 210, 237, 264–66; public representation of, 170, 195

Black Panther Party for Self-Defense, 237, 265

Black Power movement, 15, 195, 237–50, *249*, 253–54, 262–66, 308 (nn. 6, 7), 316 (n. 161). *See also* Black nationalism

Black Pride, 18, 173, 245–47. *See also* Black is Beautiful movement; Black nationalism; Black Power movement

Black racial identity, 15, 65–70, 151, 194–96

Black racial stereotypes, 58, 65, 152, 176, 236

*Black Revolution on Campus* (Biondi), 308 (n. 7)

Black skin color: black student movement, 180–82, 237–38; and female beauty, 83, 172, 174–75; political significance, 222–25, 246, 265–66, 313 (n. 109); prejudice, 78–84, 173, 191, 291 (nn. 101, 105), 318 (n. 208)

Black Skin Remover, 76, *76*

Black student movement, 150–51, 191, 242–49

Blackwelder, Julia, 94

Blackwell, Unita, 240–42

Blair, John J., 116

Blanding, Sarah, 139

Boardwalk Festival of Floats (Atlantic City), 220–21, 260

Bond, Hannah, 280 (n. 1)

Bond, Jane, *61*

*Bondwoman's Narrative, The* (Crafts), 1–5, 280 (n. 1)

"*The Bondwoman's Narrative*: Text, Paratext, Intertext and Hypertext" (Bernier and Newman), 280 (n. 1)

Bordo, Susan, 9, 215

Borglum, Gutzon, 116

Bowen, Cornelia, 66

Boyd, Elizabeth, 229

Boyd, Robert L., 293 (n. 164), 294 (n. 168)

Bra-burning, 258–59. *See also* Miss America Pageant

Brady, Tom, 210–11

Democratic Party, 200
Depression (1930s), 29, 92–95, 128, 136, 142, 283 (n. 58), 294 (n. 168)
Desegregation: beauty contests and public image of South, 13, 203–11; black beauticians' role, 232–33, 235; *Brown v. Board of Education* (1954), 192, 194, 200–202, 211, 222–25, 232, 263, 313 (n. 109); federal government initiatives, 200; opportunities for black women, 268–69. *See also* Civil rights movement; Integration; Little Rock school desegregation; Massive resistance; Ole Miss; Woolworth protests
Dessasau, Evan, 320 (n. 26)
Devlin, Rachel, 216
Dignam, Dorothy, 41
Dillard University, 170, 177, 187–89. *See also* Straight College
Disadvantage theory of business enterprise, 92, 293 (n. 164)
Dixiecrats, 200, 205
Dixon, Barbara, 250
Dollard, John, 80–82
Domestic workers, 86, 89–90, 96, 100, 167–68, 182
Duke, James "Buck," 129
Dunbar-Nelson, Alice, 74–75, 79, 99, 181
Dunson, Helen, 90, 100–101
Durr, Virginia Foster, 30

*Ebony*, 149–50, 152, 245, 255, 267
Echols, Alice, 319 (n. 7)
Edenton Peanut Festival, 136
*Ed Sullivan Show*, 139
Edwards, Paul, 167
"Effect of Prejudice and Discrimination on Personality Development" (Clark), 313 (n. 109)
Elizabeth City State College, 245
Elks, Benevolent and Protective Order of, 227
Ellis, William H. "Chubby," 208–9

Employment opportunities for women, 32, 52–53, 70–74, 88, 273–75, 283 (n. 58)
Eugenics, 121, 157, 209
"Eulogy on the Flapper" (Fitzgerald), 284 (n. 67)
Evers, Medgar, 205, 310 (n. 42)

Fair Employment Practices Commission, 200
Fairless, Janice, 122
Farm Bureau, 118, 146, 298 (n. 44)
Farmers' Institutes at Tuskegee, 156. *See also* Tuskegee Institute
Farm Security Administration, 28, 142
Fashion: black colleges and universities, 150, 178–79, 182–84, 187–90, 242; black fashion shows, 125–26, 170–72; black middle-class views, 163–64, 189; home demonstration agents, 158–63, *161*; white ideal of beauty, 54–55, 137, 154
Fass, Paula S., 284 (n. 66)
Federal Writers' Project, 29, 31, 91
Felton, Rebecca Latimer, 21
Female minstrelsy, 217–19. *See also* Blackface
*Feminine Mystique, The* (Friedan), 272, 274
Feminism: early-twentieth-century, 35–36, 115; second-wave, 9–10, 107, 115, 216–17, 257, 261–74. *See also* Women's liberation movement
Festival of States Parade, 196
Fields, Mamie Garvin: beautician business, 68–69, 74, 91, 97, 276; black ideal of beauty, 62, 80, 181; clothing, 164–65, *165*
Fiesta (San Antonio), 108
Fisk University, 177, 181–83, 226, 242, 306 (n. 124)
Fitzgerald, Zelda Sayre, 36, 284 (n. 67)
Flapper look, 30, 34–36, 182–83, *184*, 284 (n. 67)
*Florence Morning News*, 206

"Long Civil Rights Movement" (Hall), 309 (n. 26)

Lost Cause movement, 108–11, 211

Louisiana State Fair, 119

*Louisiana Weekly*, 170, 175

Lucas, Julia, 57–58, 80, 101

Lumberton Tobacco Festival, *147*, 147–48

Lumpkin, Elizabeth, 109

Lynching. *See* Racial violence

Madam C. J. Walker Company, 64–65, 72, 74–75, 77, 86, 266. *See also* Walker, Madam C. J.

Madam DeShazor's Beauty College, 87, 89–90, 231

Madam Rogers' All Queens Beauty College, 89

Maid of Cotton contest, 136–38, 140–41, 154, 205, 301 (n. 106)

Mail order business model, 24

Makeup. *See* Cosmetics

*Making Whiteness* (Hale), 282 (n. 5)

Malcolm X, 254, 316 (n. 171)

Malcolm X Liberation University, 243

Malone, Annie Turnbo, 63–65, 68–74, 76–77, 86, 174, 276

*Manliness and Its Discontents* (Summers), 306 (n. 124)

*Manning Times* (S.C.), 206, 217

Ma Rainey, 166

March on Washington (1963), 240

Mardi Gras (New Orleans), 108

Marks, Albert, 259–60

Marshall, Thurgood, 223

Martin, Ella, 87–88, 232

Martin, Janet Lane, 247

Martin, Waldo E., Jr., 316 (n. 162)

Maryland State College, 261

Mason, Bobbie Ann, 124

Massive resistance: history and tactics, 194, 200–201, 203, 221, 309 (n. 26); white ideal of beauty, 8, 15, 211, 216, 219, 281 (n. 15). *See also* Civil rights movement; Desegregation; Miss America Pageant; Segregation; White beauty contests; White Citizens' Councils of America

Mass media, 194, 198–99, 202–4, 206–8, 222, 258–59, 313 (n. 105)

May Day competitions, 108, 111, 185, *186*

McDaniel, Luella, 85

McEuen, Melissa, 52

McKimmon, Jane Simpson, 50, 122–23, 125

McKnight, Marian, 203–4, 206, 214, 217

McWilliams, Ada and Hazel, 89–91, 96–97, 100–101

Mead, Lynda Lee, 192, 205, 207–8, 211

Mebane, Mary, 62–63, 98–99, 181, 184, 225–26

"Menace of Feminism, The" (Porter), 35

Men's Business League (Atlantic City), 116

Mercury, 76, 290 (n. 77)

Meredith, James, 204, 206

*Messenger* (Spelman College), 185

*Metropolitan Magazine*, 113

Miller, Kelly, 183

Minstrelsy. *See* Blackface

Miscegenation, 210. *See also* Race mixing

Miss Alabama, 199, 207, 213

Miss America Pageant: black women's participation, 190–91, 227–29, 271, 314 (n. 129); ideal of female beauty, 257–61, 313 (n. 105); image of southern states, 15, 192, 199, 202–4, 211–12, 219–22, 270–72, 309 (n. 22); marketing goals, 116–17, 148, 198–99, 201–4; objectification of women, 257; protest (1968), 257–62, *258*, *259*, 269–71, 296 (n. 7), 319 (nn. 1, 9); racial segregation of, 174–75, 197, 221–22, 225–26; respectability, 196–99, 213–15; sexuality, 213–15. *See also* Black beauty contests; White beauty contests

ening products, *43*, 48, 78, 84, 290 (n. 77)

National Training School for Women and Girls, 66, 183

Native American women, 226

New Deal, 128–29, 141–42, 145, 309 (n. 26)

New Left, 271

*Newsweek*, 263

*New York Age*, 66

*New York Herald Tribune*, 137, 139–40

*New York Post*, 258–59

New York Radical Women, 271

*New York Times*, 215, 258, 319 (n. 1)

Nixon, Richard, 258, 260

Nixon, Tricia, 258

North Carolina College for Negroes, 181, 184, 244

North Carolina State University, 125

*Notes on the State of Virginia* (Jefferson), 4

Objectification of women, 107, 111, 128, 144, 148, 151, 194, 216–17. *See also* Commodification of women

Ole Miss (University of Mississippi), 204–5, 208–9, 217–19, 310 (n. 44)

O'Hara, Scarlett, 6, 52, 56, 277

O'Neal, Mary Lovelace, 241

One-drop rule, 68. *See also* Black racial identity

*On Habits and Manners* (Armstrong), 62

Ordinance of Secession (Mississippi), 205

*Out in Public* (Piepmeier), 281 (n. 22)

Overton, Anthony, 74, 83–84, 173

Overton Hygenic Company, 77

Ozonized Ox Marrow, 61

Pace, Debbie, 271

Pageland Watermelon Festival, 202

"Paint and Powder" (Fitzgerald), 284 (n. 67)

Palmer, Fred, 78

Palmer Memorial Institute, 75

Parks, Bert, 206, 214

Parrish, Charles H., 82–83

Passing as white, 33, 78–80. *See also* Black racial identity; Skin lightening products

Patriarchy, 3, 19, 215–16

Patriotism and national identity, 52, 197–98, 221–22, 313 (n. 105)

Pearson, Susan J., 112, 297 (n. 20)

Peiss, Kathy, 7, 22, 79

Pelican Roof Garden Club, 175

*Penthouse*, 314 (n. 129)

Pharis, Nannie, 32

Phillips, Evelyn Newman, 296 (n. 213)

Phi Mu sorority (University of Alabama), 217

Photographic beauty contests, 172–74

*Pictorial Review*, 23

Piepmeier, Alison, 281 (n. 22)

Pigee, Vera, 233, *235*

Pigmentocracy, 181. *See also* Black skin color

Pinups, 197, 213. *See also* Bathing beauty contests

Plough Chemical Company, 78–79

Points, Terry, 252–53

Poole, Marjorie, 130–31

Poro Company, 64, 71, 73

Porter, John W., 35–36, 115, 275

Potter, Eliza, 60

Powdermaker, Hortense, 68, 81–82, 93, 97, 160, 172

Pride, Cheryl, 227–29

Progressive Era, 119

*Progressive Farmer*, 25, 27–28, 37, 46–48, 50–53, 135, 146, 286 (n. 117)

Prostitution, 29, 31, 74

Pryor, William C., 144

Pure Food and Drug Act, 16

*Race and Reason* (Putnam), 209

Race mixing, 82–83, 201, 210–12, 216, 221, 225

"Racial Identification and Prefer-